Crisis

CRISIS
How to Help Yourself and Others in Distress or Danger

Lee Ann Hoff

OXFORD
UNIVERSITY PRESS

Oxford University Press is a department of the University of
Oxford. It furthers the University's objective of excellence in research,
scholarship, and education by publishing worldwide.

Oxford   New York
Auckland   Cape Town   Dar es Salaam   Hong Kong   Karachi
Kuala Lumpur   Madrid   Melbourne   Mexico City   Nairobi
New Delhi   Shanghai   Taipei   Toronto

With offices in
Argentina   Austria   Brazil   Chile   Czech Republic   France   Greece
Guatemala   Hungary   Italy   Japan   Poland   Portugal   Singapore
South Korea   Switzerland   Thailand   Turkey   Ukraine   Vietnam

Oxford is a registered trademark of Oxford University Press
in the UK and certain other countries.

Published in the United States of America by
Oxford University Press
198 Madison Avenue, New York, NY 10016

© Oxford University Press 2014

All rights reserved. No part of this publication may be reproduced, stored in
a retrieval system, or transmitted, in any form or by any means, without the prior
permission in writing of Oxford University Press, or as expressly permitted by law,
by license, or under terms agreed with the appropriate reproduction rights organization.
Inquiries concerning reproduction outside the scope of the above should be sent to the
Rights Department, Oxford University Press, at the address above.

You must not circulate this work in any other form
and you must impose this same condition on any acquirer.

A copy of this book's Catalog-in-Publication Data is on file with the Library of Congress
ISBN 978-0-19-936416-9

To victim-survivors of the April 15, 2013 Boston Marathon bombing; first responders and their healers; and to millions of others injured or killed in disasters of human origin, war, terrorism, and horrific violence worldwide over centuries and, tragically, continuing apace.

On April 15, 2013, I was working on drafts of this book's chapters on victimization and perpetrators of violence. The terrorist attack left me nearly incapable of productive work as I struggled to write meaningfully for others while following the terrorist attack in the Boston neighborhood where I lived for 24 years.

In remembrance of those who died in that terrorist attack and the millions of others in ethnic, religious, and political strife across our troubled world, and to make meaning out of the Boston Marathon bombing, I have arranged for this violence prevention goal through universities and colleges where I have affiliations.

A percentage of royalties that may accrue from this book will be dedicated to support scholarships for students with their potential for making a difference on the tragic and continuing saga of global violence. To some extent, this plan alleviates my flashes of feeling powerless in the face of so much violence worldwide.

Scholarship recipients will be eligible with this provision: Awardees must successfully complete at least one university/college course, directed study, or conduct a research or training project on crisis, violence, and abuse issues grounded in a human rights perspective and the principle of *education as prevention and intervention*. Priority for scholarship eligibility will be given to students disadvantaged by poverty, gender, race, ethnicity, sexual identity, or religion-based hatred. The plan will be augmented and continued in my estate planning. Persons interested in joining this prevention cause may contact www.crisisprograms.org

This plan is rooted in my education and research on social justice issues and crisis care, plus the healing process from vicarious traumatization in caring for victims, writing about crisis and violence, and periodic flashbacks to my personal trauma history.

Peace!
Lee Ann Hoff
Boston, Massachusetts
March 2014

CONTENTS

Acknowledgments   *ix*

Introduction: Building on a Rich History   *1*

PART I: People in Crisis: How Do They Feel, Think, and Act, and How Can We Help?

Chapter 1—Life Crises: How to Avoid Danger and Grasp Opportunity   *13*
   Crisis is a common life experience, not a psychiatric "disorder"

Chapter 2—Recognizing Different Faces of Distress on the Road to Full-Blown Crisis   *30*
   Knowing the difference between everyday upsetting events and life-or-death danger

Chapter 3—What to Do: How to Cope and Avoid Disastrous Crisis Outcomes   *54*
   When to seek professional help without shame or asking your friend to play "therapist"

PART II: Life-Threatening Crises: Suicide, Abuse, and Violence Toward Others

Chapter 4—A Cry for Help: Suicide and Other Self-Destructive Behaviors   *81*
   What everyone needs to know about clues to suicide and that there is no such thing as absolute prediction

Chapter 5—Victimization by Violence, Sexual Assault, and Emotional Abuse   *115*
   Healing from the crisis of victimization by violence or verbal abuse

Chapter 6—The Violent and Abusive Person: Preventing Violence Is Everybody's Business   *143*
   Violence and abuse: A major health and social issue worldwide

PART III: Crises Arising From Unexpected Stressful Events and Life Cycle Passages

Chapter 7—Threats to Health Status From a Serious Illness or Accident   173
   Connecting the dots between serious medical events and emotional crisis

Chapter 8—Loss of Job, Home, and Financial Security   205
   Coping with accidental and preventable loss of essentials in everyday life

Chapter 9—Life Cycle Changes, Loss and Growth: From Birth to Death   241
   Navigating and growing through challenges across the life cycle

Conclusion: Vision for Global Action: Research, Education, and Practice   298
   Learning from history, together we can make a difference across several fronts

Index   307

ACKNOWLEDGMENTS

As we go to press, I am reminded again of the struggles and victories of the people in crisis I have met over decades of practice, research, teaching, and consultation. From these patients, their families, and their therapists and counselors, I have learned so much about the suffering and triumphs of people facing the danger and opportunity of crisis.

The key features of this book are the stories of diverse persons from a range of stressful or dangerous situations, disguised here for privacy. They and their providers have found meaning in sharing their experience so that others, helped by a book like this, might learn and benefit from the lifelong lessons of both positive and negative crisis outcomes—how to avoid negative outcomes, and what to do to promote positive ones. From these stories I have been affirmed in one of my mantras: *education as prevention*. To all of these people I am deeply grateful.

Also central to this book are the lessons and wisdom of brilliant teachers, literary sources, and role models I have been blessed with for learning the basics of crisis care—its theoretical and cross-cultural foundations, and how to apply practice ideals among diverse persons in hospitals, mental health and crisis clinics, and in peoples' homes. My gratitude for these opportunities is deep and lasting.

The contextual and interdisciplinary focus of this book did not emerge from formal interdisciplinary education alone. My immersion in teaching, workshops, and practice with students and practitioners led to the dream of this book. Experience with students and practitioners in nursing, social work, psychology, policing, and pastoral care yielded wisdom and examples for this book—not only the positive outcomes we hope for our clients but also the affirmation of the centrality of collaboration, teamwork, and support among crisis workers themselves in such a challenging field. This team approach has left an indelible mark on me and many others about how best to help oneself and others in crisis situations. In workshops and formal university classes in the United States, Canada, and countries in Africa, South America, and Europe, I have met brave and generous people who have shared their experiences in personal and professional venues. Across this diverse landscape, I thank each and all, as without them, there would be no book like this.

Turning to the nitty-gritty of producing the book, I thank anonymous reviewers and my friends and colleagues who encouraged me during the process of actualizing what was only a dream through the challenges, setbacks, and finally the finish line. Some of you—Annie Leguern, my sister Marie Hoff, Lisa Brown, Judith Leconte, Betty Cragg—read sections of the book that presented particular challenges and shared valuable insights to making this a better book. Others—David Blumenkrantz, Cathleen Getty, Jesse Jones, Donna Bivens, Larry Kistler, Paul Marcus, Paula Finneran, Thalia Sidoroupolos, Susan Forward, and John Taylor—listened and offered support through dilemmas toward the finish line, while Jean Harnois, Claudia Ellis, and Don Peavy helped during the book's beginning phase. To each of you I am very grateful.

Last but not least, I thank Dana Bliss, my editor at Oxford University Press, who did so much to keep the spark alive from dream to completion. Dana, your wisdom, guidance, constructive critique, and support through the routine and rough spots mean more than I can fully express here. Thanks also to Brianna Marron at Oxford University Press, the Newgen KnowledgeWorks production team in India, and others behind the scenes for technical assistance, design, the marketing process, and for keeping me on track with deadlines. Without such teamwork, this book would never have seen the light of day. My special thanks to each and all.

Lee Ann Hoff
Boston
April 2014

Introduction

Building on a Rich History

CHAPTER OUTLINE

Experiential and Scientific Background Supporting the Book's Goals   2
Moving Forward with Kinks in the Road   4
Danger and Opportunity of Crisis and Overcoming Stigma   5
Organization   7
Who Should Read this Book?   7
References   8

Crisis signals *opportunity* and potential *danger*. The term is used in spiritual, social, and political domains. Here it refers to a psychological state—an acute emotional upset in which one's usual problem-solving ability fails. The opportunities? Learning, growth, and gaining strength to deal with future upsets. Some dangers could be health decline, suicide, violence, or substance abuse. Crisis typically occurs in response to an identifiable traumatic experience, for example, a serious accident, divorce, death of a loved one, or victimization by violence.

In itself, a crisis experience does not imply a psychiatric "disorder," although persons with true mental illness are more vulnerable than others to upsetting life events signifying crisis. Support is needed during crisis to enhance positive outcomes and avoid negative ones. Without it, substance abuse, mental illness, and/or violence toward self and others may be the unfortunate but often preventable endpoint of crisis resolution.

This book is meant for anyone facing the danger and opportunity of crisis. It is dedicated to people like Joan and Tom Brown, the distraught parents of Gary, age 16, who was arrested after killing two of his classmates with a gun brought from home. Interviews with the grieving classmates and teachers revealed that Gary was a lonely kid. As an only child of upper-middle-class parents, he possessed a lot of luxury items others kids envied, and he was also teased for his eccentric ways. One of Gary's classmates, who felt sorry for him, heard him say once: "I'm fed up and just not gonna take these guys teasing me anymore." Noteworthy here is that verbal clues like Gary's typically precede violent action.

Tragic as Gary's case is, it is, unfortunately, far too common. Years after the shock of school and other mass shootings fades, the cases of not just teenagers but also adults in crisis continue to rise at an alarming rate. National newspapers and local broadcasts are awash with stories of violent crime, fatal domestic abuse, or other tragedies. Whether they make the evening news or not, these cases can serve as a red flag signaling distress, crisis, and life-threatening behavior—patterns often picked up only *after* a tragedy occurs. They can also lead to stemming the tide of violence in our personal relationships, family, and community.

Despite advances in crisis and community mental health services for persons like Gary and his parents, and public information on varied crisis topics, there are far too many crises such as the Brown family experienced. Crises like these might be prevented through education and widespread knowledge about resolving life-threatening crises early on in a positive direction at home, school, the workplace, and neighborhoods.

This book is intended to fill a gap between college textbooks and my vision of what is needed by readers such as Gary's parents. It offers information, advice, and guidance aimed at healthy crisis resolution and preventing suicide and violence toward others. A more detailed book (primarily for college and graduate students in health and social sciences) is *People in Crisis: Clinical and Diversity Perspectives*, now in its sixth edition[1] and representing decades of research and practice in the field. As the crisis field gains momentum, many health and social service providers have benefited from a crisis course or continuing education seminars. But such academic sources typically do not reach the broader general readership.

As a translation of sorts, this book draws on the *People in Crisis* (PIC) text for major content. Its main message is for the lay reader and others who are *not* crisis specialists but often are the first contact in a crisis situation, for example, parents, teachers, clergy, police, and school counselors. It supports crisis education beyond college students and how to help one's self, family, and others in distress or danger.

Having lived through and learned from several life crises, and deeply concerned about people in crisis, I hope the book will be helpful to many others.

EXPERIENTIAL AND SCIENTIFIC BACKGROUND SUPPORTING THE BOOK'S GOALS

This book was born in several streams of learning, clinical experience with various distressed persons, research, and teaching about crisis and violence prevention in my career as a nurse-anthropologist.

First among these learning streams was on the road to my bachelor's degree in nursing with fear of flunking the Anatomy and Physiology course, a potential crisis occasion that could have cost me the degree. In the course lab, I was nearly frozen with dread of touching and dissecting frogs, while my college teammate struggled to master the theory base. So we struck a deal: She would do my dissecting, and I would help her with the conceptual base. Our team approach resulted in a better outcome for both of us—just as in effective crisis care!

During the second stream, I worked as a therapist and manager in a hospital psychiatric ward, a period coinciding with US national survey data supporting the National Institute of Mental Health ideal of 24-7 crisis services available nationwide and close to home in all communities. During this same era, I was deeply influenced by the theoretical work and publications of three giants in the field: Harry Stack Sullivan's *Interpersonal Theory of Psychiatry* served as a firm base for community mental health and a centerpiece of psychotherapy for acutely distressed persons;[2] Hildegard Peplau's nurse–patient relationship theory;[3] and Gerald Caplan's *Principles of Preventive Psychiatry*[4] provided a baseline for crisis theory and practice.

Applying Peplau's theory, I guided the nurses to plan for at least a half hour during day and evening shifts for one-to-one interaction with their assigned patients in addition to administering medications, doing safety checks, and related nursing tasks. This approach had a noteworthy result: Upon discharge, distressed patients needing support typically called the hospital asking to speak with their nurse. Observing this pattern, I considered: If these discharged psychiatric patients need someone to talk with in middle of the night, what about others in crisis who had never been hospitalized?

As a consequence, under this assumption, the entire team and hospital administration opened our 24-hour telephone service as a crisis hotline available to *all* distressed persons in our community—not just for our discharged patients—with linkage to follow-up and comprehensive mental health service. The Los Angeles Suicide Prevention Center was "ground zero" and a model for other communities nationwide. Still today, and influenced by the Samaritan movement in London, trained volunteers (not psychiatric specialists) remain typical as first-contact providers responding 24/7 to suicidal and other distressed callers. This was the forerunner to today's front-page telephone directories that routinely include hotline numbers for suicidal and other dangers (National Suicide Prevention Lifeline: 1-800-273 TALK [8255]). It lays the foundation for community-based face-to-face crisis services across the United States and many other countries.

Together, these experiences and an interdisciplinary literature base led to my vision for this book, an evidence-based resource that translates the *People in Crisis* college text for nonspecialists in crisis care—*lay readers, front-line health and social service providers, pastors, and public safety officers.* Increasingly, these dedicated workers need reliable information for supporting people in their everyday crisis encounters at home, work, and in the community.

MOVING FORWARD WITH KINKS IN THE ROAD

Yet, since the early 1980s, with widespread inadequate funding of mental health services close to home, for many in acute distress, the nearest hospital emergency room has emerged as the first resort and a "revolving door" for many psychiatric patients. The sometimes scant training of front-line health providers compounds this sad scenario in crisis care. A major challenge is assuring a smooth transition from crisis intervention in emergency situations (or during typical 15- to 20-minute primary care visits) to important follow-up counseling or psychotherapy.[5]

The professional psychiatric literature and even magazines like *Time* and *The New Yorker* address this interconnected socioeconomic and politicized process. The lack of early intervention can lead to lethal crisis outcomes. Another serious outcome of these shortcomings is the use of physical and chemical restraint of a violent patient—sometimes the major intervention in high-risk situations.

And so, to another stream of this book's birth. Struck by the travel and learning bug, the outcomes of crisis care workshops conducted on several continents, responding to my affinity for diversity issues, and deeply influenced by the Peplau, Sullivan, and Caplan giants in the psychiatric/ mental health arena, I was lucky to study social anthropology abroad that included immersion in social network theory. My doctoral dissertation research with abused women and their families in metro Boston uncovered the sociocultural context of domestic violence and how to prevent it.[6]

Coupled with this research was my day job teaching police and nurses (typical first-contact providers) the basics of crisis care and violence prevention. That experience has been pivotal to writing about crisis, violence, and suicide and how these topics are so deeply intertwined.[7] Building on my Crisis and Suicidology Fellowship clinical practicum at Johns Hopkins University and ride-along experience with Los Angeles police, a key observation emerged: *the wide gap in collaboration between psychiatric crisis specialists and front-line police work.*

Similar ride-along experience with Boston police officers affirmed the importance of teamwork in crisis care. Clearly, responding to domestic violence and related crises reveals not only the danger to police but also their frustration with such policing challenges. At this interface between police and professional psychiatric work I saw a deep hole: While public order and safety will always be the primary work of police, they may find themselves filling in by default when 24/7 professional crisis services are not readily available. This staffing issue appears as a frustrating loop in the "revolving door" of psychiatric treatment: premature discharge, readmission during crisis and discharged again, as the cycle continues.

Beyond this common emergency experience and revolving door is one of society's serious drug problems: abuse or misuse of prescription medications. It also speaks to the severe stress and danger toward police and hospital emergency staff caring for seriously disturbed or out-of-control patients. A related hazard in this scenario is the overreliance on psychotropic drugs for desperate patients brought by police or arriving alone from the streets. When time and staffing are short, chemical restraint with powerful drugs is often the first resort for a potentially dangerous patient, with little time for listening to the plight of desperate persons. Several pages of this book are devoted to this issue, especially for front-line professionals and well-intentioned but frustrated family members seeking help for a loved one (see Chapter 1). Journalists Pete Earley[8] and Robert Whitaker[9] present vivid accounts of the personal and social costs when psychiatric and mental health care (beyond psychotropic drug use) is not readily accessible.

The nationwide massive discharge of patients from psychiatric hospitals, coupled with insufficient funding of community mental health services, has threatened further development of mental health service ideals from the 1960s and 1970s.[10] Currently, with tragic and highly publicized gun-related deaths, injuries, and other crises, it seems clear that at least some of these deaths might have been prevented—this, especially if we close the gap in what appears as a knowledge deficit in *detecting early danger signals of possible injury to self and others*, and urge people to seek crisis care as early as possible. Responding to these needs, a major aim of this book is to close this knowledge gap for a broad range of readers—from first responders to the general public.

DANGER AND OPPORTUNITY OF CRISIS AND OVERCOMING STIGMA

The task of helping people heal from stressful life events, the wounds of war, and other trauma to prevent suicide or violence whenever possible is very challenging for someone who cares but does not recognize danger clues early on or know best responses to high-risk crisis situations. Also, a short office visit with health providers may not be enough to prevent tragic crisis outcomes, so we should never hesitate to ask for whatever help is needed, and that help should be easily accessible 24/7 in every community. Clearly, awareness of subtle clues to life-threatening crises is everybody's business at home, at work, and in schools, as Gary's case illustrates.

Typically and unfortunately, as press accounts of violence reveal, distress signals were there, but observers did not take them seriously or know how to respond and engage professional helpers. It wasn't until after it was too late that Gary's fellow students reported Gary's boasting about his knowledge of Internet sites for purchasing weapons. He had also frequently asked the forensic science teacher about the best way to cover up a murder.

Together, these were missed clues and opportunities for crisis intervention and violence prevention. Apparently no one thought to seek guidance from school counselors or the principal, alert Gary's parents, or talk with Gary directly about his violence-laced remarks. As is often the case, such language is dismissed as just another facet of today's "culture of violence" or "that's just the way kids talk these days." These classical clues to the danger and opportunity of crisis are elaborated in the book's three parts and nine chapters.

Thus, with examples like Gary and the Newtown massacre of children and teachers, and steeped in the history of social psychiatry and the potential of nurses and other front-line providers to make a difference on behalf of people in crisis, I am deeply saddened by current setbacks and financial challenges in the mental health field. But I am also encouraged to move forward when considering historian George Santayana's wisdom: "Those who do not learn from history are doomed to repeat it".[11] Another inspiration is the wisdom and ideal of renowned sociologist C. Wright Mills, who said: "It is the political task of the social scientist. . . continually to translate personal troubles into public issues, and public issues into the terms of their human meaning for a variety of individuals" (p. 187).[12] I believe that some tragic injuries and deaths might be avoided in a framework of "knowledge as prevention" applied by this book's readers.

For example, one of my responses to setbacks since the earlier ideals of social psychiatry is encouraging all students and workshop attendees embracing a mental health or social service career to arrange a "ride-along" in their local police department—this allows not only for one to observe serious life crises firsthand in the community and homes but also to strengthen links between police training in crisis intervention and important follow-up counseling around life-threatening events. Such experience observing police officers' keen sensitivity to danger is a reminder that police and firefighters rate first and second in job-related injuries and deaths, with nurses and nursing assistants ranking third in national statistics regarding workplace safety.[13]

Considering the rich terrain of sociocultural theory and its contribution to professional crisis care, its "second cousin" status among health care models is noteworthy for confronting the continuing social stigma of mental illness and its treatment. It is a sober reminder that despite progress, some distressed persons refrain from seeking help because of remaining historical stigma associated with psychiatric illness. No one should experience shame and stigma or hesitate to accept help when in crisis or suffering around serious mental health issues.

It is particularly tragic when reading about veterans and others even today who may avoid seeking help, blame themselves for perceived weakness, cope alone with alcohol or other drugs, or choose suicide rather than accepting counseling or psychotherapy—this, often because of lingering bias around mental health service. Similar isolation and self-blame may haunt a victim of rape by a stranger or trusted partner: "What did I do wrong?" "How could I have been so stupid trusting him or her?" "He was such a sweet nice kid [a teacher notes after a school shooting]...What did I miss?"

It is my sincere hope that this book will help to correct and dispel the unfortunate backwater of mental health service and thereby contribute to a vision of crisis and psychiatric care in the framework of *basic human rights*. Social networking and teamwork are essential for successful crisis care (i.e., collaboration vs. competition, power and control). I therefore value greatly a self-defined role as "bridge builder." In C. Wright Mills' ideal of action linking personal troubles and public issues, together we can help close the gap between the social and health sciences. This book is one spoke in the wheel of education and service so central to the health and happiness of our patients, especially those in despair or danger.

ORGANIZATION

The book is organized into three parts. Three chapters in Part I present an overview of emotional crisis as an essentially *normal* life experience, how it differs from everyday stress and serious mental illness, and what to do when aware of impending crisis in oneself and/or others. It lays the foundation for three chapters in Part II, in which life-threatening crises (suicide and violence) are addressed. Chapters in Part III deal with the heightened vulnerability of persons facing unexpected events such as divorce, serious illness, job loss, and the stress encountered during major life cycle transitions. Brief cross-referencing between chapters will help readers concerned about a particular topic, for example, life-threatening illness, a troubled child, or threats of suicide or murder.

The book's nine chapters address the multilayered field of crisis care. Depending on a reader's interest and needs, each chapter stands alone, with easy cross-referencing about common crises addressed in the three parts.

Readers will note throughout the book a blended or middle ground between complex psychiatric and other scientific literature and life stories typifying the topic. Themes and issues from the stories are translated from dense psychiatric prose to key points the average reader can relate to from personal, family, or work experience. Each chapter includes a Discussion Guide and action items relevant to a story line that we can take on behalf of ourselves and others.

WHO SHOULD READ THIS BOOK?

The general reader and front-line health and social service providers who are not specialists in psychiatric and mental health care might especially benefit from this book. Psychiatric specialists may find it helpful in their consulting work with front-line providers or perhaps suggest it to some of their clients. The book is also intended as self-help during critical life events with would-be victims and their families and for brave first responders like police or a next-door neighbor called on to help someone in distress.

Undergraduate students in health and social science majors may decide to enroll in a crisis-related course after reading this book and considering the Further Reading and Discussion Guides. These sources may also be useful for readers pursuing graduate degrees in psychiatric and mental health disciplines—medicine, nursing, clinical and counseling psychology, social work, and pastoral ministry.

Finally, the book is meant to empower distressed persons to work in *active partnership* with front-line responders and crisis care professionals. Hence, readers can advance their own mental health by *knowing what to clearly expect of providers*—doctors, nurses and others—when finding themselves in acute distress or crisis. Chapter Discussion Guides may facilitate such activism.

The bottom line is that no acutely distressed person should have to suffer alone during crisis. Nearby compassion and support can often prevent disastrous crisis outcomes with recognition of both the *opportunity and danger* of crisis. Sometimes the outcome is tragic despite our best efforts and serious attention to crisis clues. But in such disappointing circumstances, it is important to avoid a misplaced "savior" complex and remember that there is *no such thing as absolute prediction of suicide or violence toward others*.

And so I hope that whether at home, at work, or out and about, you will find this book helpful in your personal and family lives, your professional work, and in your neighborhood—especially if it is one of those communities plagued by violence and/or lacking sufficient sources of support, good jobs, and safety during life's challenges.

While aiming to be helpful to people in distress or crisis, this book is *not* the bible of crisis care. Readers are encouraged to share their crisis experience and add words of wisdom to this growing and important field.

REFERENCES
1. Hoff, L. A., Hallisey, B. J., & Hoff, M. (2009). *People in crisis: Clinical and diversity perspectives* (6th ed.). New York: Routledge.
2. Sullivan, H. S. (2012). *Interpersonal theory of psychiatry.* New York: W.W. Norton. (Original work published 1953)
3. Peplau, H. (1991). *Interpersonal relations in nursing.* New York: Springer. (Original work published 1952)
4. Caplan, G. (1964). *Principles of preventive psychiatry.* New York: Basic Books.
5. Hoff, L. A., & Morgan, B. (2012). *Psychiatric and mental health essentials in primary care.* London: Routledge.
6. Hoff, L. A. (1990). *Battered women as survivors.* London: Routledge.
7. Hoff, L. A. (2010). *Violence and abuse issues: Cross-cultural perspectives for health and social services.* London: Routledge.
8. Earley, P. (2006). *Crazy: A father's search through America's mental health madness.* New York: Berkley Books.

9. Whitaker, R. (2010). *Anatomy of an epidemic: Magic bullets, psychiatric drugs, and the astonishing rise of mental illness in America.* New York: Crown Publishers.
10. Levine, M. (1981). *The history and politics of community mental health.* New York: Oxford University Press.
11. Santayana, G. (2013). *Quotes from Stanford encyclopedia of philosophy.* Retrieved from w.w.w. Santayana, Historian. George Santayana's Warnings.
12. Mills, C. W. (1959). *The sociological imagination.* London: Oxford University Press.
13. Mayhew, C., & Chappell, D. (2007). Workplace violence: An overview of patterns of risk and the emotional/stress consequences on targets. *International Journal of Law and Psychiatry, 30,* 327–339.

PART I
People in Crisis: How Do They Feel, Think, and Act, and How Can We Help?

CHAPTER 1

Life Crises

How to Avoid Danger and Grasp Opportunity

Crisis is a common life experience, *not* a psychiatric "disorder"

CHAPTER OUTLINE

What Is Crisis?   14
What Is Crisis Intervention?   17
Some Common Notions About People in Crisis and How to Help Them   18
Avoiding Danger and Taking Advantage of the Opportunity in Crisis   20
Diverse Approaches to Crisis   21
A Continuum of Crisis Services   23
Fruits of Coordinated Care Versus the "Revolving Door"   24
Example: Home-Based Crisis Care—Ray and Family   26
Basic Steps in Crisis Care   27
References, Further Reading, Discussion Guide   28

Sharon, a 55-year-old insurance manager, sits at her desk while putting the finishing touches on her presentation for the usual Monday morning staff meeting. Her typing is occasionally interrupted as she sips her coffee. This morning she got a *grande* because she has been feeling a bit fatigued lately, even though she has continued her twice-weekly health club visits.

In addition to fatigue, Sharon noticed some heart palpitations and a couple of dizzy spells over the weekend, which she traced to helping her two teenage daughters load their soccer equipment into the family van. Sharon hears her telephone ring and turns around from the computer to answer it, but she is stopped by a sudden onset of lightheadedness. She manages to pick up the handset, drops it, picks it up again, and mumbles something into it as the room begins to spin her world out of control. When Sharon regains her senses, she finds herself in the intensive care unit of a local hospital, where she is told she has just suffered a mini-stroke.

Sharon is in an acute medical situation that may include emotional crisis. As defined and explained later, Sharon is facing both *opportunity* and *danger*. Her world has been turned upside down, and her life as she has known it is threatened. Even though she has survived the stroke with no impairment thanks to rapid medical treatment, this sudden threat to her health will cause disruptions in her life and work which, depending upon the intervention skills of her family and health care workers, could spiral downward into chaos or outright dysfunctioning. Her situation affects not only herself but also her family, her work, and life as a whole. Most immediately, however, Sharon's stroke precipitates unusual stress and confusion for her family as they try to find ways to cover the everyday activities Sharon usually performs for the family.

Chronic stress following Sharon's physical illness could lead to an emotionally troubled family or mental breakdown of individual family members, depending on the various psychological, social, and cultural factors involved in the fallout from Sharon's stroke. It is like a car wreck which, unnerving as it is, can have far-reaching psychological and economic implications depending on whether one has appropriate insurance and contingency plans. Some people walk away from an automobile accident without losing any time off work or suffering disruption of their usual activities, while others fall into a state of crisis. What then is a "crisis"? And what is it that enables one person to manage and learn from a crisis while others are pulled into a vicious emotional storm?

WHAT IS CRISIS?

Initially, Sharon and members of her family will no doubt become very upset as a result of her stroke, and they may feel emotionally unable to handle the event. Their lives will have to be reordered and changes will occur in their daily activities. Depending on what happens next, Sharon and her family can avoid the potential negative fallout of a distressful situation. In this book, *crisis* refers to *an acute emotional upset arising from situational, developmental, or social sources that results in a temporary inability to cope by means of one's usual problem-solving devices.* A crisis does not last long and is self-limiting. *Crisis management* refers to the entire process of working through a crisis to its end point of *crisis resolution*.

This process typically includes activities of the individual in crisis and various members of the person's natural and institutional social network. It is an integral facet of holistic health care, which addresses the psychological as well as social needs of patients. Holistic, comprehensive health care recognizes that humans are social beings living in a network of relationships which affect and are affected by the injuries, illnesses, and diseases of patients. Thus, health care workers must be attuned to the personal needs of the patient and also direct concern and attention to those affected by the patient's challenging situation. Most important, this includes relationships that may be contributing to the patient's condition. And it means that everyone concerned about a loved one in crisis needs to know what to expect from health care professionals.

To understand crisis more clearly, it is helpful to explore a few misconceptions about crisis to emphasize *what crisis is not*:

- *Stress* is not crisis; stress is tension, strain, or pressure. Stress can occur whenever we face change whether that change is positive or negative, such as getting married or being fired from a job. Stress can also ensue from moments of difficult decision making such as balancing a budget.
- *Predicament* is not crisis either; predicament is a condition or situation that is unpleasant, dangerous, or embarrassing. Having your credit card declined after an evening of dining with friends is a predicament.
- *Emergency* is not crisis; emergency is an unforeseen combination of circumstances that calls for immediate action, often with life-or-death implications. Running out of gas on a freeway while traveling in the center lane is an emergency. Choking on food lodged in your throat is also an emergency.
- Finally, crisis is *not* emotional or mental illness.

The crisis experience typically includes an upset in cognitive, psychological, and behavioral functioning that influences crisis outcomes. The *cognitive* aspect of crisis resolution includes thinking and planning next steps following an upsetting event. *Psychological* functioning is revealed in the expression of our *feelings* about what has happened; for example, high anxiety or fear of "going crazy" when realizing one's inability to solve a vexing problem as usual. *Behavioral* functioning involves one's ability to control impulsivity (e.g., suicide or violence toward others) and engage in safety planning. Thus, for example, treatment of an intoxicated person in the emergency department includes ascertaining *cognitive* functioning (i.e., the person's ability to accurately describe the source of current distress and history of managing crisis situations); the severity and source of *psychological or emotional* pain; and the *behaviors* required for following through with a crisis resolution plan. Sensitivity to these points is central to helping ourselves and others in distress or crisis.

Simply stated, *crisis* is a serious situation or turning point in one's life that presents both *danger and opportunity*. For Sharon, she faces the dangers of a serious medical event that also presents opportunities to rethink her priorities and the degree to which her family is dependent upon her. She also faces the opportunity to make adjustments in her schedules and commitments, and perhaps to lighten up on the many demands she makes on herself.

Whether this hazardous situation results in growth and enrichment for Sharon and her loved ones or in a lower level of functioning for one or all of them depends largely on their problem-solving abilities, cultural values regarding illness and health, and current levels of social and economic support. Sharon, it turns out, recently received a promotion that elevated her status at work. Coming from a working-class family challenged to meet their financial demands, Sharon has vowed to avoid the struggles and stresses of her childhood. She is determined to provide a better life for her children than her parents were able to provide her and her siblings.

However, it is not enough for Sharon to achieve professional success. She also seeks to maintain a stable family life. It is no wonder then that her husband and children are devoted to her. However, that devotion comes with a price—it puts constant pressure on Sharon to set an example of strength and perform to an exacting standard. These facts of Sharon's life and the lives of people like her signify the *subjectivity* of the crisis experience, that is, how each individual interprets a stressful event. This subjectivity contributes to some difficulties and misunderstandings about crisis.

Even as Sharon's family faces the *danger* of a family breakdown and severe stress and disruptions to their daily lives, they are presented with an *opportunity* to learn new skills, develop existing talents, and discover a new and deeper appreciation for the worth of their spouse and mother. They might decide to hire a housekeeper or driver or some other helper to reduce the many tasks which Sharon has performed.

Sharon's employer will also face danger and opportunity. The employer's regular routine has already been disrupted and further tensions might be experienced as a result of the sudden loss of one of their key workers—at least temporarily. Personnel will have to be reshuffled and perhaps some interim help will be hired. Nevertheless, Sharon's employer has an opportunity to access its own crisis management strategy and how it relates to the health crisis of a key manager and the amount of work expected from administrators like Sharon.

Fortunately for Sharon and her family, she recovered fully from the stroke—thanks to her husband's recognition of early symptoms—some slurred speech and dropping things as she prepared dinner. They rushed to the hospital emergency department, where she received the "clot-busting" medication that disrupts the lasting physical damage caused by stroke. Everyone should know about emergency treatment of stroke and the chances of full recovery if treated within the 3- to 4-hour window from time of symptom onset. Given Sharon's full life at home and at work, she and her family were extremely grateful for their easy access to medical emergency care and its successful outcome. In this book, Sharon's medical emergency treatment sets an example of the parallel services everyone deserves if experiencing *acute emotional distress and/or the danger of suicide or violence*. Unfortunately, mental health emergency care does not always measure up to standards of holistic emergency treatment for avoiding disastrous outcomes.

WHAT IS CRISIS INTERVENTION?

How well Sharon, her family, and her employer respond to this critical event often depends on *crisis intervention* or *crisis care,* that aspect of health service carried out by a crisis worker—nurse, social worker, police officer, physician, counselor, or minister. Crisis care is a short-term helping process. It focuses on *resolution of the immediate problem* through the use of personal, social, and environmental resources. *Crisis counseling* is a time-limited aspect of crisis resolution focusing on the emotional, cognitive, and behavioral ramifications of the crisis. It is usually done by providers with formal preparation in counseling techniques.

Psychotherapy is a helping process, brief or longer term, directed toward changing a person's feelings (sometimes unconscious) and patterns of thought and behavior. Whether both or either of these interventions will be needed in a situation such as Sharon's is part of the assessment done by crisis care managers in consultation with those involved in the crisis. The earlier this assessment can be made, the better the chances are for a favorable resolution of the crisis in a timely manner.

A crisis can resemble an earthquake in some respects. It is a sudden eruption in a person's or institution's life that typically is followed by several aftershocks of varying intensity such as those experienced by Sharon, her family, and employer after her stroke. If care is not taken and people are not attended to by appropriate caregivers, such stress can evolve into a crisis state. Although stress is a common denominator in everyone's passage from infancy through childhood to adolescence, adulthood, and old age, its effects vary. For example, your son finds himself in turmoil during adolescence; your son's friend does not. You face midlife as a normal part of human development; your friend becomes depressed; a neighbor becomes suicidal. Part of the beauty of life, though, is the rebirth of peace following turmoil and pain; few escape the lows—and the subsequent highs—of living through stressful events or victimization by violence or abuse.

Likewise, people react to stress in different ways. For instance, if Sharon is the coach of her teenagers' soccer team, the team may experience stress as they struggle to find a replacement and avoid missing any scheduled games and events. If Sharon's assistant was planning a vacation before Sharon's stroke, the assistant will experience stress in having to delay or even postpone such a vacation. It is virtually impossible to envision all the people who may be affected by Sharon's medical emergency, but it is important for those who come to her aid to look as far as possible for any unaddressed stress that could reverberate back to Sharon.

This relationship between crisis and stress cannot be overemphasized. Although stressful events, emotional upsets, and emergency situations are parts of life that have a potential for crisis, a *crisis does not necessarily follow a traumatic event.* Nor does crisis imply or inevitably lead to emotional or mental breakdown. Something that is a crisis for one person may not be for another. As long as we are able to handle stressful life events, we will not experience a crisis. But if stress overwhelms us, and we are unable to find a way out of our predicament, a crisis may result. Crises must be resolved constructively or emotional or mental illness, addictions, suicide, or violence against others can be the unfortunate outcome. And once emotional breakdown occurs, a person is more vulnerable to other stressful life events, thus beginning an interacting cycle of stress, crisis, and destructive crisis outcomes. Crisis does not occur in isolation but is usually experienced in dynamic interplay with stress and illness in particular cultural contexts.

Note that the events of our lives do not themselves activate crisis. Crisis occurs when our interpretation of these events, our coping ability, and the limitations of our social resources lead to distress so severe that we cannot find relief. Accordingly, understanding people in crisis and knowing how to help them involves attention not only to the emotional tension experienced but also to the social, cultural, and material factors that influence how people respond to stressful life events. The heart of successful crisis resolution consists of *reducing one's vulnerability while enhancing one's resilience and capacity for emotional growth.*

For no matter how much we carefully plan, we cannot always avoid a crisis. What we can avoid, however, is the *danger* lurking beneath the surface of every crisis, which seeks to pull us down toward the darkness and gloom of depression and dysfunction. The challenge for everyone in crisis is to see and to grasp the *opportunity* presented by the crisis so that the crisis will be short lived, that we learn from it, and can return to our normal lives as soon as possible but better than before.

SOME COMMON NOTIONS ABOUT PEOPLE IN CRISIS AND HOW TO HELP THEM

People, much like Sharon, have been experiencing stress, predicaments, and life crises from the beginning of time. They have also found a variety of ways to resolve predicaments and live through crises. People have always helped others cope with stressful life events as well. The biblical Noah anticipating the great flood is an example of how our ancestors handled crises. Noah was warned of the serious predicament he and his family would be facing shortly. They prepared for the event by working together even in the face of ridicule and jesting from their neighbors. Through various creative problem-solving techniques, they avoided being overwhelmed by the floodwaters.

Insights developed through the psychological and social sciences have helped people understand themselves and others in crisis. The advent of a more enlightened view of people in crisis has helped put to rest some old myths about "upset people." It is not so easy anymore to write a person off as "crazy" and institutionalize someone who is behaving strangely in the face of an upsetting event. However, the constraints of health care restructuring in the United States, and sometimes bias against those needing psychiatric treatment, can result in serious consequences when necessary treatment is shortchanged. The growing acceptance of crisis care as an essential facet of comprehensive health services is a promising development for people with problems or who are experiencing acute emotional distress.

Views about people in crisis and how to help them vary among health care workers as well as those involved in crisis management and intervention. Likewise, those in the midst of a crisis will have their own values and assumptions, which may affect how they handle their situation and the degree to which they can accept needed help. People involved in crisis intervention—parents, spouses, social workers, nurses, doctors, police, counselors, teachers—can be most helpful if they recognize that everyone has vast potential for growth and that crisis is a point of *opportunity* as well as *danger*.

For most of us, our healthiest human growth and greatest achievements can often be traced to the trust and hopeful expectations of significant others. Successful crisis intervention involves helping people take advantage of the opportunity and avoid the danger inherent in crisis. Our success in this task may hinge on our values and beliefs about persons experiencing crisis. In this book, the following values are assumed.

- People in crisis—while in a state of high tension and anxiety—are basically *normal* from the standpoint of diagnosable illness. However, the precrisis state for some persons in crisis may be that of emotional turmoil or mental illness. In these instances, the person can be viewed as ill while simultaneously experiencing a crisis. In some cases, emotional or mental breakdown is the result of a negative resolution of crisis, often because of inadequate social support. So even though crisis is related to emotional or mental disturbance, it is important to distinguish between crisis and diagnosable emotional and mental states—that is, psychiatric *disorders* in the biomedical paradigm.
- People in crisis are social by nature and live in specific cultural communities by necessity. Their psychological response to hazardous events therefore cannot be properly understood apart from a sociocultural context. Cultural sensitivity by crisis workers does not require detailed knowledge of another's cultural system. But it does include *withholding judgment* about behaviors that may appear "strange." It also involves sensitive inquiry about the meaning of customs and beliefs that inform a person's response to stressful life events.
- People in crisis generally are capable of helping themselves when facing critical events, although this capacity may be impaired to varying degrees. Their need for self-mastery and capacity for growth from the crisis experience are usually enhanced with timely help from friends, family, neighbors, and sometimes trained crisis workers. But failure to receive such help when needed can result in diminished growth and disastrous crisis resolution in the form of addictions, self-harm, suicide, assault on others, or mental breakdown. The strength of a person's desire for self-determination and growth, one's resilience, and available help from others will usually influence the outcome of crisis in a favorable direction.

- The prevention of burnout in human service workers is tied to their recognition of people's basic need for self-determination, even when in crisis. This implies resisting the tendency to rescue or "save" distressed people. Such tactics compromise the possibilities of a healthy crisis outcome. In contrast, actively fostering self-sufficiency contributes to an upset person's sense of control needed for positive crisis resolution. This is true especially when a fear of losing control is a major part of the crisis experience.
- The greatest economy and effectiveness of crisis care for health promotion and the prevention of suffering results when clinical care of individuals occurs in a public health and human rights framework. Crisis intervention is recognized as the third of three revolutionary phases during the last century in the mental and public health fields: (1) Freud's discovery of the unconscious, (2) the discovery of psychotropic drugs in the 1950s, and (3) crisis intervention in the 1960s and after.
- Although crisis intervention is not merely a Band-Aid (as it was formerly deemed) or simple preliminary action trivial in comparison with treatment by professional psychotherapists, *neither is it psychotherapy*. The fact that some of the same techniques, such as listening, are used by both psychotherapists and crisis workers does not mean that psychotherapy and crisis intervention are equated, any more than either can be equated with friendship or consultation, which also employ listening. Crisis intervention focuses on timely problem solving around hazardous life events and avoids probing into unconscious conflict and deep-seated psychological problems—the province of psychotherapy.

Growing numbers of counselors, family members, and others regard the stress and crises of human life as normal, as opportunities to advance from one level of maturity to another. Such was the case for the self-actualized individuals studied by the psychologist Abraham Maslow[1] decades ago. His study, unique in its time for its focus on normal rather than disturbed people, revealed that people are resilient and capable of virtually limitless growth and development. Growth, rather than stagnation and emotional breakdown, occurred for these people in the midst of pain, adversity, and the turmoil of events such as divorce and physical illness. This optimistic view of people and their problems is becoming a viable alternative to the popular view of life and human suffering in an illness or psychiatric disorder paradigm. Interpreting crisis as illness implies treatment or tranquilization, whereas viewing it as opportunity invites a human, growth-promoting response to people in crisis.

AVOIDING DANGER AND TAKING ADVANTAGE OF THE OPPORTUNITY IN CRISIS

The Chinese character for crisis represents both *danger* (of health decline, suicide, violence, substance abuse) and *opportunity* (for growth, development, and strength during future crises). Thus, even when we do not know what lies ahead, we can take advantage of the opportunity presented in every crisis. When we do know what lies ahead, we can prepare for stressful life events and usually avoid the potential danger in critical situations and life's turning points.

Unfortunately, far too many people fail to grasp the opportunity of crisis and instead fall into danger and emotional chaos. Although we cannot predict events such as the sudden death of a loved one, the premature birth of a child, or natural disaster, we can anticipate how people will react to them. In his study of survivors of the Cocoanut Grove fire, crisis pioneer Erich Lindemann[2] demonstrated the importance of recognizing crisis responses and preventing negative outcomes of crisis. Once a population or individual is identified as being at risk of crisis, we can use a number of time-honored approaches to prevent crisis and enhance growth. In addition, where a population or individual is already in the grip of crisis, we can help them loosen that grip so they can grasp the opportunity rather than the danger inherent in every crisis. The danger of crisis can also be avoided by interrupting the "downward spiral" of an acutely distressed person toward suicide, assault, or psychiatric disorder. See Figure 5.1 in Chapter 5 (Abuse and Downward Spiral), which links positive crisis outcomes to avoiding victim blaming and instead holding abusers accountable for their behavior.

DIVERSE APPROACHES TO CRISIS

Although "natural" crisis care is as old as recorded history, as a formal element of multilevel mental health services, the crisis field is fairly new. Because human beings encompass physical, emotional, social, and spiritual functions, no single theory is adequate to explain the crisis experience, its origins, or the most effective approach to helping people in crisis.

Accordingly, this book includes insights and strategies from psychology, nursing, sociology, psychiatry, anthropology, philosophy, political science, and critical analysis that feature a dynamic interdisciplinary framework emphasizing the following[3]:

- The individual, social, and cultural origins of crisis
- How a crisis develops from early warning signs to acute distress
- The emotional, behavioral, and other signs of an impending crisis and/or risk to life
- How stress, crisis, and illness (physical and mental) are interrelated
- The skills needed to deal with major life changes and the risk of violence toward self or others, and disaster

- The positive resolution of crises using psychological, social, material, and cultural resources
- How a person or family in crisis and significant others can work together toward positive crisis resolution
- The global social-political task of reducing the crisis vulnerability of various disadvantaged groups through social change strategies and health care advocacy in a public health and human rights framework

These elements of crisis theory and practice are illustrated relationally in the Crisis Paradigm (Fig. 1.1). The Crisis Paradigm depicts (1) the *crisis process* experienced by the distressed person from origin through resolution and (2) the place of natural and formal crisis intervention in promoting growth and avoiding negative crisis outcomes. This paradigm is based on research and clinical experience with survivors of violence, other life event research, and work with survivors of human-made disasters.[4] The inclusion of sociocultural origins of crisis extends the

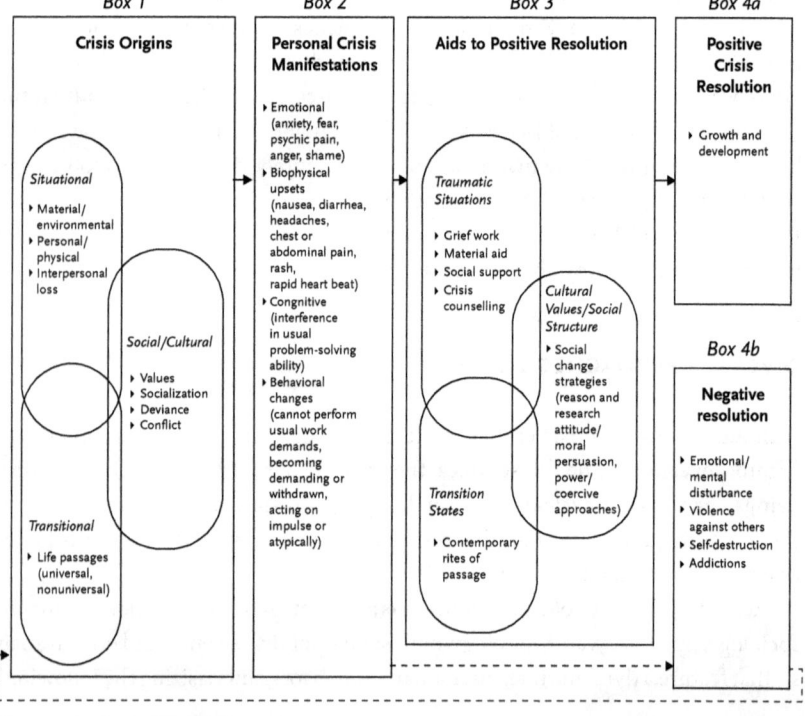

Figure 1.1 Crisis Paradigm
Crisis origins, manifestations, and outcomes and the respective functions of crisis care have interactional relationships. The intertwined circles represent the distinct yet interrelated origins of crisis and aids to positive resolution, even though personal manifestations are often similar. The arrows pointing from origins to positive resolution illustrate the *opportunity for growth and development* through crisis. The broken line at the bottom depicts the potential *danger of crisis* in the absence of appropriate aids. The loop between Box 4b and Box 1 denotes the *vulnerability* to future crisis episodes following negative outcomes.

traditional focus of crisis intervention on situational and developmental life events. The paradigm's inclusive framework is intended to guide crisis care for people who are *intentionally* injured through violence, prejudice, neglect, or preventable disaster.

The paradigm suggests a tandem approach to crisis care—that is, attending to the immediate problem while not losing sight of the social change and public health strategies needed to address the complex sociocultural origins of certain crisis situations. This perspective serves as the framework for the life crisis situations presented throughout this book.

A CONTINUUM OF CRISIS SERVICES

The key goals of crisis service are to save lives and offer distressed persons the most effective and least costly care available while enhancing client independence and family stability to the greatest extent possible. This implies a major emphasis on crisis prevention and early intervention close to the person's residence and community.[5] For example, college student health and counseling services should be tightly linked to psychiatric follow-up care for students at risk of suicide and/or violence toward others. Figure 1.2 illustrates this point and the public health principles and relationship between primary, secondary, and tertiary prevention. Public education, consultation, and emergency mental health services encompass *primary prevention*, which aims to reduce the prospect of mental disability and assist distressed people to learn and grow stronger through a hazardous event such as Sharon's stroke.

Secondary prevention implies that some form of mental disability has already occurred because of the absence of primary activities or because a person is unable to profit from these activities. In Sharon's case, there is no evidence of mental disability, while family and formal supports will help her avoid mental breakdown or

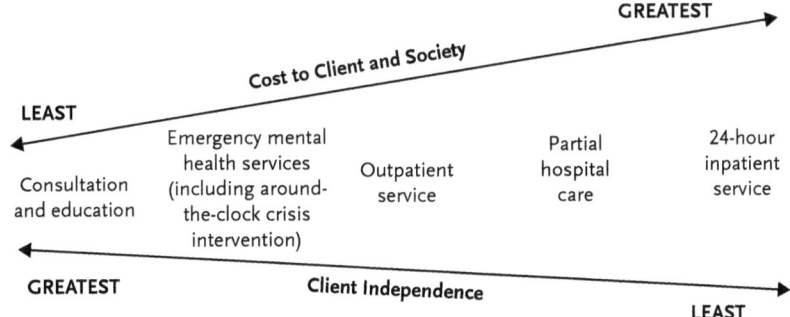

Figure 1.2 Continuum of Mental Health Services: Cost and Client Independence
Assisting distressed people in their usual social roles (homemaker, paid worker, student) through consultation, education, and crisis services is the *least* costly means of service and allows the *greatest* client independence; institution-based care is the *most* costly means and allows the *least* client independence.

dysfunction. *Tertiary prevention* aims to reduce long-term disabling effects for someone recovering from a mental disorder. It includes clinic-based counseling or psychotherapy, and partial or 24-hour inpatient psychiatric care. Public education programs should ensure that all community residents are aware of the continuum of crisis services they are entitled to as a basic human right and which they and their neighbors might need in dangerous or life-threatening situations. They also speak to the importance of crisis care available in every community and in primary care settings.

The continuum suggests that people with problems vary in their dependency on other people and agencies for help. It also illustrates the economic implications of crisis intervention in addition to its clinical and humanistic benefits. However, in the United States, health and human service workers trying to implement community-based crisis approaches in their individual practices are often frustrated by insurance reimbursement policies that underscore persistent disparities in coverage for those needing mental health care.

The five essential services illustrated in the continuum, including crisis care, were originally mandated by the Community Mental Health Acts of 1963 and 1965 in the United States.[6] Later federal guidelines for basic services include rehabilitation, addiction services, victim services, specialized care for the elderly and children, and evaluation programs. Unfortunately, various policy decisions and financial constraints have curtailed many of these programs, including mental health and crisis care, which have a sort of "second-cousin" status in the health care system.

FRUITS OF COORDINATED CARE VERSUS THE "REVOLVING DOOR"

To underscore the social and cultural concepts central to the Crisis Paradigm presented here and to affirm current emphasis on community-based crisis care, let us consider the economy of early preventive intervention in the home, timely psychiatric treatment, and smooth linkage among other elements of comprehensive health service.

In the United States, a much publicized dramatic swing of the pendulum has occurred as a result of failed policies around "deinstitutionalization" of persons with serious mental illness. The original goal was to provide community-based services for such persons and to use psychiatric hospitalization only when there was serious danger of suicide or homicide and cognitive impairment resulting in life-threatening neglect of basic self-care due to serious mental illness with which a family member could no longer cope. A key factor in this failed policy is that money (public funding of mental health services) did not follow the discharged patients to the community. The tragic result is confinement of thousands of mentally ill persons to the street, jails, and prisons often under deplorable conditions.

When public education and knowledge of necessary mental health services (as originally mandated) are lacking, a vicious cycle and all-too-common "revolving door" syndrome can occur, with these spokes in the wheel:

1. Psychiatric patients are discharged prematurely to the streets or home (based on pressure from the insurance industry and "cheaper" costs, *not* clinical judgment about the patient's needs) with minimal or no treatment for serious mental illness or substance abuse.
2. The patient enters a general hospital emergency department when in crisis.
3. De-escalation and/or restraint is applied—typically with powerful psychotropic drugs; while chemical restraint may be necessary in a dangerous situation, it can also serve as a Band-Aid for the serious policy issue of underfunded psychiatric treatment.
4. The vulnerable patient is discharged (sometimes prematurely and just back to the streets) with minimal or no psychiatric follow-up.
5. The patient experiences a repeat crisis episode and readmission to the emergency department—and the revolving door continues at great personal and social cost.

Across the country and internationally there is progress toward interrupting the "revolving door" cycle out of commitment both to service ideals and cost containment. One example of this effort is at Boston Medical Center, a private nonprofit facility and major trauma treatment center, with nearly 500 beds. Its Violence Intervention Advocacy Program was launched in 2006 with support of the Public Health Commission. As program director Dr. Thea James says: "We try to break cycles because if we don't people just come back." The hospital cites significant improvement in the rate of return to the emergency department by persons living on the edge and at risk of violence.[7]

Journalist Pete Earley dramatically illustrates this syndrome in his attempt to obtain appropriate treatment of his son Mike who was diagnosed with bipolar illness. Every family seeking appropriate psychiatric treatment for a loved one would feel empowered (and perhaps inspired toward action for reform) by Mr. Earley's book: *Crazy: A Father's Search Through America's Mental Health Madness*.[8]

Instead of appropriate treatment—in this case, inadequate and dictated by the insurance industry, *not* professional mental health standards—Mike was subjected to the "revolving door" between hospital and jail. This heart-rending saga, and Mr. Earley's later extensive investigation of the bigger picture citing thousands of similar cases, reveals the enormous and tragic human costs of failed policies and inadequate funding of the federally mandated community mental health services.

Mr. Earley's account dramatically illustrates this sad reality: *Jails and prisons are now de facto psychiatric institutions for thousands of inmates*—new "cages" that humane and reform-minded mental health professionals and others believed were a horrific relic of the past. But instead these cages provide a bare minimum of treatment for many whose crimes are related to inadequate crisis services and untreated psychiatric disorders. Earley's work and that of many others support this unfortunate reality that is compounded by race, class, and gender factors.

That is, if a well-situated journalist like Mr. Earley could experience such a nightmare trying to get appropriate treatment for his son Mike—only to see him land in prison—think of the thousands of people in crisis who are disadvantaged because they are poor or are struggling as an immigrant. A stark and shameful reality is that the large majority of these caged inmates are young and poor Black or Latino males with limited chances of community-based treatment or jobs in the event of their release—traceable in part to the remnants and unfinished business of the civil rights era.

Research thus not only supports the hazards of being uprooted from natural social settings but also provides a sober reminder of this social reality: Health and criminal justice agencies are indeed subcultures of the larger society in which crisis intervention by family members, friends, police, and neighbors is an everyday occurrence. This does not preclude the need for formal crisis intervention by persons specially trained for this task. Rather, it highlights the fact that the prospects for positive crisis resolution by individuals, families, and peer groups are enhanced and negative complications are reduced when *formal crisis care occurs early and as close as possible to natural settings.*

It also means that when crisis assessment reveals the need for psychiatric inpatient treatment, the crisis worker and family members should not be burdened with insurance and other obstacles such as Pete Earley encountered in trying to get help for his son stricken by a serious mental illness. The following account of a counselor doing crisis work in a home supports these points.

The example of Ray and his family illustrates how a crisis counselor offered help at home to avoid more costly secondary and tertiary levels of care, and possible imprisonment. It underscores the importance of prevention and 24-7 crisis intervention in home and community settings.

EXAMPLE: HOME-BASED CRISIS CARE—RAY AND FAMILY

Recently, another counselor and I made a home visit to a family that was very upset because the parents thought their 22-year-old son Ray had "flipped out" on drugs. The parents had called with the express purpose of getting their son into psychiatric hospital care, even though he had refused to go before. When they called, I said that we would not automatically put Ray in the hospital but that we would come over to assess the situation and help the entire family through the crisis. We worked out a strategy for telling Ray directly and clearly the reasons for our visit. Ray refused to come to the phone, shouting, "They're the people who will take me to the hospital in an ambulance."

When we got there, a family session revealed that Ray was the scapegoat for many other family problems. This assertion does not mitigate the impact of Ray's drug abuse. We assisted each family member in accepting responsibility for her or his own actions while at the same time helping Ray to see and accept his role in precipitating the family crisis in which he was now embroiled.

We also succeeded in helping the family to recognize the extent to which they were enabling Ray in his drug abuse by blaming him for just about every stressful event experienced in this family. The family was locked in a revolving cycle from which none of them could escape without formal crisis intervention.

Ray's situation shows that previous strategies to break that cycle had failed because attention was *focused solely on Ray with little attention to his environment and relationships*. As noted in the case of Sharon and her relations with her family, job, and soccer club, Ray's crisis cannot be managed successfully without attention paid to his family, which is affected by Ray's drug use even as family problems appear related to that drug use.

Again, this crisis cycle usually cannot be broken from within. But it can be pierced and effectively dissolved by competent crisis intervention and follow-up counseling. With that in mind, the crisis counselors worked out a crisis service plan, and Ray started to show some trust in them after about 2 hours with the whole family. He could see that the counselors did not come there just to whisk him off to a mental hospital. In the end, even Ray's family was relieved that he did not have to go to the hospital. Before the home visit, they had seen no other way out. They had talked with several therapists before, but *no one had ever come to the house or worked with the whole family*.

Although psychiatric hospital treatment is necessary in some cases, its cost in both human and economic terms may be even greater if discharge is premature and community and family supports are inadequate. The example of Ray and his family reveals the importance of integrating biomedical with development approaches in acute crisis situations. In the event that psychotropic medication is indicated, the long-term results will almost certainly be enhanced if used in combination with crisis counseling, an intensive home treatment plan, and possibly rehabilitation services.

BASIC STEPS IN CRISIS CARE

As seen in Ray's case, family members facing a crisis at home are typically the first responders—offering "natural" crisis care. But for many, "formal" crisis service is needed. When that is the case, significant others (family, friends, and neighbors) *should know what to expect* from crisis care providers in health and social service agencies. They need to recognize the basic steps in professional crisis care as a baseline for evaluating whether they received the service they are entitled to.

Because of needing relief from the acute emotional pain of crisis, resolution (either positive or negative) will occur in a short time frame (typically 1–6 weeks) with or without the assistance of others. For example, if help is not available, some crises are resolved by suicide or violence toward others (see Fig. 1.1). Ray's case illustrates that crisis care can be offered in a variety of settings, some natural, some institutional. Regardless of the context or variations in personal style, the probability of positive crisis outcomes is greatly enhanced by careful attention to the basic steps of crisis care, which include the following:

1. Psychosocial assessment of the individual or family crisis, including evaluation of victimization trauma and the risk of suicide or assault on others
2. Development of a plan with the person or family in crisis
3. Implementation of the plan, drawing on personal, social, and material resources
4. Follow-up and evaluation of the crisis care process and outcomes
5. Referral of the individual or family for follow-up counseling or family therapy where appropriate

Broadly these basic steps of crisis care correspond to the *problem-solving process* used in medical, nursing, and social work practice, as well as in other human service protocols. The example of Ray and his family illustrates both "natural" crisis intervention as employed by his family, as well as a formal, structured process (see Fig. 1.1). It underscores the fact that everyone recognizes when someone is "crazy," that is, not acting according to commonly accepted social norms—at home, in school, on the bus or streets. The home visit to Ray's family revealed their inability to handle the crisis alone. They managed the crisis by calling for and receiving professional help. In sharp contrast, despite Pete Earley's repeated efforts on behalf of his son, Mike landed in the criminal justice system *explicitly traceable to denial of the psychiatric treatment he needed.*

A focus on early intervention and prevention of negative crisis outcomes includes providing the average person, through public education programs, with more skills in detecting victimization and the risk of suicide, assault, or homicide, and in assessing the advantages and limits of psychiatric hospitalization. Professional providers would then be less likely to simply discount what people in crisis say. After all, professional assessments must in the end rely on data presented by the traumatized, suicidal, or disturbed person; the family; police; and other laypersons.

REFERENCES, FURTHER READING, DISCUSSION GUIDE

REFERENCES
1. Maslow, A. (1970). *Motivation and personality* (2nd ed.). New York: HarperCollins.
2. Lindemann, E. (1944). Symptomatology and management of acute grief. *American Journal of Psychiatry, 101*, 101–148. (Reprinted from *Crisis intervention: Selected readings*, by H. J. Parad (Ed.), 1965, New York: Family Service Association of America)
3. Hoff, L. A., Hallisey, B. J., & Hoff, M. (2009). *People in crisis: Clinical and diversity perspectives:* New York: Routledge.

4. Hoff, L. A. (1990). *Battered women as survivors*. London: Routledge.
5. Caplan, G. (1964). *Principles of preventive psychiatry*. New York: Basic Books.
6. Levine, M. (1981). *The history and politics of community mental health*. New York: Oxford University Press.
7. Irons, M. E. (January 9, 2014). Walsh's hospital tour focuses on victims of violence. *The Boston Globe*, B3.
8. Earley, P. (2006). *Crazy: A father's search through America's mental health madness*. New York: Berkley Books.

FURTHER READING

Antonovsky, A. (1980). *Health, stress, and coping*. San Francisco: Jossey-Bass.
Becker, D. (2013). *One nation under stress: The trouble with stress as an idea*. New York: Oxford University Press.
Freeman, D., & Freeman, J. (2013). *The stressed sex: Uncovering the truth about men, women & mental health*. Oxford, UK: Oxford University Press.
Graham, L. (2013). *Bouncing back: Re-wiring your brain for maximum resilience and well-being*. Novato, CA: New World Library.
Hanson, R. (2009). *Buddha's brain: The practical neuro-science of happiness, love and wisdom*. Oakland, CA: New Harbinger.
Hoff, L. A. (1993). Review essay: Health policy and the plight of the mentally ill. *Psychiatry*, 56(4), 400–419.
Johnson, A. B. (1990). *Out of bedlam: The truth about deinstitutionalization*. New York: Basic Books.
Sobo, E. J., & Loustaunau, M.O. (2nd ed.) *The cultural context of health, illness, and medicine*. Santa Barbara, CA: Praeger.

DISCUSSION GUIDE

1. From reading this chapter (and perhaps References and Further Reading), explore with your family or trusted friends a stressful situation of your own or of someone you love, and consider this question: Do you think this was an example of acute crisis, a sign of mental illness, an occasion of everyday life stress, or a combination of these factors? If a combination, which event or circumstance do you think most clearly explains Sharon's situation? Or consider something similar in your own life.
2. How have common notions about crisis influenced your decisions to either seek help or "go it alone" through life's ups and downs? If you have looked for help, which approaches were most useful to you and your family (e.g., counseling, medication)? Which did you experience as inadequate or disappointing, and why? And what were you able to do to correct the inadequacy?
3. In exploring the Crisis Paradigm (Fig. 1.1), how helpful is it in understanding yourself or someone else in distress or life-threatening danger?
4. If you or someone you care about needed help in an acutely stressful or dangerous situation, how well were the services coordinated to avoid "falling through the cracks" of a complex health care system?
5. Do you know an acutely distressed person who landed in jail or prison because 24-hour community-based crisis services were lacking? If yes, consider what you, your family, and others might do to address this serious issue in mental health care.

CHAPTER 2

Recognizing Different Faces of Distress on the Road to Full-Blown Crisis

Knowing the difference between everyday upsetting events and life-or-death danger

CHAPTER OUTLINE

The Faces of Distress   *31*
Why People Go Into Crisis   *32*
How a Crisis Develops   *32*
Example: John—Positive Outcome   *33*
Example: George—Negative Outcome   *35*
The Duration and Outcomes of Crisis   *37*
Recognizing an Impending Crisis: Asking the Right Questions   *41*
Triage Questions: Screening for Victimization and Life-Threatening Behaviors   *42*
Typical Feelings and Other Responses During Crisis   *45*
Navigating the Assessment Process   *46*
Example: Delaine's Multiple Losses   *46*
Knowing the Difference Between a Stressful Event and a Crisis State   *48*
No Such Thing as Chronic Crisis   *51*
References, Further Reading, Discussion Guide   *52*

We have seen how crisis originates from physical, material, personal, social, and cultural sources, as well as how it fits into the larger picture of life's ups and downs. While everyone experiences stressful moments at some point, several factors influence whether a person falls into a crisis state. Among these are available resources and the reactions and actions of those close by: family, friends, and others who may be in a position to help.

THE FACES OF DISTRESS

Edward, age 45, had been an outstanding assistant director of his company. When he was promoted to the vacated position of executive director, instead of rising to the challenge in his customary, easy-going manner, he became depressed and virtually nonfunctional: He would not answer phone calls and stopped seeing his friends. A long-time competitive player, he even discontinued his weekly squash game at the local gym. Edward, despite external signs of success, lacks basic self-confidence; he cannot face the challenge of his new job. He found the possibility of failure in his new position unbearable, and his anxiety prevented him from achieving the success he desires. If he gets help quickly, Edward is one among many people who, with the help of family and friends and perhaps a crisis counselor, can get through this episode without falling into a full-blown crisis state. He has his whole past career, including many successes, to draw on profitably in his present job. With help, he might see that even if he did fail in his present position, it need not mean the end of a happy and productive life.

Shock and a resulting crisis state can also occur during normal role transitions, whether or not a stressful event occurs. Mary, age 21, relied very heavily on her mother for advice and support in all aspects of her life. One month after her honeymoon and the move into an apartment with her husband, she became depressed and suicidal and was unable to function at home or work. Her new husband, also facing a transition to adult responsibilities, did not know how to deal with Mary, who seemed to him totally alien from the fun-loving, high-spirited woman he had married. Mary was obviously not ready for the move from adolescence into the more independent role of a young married adult.

Joan, also age 21, is another person who cannot meet the challenge of increasing her personal and social resources. Even though she had always dreamed of becoming a teacher since she was a little girl, she became paralyzed by her fear of the responsibilities involved in a teaching career and so has difficulty obtaining her degree. At examination time, she is unable to study and fails over half of her college courses. At the same time, she worries about coming out as a lesbian. The conflict that Joan experiences around revealing her sexual identity is compounded by the regular transition to adulthood faced by all adolescents. Joan's challenge to increase her social/psychological "supplies" in preparation for an adult teaching responsibility is more than she can face without additional resources. She feels like a failure—she does not realize that help is available, let alone how to find that help.

What these two young women have in common with Edward, over 20 years their senior, is that they are all on the threshold of crisis. The steps that they and those around them take during this vulnerable time can make the difference between healthy stress management and facing it as a time of learning and growth, or sinking into a full-blown crisis.

WHY PEOPLE GO INTO CRISIS

A happy, healthy life implies an ability to solve problems effectively. It also implies that basic human needs are fulfilled. Our basic needs include a sense of physical and psychological well-being; a supportive network of friends, family, and associates; and a sense of identity and belonging to one's society and cultural heritage. People in crisis can find themselves in a vulnerable state, whether it be by a sudden shock following death of a child, being victimized by a crime, or by a gradual change such as suffering years of abuse. Emotionally upset, they are unable to solve life's problems in their usual way.

Typically, people in crisis suffer a *sudden loss or threat of loss* of a person or thing considered essential and important. One or several of their basic attachments are severed or are at risk of being severed. For example, if Edward cannot handle the responsibilities of his new job, he risks losing the respect and esteem of his colleagues. Likewise, if Joan comes out of the closet, she risks possible abandonment by her friends and family. This fear, or dread, whether or not it materializes, can have the same impact as a sudden loss of connections, for example, through the unexpected death of a loved one by car accident or heart attack where the person's familiar source of support and comfort disappears without warning, with no time to adjust to the change. Similar shock occurs in response to the suicide of a friend, threat of divorce, diagnosis of a terminal illness such as Lou Gehrig's disease, or a serious operation for cancer. A person with AIDS, for example, not only loses health and faces the probability of a shortened life cycle but also may be abandoned by friends and family or scorned by would-be helpers.

When these events happen while the individual is going through a normal, life-stage transition such as adolescence to adulthood, the extra stress may compound the situation and push a person over the edge. While most of us adapt to transitions with fairly minor disruptions—from college to professional life, from life with children to an empty nest—these changes can leave us vulnerable to crisis. Remember the all-too-familiar stereotype of the middle-age man who reacts to his receding hairline by buying a fancy sports car or having an affair? In the case of Mary and Joan, they are both in these vulnerable, transitory states. Joan is at even more risk for crisis because, in addition to finishing her college work and planning a career, she is also sharing her sexual identity with her family and friends—and confronting how that might change these relationships, some of which she has had her whole life.

HOW A CRISIS DEVELOPS

A crisis does not occur instantaneously. There are identifiable phases of development that lead to an active crisis state. These phases were first described in 1957 by James

Tyhurst[1] in his study of people responding to community disaster. He found that survivors experience three overlapping phases: (1) a period of impact, (2) a period of recoil, and (3) a posttraumatic period. The breakdown of phases applies most appropriately to crises originating from catastrophic or shocking events such as rape and other violent attacks, or war-related devastation (discussed in Chapters 5 and 8).

Several years later, psychiatrist Gerald Caplan[2] described four phases in the development of extreme anxiety and crisis. His description of phases is helpful when looking at more gradually increasing stress levels that, if left unchecked, can leave one more vulnerable to crisis when faced with "one more thing": *the straw that breaks the camel's back*. Recognizing these phases of crisis development is useful in *preventing* stressful life events from spiraling into full-blown crises.

EXAMPLE: JOHN—POSITIVE OUTCOME

Phase One

A traumatic event causes an initial rise in one's level of anxiety. To get rid of this anxiety, the individual responds with familiar problem-solving mechanisms to reduce or eliminate the stress and discomfort. During this phase, the level of stress may or may not be seen as egregious. This phase is marked more by the person's *capacity to cope* with the stress than by the degree of stress. Take the case of John, age 34, who is striving toward a career as an executive in his company when he receives a diagnosis of multiple sclerosis. Fortunately, his wife, Nancy, is very supportive. He adjusts to this potentially devastating event by continuing to work as long as he can. John also has the advantage of comprehensive health insurance that helps provide him with the most advanced medical treatment available. In addition, John's physician is skillful in applying his knowledge of the emotional impact of John's diagnosis. As a result, John is able to cope with his illness so he does not slip into a crisis state at this time. His friends remark how well he has taken this news and how the family seems to have taken it all in stride.

Phase Two

In this phase, the person's usual problem-solving ability fails, while the stimulus that caused the initial rise in tension continues. Despite the excellent care he has been receiving, John's disease continues to advance. His wife begins to participate less and less in some of her own interests—including volunteer work—so she can spend more time with her husband. The accumulating medical expenses and loss of work time strain the family's financial resources. This strain affects the whole family: John and Nancy receive a report from school that their teenage son, Larry, is having behavioral problems. At this stage, the level of stress is clearly increasing, warning signs are also present, but a crisis is not inevitable. There is an opportunity here for crisis prevention. Whether John slips into a full-blown crisis state depends on what happens next in his life, both the steps that he himself takes and those that family and friends take on his behalf.

Phase Three

Unable to resolve the stressful pattern, in this phase the individual's anxiety level rises further. The increased tension moves the person to use every resource available—including unusual or new means—to solve the problem and reduce the increasingly painful state of anxiety. We often hear of people who have come out of a state of crisis saying that they found strength or resources they did not know they had—a common characteristic of this phase.

In John's case, he fortunately has enough inner strength, confidence, and sensitivity to recognize the strain of his illness on his wife and child. He looks for new ways to cope with his increasing stress. First, he confides in his physician, who responds by taking time to listen and offer emotional support. His physician also arranges for home health services through a visiting nurse agency. This outside health assistance frees Nancy from some of her steadily increasing responsibilities. The physician also encourages John and Nancy to seek help from the school guidance counselor regarding their son, Larry, which they do.

Flexibility is key to averting a crisis during this phase. In addition to utilizing inner resources and seeking and accepting help from others, success in this phase often depends on changing the rules of the game by redefining or changing one's goals. This means of avoiding crisis is not usually possible for someone who is emotionally isolated from others and feels locked into solving a problem alone.

Prior to his illness, John defined himself in terms of what he could do. After his diagnosis, he at first was tempted to see the limitations his illness imposed on him, seeing only what he could no longer do. He began to feel sorry for himself, but then saw the effect this had on his family. When he saw the changes his wife had been willing to make in order to support him, he decided to change his approach. Gradually, John began to realize that changing his attitude required developing a positive image of himself.

As John's illness progressed, it became necessary to change his role as the family's sole financial provider. John and Nancy began to talk openly with each other about the situation. Together, they decided that Nancy would take a job to ease both the financial strain and her encroaching sense of isolation. They also asked the nursing agency to increase the home health services, since Nancy was beginning to resent the increasing demands of being both nurse to her husband and supplemental income provider.

Phase Four

This final phase is the state of active crisis that results when internal strength and social support are lacking, the person's problem remains unresolved, and the tension and anxiety rise to an unbearable degree.

John successfully averts this stage and does not go into a full-blown crisis state because he is able to respond constructively to his unanticipated illness. The news here is that *crisis is not inevitable*. The various decisions and actions one takes during any one of the three preceding phases can derail the movement toward acute crisis. John has natural social supports and is able to use available help, so his stress does not become unbearable.

EXAMPLE: GEORGE—NEGATIVE OUTCOME

Not all outcomes are as fortunate. Take the following example of George, which is in sharp contrast to the earlier example of John. George, age 48, works as a machinist with a construction company. Four evenings a week he works a second job as a taxi driver in a large metropolitan area; his beat includes high-crime sections of the city. He has just come home from the hospital after his third heart attack. The first occurred at age 44 and the second at age 47.

Phase One

George is advised by his physician to cut down on his work hours. Specifically, the doctor strongly recommends that he give up his second job and spend more time relaxing with family and friends. George's physician recognizes his patient's vulnerability to heart attacks, especially in relation to his lifestyle. George rarely slows down. He is chronically angry about things going wrong and not being able to get ahead financially. George receives his physician's advice with mixed feelings. He understands the relationship between his heavy work schedule and his heart attacks; however, he still reacts to the news emotionally. He feels that he does not deserve what is happening to him, and he resents what he acknowledges as a necessary change to reduce further risk to his health and possibly an early death.

George becomes locked in a vicious cycle. His health and financial problems markedly increase his usual level of anxiety, which increases his health problems. Having grown up in a home where his parents did not talk openly to one another in front of him and his two brothers, he talks only superficially to his wife, Marie, about his dilemma, subsequently receiving little support or understanding from her and further straining their relationship. Marie suggests that in place of George's second job, she increase her part-time job to full time. George reacts with anger because of what this implies about his image of himself as the chief provider.

George's discouragement and anger about not getting ahead are aggravated by Marie's complaints of never having enough money for the things she wants. George also resents what he perceives as the physician's judgment that he is not strong enough to do two jobs.

Phase Two

George fails to obtain relief from his anxiety by talking with his wife. In addition, he does not feel comfortable talking with his physician about his reluctance to cut down the work stress as advised. When he attempts to do so, he senses that the physician is rushed. So he concludes that his doctor is only concerned about giving technical advice, not about how George handles the advice. The prospect of quitting his second job, which he happens to enjoy, and bringing home less money leaves George feeling like a failure. Unable to resolve these conflicting tensions, his tension escalates. If he quits his second job, he cannot preserve his image as adequate family provider; yet he cannot reduce the risk of death by heart disease, if he continues at his present pace. He sees no possible solution. Help from other resources seems hopelessly out of reach.

Phase Three

George's increased anxiety moves him to again try talking with his wife. Ordinarily, he would have abandoned the idea based on the response he received earlier. Thus, this action—characteristic of Phase Three creative problem-solving approaches—constitutes an unusual effort for him, but he fails again in getting the help he needs. To make matters worse, George and Marie learn that their 16-year-old son, Arnold, has been suspended from school for a week due to suspected drug involvement. Instead of seeing this event in relation to the problems he is already experiencing, George and Marie see this as "one more thing"—as an additional problem they have to confront. This leaves George feeling like even more of a failure, as he is seldom home during normal family hours, and it seems to prove Marie's point that he does not spend enough time with the children. George's high level of anxiety becomes so obvious that Marie finally suggests that he talk to a psychologist about his problems, since he does not seem able to talk with her. George knows that this is a good idea but cannot bring himself to do it, as he has always taken pride in solving his own problems. In addition, he cannot accept his wife's proposal to start working full time. Personality and social factors block him from redefining or changing his goals as a means of problem resolution and crisis prevention. Financial concerns, along with the new problem of his son, further increase his anxiety level. George is in a predicament he does not know how to resolve.

Phase Four

George is at a complete loss about how to deal with all the stress in his life: the threat to his health and life if he continues his present pace, the threat to his self-image if he quits the second job, the failure to communicate with his wife, and the sense of failure and guilt in his role as a parent. He is in a state of active crisis.

George's case highlights the subjective elements that contribute to a crisis state at different times in people's lives. George's heart disease was clearly an unanticipated, stressful event. His son Arnold's threat of suspension was unanticipated and a source of added stress. Yet Arnold's adolescence should have been anticipated as a normal phase of human development. Furthermore, if George's heart disease had developed at a time when his marriage was less strained, he might have received more help and support. Also, Arnold might have made it through adolescence without school suspension if there had been regular support from both parents. As it turned out, George and Marie had their first report of Arnold's behavior problems in school shortly after George's first heart attack 4 years earlier. They were advised at that time to seek family or marital counseling, which they did, but only for a single session. Finally, because George and Marie were firmly entrenched in stereotypical male and female roles, this created an added source of stress and was a barrier to constructive crisis resolution.

For another person, such as John in the previous case, or for George at another time of life, the same medical diagnosis and the same advice could have had an altogether different effect. This is also true for Arnold. A different response from his parents when he gave his first signals of distress, or a more constructive approach from school officials and counselors, might have prevented the additional stress of Arnold's school suspension. The interview example in Table 2.1 reveals the build-up toward suicidal crisis.

THE DURATION AND OUTCOMES OF CRISIS

People cannot stay in crisis forever. The state of crisis and the accompanying anxiety are too painful. Because one cannot survive indefinitely in such a state of psychological pain and turmoil, there is a natural time limitation to the crisis experience. The emotional distress stemming from extreme anxiety moves the person toward action and reducing the anxiety to an endurable level as soon as possible. As a result, the person in crisis is at the proverbial fork in the road. This aspect of the crisis experience underscores the *danger* and the *opportunity* that crisis presents.

Table 2.1 BUILD-UP TO SUICIDAL CRISIS—INTERVIEW EXAMPLE

Assessment Techniques		Interview Between George Sloan and Emergency Department Nurse
Signals of Distress and Crisis to Be Identified	*Nurse:*	Hello, Mr. Sloan. Would you like to be called Mr. Sloan or George?
	George:	George is fine.
	Nurse:	Will you tell me what happened, George?
	George:	I had a car accident. Can't you see that without asking? (slightly hostile and seemingly reluctant to talk)
	Nurse:	Yes, I know, George. But the police said you were going the wrong way on the expressway. How did that happen?
Active Crisis State: Extreme anxiety to the breaking point	*George:*	Yes, that's right. (hesitates) Well, I just couldn't take it anymore, but I guess it didn't work.
	Nurse:	Sounds like you've been having a rough time, George. Can you tell me what it is you can't take anymore?
Hazardous Event/ Situation: Physical illness	*George:*	Well, I've got heart trouble...
Vulnerable State: Loss of external social supports or inability to use them		It's gotten to be too much for my wife. I can't expect her to do much more.
Loss of personal coping ability		We're having trouble with our 16-year-old son, Arnold.
Inability to communicate stress to significant others		I just couldn't take it anymore. I figured I'd do everybody a favor and get rid of myself.
High-lethal suicide attempt	*Nurse:*	So your car accident was really an attempt to kill yourself?
	George:	That's right. That way, at least my wife wouldn't lose the insurance along with everything else she's had to put up with.
	Nurse:	I can see that your heart trouble and all your other troubles have left you feeling pretty bad.
Depression	*George:*	That's about it, too bad I came out alive. I really feel I'm worth more dead than alive.
	Nurse:	I can see that you're feeling desperate about your situation. How long have you felt this way?
	George:	I've had heart trouble for about 4 years. After my last heart attack, the doctor told me I had to slow down or it would probably kill me. Well, there's no way I can change things that I can see.

(Continued)

Table 2.1 (CONTINUED)

Assessment Techniques	Interview Between George Sloan and Emergency Department Nurse	
Precipitating Factor: Inability to perform in expected role as father	*Nurse:*	What happened this past week that made you decide to end it all?
	George:	Well, our kid Arnold got suspended from school—that did it! I figured if a father can't do any better with his son than that, what's the use?
	Nurse:	I gather from what you say that you just couldn't see any other way out.
State of Active Crisis: Vulnerability: Fixation on role expectations, inability to use outside helping resources	*George:*	That's right. Money is really getting tight; my wife was talking about getting a full-time job, and that really bothers me to think that I can't support my family anymore. And if she starts working more, things might get even worse with Arnold. There was no one to talk to. Suicide's the only thing left.
	Nurse:	With all these problems, George, have you ever thought about suicide before?
History of poor coping ability	*George:*	Yes, once, after my doctor told me to really watch it after my last heart attack. I felt pretty hopeless and thought of crashing my car then. But things weren't so bad then between me and my wife, and she talked me out of it and seemed willing to stick with me.
	Nurse:	I see, but this time you felt there was nowhere else to turn. Anyway, George, I'm glad your suicide attempt didn't work. I'd really like to help you consider some other ways to deal with all these problems.
	George:	I don't know what they could be. I really feel hopeless, but I guess I could see what you've got to offer.
	Nurse:	There are several things we can discuss.

Experience with people in crisis has led to the observation that the acute emotional upset of crisis lasts from a *few days to a few weeks*. The person must then move toward some sort of resolution; this is often expressed in terms such as: "I can't go on like this anymore… something has got to give"; "Please, tell me what to do to get out of this mess… I can't stand it"; or "I feel like I'm losing my mind."

What, then, happens to the person in crisis? Several outcomes are possible:

1. The person can return to his or her precrisis state. This happens through effective problem solving and one's inner strength, values, and social

supports. Such an outcome does not necessarily imply new psychological growth as a result of the experience; the person simply returns to his or her *usual* state of being.

2. The person may not only return to the precrisis state but can grow from the crisis experience through discovery of new resources and successful problem solving. These discoveries result from the crisis experience itself, as John's case illustrates. He took advantage of available resources such as his physician and the school guidance counselor. He found new ways to solve problems. The result for John was positive. His concept of himself as a worthwhile person was reinforced despite the loss of physical integrity from his illness, and he strengthened his marriage relationship. John also developed in his role as a father by constructively handling the problem with his son.

3. The person responds to his or her problem by lapsing into neurotic, psychotic, or destructive patterns of behavior. For example, the individual may become very withdrawn, suspicious, or depressed. A distorted perception of events can reach the point of blaming others inappropriately for the misfortunes experienced. Others in crisis resolve their problems, at least temporarily, by excessive drinking or other drug abuse, or by impulsive, disruptive behavior. Still others resort to more extreme measures by attempting or committing suicide or by abusing or even killing others.

The negative and destructive outcomes of the crisis experience described in outcome 3 occur among those who lack constructive ways to solve life's problems and relieve intolerable anxiety. George, for example, eventually concluded in his despair that he was worth more dead than alive. Feeling that he had already overburdened his family, George did not know where else to turn, so he deliberately crashed his car in order to spare them the stigma of suicide. But he did not die as planned, and instead he was brought to the hospital emergency department. (George's case is continued in Chapters 3 and 4 in respect to his emergency treatment and follow-up care.)

Considering all the possible outcomes of a crisis experience, it becomes clear that the actions and motives of family, friends, and others involved with someone in crisis are meaningful and can significantly affect which outcome the distressed person ultimately leans to. For those in a position to help, the following goals are clear:

- Help people in crisis to at least return to their precrisis state.
- Do everything possible to help a person grow and become stronger as a result of the crisis and effective problem solving.
- Be alert to danger signals in order to prevent negative, destructive outcomes of a crisis experience.

(See Fig. 1.1 in Chapter 1, Crisis Paradigm, Boxes 4a and 4b.)

RECOGNIZING AN IMPENDING CRISIS: ASKING THE RIGHT QUESTIONS

When faced with someone who may be approaching a crisis state—be it a family member, friend, or colleague, you may have many questions: What do I say? What questions should I ask? How do I find out what is really happening with someone who seems so confused and upset? How do I recognize a person in crisis? If the person in crisis is not crazy, what is the difference between mental illness and acute crisis? What roles do the family and community play on behalf of the person in crisis? I am not a professional, but how can I help?

The answers to assessment questions provide a broad picture of what psychiatrist Norris Hansell[3] proposes that we look for in what he calls "crisis plumage"—signs revealed by a person in crisis compared with one who is not. This plumage consists of distress signals that people send to others when experiencing a loss, are abused or in danger, or otherwise challenged to meet their basic needs, including the following:

1. Difficulty in managing one's feelings
2. Suicidal or homicidal thoughts
3. Using alcohol or other drugs to cope with anxiety
4. Trouble with the law
5. Inability to use available help effectively

The four phases of crisis development reveal people proceeding through life with varying levels of material, personal, and social/cultural resources or "supplies" (as Gerald Caplan puts it), as well as problem-solving skills to deal with various stressors. When these resources are intact, people generally avoid the possible negative outcomes of stressful life events and can adapt more easily. But when lacking such resources, the person in crisis usually seeks help—either directly or indirectly—through actions commonly referred to as "cries for help" from others to compensate for one's temporary inability to cope. However, in order to be part of the crisis solution rather than the problem, it is important to recognize the degree of the distressed person's vulnerability. This requires our understanding of the typical emotional, biophysical, cognitive, and behavioral responses to stressful or dangerous events (see Fig. 1.1 in Chapter 1, Crisis Paradigm, Box 2).

At this stage, simply suggesting that an upset person should seek help may not be the most productive approach, because appropriate help may not be immediately available. Or the person may resist help because "nothing's wrong" or such help is for "other people." The distressed person may need guidance to either resolve the crisis with available resources (inner fortitude or family support, for example) or accept the fact that outside resources are available.

Mental health experts typically follow a standard procedure, or protocol, when encountering a person in impending crisis. Whether you are approaching someone in crisis as a concerned friend or family member, or at your job as a front-line professional (police officer or social service worker, for example), or as a manager or supervisor, it is helpful to know this two-level assessment process so that your intercession can have the best possible outcome.

As you encounter someone in distress, the most important first step is *find out what happened* that led to the person's distress. For example, in the cases of John and George, the precipitating event was the sudden change in their health. In the case of Edward, whom we met earlier in the chapter, it was his promotion that unleashed the feelings of doubt and insecurity. Finally, in the cases of Mary and Joan, it was their transition from students to career women that brought out their feelings of distress. Knowing the exact source of distress allows us to tailor our approach. If you do not know, do not be afraid to simply ask, "What happened?" Sometimes people are so upset or overwhelmed by a series of things that they cannot clearly identify the sequence of events or pinpoint exactly what triggered the acute distress. In these instances, it is helpful to ask when the person began feeling so upset. Putting events in order has a calming effect; the person experiences a certain sense of self-possession in being able to make some order out of confusion... "Oh, now I remember." But once you know what happened, then what?

The mental health crisis care framework consists of two levels of assessment. The following questions must be asked at each level:

Level 1

Key questions for this first level include the following: Is there an obvious or potential threat to life, either that of the person in crisis or the lives of others? Has he or she been abused? And what are the risks of suicide, assault, and homicide?

Level 1 assessment can be done by anyone, including people in their natural roles of friend, neighbor, parent, and spouse, as well as people in various professional positions: physicians, nurses, teachers, police, clergy, welfare workers, and prison officials. *This level of assessment is critical*—with life and death dimensions that are the basis for mobilizing emergency services on behalf of the person, family, or community in crisis. In emergency medical and disaster situations, "triage" refers to the process of determining who is in danger and most in need of help. The key information to uncover at this stage is whether the person is being victimized and/or is a danger to self or others. Here is an example of triage questions in crisis care.

TRIAGE QUESTIONS: SCREENING FOR VICTIMIZATION AND LIFE-THREATENING BEHAVIORS

Whether at home, the community, or formal institutional settings, the following questions are basic for preventing injury and potentially saving lives.

1. Have you been troubled or injured by any kind of abuse or violence? Yes___ No___ If yes, check one of the following: By someone in your family___ By an acquaintance or stranger___
2. If yes, has anything like this ever happened before? Yes___ No___ If yes, when?_____
3. Do you have anyone you can turn to or rely on now to protect you from possible further injury? Yes___ No___ If yes, who? _____
4. Do you feel so bad now that you have thought of hurting yourself/suicide? Yes___ No___ If yes, what have you thought about doing?_____
5. Are you so angry about what's happened that you have considered hurting someone else? Yes___ No___ Describe: _____

How many stories of suicide or violence appear in the regular news along with "surprise" by those familiar with the person? These "surprise" reactions are often rooted in the failure of triage questioning in Level 1 assessment. Such failure could be avoided by wider general knowledge of "signals of distress" that typically precede life-threatening behavior. (Techniques for assessing suicidal danger are presented in Chapter 4; assessment for victimization trauma is presented in Chapter 5; and assessing the risk of assault or homicide is discussed in Chapter 6.)

The following point cannot be emphasized enough: If a lay person or a professional without special crisis training suspects that a person is a *probable risk for abuse, suicide, assault, or homicide*, an experienced professional crisis worker should be consulted for Level 2 in-depth assessment and follow-through. No matter how well intentioned you may be, it is no substitute for seeking professional help in such cases. Some life-threatening situations must be approached collaboratively with the police and/or mental health experts (see Chapter 6). Most crisis and psychiatric emergency services have such collaborative relationships in place for handling high-risk crises.

Level 2

This more extensive assessment involves considering personal and social characteristics of the distressed person and his or her family. It is usually done by a trained crisis counselor or mental health professional. Here it can serve as a guideline for nonexperts to evaluate professional crisis care for yourself or others. These questions build on all Level 1 screening for victimization, trauma, and risk of harming self and others, including the following: Is the person unable to function in his or her usual life role? Is the person in danger of being removed (either by preference or circumstance) from his or her natural social setting? What are the psychological, socioeconomic, and other factors related to the person's coping with life's problems and stressors? Level 2 assessment corresponds to the elements of the total crisis experience:

1. *Identification of crisis origins.* What hazardous events occurred? Is there turmoil associated with a major transition state such as adolescence or divorce? What sociocultural or diversity issues are involved?
2. *Development of crisis.* How far along is the individual in moving through the four phases of crisis development as described earlier? Is the person in the initial or acute phase of crisis?
3. *Manifestations of crisis.* How does the person interpret and react to hazardous events or situations? Are the events perceived as threat, loss, or challenge? Does the person deal with the accompanying stress effectively?
4. *Identification of personal, family, interpersonal, and material resources.* Are there individuals who can help pull the person through? How effective are they? Can the person afford to pay for certain help or have adequate insurance?
5. *Determination of the social/cultural milieu of the person or family in crisis.* Are there cultural or other barriers that may prevent the individual from seeking out or accepting help?

The chances for a successful risk assessment depend on our personal level of self-confidence, general experience, and our previous success doing risk assessment and helping others with problems. At some point, depending upon the level of crisis you are faced with, consultation with professional crisis counselors may be the best course. The different foci and performances of Level 1 and 2 assessments are summarized in Table 2.2.

Table 2.2 CRISIS ASSESSMENT LEVELS

	Focus of Assessment	Assessment Done by
Level 1	Risk to life • Victimization • Suicide (self) • Assault and/or homicide (against child, partner, parent, health provider, police officer)	Everyone (natural and formal crisis managers) • Family, friends, neighbors • Hotline workers • Frontline workers: clergy, police officers, nurses, physicians, teachers • Crisis and mental health professionals
Level 2	Comprehensive psychological and social aspects of the person's life pertaining to the hazardous event, including assessment of chronic self-harm	Counselors or mental health professionals formally trained in crisis and assessment strategies

TYPICAL FEELINGS AND OTHER RESPONSES DURING CRISIS

People in crisis experience a high degree of anxiety and tension—in short, *severe emotional pain*. Another common theme is a sense of loss or emptiness. This feeling springs directly from an actual or threatened loss in self-esteem, material goods, social relationships, or a failure to reach a life goal such as promotion or retirement. Other feelings frequently experienced are fear, shock, anger, guilt, embarrassment, or shame. Fear is often expressed in terms of losing control, "going crazy," or not understanding why one is responding in a certain way.

This flood of emotions can interfere in a person's cognitive functioning for usual problem solving or carrying on with work and family affairs. Anger is often directed inward for not being able to manage one's life, or at a significant other for leaving, dying, or inflicting physical or sexual abuse. Guilt and embarrassment often follow anger that does not seem justified. How can we be angry at a dead person when considering our luck in being alive from an accident or disaster? People who are abused by someone they love often feel ashamed—an outcome of the victim-blaming legacy.

Of all feelings common to the crisis experience, *anxiety* is probably the most familiar. A certain degree of tension is a normal part of life; it serves to move us to make plans for productive action. Without it, we become nonproductive. For example, Barry, a student, has no anxiety about passing or failing a course. Therefore, he does not exert the effort required to study and achieve a passing grade. When a person is excessively anxious, however, negative results usually occur, as in the case of Joan, whom we met earlier in this chapter.

Anxiety is manifested in a number of ways. Some anxiety signals will be peculiar to the person concerned. Commonly experienced signs of anxiety are as follows:

- Sense of dread
- Fear of losing control
- Inability to focus on one thing
- Physical symptoms: sweating, frequent urination, diarrhea, nausea and vomiting, rapid heartbeat, headache, chest or abdominal pain, rash, menstrual irregularity, and sexual disinterest

Acute anxiety is one of the most painful experiences a human being can have. However, this does not necessarily imply the presence of a psychiatric "disorder." Following the assessment process discussed earlier, one can more easily discern whether acute anxiety is the result of a stressful situation and signals of an impending crisis, or a serious psychiatric disorder. It is important for everyone to *understand the difference between a crisis state and diagnosable mental illness*.

Clearly, there is such a thing as true mental illness, for example, schizophrenia and bipolar illness, but everyday stressful events should not require a psychiatric "label" as grounds for getting professional help. Psychotherapist Richard

McNally[4] has joined his voice in the growing critique of the *Diagnostic and Statistical Manual of Mental Disorders* (*DSM*), often referred to as the bible of psychiatry. This critique follows decades of work in sociology citing the dangers of stigma, psychiatric "labeling," and the "social construction of illness" by authors Cooksey and Brown,[5] Goffman,[6] Link,[7] Rosenhan,[8] and others.

Despite scientifically grounded critique regarding *DSM*-based prevalence rates of mental illness, the *DSM* is used worldwide by psychiatric specialists and by practitioners who lack specialty training in psychiatry. This complex issue is intertwined with continued bias regarding mental illness and psychosocial care, the power of the pharmaceutical industry, and health insurance policies in the United States that require a *DSM* diagnosis for reimbursement of professional crisis services for acutely distressed persons needing psychosocial care but who are not "mentally ill." Despite these controversies in the mental health arena, a person suffering from acute anxiety—whether the result of an unanticipated stressful situation or a psychiatric "disorder"—should be advised to get help.

NAVIGATING THE ASSESSMENT PROCESS

Human service providers on the front lines (e.g., emergency medical, police) are skilled in quickly determining the urgency and level of danger in various stressful situations. The example of Delaine shows typical mind/body connections when one loss is soon followed by another and is complicated further by its occurrence during a major life cycle change, or when primary care providers are seriously pressed for time. Here it reveals what a friend can do to help bridge the gap between what one needs during stressful times, the constraints of a very busy health care system, and how to avoid the overuse of psychotropic drugs during crisis (see Chapter 3).

EXAMPLE: DELAINE'S MULTIPLE LOSSES

Delaine, age 45, feels bereft after the recent death of her husband from chronic heart disease. Her friends have been supportive, but she still chides herself and feels guilty about not being able to take the loss any better. She knew her husband's condition was precarious; nevertheless, she had depended on him as a readily available source of reassurance. Since she is basically a cheerful person, always on hand to support others in distress, she is embarrassed by what she perceives as a weakness following her husband's death.

Because she cries more than usual, Delaine is afraid she may be losing control. At times she even wonders whether she is going crazy. In addition, she is in a major developmental transition to middle age, and the oldest of her three children is about to be married, leaving her with a sense of impending loss in her usual mother role. To further compound her eroding base of support and sense of purpose, she recently learned that one of her close friends will soon be moving to another state. Delaine feels angry about all the losses in her life, asking, "Why does all this have to happen to me all at once?" But she also feels guilty about her anger; after all, her friend deserves the opportunity that the move will afford her, and she knows her daughter has every right to get married and live her own life.

Complicating Delaine's emotional upheaval, she developed gastrointestinal symptoms, including bouts of lower abdominal pain and diarrhea. She made an appointment with her primary care provider about her physical symptoms and requested something to ease her "embarrassing" crying bouts (to be continued in Chapter 3). However, because the doctor's time was limited and he was unfamiliar with her particular circumstances, he recommended an over-the-counter medication and prescribed a mild sleeping pill, telling her to come back in a couple of weeks if the symptoms persisted. This lack of validation created further isolation for Delaine who never made a follow-up appointment.

Delaine is at a critical juncture. Her husband's death alone may not have led her to a crisis state, but the surrounding events and consequences have had a profound impact, disrupting her stability:

- Her role as wife was changed to that of widow.
- Her role as mother of her oldest daughter was altered by her daughter's marriage.
- Her attachment to her husband was completely severed.
- Attachment to her friend will be altered in terms of physical distance and immediacy of support.
- Her notion of a full life includes marriage, so she must adjust—at least temporarily—to a change in that perception.
- Her unanticipated physical symptoms need medical attention.

Delaine's friends and children, concerned about the changes they see in her, regularly ask whether she is OK. At first, she pacifies them with vague reassurances, and they give her time to "get over" her husband's death. But they soon notice that she is becoming increasingly wan, with dark circles under her eyes that are constantly red from crying. She is unable to focus, and at home she has become short-tempered and no longer expresses interest in her younger children's school activities. Her oldest daughter, realizing that her mother does not seem interested in the wedding plans, calls on a friendly neighbor for help.

The friend, realizing that Delaine is not "getting over it" and may drift into serious depression, takes an interest in her care. Through a series of gentle conversations over lunch and other visits, she asks the questions covered in the two-level assessment process reviewed earlier. Together they determine a course of action that leads Delaine to realize that help is available, that she is not crazy, and that there are other options available to her—for example, that she does not need to see a "shrink." The friend drives Delaine to her first session with a grief counselor. With the right help, she is able to realize the following:

- She also has a right to her feelings about these disturbing events.
- She has a right and a need to express those feelings.
- Her feelings of loss and anger do not cancel the good feelings and support she can continue to have from her daughter and friend, though in an altered form.
- Her physical symptoms are probably related to the distressing psychosocial facets of her life.

Delaine's situation reveals the intermingling of stressful life events that can result in acute crisis. But suppose that instead of widowhood, Delaine or someone like her is grieving the death of her child from serious illness or violence, or that she is now alone because her life was threatened by an abusive husband. Building on the Crisis Paradigm (Fig. 1.1 in Chapter 1), Table 2.3 illustrates these examples of crisis and the typical emotional, biophysical, and behavioral responses to stressful life events relative to their origins. It distinguishes between effective and infective coping by the distressed individual in need of assistance to avoid potentially dangerous crisis outcomes, for example, suicide, substance abuse, or violence against others.

KNOWING THE DIFFERENCE BETWEEN A STRESSFUL EVENT AND A CRISIS STATE

Clearly, then, a stressful or hazardous event is not in itself a crisis. After all, just getting on with our lives implies the everyday management of such events. Even an extremely stressful event does not guarantee a fall into crisis.

Researcher Aaron Antonovsky[9] identified the "sense of coherence" that influenced Holocaust survivors, leading some to kill themselves, while others went on to live extraordinary and fruitful lives. And extensive experience and research with many abused women, for example, reveals them as capable survivors despite the daunting odds. While the severity level of a stressful life event does indeed have an effect on a person's ability to deal with it effectively, a more comprehensive question is: How is *this* particular event unusual in terms of its *timing, severity, danger, or the person's ability to handle it successfully*? As we have seen from the discussion of John and George, early prevention and strategic intervention are pivotal in avoiding a full-blown crisis.

While they may not make an individual more vulnerable, hazardous events *alone* do not constitute a crisis state or warrant a psychiatric diagnosis. We need to pay attention to the *immediacy* of the person's stress: What is the precipitating factor?

Table 2.3 DIFFERENTIATION: EFFECTIVE AND INEFFECTIVE CRISIS COPING ACCORDING TO CRISIS EPISODE

Crisis Episode			Crisis Coping	
Hazardous Event	Origin	Personal Manifestations	Ineffective	Effective
Loss of child by death	*Situational*: Unexplained physical malfunctioning or death of child, for example, SIDS	Emotional	Depression	Grief work
		Biophysical	Stomach or other ailments	
		Cognitive	Conviction of having done something wrong to cause death of the child	Recognizing and accepting that one used all available knowledge to prevent the death
		Behavioral	Inability to care for other children appropriately (for example, overprotectiveness)	Attending peer support group
Physical battering by partner	*Sociocultural*: Values and other factors affecting relationships	Emotional	Crying, depression, feelings of worthlessness, self-blame, and helplessness	Anger, shock (How could he do this to me?), outrage at the fact that it happened
		Cognitive	Assumption that the beating was justified: inability to decide what to do	Conviction of inappropriateness of violence between men and women, decision to leave and/or otherwise reorder one's life free of violence
		Behavioral	Alcohol abuse, abuse of children, excusing of partner's violence	Seeking refuge in nonviolent shelter, initiating steps toward economic independence, participating in peer group support and social change activities

That is, what is the *final, stressful event in a series of such events, or a situation that can catapult a person from serious vulnerability into crisis*? When the presenting problem seems to have been hazardous for a long time, and the proverbial "last straw" is not immediately apparent, we might ask, for example, "What happened *today*—or this week—that is so upsetting now?" In George's case, the stressful event that he could overcome—his heart attack—was the precursor of his crisis state leading to a suicide attempt. The precipitating factor, the one that pushed him over the edge, was learning about his son's suspension from school because of drug involvement.

The *precipitating factor* is often a minor incident. Nevertheless, it can take on crisis proportions in the context of other stressful events and the person's inability to solve problems effectively. In George's case this could be his wife's decision to take on a full-time job and his refusal to seek professional help. For a person experiencing a series of crises, the precipitating factor in one crisis episode may be the hazardous event in the next—the "one thing after another" scenario. In short, we need to *recognize the "signal"* in an acutely stressful situation that typically is beyond the ability of the individual alone to resolve. For example, in Delaine's case, missing the wedding dressmaker's appointment (atypical for her) signaled to her daughter that the situation was beyond her mother's control.

Hazardous events or situations (those final "straws") must be placed in a meaningful context in order to judge their relative importance to the individual. When, for example, is a missed dressmaker's appointment simply a missed appointment, and when is it something more serious? This can be done by ascertaining the subjective or typical reaction of the person to stressful events. How does a person *usually* respond to these events, either directly or as noticed in a conversation about them? A person's subjective response can be elicited through a guided conversation and asking questions such as those illustrated in Table 2.4.

The answers to questions like these are important for several reasons:

- They provide essential information to determine whether a person is in crisis.
- They suggest whether the person's problem-solving ability and usual coping devices are healthy or unhealthy, and how these ways of coping are related to what psychiatrist Gerald Caplan calls the personal, material, and social/cultural supplies needed to avoid crisis.
- They provide information about the *meaning of stressful life events to various people* and about the individual's particular definition of the situation, which is essential to a personally tailored intervention plan.
- They link the assessment process to intervention strategies by providing baseline data for action and learning new ways of coping.[10]

Recognizing the relationship between hazardous events or situations, people's response to them (their vulnerability), and signals of distress lays the foundation for helping a person in impending or acute crisis, discussed in Chapter 3.

Table 2.4 ASSESSING PERSONAL RESPONSES

Sample Assessment Questions	Possible Verbal Responses	Interpretation in Terms of Personal Crisis Manifestations (Emotional, Cognitive, Behavioral)
How do you feel about what happened? (for example, divorce or rape)	*Divorce:* I don't want to live without her. If I kill myself, she'll be sorry.	Feelings of desperation, acute loss, revenge (emotional)
(Or if the feelings have already been expressed spontaneously), I can see you're really upset.	*Rape:* I shouldn't have accepted his invitation to have a drink. I suppose it's my fault for being so stupid.	Guilt, self-blame (emotional, cognitive)
What did you do when she told you about wanting a divorce?	I figured, good riddance. I only stayed for the kids' sake. But now that she's gone, I'm really lonely, and I hate the singles' bar scene.	Relief, ambivalence (emotional, cognitive)
	Or: I went down to the bar and got drunk and have been drinking a lot ever since.	Unable to cope effectively, desire to escape loneliness (emotional, behavioral)
How do you usually handle problems that are upsetting to you?	I generally talk to my closest friend or just get away by myself for a while to think things through.	Generally effective coping ability (behavioral, cognitive)
Why didn't this work for you this time?	My closest friend moved away, and I just haven't found anyone else to talk to that I really trust.	Realization of need for substitute support (cognitive, behavioral)

NO SUCH THING AS CHRONIC CRISIS

This chapter highlights the distinction between a crisis or a potential crisis state evolving from a single upset or successive stressful events. But what happens when an individual seems to be in a *chronic* state of crisis? While we may be tempted to dismiss this by referring to the person as a "drama queen" or a "crisis magnet" (often with a knowing sigh or shake of the head!), it is important to realize that such people often exhibit a multifaceted "wave" of the same underlying problem. For example, while they may always seem to be losing a job or moving from place to place, each of these events may not be the initial stressful event devolving into crisis. More likely, it is *some other, earlier hazardous event or trauma that has gone unresolved*—childhood abuse, for example. This can result in damaging a person's ability to cope with future stressors, and thus heighten one's vulnerability to crisis. "Chronic crisis" is essentially a contradiction in terms. That is, repeated critical life events minus appropriate crisis care can lead to a downward spiral toward *chronic emotional, cognitive, and behavioral dysfunction*, as discussed in Chapter 3.

This chapter uncovers the relationship between a stressful event and a fall into full-blown crisis, and it reveals the opportunity to intervene and break the connection. But what is the best way to intervene and offer help without making the situation worse? The next chapter addresses techniques that aid in fruitful communication and other crisis care strategies.

REFERENCES, FURTHER READING, DISCUSSION GUIDE

REFERENCES

1. Tyhurst, J. S. (1957). The role of transition states—including disasters—in mental illness. In *Symposium on preventive and social psychiatry*. Washington, DC: Walter Reed Army Institute of Research and the National Research Council.
2. Caplan, G. (1964). *Principles of preventive psychiatry*. New York: Basic Books.
3. Hansell, N. (1976). *The person in distress*. New York: Human Sciences Press.
4. McNally, R. J. (2011). *What is mental illness?* Cambridge, MA: The Belknap Press of Harvard University Press.
5. Cooksey, E. C, & Brown, P. (1998). Spinning on its axes: DSM and the social construction of psychiatric diagnosis. *International Journal of Health Sciences, 28*(3), 525–554.
6. Goffman, I. (1963). *Stigma*. Englewood Cliffs, NJ: Prentice Hall.
7. Link, B. G., Phelan, J. C., Bresnahan, M., Stueve, A., & Pescosolido, B. A. (1997). Public conceptions of mental illness: Labels, causes, dangerousness, and social distance. *American Journal of Public Health, 89*(9), 128–133.
8. Rosenhan, D. L. (1973). On being sane in insane places. *Science, 179*, 250–258. (Also reprinted in H. D. Schwartz & C. S. Kart. (1976). *Dominant issues in medical sociology*. Reading, MA: Addison-Wesley; and in P. J. Brink (Ed.). (1976). *Transcultural nursing*. Englewood Cliffs, NJ: Prentice Hall.)
9. Antonovsky, A. (1980). *Health, stress, and coping*. San Francisco: Jossey-Bass.
10. Hoff, L. A., & Brown, L. (2011). Mental health assessment and service planning. In L. A. Hoff and B. D. Morgan, Psychiatric and mental health essentials in primary care (pp. 20-48). London & New York: Routledge. Illustrates a clinically tested and user-friendly assessment tool as an alternative to the DSM and psychiatric labeling. See also Hoff, L. A., Hallisey, B. J. & Hoff, M. (2009) *People in Crisis*, for philosophy, context and genesis of a comprehensive mental health record system, pp. 96-100.

FURTHER READING

Earley, P. (2006). *Crazy: A father's search through America's mental health madness*. New York: Berkley Books.

Greenberg, G. (2013). *The book of woe: The DSM and the unmaking of psychiatry*. New York: Blue Rider Press (Penguin).

Grosz, S. (2013). *The examined life: How we lose and find ourselves*. New York: W.W. Norton.

Johnson, A. B. (1990). *Out of bedlam: The truth about deinstitutionalization.* New York: Basic Books.

Luhrmann, T. M. (2000). *Of two minds: The growing disorder in American psychiatry.* New York: Knopf.

Sobo, E. J., and Loustaunau, M. O. (2010). *The cultural context of health, illness, and medicine* (2nd ed.). Santa Barbara, CA: Praeger.

Watters, E. (2010). *Crazy like us: The globalization of the American psyche.* New York: Free Press.

Whitaker, R. (2010). *Anatomy of an epidemic: Magic bullets, psychiatric drugs, and the astonishing rise of mental illness in America.* New York: Crown Publishers.

DISCUSSION GUIDE

1. With your family or a couple of trusted friends: Recall a situation in which you or someone you know experienced a very stressful life event, and consider these points: How successful were you in helping yourself or another person who was so acutely upset? If successful, what helped you most? If disappointed in the outcomes, how do you think you might have been more helpful to size up and defuse the situation?

2. How comfortable do you feel in asking (or being asked) the kind of questions proposed in this chapter for identifying an impending or acute crisis state?

3. Consider from your experience (or that of someone you know) the difference between everyday stressful events and a crisis or acute psychiatric disturbance requiring professional help. Put another way: Discuss the differences and/or similarities between acute crisis and mental illness.

4. Do you know someone who seems to be in "chronic crisis"? From reading this chapter, what might you do as a family member or friend to avoid the trap of playing "therapist" with a person who resists seeking professional help?

CHAPTER 3
What to Do

How to Cope and Avoid Disastrous Crisis Outcomes

When to seek professional help without shame or asking your friend to play "therapist"

CHAPTER OUTLINE

Social Change and Crisis Prevention   55
Communication as a First Step in Helping   57
Example: Interview With a Suicidal Patient in the Emergency Room   58
Loss, Grief, and Bereavement   59
Decision Counseling: A Key Coping Strategy   62
Other Crisis Coping Strategies   63
Enabler or Helpful Interviewer? Victim-Rescuer-Persecutor Triangle   65
Talking It Through to an Action Plan   66
Features of a Good Crisis Care Plan   67
Example: Crisis Care in an Emergency Setting   70
Purpose of a Service Contract   72
Psychotropic Substance Use: Historical Context and Questions   73
Prescription Drugs: Their Place in Crisis Intervention   75
References, Further Reading, Discussion Guide   76

In Chapter 2 we saw the faces of distress and how a crisis can evolve from a stressful event to a full-blown crisis. We saw that a stressful event, no matter how severe, does not have to set the stressful cycle in motion—it can be broken. The help of family and friends or others can make the difference. We saw this vividly in the contrasting examples of John—who was dealing with multiple sclerosis (a serious neurological condition)—and George, who had had a heart attack.

In these and other examples, many factors come into play, and there are many opportunities to intervene. In this chapter, we explore the best ways to offer assistance to someone in distress. These are tried and true methods and tactics, including communication skills, cautions about psychotropic drugs during crisis, and how not to be an enabler with a person who repeatedly suffers a crisis.

In Chapter 1, the Crisis Paradigm was introduced as a guide to understanding crisis—from its beginnings to positive or negative resolution. A key to understanding and helping a person in crisis is uncovering the *origins* of the person's distress as depicted in the intertwined circles that guide our action.

Chapter 2 features the typical responses to distressful events, while here the focus is on how to help with keen sensitivity to the roots of the person's distress or danger. The aim, of course, is a positive resolution—learning and growth from the crisis experience—and avoiding negative outcomes such as suicide or violence toward others. Typically, our helping strategies fall into immediate action as in life or death situations, and preventive or long-term action.

SOCIAL CHANGE AND CRISIS PREVENTION

Before considering in detail what to do on behalf of someone in acute crisis—the bulk of this chapter—let's turn briefly to the sociocultural context of crisis and what we can do to *prevent* crisis in the first place. Understanding social change as a prevention strategy is central to positive crisis resolution, particularly those crises originating from sociocultural sources. Social action as crisis prevention typically draws on (a) reason and research, (b) reeducation and attitude change, and/or (c) power tactics.

Action based on *reason and research* rests on the assumption that people are reasonable and that, when presented with evidence, they will take appropriate action to bring about needed change. But this strategy alone is usually not enough to move people toward needed change: Most people in or approaching a crisis state will not be moved by an intellectual argument. Prominent social action based on reason and research includes the mediation and nonviolent conflict resolution programs aimed at stemming the tide of youth violence or programs that teach tolerance and respect of others. Through such programs, the psychic pain of crisis (in contrast to violence or chronic unhealthy coping) often moves people to learn new ways of coping with life's problems.

Action based on *reeducation and attitude change* assumes that people are guided by internalized values and habits and that they act according to expected social roles and self-image. For example, some parents remain in unhappy marriages for the sake of the children. Some are in crisis because of greater vulnerability originating from their disadvantaged position in society, for example, bias based on race or gender. These disadvantages may tie into negative coping devices such as learned helplessness, excessive drinking, or violence toward self and others.

When barriers to receiving help are social, cultural, or political, it is helpful to understand the individual's role, real or perceived, in a charged sociopolitical climate. Here, *power-coercive* strategies are useful since the focus is on political and economic sanctions, along with moral power moves such as playing on sentiments of guilt, shame, and a sense of what is just and right. However, political action approaches probably will not succeed apart from *reeducation and attitude changes*. Power strategies are more global in nature and reflect an effort to make broad changes to remove barriers and crisis-producing stressors that affect larger segments of society. This presumes collective planning with those who are distressed or in crisis because of discrimination and repressive policies: feminists; racial equity groups; gay, lesbian, and bisexual activists; disabled persons; and others.

Larger models of social change are pivotal when intervening with a person in crisis and tailoring intervention strategies accordingly. For example, in their discussion of female deviance, researchers R. A. Cloward and F. F. Piven[1] claim that women's coping through depression, passive resistance, and lower rates of violence is related to the *origin* of their stress. Some women have been socialized to accept the view that their stress is determined biologically and stems from natural psychic weakness. When experiencing stress in job or marriage, these women may expect to simply endure what nature offers—not unlike survivors of natural disaster. However, social sources of stress can be resisted, as can the threat of human-made disaster. These ideas support the importance of consciousness-raising and a human rights perspective in crisis work.

From Chapter 2 in the case of George, we can see that his crisis state is more acute than John's because, while both are confronted with a serious health issue, George also faces *social and cultural barriers* that make intervention both more difficult and more pressing. In contrast, John's wife and physician offered significant social support that contributed to the positive outcomes of his crisis. The contrasting examples of John and George show that people will resolve their crises—one way or another—with or without the help of significant others.

The question is *how* they will resolve it, that is, whether they come through the experience stronger and more self-aware, or damaged with weakened self-esteem or other, possibly permanent, scars. People rich in personal, social, and material resources are often able to resolve crises positively in a natural (as opposed to institutional) context with the help of family, friends, and neighbors. Many, however, lack such resources or for personal, cultural, and political reasons cannot mobilize them successfully on their own during crisis. In these instances, with intervention by family, friends, and coworkers to guide them, more formal help from trained crisis workers may be needed to see them through this potentially dangerous period and promote positive crisis resolution.

COMMUNICATION AS A FIRST STEP IN HELPING

When found in a stressful or even an uncomfortable situation, a common response is to look for ways to protect ourselves. Denial is the most common. As a way of coping, denial involves convincing ourselves that everything is fine, thereby shutting us off from seeking or receiving help. Intervention then is most needed for persons unable to reach out.

This was the main difference between John and George. John was able to talk openly with his wife—to share his concerns and fears. George was not. Social or gender factors, as is the case with George, can be internalized so totally that the individual is not even aware of it. Or behaviors such as excessive drinking or other substance abuse can cloud a person's perception of the event and serve as barriers to healthy coping. These are all cloaks that a distressed person can hide behind, but they end up doing more harm than good. Even if not hampered by such unhealthy self-protections, the person may just be overwhelmed by the stressful event, stops communicating, and sacrifices the help of available resources.

Human beings are distinguished from the nonhuman animal kingdom by our ability to produce and use symbols and create meaning out of the events and circumstances of our lives. Through language and nonverbal communication, we let our fellow humans know what we think and feel about life and each other. When dealing with someone in crisis, basic communication skills, such as listening and asking open-ended questions, is a way to build rapport, empathy, and trust. This rapport with the person in crisis is a key ingredient of positive crisis outcomes.

A man might say, "Life is not worth living without her." He may be contemplating suicide after divorce because he sees life without his cherished companion as meaningless. A rape victim or fatally ill woman might say, "What did I do to deserve this?" thus accounting for the situation by blaming herself. Communication is the medium through which we do the following:

- Struggle to survive (for example, by giving away prized possessions or saying, "I don't care anymore" as a cry for help after a serious loss)
- Develop and maintain meaningful human connections (such as by giving and receiving support during stress and crisis)
- Bring stability and organization into our lives (for example, by sorting out the chaotic elements of a traumatic event with a caring person)
- Negotiate social and political struggles at national and international levels

When communication fails, a person may feel alone, abandoned, worthless, and unloved, or conflict and tension may be created in interpersonal relations. The most tragic result of failed communication is violence toward self and others. We saw this in the case of George: Because he could not communicate effectively with his wife or even his doctor, he became stuck in a state of despondency. He felt that he was letting everyone down, when all they wanted was to help him. Neither side was able to bridge the gap, which led George to deliberately crash his car.

The contrasting examples of John (with multiple sclerosis) and George (with a heart attack) illustrate both the success and limitations of individual approaches to life crises. Let us suppose that John and George each had identical help available from human service agencies. The key difference is how they approached that care. John approached it head on. He was scared, but he was open to the challenge. George's crisis response, however, was rooted partially in social and cultural sources, which limited his ability to get help by himself. Just as these protective measures act as barriers to the individual in crisis, they are also barriers to those seeking to intervene and help. It is all too easy to back down. Kate, for example, in a stressful job as a 911 operator was in denial about needing help, assuring her husband and her family that everything was OK when they tried to help. So once rebuffed, they backed off, reluctant to intervene any further and not wishing to alienate her. "That's how she is, she doesn't like it when people try to help," they said when talking among themselves. Of course, there is no plain-vanilla approach to dealing with a person in crisis. But successful intervention demands that we consciously address these factors rather than be rebuffed by them. We need to find a level of communication that reaches around or through the barriers that block a person from getting the care needed.

This more holistic approach to dealing with crisis is part of a larger strategy for crisis resolution: understanding the traumatic event, its origins, and how it affects the way one feels during crisis. For example, a rape victim can be helped to understand that she feels guilty and dirty about being raped not because she is in fact guilty and dirty, but because of the widely accepted social value that women are responsible if they are raped because they dressed provocatively or otherwise provoked the attack. The excerpt from an interview with George reveals communication as pivotal to understanding the inner pain and turmoil that led to his decision to end it all by crashing his car.

EXAMPLE: INTERVIEW WITH A SUICIDAL PATIENT IN THE EMERGENCY ROOM

GEORGE: Hello, Mr. Sloan. Would you like to be called Mr. Sloan or George?
GEORGE: George is fine.
NURSE: Will you tell me what happened, George?
GEORGE: I had a car accident. Can't you see that without asking? (slightly hostile and seemingly reluctant to talk)
NURSE: Yes, I know, George. But the police said you were going the wrong way on the expressway. How did that happen?
GEORGE: Yes, that's right. (hesitates) Well, I just couldn't take it anymore, but I guess it didn't work.
NURSE: Sounds like you've been having a rough time, George. Can you tell me what it is you can't take anymore?

GEORGE: Well, I've got heart trouble...It's gotten to be too much for my wife. I can't expect her to do much more. We're having trouble with our 16-year-old son, Arnold. I just couldn't take it anymore. I figured I'd do everybody a favor and get rid of myself.

NURSE: So your car accident was really an attempt to kill yourself?

GEORGE: That's right. That way, at least my wife wouldn't lose the insurance along with everything else she's had to put up with.

NURSE: I can see that your heart trouble and all your other troubles have left you feeling pretty bad.

GEORGE: That's about it, too bad I came out alive. I really feel I'm worth more dead than alive.

NURSE: I can see that you're feeling desperate about your situation. How long have you felt this way?

GEORGE: I've had heart trouble for about 4 years. After my last heart attack, the doctor told me I had to slow down or it would probably kill me. Well, there's no way I can change things that I can see.

NURSE: What happened this past week that made you decide to end it all?

GEORGE: Well, our kid Arnold got suspended from school—that did it! I figured if a father can't do any better with his son than that, what's the use?

NURSE: I gather from what you say and feel that you just couldn't see any other way out.

GEORGE: That's right. Money is really getting tight; my wife was talking about getting a full-time job, and that really bothers me to think that I can't support my family anymore. And if she starts working more, things might get even worse with Arnold. There was no one to talk to. Suicide's the only thing left.

NURSE: With all these problems, George, have you ever thought about suicide before?

GEORGE: Yes, once, after my doctor told me to really watch it after my last heart attack. I felt pretty hopeless and thought of crashing my car then. But things weren't so bad then between me and my wife, and she talked me out of it and seemed willing to stick with me.

NURSE: I see, but this time you felt there was nowhere else to turn. Anyway, George, I'm glad your suicide attempt didn't work. I'd really like to help you consider some other ways to deal with all these problems.

GEORGE: I don't know what they could be. I really feel hopeless, but I guess I could see what you've got to offer.

LOSS, GRIEF, AND BEREAVEMENT

Given the importance of communication in crisis development and resolution, here are some typical themes that influence our interactions with people in crisis. No matter what the origin of distress, a common theme observed among people in crisis is that of *loss*, including loss of the following:

- Spouse, child, or other loved one
- Health, property, and physical security
- Job, home, and country
- A familiar social role
- Freedom, safety, and bodily integrity
- The opportunity to live beyond youth

When looked at this way, we see that working through any type of crisis is a lot like dealing with grief or bereavement, the basic response to any acute loss. Human beings are social creatures, drawn to connections and attachments to people and things that embody that social view. We tend to view ourselves in relationship to the rest of the world: our family, friends, pets, and home. Death and the changes following any loss are as inevitable as the ocean tide, but because loss is so painful emotionally, our natural tendency is to avoid coming to terms with it immediately and directly.

Dealing with grief, therefore, takes time. Grief is not a set of symptoms to be treated. Rather, it is a process of suffering that a bereaved person goes through on the way to a new life without the lost person, status, or object of love. Grief experts Erich Lindemann[2] and Colin Murray Parkes[3] identified the various stages of grieving. It includes numbness and bodily distress (tightness in the throat, need to sigh, shortness of breath, lack of muscular power), pining and searching, anger and depression, and finally a turning toward recovery. Sometimes people in or approaching crisis may act in unpredictable or confusing ways. But these behaviors are typical for someone going through grief following a loss. So, even though the person may not seem to be suffering from traditional bereavement (i.e., a death in the family), the reactions are similar and typically include the following:

- Acceptance of reality eventually replaces denial around the memory of the lost person, status, or object.
- An alarm reaction sets in, including restlessness, anxiety, and various somatic (physical) reactions that leave a person unable to initiate and maintain normal everyday activities.
- The bereaved has an urge to search for and find the lost person or object in some form. Painful pining, preoccupation with thoughts of the lost person or role and events leading to the loss, and general inattention or distraction are common.
- Anger may develop toward the one who has died, toward oneself, or toward others: "Oh John, why did you leave me?" or "Why didn't I insist that he go to the hospital?" are typical reactions.
- Guilt about perceived neglect is also typical—neglect by self or others—as is guilt about having said something harsh to the person now dead or guilt about one's own survival. There may also be outbursts against the people who press the bereaved person to accept the loss before being ready psychologically.

- Feelings of internal loss or mutilation are revealed in remarks such as "He was a part of me" or "Something of me went when they tore down our homes and neighborhood." For example, the "urban villagers" in Boston's West End across decades mourned the loss of their community to an urban renewal project.
- By adopting the traits and mannerisms of the lost person or by trying to build another home of the same kind, the bereaved person re-creates a lost world. This is typical for refugees who have lost family members and everything but the clothes on their backs.
- Sometimes, especially if there is little social support or where the loss is ambiguous and closure is difficult, a pathological variant of normal grief may emerge. In such instances, the aforementioned reactions may be excessive, prolonged, inhibited, or appear in a distorted form.

All of these reactions can be influenced by factors existing before, during, or after a loss whether personal, material, demographic, cultural, or social, and can affect the outcome of a crisis by influencing the grieving person, either knowingly or not. Interference with normal grieving can result from a person's inflexible approach to problem solving, poverty, the dependency of youth or old age, cultural inhibition of emotional expression, and the unavailability of social support.

Grief work, then, is integral to the healthy resolution of any crisis in which loss figures as a major theme. Normal grief work includes the following:

1. *Acceptance of the pain of loss.* This means dealing with memories of the deceased.
2. *Open expression of pain, sorrow, hostility, and guilt.* The person must feel free to mourn his or her loss openly, usually by weeping, and to express feelings of guilt and hostility without fear of reproach.
3. *Understanding the intense feelings associated with loss.* For example, the fear of going crazy is a normal part of the grieving process. When these feelings of sorrow, fear, guilt, and hostility are worked through in the presence of a caring person, they gradually subside. The ritual expression of grief, as in funerals, greatly aids normal grief work.
4. *Resumption of normal activities and social relationships without the person lost.* By working through the memories and feelings following a loss, the grieving person typically acquires new patterns of social interaction apart from the deceased.

Many bereaved persons find support groups particularly helpful. Being with others who have suffered a similar loss provides understanding as well as some relief of the social isolation that may follow an acute loss. People unsupported during grief work following any profound loss may suffer serious emotional, mental, and social problems.

DECISION COUNSELING: A KEY COPING STRATEGY

Working through a crisis involves making decisions. As we saw with John (Chapter 2), he successfully negotiated his way through his health crisis by making strategic decisions about how to approach his illness, meet his medical needs, and work with his wife to meet the family's financial needs.

When a person is unable to figure these things out, it is often impossible to come up with an action plan to avert crisis—as was the case with George. As psychiatrist Norris Hansell[4] notes, help with making decisions is intrinsic to positive crisis resolution. Decision counseling is *not making the decisions for others*, but rather, it allows the upset person to put distorted thoughts, chaotic feelings, and disturbed behavior into some kind of order and make one's own decisions. These techniques are central to helping a person in crisis to develop a plan of action:

- *Search for boundaries of the problem.* If the roots of the crisis are multifaceted, it is helpful to examine each component of the crisis separately. ("How long has this been troubling you?" or "In what kind of situation do you find yourself getting most upset?")
- *Appraise the meaning of the problems and how they can be mastered.* ("How has your life changed since your wife's illness?")
- *Make a decision about various solutions to the problem.* ("What do you think you can do about this?" or "What have you done so far about this problem?")

The goal here is to help the distressed person consider key questions and decide the following:

- What problem is to be solved? ("Of the things you are troubled by, what is it you want help with now?")
- How can it be solved? ("What do you think would be most helpful?")
- When should it be solved? ("How about coming in after school today with your husband and your son?")
- Where should it be solved? (This can be anything from "Do you want to go to a family crisis center or a regular counselor?"... "Do you think you could get perspective on your problem if you stayed with a friend or other family member?")
- Who should be involved in solving it? ("Who else have you talked to about this problem who could be helpful?")

Decision counseling also includes establishing benchmarks and a timetable, and setting goals for the future. An alternative action plan should also be considered in case the current plan fails or goals are not achieved.

Used effectively, decision counseling honors a person's strengths, contributes to the basic human need of self-mastery, and makes maximum use of the turmoil of crisis to (1) assess the person's current coping ability; (2) develop new problem-solving skills; (3) establish more stable emotional attachments; (4) improve the person's social skills; and (5) increase the person's competence and life satisfaction. It also serves as a framework to evaluate the kind of crisis care offered—for ourselves and for our family and significant others in distress.

OTHER CRISIS COPING STRATEGIES

We have seen that effective communication strategies form the bedrock for helping a person in crisis. Broadly, successful crisis coping involves empathic engagement with the distressed person and his or her feelings, attitudes, values, behavior, and thoughts about what has happened. Here are several important ways of doing that.

Listen actively and with concern. If we are ashamed of our inability to cope with a problem or feel that the problem is too minor to be so upset about it, a good listener can dispel some of these feelings. Listening helps a person feel important and deserving of help no matter how trivial the problem may appear. Effective listening demands attention to possible listening barriers such as internal and external noise. Comments such as "Hmm," "I see," and "Go on," are useful in acknowledging what a person says; they also encourage more talking and build rapport and trust. We can also encourage communication by asking follow-up questions—especially questions that require more than a simple yes or no answer. The failure to listen, on the other hand, can be a barrier to everything else we might do to help.

Encourage the open expression of feelings. Listening is a natural forerunner to positive crisis outcomes. One reason some people are crisis-prone is that they habitually bottle up feelings such as anger, grief, frustration, helplessness, and hopelessness. Negative associations with expressing feelings during childhood seem to put a damper on the open expression of feelings when traumatic events occur later in life. Accepting a distressed person's feelings often helps him or her feel better immediately. It also can be the beginning of a healthier coping style in the future. This is one of the rewarding growth possibilities for people in crisis who are fortunate enough to get the help they need.

A useful way to foster emotional expression is role modeling. For example, saying, "If that happened to me, I think I'd be very angry," gives the distressed person permission to express feelings that he or she may hesitate to share, perhaps out of misdirected shame. This also lets someone like George know that it is okay to feel the way he does, especially if those feelings are strong or unusual.

George is stymied by gender barriers that make it difficult for him to talk to his wife about his feelings surrounding his heart attack and the best route for his recovery. It may therefore take more of an effort for George's wife to create a climate where George can feel at ease to discuss what is bothering him. If she recognizes these gender barriers, it will be easier to understand and be patient. She may need to enlist the help of a close, male friend or relative to encourage him to talk. John, on the other hand, who is more comfortable talking to his wife, would approach the conversation more naturally.

As important as listening and emotional and physical expression are, more is needed for positive crisis resolution. Here are several additional ways to assist a person coping with a crisis.

Help the person gain an understanding of the crisis. When John was first diagnosed, he was understandably shaken and confused, asking questions such as "Why did this awful thing have to happen to me?" This perception of a traumatic event implies that the event occurred because the person in crisis was bad and deserving of punishment. Helping the person see the many factors that contribute to a crisis situation can help curtail this self-blaming. The individual is encouraged to examine the total problem, including his or her own behavior or physical symptoms that may be related to the crisis. As we saw with John, such thoughtful reflection can lead to growth and change rather than self-deprecation and self-pity.

Help the person gradually accept reality. This includes explicit attention to a person who adopts a victim role or blames one's problems on others. It may be tempting to agree with someone who is blaming others, especially if the person's story, as well as the reality, reveal very cruel attacks, rejections, or other unfair treatment. People whose crises stem primarily from social sources do not just *feel* victimized; they *are* in fact victimized. Such abused people, though, are also brave survivors.

Help the person explore new ways of coping with problems. Instead of responding to loss and crises as helpless victims or with suicide and homicide attempts, people can learn new responses. Some troubled persons have given up on problem-solving devices that used to work for them. Unfortunately for George, he could not take advantage of professional crisis counseling and chose suicide as the best answer to his serious problems. But since his high lethal attempt failed, there is still a chance for another way out of his crisis.

Link the person to a social network. Exploring new coping devices leads naturally to social networking for positive crisis resolution. Just as disruption of social ties is an important precursor of crisis, so the restoration of those ties—or, if permanently lost, the formation of new ones—is one of the most powerful means of resolving a crisis in a healthy way. This can be done by encouraging social interaction, for example, asking about family and friends that a troubled couple may have in common, or asking the person, if this is a work situation, about attending a planned gathering, such as a department lunch.

Reinforce the newly learned coping devices, and follow up after crisis resolution. A person in crisis needs time to follow through with an action plan. Regularly asking, "How is it going?" or similar questions helps to reinforce successful problem solving and perhaps discard unworkable solutions, and seek out new ones. Communication for healthy crisis resolution is more of a process than a one-time event. While helping a distressed person should not be a full-time job, it may take repeated efforts to observe positive results. For example, we might call regularly and "check in" with the upset person.

Human service workers and community caretakers, volunteer counselors, social workers, nurses, physicians, police officers, teachers, and clergy increasingly incorporate crisis intervention as a part of their professional training in caring for distressed people. But these crisis care approaches can be mastered by any helping person who chooses to learn them. Whether in offices, institutions, homes, or mobile outreach programs, effective crisis care saves time and effort spent later on negative crisis outcomes such as substance abuse or mental health breakdowns. In highly charged and potentially violent crisis situations (both individual and group), it is advisable to get professional help to avoid putting yourself or the upset person in further danger.

ENABLER OR HELPFUL INTERVIEWER? VICTIM-RESCUER-PERSECUTOR TRIANGLE

Sometimes, despite sincere desires to help, both the troubled person and the helper may fall into what M. James and D. Jongeward,[5] from their work in transactional analysis (*Born to Win*), describe as the victim-rescuer-persecutor triangle (VRP; see Fig. 3.1). In a complementary vein, psychotherapist Jay Haley[6] cites a similar pattern in which the egalitarian aspects of a service contract are sabotaged. For example, if person A acts helpless and repeatedly begs Person B for help, but fails to follow through on suggestions or agreed actions, person A is actually in control while also being dependent. This is why the VRP cycle is so difficult to disrupt once started.

Well-intentioned laypersons (e.g., friends and family trying to be compassionate) and primary care providers not formally trained in mental health and crisis

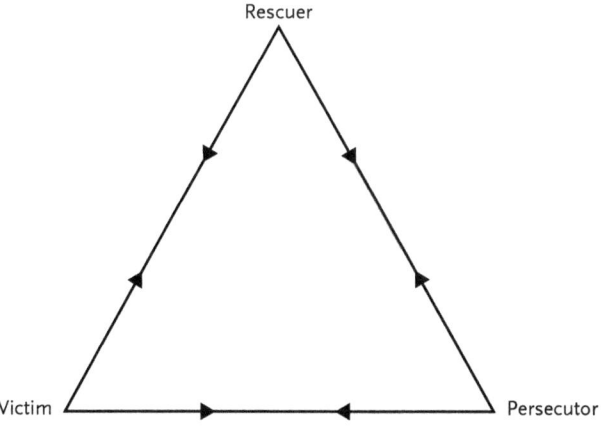

Figure 3.1 Victim-Rescuer-Persecutor Triangle. (Adapted from *Transactional Analysis*).

care are particularly vulnerable to falling into the VRP trap. This may occur especially with a person who refuses referrals for professional counseling but begs for "help" during repeated crisis and self-destructive episodes. So here is how client and helper roles are seriously compromised in the VRP triangle:

Rescuer Role:
- Cannot be enacted without a complementary "victim"
- May suggest the helper's excessive "need to be needed"
- Impedes growth and empowerment of the distressed person

Victim Role:
- Threatens basic need for self-mastery and self-determination
- Even if the overt message is a demand for rescue, more help can covertly lead to resentment and role switch to "persecutor"
- Typically includes repeated demands for rescue

Perpetrator Role:
- Would-be rescuer is frustrated and resents "failure" in meeting victim's demands
- The victim's needs and demands appear unending and implacable
- Switches to persecutor role, essentially "punishing" the victim for failing to use help

Practice Implications: How to Avoid the VRP Triangle:
- Emphasize self-awareness and focus on *empathy* versus sympathy
- Conduct data-based assessment of the person's actual needs
- Provide neither more nor less than needed
- Be honest and forthright about what you can and cannot do
- Promote *interdependence* (versus excessive dependence or independence)
- Avoid power and control tactics

TALKING IT THROUGH TO AN ACTION PLAN

When dealing with someone who is either distressed or in crisis, and avoiding the VRP trap, coming up with a realistic plan is key to positive outcomes. A useful plan consists of more than vague or haphazard intentions. Here are some questions we can ask—whether it is about seeking help for ourselves or others—that may be helpful for assessing not just the type of plan but also an action timetable as follows:

- To what extent has the crisis disrupted the individual's normal life pattern?
- Is she or he able to go to school or hold a job?

- Can the person handle the responsibilities of daily life, for example, eating and personal hygiene?
- Has the crisis situation disrupted the lives of others?
- Has the person been victimized by crime?
- Is the person suicidal, homicidal, or both?
- Is the person coping through substance abuse?
- Does the person seem to be close to despair?
- Has the high anxiety level distorted the person's perception of reality?
- Is the person's usual support system present, absent, or exhausted?

The answers to these questions can provide essential information for a workable action plan. This involves considering the relationships between events and the way the person is thinking, feeling, and acting and then helping to formulate some possible solutions—including if and when it is necessary to find professional or more specialized help. A timetable with benchmarks should be part of any action plan.

It may also be helpful to set priorities around areas that appear most critical. You can ask the person which problem or issue is most urgent, for example, "It seems there are a lot of things upsetting you right now. . . .. Which of these is the most important for you to get help with immediately?"

Once you have the person's attention, the goal is to work toward successful crisis resolution. Communication skills should richly imbue the action plan. We may have to guide the individual in crisis, but this is not about telling someone what to do. Rather, it is about helping the person with what needs to be done and developing our own course of action as a helper. Since most stressful situations involve loss, grief work is a good start, with decision counseling following, as already discussed.

FEATURES OF A GOOD CRISIS CARE PLAN

A plan can be used in several ways: (1) as a self-evaluation tool; (2) as a checklist for evaluating professional crisis workers and determining with them what might be missing or why progress seems elusive; (3) as a way to brainstorm about complex or difficult crisis situations. Whether evaluating for ourselves or on behalf of others, a good crisis care plan should have the following characteristics:

1. *Developed with the person in crisis.* An effective plan is developed in active collaboration with the person in crisis and significant people in his or her life. The underlying philosophy is that people can help themselves with varying degrees of help from others. Making decisions *for* rather than *with* the person in crisis will put a damper on the growth, development, and empowerment that are essential for healthy crisis resolution. If we try to take over, this implies that the distressed person is incapable of participating actively in matters of vital

concern. The person in crisis may feel devalued. Also, an inappropriate power grab may threaten other important characteristics of the plan, for example, attention to the person's cultural identity and values.

2. *Problem-oriented.* The plan focuses on immediate, concrete problems that directly contribute to the crisis, that is, the hazardous event or situation, and that "final straw" leading to crisis. For example, a teenage daughter has run away, a woman gets a diagnosis of breast cancer, or a man learns he has AIDS. The plan should avoid probing into personality patterns or underlying psychological or marital problems contributing to the risk of crisis. This is not the time to solve long-standing issues which are properly the aim of psychotherapy or ongoing counseling following successful resolution of the immediate crisis. The goal is to get the individual out of immediate danger of suicide or harm to others.

3. *Appropriate to a person's functional level and dependency needs.* The plan is based on how the person is *thinking, feeling, and acting.* If the individual's anxiety level impedes straight thinking and problem solving, we might take a more active role. But in general, we should never make a decision for another. If the person is unable to make decisions independently, or the person has a guardian, decision making should be done with the person's guardian.

    If the person is feeling pent up with emotion, the plan should include adequate time to express feelings. It is legitimate to give directions for action if the person's behavior and thinking are chaotic, or perhaps psychotic. Success in a crisis care plan is based on the belief in a person's ability for usual independence once the acute crisis phase is over. We need to know when to let go so the person can once again take charge of his or her life.

4. *Consistent with a person's culture and lifestyle.* Inattention to a person's lifestyle, values, and cultural patterns can result in the failure of a seemingly perfect plan. Various cultural, ethnic, and religious groups have distinct patterns of response to events such as death, physical illness, divorce, and pregnancy out of wedlock. Sensitivity to the person's total situation, value system, and lifestyle is essential. A sincere interest in people different from ourselves conveys respect, elicits information relevant to health, and curbs ethnocentric or culturally based bias.

5. *Inclusive of the person's significant other(s) and social network.* Since crises occur when there is a serious disruption in normal social transactions or a person's self-perception in interpersonal situations, planning must attend to these important social factors. This is true even when the closest social contacts are hostile or in other ways are contributing significantly to the crisis.

    It is tempting to avoid dealing with family members who appear to want a troubled person out of their lives or to let our own bias toward these people influence the guidance we may provide. (In other words, saying "He's no good for you," is counterproductive.) Significant others are vital to the planning process—at least to clarify whether they are a future source of help. In the event a person in crisis is no longer wanted (for example, by a divorcing spouse or parents who abandon their children), the plan will include a means of helping the individual accept this reality and identify new social contacts. A child not helped to face such harsh realities may spend years fantasizing about reuniting a broken family. Put another way, the plan should include information about whether the family (or other significant person) is part of the problem or part of the solution (see Chapter 9).

6. *Realistic, time limited, and concrete.* A good crisis care plan is realistic about needs and resources. For example, a person who is too sick or lacks transportation or money should not be expected to go to a counseling center for help without arranging for transportation. The plan should also contain a clear time frame. The person or family in crisis needs to know that actions A, B, and C are planned to occur at points X, Y, and Z. This kind of structure is reassuring to someone in crisis. It provides concrete evidence that:

- Something definite will happen to change the present state of discomfort.
- The seemingly endless confusion and chaos of the crisis experience can be handled in terms familiar to the person.
- The entire plan has a clearly anticipated ending point.

When someone who fears going crazy, is threatened with violence, or who finds it difficult to depend on others, it is reassuring to look forward to having events under control again within a specified time.

7. *Dynamic and renegotiable.* A dynamic plan is not carved in marble; it is alive, meaningful, and flexible. It is specific to a particular person with unique problems and allows for ongoing changes in the person's life. It should also include a mechanism for dealing with changes if the original plan no longer fits the person's needs so that expected outcomes will not be perceived as failures.

   A person who doubts whether anything can be done to help should be assured, "If this doesn't work, we'll examine why and try something else." This feature of a plan is particularly important for people who have experienced repeated disappointment or are in despair around efforts to obtain help.

8. *Inclusive of follow-up.* Finally, a good plan includes an agreement for follow-up contact after apparent resolution of the crisis. The person in crisis needs to know that you will be there and that you care about him or her and the outcome of the plan. In life-threatening crisis situations such as threats of violence and/or suicide, a *follow-up plan literally can mean the difference between life and death.*

   Careful attention to planning reduces the probability of negative crisis outcomes and lowers the risk of future vulnerability to crisis episodes. It also helps a concerned family member, friend, or anyone who is not a crisis specialist to evaluate whether a person in crisis is receiving crisis care that is up to standards in the mental health field.

EXAMPLE: CRISIS CARE IN AN EMERGENCY SETTING

See Table 3.1.

Table 3.1 CRISIS CARE IN AN EMERGENCY SETTING

Intervention Techniques		Interview Between George Sloan and Emergency Department Nurse
Exploring resources	Nurse:	You said you really can't talk to your wife about your problems. Is there anyone else you've ever thought about talking with?
	George:	Well, I tried talking to my doctor once, but he didn't really have time. Then a few months ago, my minister could see I was pretty down and he stopped by a couple of times, but that didn't help.
Facilitating client empowerment and decision making	Nurse:	Is there anyone else you think you could talk to?
	George:	No, not really—nobody, anyway, that would understand.
Suggesting new resources	Nurse:	What about seeing a regular counselor, George? We have connections here in the emergency room with the psychiatric department of our hospital, where a program could be set up to help you work out some of your problems.
	George:	What do you mean? You think I'm crazy or something? (defensively) I don't need to see a shrink.
Listening, accepting client's feelings	Nurse:	No, George, of course I don't think you're crazy. But when you're down and out enough to see no other way to turn but suicide—well, I know things look pretty bleak now, but talking to a counselor usually leads to some other ways of dealing with problems if you're willing to give it a chance.
	George:	Well, I could consider it. What would it cost? I sure can't afford any more medical bills.

(Continued)

Table 3.1 (CONTINUED)

Intervention Techniques		Interview Between George Sloan and Emergency Department Nurse
Involving client in the plan Facilitating client decision making Making the plan concrete and specific Involving significant other	Nurse:	Here at our hospital clinic, if you can't pay the regular fee, you can apply for medical assistance. How would you like to arrange it? I could call someone now to come over and talk with you and set up a program, or you can call them yourself tomorrow and make the arrangements.
	George:	Well, I feel better now, so I think I'd just as soon wait until tomorrow and call them—besides, I guess I should really tell my wife; I don't know how she'd feel about me seeing a counselor. But then I guess suicide is kind of a coward's way out.
Reinforcing coping mechanism Actively encouraging client action	Nurse:	George, you sound hesitant, and I can understand what you must be feeling. Talking again with your wife sounds like a good idea. Or you and your wife might want to see the counselor together sometime. But I hope you do follow through on this, as I really believe you and your family could benefit from some help like this. After all, you've had a lot of things hit you at one time.
Expressing empathy	George:	Well, it's hard for me to imagine what anyone could do, but maybe at least my wife and I could get along better and keep our kid out of trouble. I just wish she'd quit insisting on things I can't afford.
Conveying realistic hope that things might get better	Nurse:	That's certainly a possibility, and that alone might improve things. How about this, George: I'll call you tomorrow afternoon to see how you are and whether you're having any trouble getting through to the counseling service?
Initiating follow-up plan	George:	That sounds fine. I guess I really should give it another chance. Thanks for everything.
	Nurse:	I'm glad we were able to talk, George. I'll be in touch tomorrow.

PURPOSE OF A SERVICE CONTRACT

In a professional therapeutic setting, a service contract is a method of establishing trust. The contract is a formalized action plan that is agreed on by the person in crisis and the crisis worker, and spells out client and counselor responsibilities. The service contract implies that it is mutually arrived at by the helper and the distressed person. It should be formalized in writing and include these elements:

- The person is essentially in charge of his or her own life.
- The person is able to make decisions.
- The crisis counseling relationship is one between partners.
- Both parties to the contract—the person in crisis and the crisis counselor—have rights and responsibilities, as spelled out in the contract.
- The relationship between the helper and person in crisis is complementary rather than between a superior person and a subordinate.

People have the right to either use or refuse services; the formal service contract protects that right. In addition, the contract establishes:

- What the client can expect from the counselor
- What the counselor can expect from the client
- How the two parties will achieve the goals on which they have agreed
- The target dates for achieving the goals defined in the contract

Nothing goes into a contract that is not mutually developed by the client and counselor through decision counseling. Both parties sign the contract and retain copies. Receiving help on a contractual basis: (1) reduces the possibility that the helping relationship will degenerate into a superior/subject or rescuer/victim stance; (2) enhances the distressed person's self-mastery and social skills; (3) facilitates growth through a crisis experience; (4) reduces the incidence of failure in helping a person in crisis; (5) documents for clinical supervision and insurance purposes the goals and outcomes of crisis care if expert help is sought.

While helping a family member or friend through a crisis may not warrant this formality, it is helpful to know about these steps when seeking expert help. An informal agreement is also helpful. For example, "I will help you if you tell me the truth and do not hurt yourself or others" (see VRP triangle).

The goals of an effective action plan during crisis are to foster growth and healthy coping, and avoid negative, destructive outcomes of traumatic events. We can best assist individuals and their families by helping them carry out an action plan that follows from the way the person in crisis is thinking, feeling, and acting and is tailored to the distinct origins of the crisis.

Ignoring crisis flags can take a heavy toll, as we have seen in George's inability to cope with his series of heart attacks. George clearly needs help, especially formal crisis assistance and medical care. But George most likely will not get there by himself. Carefully planned intervention with persons like George will help avoid negative outcomes and move toward growth and development while resolving the crisis. Other common instances of such intervention are in the event of self-inflicted injury, victimization by crime, or injury by accident, as discussed in Chapters 4, 5, and 6.

PSYCHOTROPIC SUBSTANCE USE: HISTORICAL CONTEXT AND QUESTIONS

Once an acutely distressed person seeks professional help, questions about prescription drugs may come up. There are many factors to consider about medication use during crisis, their role in a comprehensive treatment plan, and the individual's ability to handle them—both physically and psychologically. Drugs can be helpful in the beginning, but the ultimate goal should be getting the person off drugs and moving forward on one's own.

Advertisements bombard us constantly with the idea that drugs are a solution for many problems. We hear: Do you feel down or upset? Can't sleep? Can't control your kids? Take pills. These controversies—prominent across media sources—are situated in historical, cultural, and economic realities commonly discussed by patients, their families, health and mental health providers, policy makers, and others. The discussion of prescription drugs here is about their usefulness and how they can be used responsibly or misused in crisis care. The aim is to provide facts about what to expect if drugs are used to resolve a crisis. Here, then, are some common historical facts, related questions, the results of research and practice, and guidelines for medication use during crisis:

1. People have been using mind-altering substances over many centuries. It is therefore unlikely that a particular "war on drugs" will significantly alter this pattern. What, then, is the significance today of legalizing one of these substances, alcohol (at one time legally "prohibited" in the United States) but not others?
2. How did so many people, both professionals and the general public, come to believe that chemical tranquilization is a preferred way to deal with life's stresses and crises? For example, some parents and teachers insist on drugs for attention-deficit/hyperactivity disordered (ADHD) children. When confronted with a client's demand for drugs, it is not uncommon to hear practitioners say, "But they want the pills... They don't want to talk about or deal with what's troubling them or what's going on in the family." Of note here is that the advertising industry and professional practice have enormous influence on what the public comes to accept as a norm. Also of note is the national

crisis in the United States of inadequate counseling and psychiatric services for disturbed children—services which would alleviate excessive reliance on drugs for children—as well as policy decisions within the insurance industry that support medication versus longer term psychiatric treatment protocols. Among other facts about this issue, the chapters on children in Robert Whitaker's[7] book, *Anatomy of an Epidemic*, are particularly poignant. Whitaker explores in depth the yet-to-be determined outcomes of psychotropic drugs on the developing brains of children. This issue has also commanded public attention to the practice of *keeping teenage children on ADHD drugs as a qualifying ticket for continued government assistance* to poor families for such basics as food and shelter.

3. Media exposures increasingly address the problem of prescription drugs, their overuse, and their escalating costs; many Americans go to Canada to purchase an identical drug at a fraction of the cost. What does the profit motive have to do with the overuse of some drugs and the prices US citizens are expected to pay in comparison to others? Given this pattern of dependency on and overuse of prescription drugs, why does the political "war on drugs" continue to focus on foreign production of illegal drugs rather than prevention and treatment among users at home? And why—in the United States—are the main victims of this war mostly poor inner-city black youth rather than those profiting from the illegal drug traffic?

4. At least a half-century of research-based knowledge and experience regarding psychotropic drugs establishes that their *greatest efficacy is when used in combination with other treatments such as psychotherapy and support* in rehabilitation programs. These outcomes have been demonstrated even in the treatment of bipolar illness and schizophrenia, the mental disorders with strong biological correlates. Yet the disparity in insurance coverage for psychosocial treatment and rehabilitation of mentally ill persons beyond psychotropic medications continues.

These questions are widely addressed in separate books and public discourse, with slow progress on the issues. The point here for individuals and their family members is to thoughtfully consider questions that swirl around prescription drug use, including the knee-jerk reaction that all drugs are bad. And so it is important to remember that the benefits of prescription drugs, when used responsibly, are accepted by professionals and lay persons alike. It is their *misuse and overdependence that are in dispute*.

With this overview of the problem, the following criteria can be helpful when considering prescription drugs for individuals in crisis—usually, antianxiety agents and antidepressants. And everyone should know about this fact: The most serious drug problem is not about those sold on the street. Rather, as M. J. Rogers[8] noted decades ago, this point is even more apt today: "Drug abuse: Just what the doctor ordered."

PRESCRIPTION DRUGS: THEIR PLACE IN CRISIS INTERVENTION

Tranquilizers taken during crisis temporarily relieve anxiety but do nothing about the problem's origin or root cause. At best, they are a crutch. At worst, they can be addictive and displace effective problem solving at the psychosocial level. For someone in crisis, prescription drugs should never be used as a substitute for crisis counseling and problem solving. However, there are times when a tranquilizer can be used in addition to the crisis care discussed in this book. These instances are:

1. When a person is experiencing extreme anxiety, has frequent crying spells, or fears losing control
2. When a person is so emotionally distraught that it is impossible to engage him or her in the problem-solving process
3. When extreme anxiety prevents sleep for a significant period of time. Sleeping pills should be used very cautiously. Exercise and nonchemical means of relaxation are encouraged instead (see Chapter 4). The increasingly popular alternative or complementary medical techniques are also encouraged, for example, biofeedback, acupuncture, herbal remedies, and so on for certain bodily responses to stress.

Apart from these special circumstances, prescription drugs should be avoided whenever possible while dealing with a critical life event. By relieving anxiety on a temporary basis, tranquilizers can have the effect of reducing a person's motivation to resolve a crisis effectively. With chemical tranquilization, the person loses the advantages of the increased energy that typically occurs during crisis coping. The *opportunity* for psychosocial growth is often lost due to the temporary tranquility of a drugged psyche, while the *danger* is increased—including possible overdose or unpleasant and even dangerous side effects from interactions among drugs that are not carefully monitored. Some drugs can complicate rather than alleviate the original symptoms for which they were sought.

A comprehensive plan for persons in crisis may include measures available only through the professions of medicine and psychiatry. A psychiatrist has a medical degree and possesses skills and legal powers unique to training and position in the field of medicine. Unlike the nonmedical counselor or psychiatric practitioner—for example, a social worker—a psychiatrist can prescribe medications, admit people to hospitals, and make distinctions between psychological, psychiatric, and neurological disturbances. Psychiatrists also diagnose and treat the symptoms of drug overdose. In the United States, advanced practice registered nurses (APRNs) and clinical psychologists can also prescribe medication in some jurisdictions.

Remember Delaine from Chapter 2? Applying crisis care to Delaine's case, the primary care provider (MD or APRN) would have made a mental connection between her request for something to ease her crying bouts, her gastrointestinal symptoms, and the series of losses she has suffered. Without discounting or minimizing any of Delaine's presenting symptoms, the provider would listen attentively, make an empathic response affirming the realistic basis for her distress (e.g., "You've certainly been through a lot in a very short time... It's not surprising that you feel sad and a bit overwhelmed with the many losses and big changes from what you're used to.")

The provider would also use an office visit to teach about the essential *normality* of physical symptoms like Delaine's in response to coping with major life stressors. Such teaching provides a context for explaining to Delaine the limitations of psychotropic medication if not accompanied by social support and counseling around her many losses.

Delaine's history of coping suggests her positive response to this approach. Ideally, here is what to expect an MD or APRN (primary care providers) to develop with Delaine:

1. Laboratory tests to aid diagnosis and follow-up treatment of gastrointestinal symptoms
2. A referral to the on-site mental health service (usually staffed by a social worker, psychologist, or advanced practice psychiatric-mental health nurse) for crisis counseling around loss, guilt, and so on
3. A 1-week prescription of an antianxiety medication to be monitored in concert with follow-up counseling by the mental health specialist
4. A recommendation to consider joining a support group for widows (resource information is given, with the suggestion to discuss this further in follow-up counseling)
5. A follow-up appointment for review of laboratory results and general progress

Family members, friends, and anyone concerned about a person in crisis should be familiar with these crisis care ideals on the front lines in primary care. And by being informed, clients and their families can raise questions with health providers who may not attend to them or who cut corners in essential care.

REFERENCES, FURTHER READING, DISCUSSION GUIDE

REFERENCES
1. Cloward, R. A., & Piven, F. F. (1979). Hidden protest: The channeling of female innovations and resistance. *Signs: Journal of Women in Culture and Society, 4*, 651–669.
2. Lindemann, E. (1944). Symptomatology and management of acute grief. *American Journal of Psychiatry, 101*, 101–148. (Reprinted from *Crisis intervention: Selected readings*, by H. J. Parad, Ed., 1965, New York: Family Service Association of America)
3. Parkes, C. M. (1975). *Bereavement: Studies of grief in adult life*. Harmondsworth, England: Penguin Books.
4. Hansell, N. (1970). Decision counseling. *Archives of General Psychiatry, 22*, 462–467.
5. James, M., & Jongeward, D. (1971). *Born to win*. Reading, MA: Addison-Wesley.

6. Haley, J. (1987) *Problem-solving therapy.* San Francisco: Jossey-Bass.
7. Whitaker, R. (2010). *Anatomy of an epidemic: Magic bullets, psychiatric drugs, and the astonishing rise of mental illness in America.* New York: Crown Publishers.
8. Rogers, M. J. (1971). Drug abuse: Just what the doctor ordered. *Psychology Today, 5,* 16–24.

FURTHER READING

Antonovsky, A. (1987). *Unraveling the mystery of health: How people manage stress and stay well.* San Francisco: Jossey-Bass.

Becker, D. (2013). *One nation under stress: The trouble with stress as an idea.* New York: Oxford University Press.

Bishop, E. E., & McNally, G. (1993). An in-home crisis intervention program for children and their families. *Hospital and Community Psychiatry, 44*(2), 182–184.

Brownlee, S. (2007). *Overtreated: Why too much medicine is making us sicker and poorer.* New York: Bloomsbury.

Burge, M. (2012). *The ADD myth: How to cultivate the unique gifts of intense personalities.* San Francisco: Conari Press.

Cain, S. (2013). *Quiet: The power of introverts in a world that can't stop talking.* New York: Broadway Paperbacks.

Chansky, T. E. (2012). *Freeing yourself from anxiety: 4 simple steps to overcomes worry and create the life you want.* Cambridge, MA: DaCapo Press.

Dubowsky, S. L., & Dubowsky, A. N. (2007). *Psychotropic drug prescribers' survival guide: Ethical mental health treatment in the age of Big Pharma.* New York: W.W. Norton.

Earley, P. (2006). *Crazy: A father's search through America's mental health madness.* New York: Berkley Books.

Elliot, G. R. (2006). *Medicating young minds.* New York: Stewart, Tabori, & Chang.

Fast, J. A. & Preston, J. D. (2012). *Loving someone with bipolar disorder.* Oakland, CA: New Harbinger Publications.

Greif, G. L. (2009). *Buddy system: Understanding male friendships.* New York: Oxford University Press.

Luhrmann, T. M. (2000). *Of two minds: The growing disorder in American psychiatry.* New York: Knopf.

Sobo, E. J., & Loustaunau, M. O. (2010). *The cultural context of health, illness, and medicine* (2nd ed.). Santa Barbara, CA: Praeger.

Tschudi, S. (2012). *Loving someone with attention deficit disorder.* Oakland, CA: New Harbinger Publications.

Wolin, S. (1993). *The resilient self: How survivors of troubled families rise above adversity.* New York: Random House.

DISCUSSION GUIDE

1. If you were in crisis and confided your distress to your primary care provider (PCP), think back to how the PCP questioned you about your problem and whether you were helped to make important decisions. Did you feel respected, included, and empowered in the decision-making process? Or if you were disappointed, why, and what—if anything—did you do about it?

2. Consider and discuss other crisis coping strategies with a trusted friend. Evaluate the successful or frustrating outcomes you have experienced when trying to help an acutely distressed person. For example, if you are not a patient listener, or if you are also prone to bottle up painful feelings, what might you do to correct these traits? For example, consider practicing some listening skills with a friend who will give you honest answers without feeling put down.
3. Recall whether you have ever found yourself caught in the Victim-Rescuer-Persecutor triangle. If yes, discuss with someone you trust how you fell into this trap and your efforts to extract yourself without feeling that you were being cruel or indifferent to a distressed person. Discuss how you might interrupt the triangle and perhaps persuade the distressed person to obtain professional help without feeling like you betrayed this person. For example: What might you say about your limits to helping in such a situation? If the needy person accuses you of indifference or betrayal of "normal" friendship norms, how might you respond? Would you consider professional help to examine how you got caught in this triangle in the first place? For example, do you perhaps have an unconscious "need to be needed"?
4. Consider the serious issue of dependency on drugs or alcohol in response to crisis and/or everyday problems. If such dependency is a problem for you or someone you care about, discuss with a person you trust some social and other actions that might address this unhealthy dependency issue.

PART II
Life-Threatening Crises: Suicide, Abuse, and Violence Toward Others

CHAPTER 4

A Cry for Help

Suicide and Other Self-Destructive Behaviors

What everyone needs to know about clues to suicide and that there is no such thing as absolute prediction

CHAPTER OUTLINE

The Messages of Suicidal People   82
Facts and Feelings About Self-Destructive Persons   83
The Social, Psychological, and Cultural Context of Suicide   84
Ethical Issues: Suicide and the Right to Die   87
Example: John—Mental Health Commitment   88
Recognizing Typical Behaviors of Self-Destructive People   89
The Path or "Highway" to Suicide   92
Example: Sally—Responding to Her Cry for Help   94
Detecting Clues to Suicide and What They Mean   95
Major Signs Revealing Immediate and Long-Range Risk of Suicide   96
What To Do: Essential Services for Self-Destructive Persons   102
Precautions: Psychotropic Drug Use for Suicidal Persons   104
Example: Jack—Drug Treatment for Depression   105
Illustrations: Suicide Risk Levels, Safety Planning, Crisis Care, and Follow-Up Counseling   106
How to Help Family and Other Survivors of Suicide   111
References, Further Reading, Discussion Guide   112

"He was such a nice guy... I knew they were getting a divorce but am just shocked that he killed himself" (friend's reaction after reading about this suicide in the neighborhood newspaper). "I can't help wondering what's going on at that hotline I thought we had... Maybe she just didn't know about it... How could that possibly be?"

This chapter addresses typical reactions of people surprised by a suicide and wondering what may be missing in their community for distressed families, neighbors, and others. It shares recent decades of progress toward suicide prevention that has moved past a centuries-old era when suicide was a taboo topic, forbidden by major religions, and survivors were "punished" for the "sin" of suicide—for example, by denying Christian burial of their loved one lost to suicide. It shows how family, friends, and others can prevent suicide by recognizing significant clues. Also important is refraining from playing "therapist" with suicidal people, and letting go of well-intended but misplaced "rescue" scenarios that can boomerang. Examples of essential services show what should be available in all communities, so that acutely distressed persons can benefit from crisis care and choose life instead of self-injury or death.

THE MESSAGES OF SUICIDAL PEOPLE

- "You won't be seeing me around much anymore."
- "I've about had it with this job. I can't take it anymore."
- "I'm angry at my mother. She'll really be sorry when I'm dead."
- "I can't take any more problems without some relief" [and may request psychotropic medication from a primary care provider]
- "I can't live without my boyfriend. I don't really want to die; I just want him back or somebody in his place."
- "I can't take the pain and humiliation anymore [from AIDS, for example]."
- "There's nothing else left since my wife left me. I really want to die."

After a person's first suicide threat or attempt, family members and others are usually shocked and more disturbed by a suicidal message than by anything else the person might have done. Typically, a parent, spouse, friend, or primary care provider (PCP) will say, "I knew she was upset and not exactly happy, but I didn't know she was *that* unhappy." In other words, the first suicide attempt is a distressed person's message among clues typically given over a period of time. Interrupting the path to suicide depends on understanding and responding appropriately to the person's messages of psychic pain, distress, or despair.

The communication problems of suicidal people follow two general patterns:

1. In the first pattern, people habitually refrain from expressing feelings and sharing their concerns with significant others, and use the "stiff upper lip"

approach to life's problems. Suicide by someone in this group elicits great shock and consternation: "He seemed to have everything... I wonder why? There doesn't seem to be any reason." Yet hindsight usually reveals clues that went unrecognized. Subtle changes in behavior, along with a tendency to repress feelings, are *quiet cries for help*, often with no explicit history of suicidal behavior.
2. The second communication problem is less subtle than the first. Typically, people in this group threaten suicide or have already injured themselves.

Behavioral clues may include making out a will, taking out a large life insurance policy, giving away precious belongings, being despondent after a financial setback, or engaging in unusual behavior. These behavioral, verbal, and emotional clues can be interpreted in two general ways: (1) "I want to die" or (2) "I don't want to die, but *I want something to change in order to go on living*," or "If things don't change, life isn't worth living. Help me find something to live for." We can ascertain the *meaning* of suicidal behavior and identify clues in the distressed person's words and attitudes by *asking*, for example,

- "What do you mean when you say you can't take your problems anymore? Are you thinking of suicide?"
- "What did you hope would happen when you took the pills (or cut your wrists)? Did you intend to die?"

There is no substitute for *simple, direct communication* by any caring person—family member, friend, police, or health care professional (HCP). Besides providing important clinical information, this tells the person we are interested and concerned about her or his motives for the contemplated suicide. Experience reveals that suicidal people are relieved when a primary care provider, for example, is sensitive enough to detect and respond to their despair and help protect them from themselves. This includes referral for counseling after initial risk assessment and crisis intervention, plus careful follow-up.

FACTS AND FEELINGS ABOUT SELF-DESTRUCTIVE PERSONS

Suicide is generally considered the most stigmatizing sort of death. It is viewed as a major public health problem and leading cause of death in many countries, while suicide among adolescents continues as a serious problem. The incidence and rates of suicide presented here are drawn from World Health Organization (WHO)[1] sources and the American Association of Suicidology[2], which summarizes the most current data from the National Center for Health Statistics, and the American Foundation for Suicide Prevention, funded by SAMHA (Substance Abuse and Mental Health Services Administration).

The highest rates of suicide in the United States are among older White males. Among adolescents, suicides account for about 20% of all suicides nationwide in the United States. Among Black men, American Indian, and Alaska Natives, however, the highest rates occur between ages 20 and 29 years. This suggests racial minority groups' continuing struggle with devastating social and individual circumstances. There is a strong association between suicide risk and bisexuality in males that is only recently commanding research attention.

The rate of suicide for all ages and groups in the United States is about 12 per 100,000 (around 30,000 annually and the majority of deaths by guns). In the United States, firearms are the suicide method of choice for both men and women; the second most common method used by men is hanging and by women is poisoning. White women's rates peak at around age 50, whereas rates for non-White women remain low and fairly constant through old age. Internationally, the wide range of suicide rates reveals the complexity of the suicide problem. In Canada, the age-adjusted suicide rate is 13.6. In England, France, Italy, Denmark, and Japan, the rates for men are consistently higher than for women. England has the lowest rate for old people, Hungary the highest rates in the world, and Italy the lowest rate for the young.

Suicide attempts occur at least 10 times more frequently than suicides, with a total of approximately 300,000 annually in the United States. Among adolescents, particularly females, the attempt rate may be 20–50 times higher. Many of these adolescents have been physically or sexually abused. Among suicidal women there are strong links to conflict and abuse in intimate relationships, while women with histories of exaggerated passivity may be at greater risk of suicide than those who are rebellious. Women have higher rates of depression than men, traceable to socioeconomic disadvantage. However, the question that remains and invites further research is why greater numbers of women who are abused or otherwise disadvantaged do *not* kill themselves.

Over the past several decades suicide rates have increased by around 60% worldwide, although some of this increase may reflect more accurate reporting and public health attention to the issue. The WHO reports for 2008 revealed suicide among the three leading causes of death for both sexes aged 15–44. Because reporting systems differ widely, there are probably more suicides than are reported. Cultural taboos, insurance policies, and other factors strongly influence the reporting of suicide.[1,2]

THE SOCIAL, PSYCHOLOGICAL, AND CULTURAL CONTEXT OF SUICIDE

Understanding suicide and responding compassionately to an acutely distressed person is complex. And because it is also emotion laden, and "guilt" among survivors is so common, it is important to consider the psychological, social, and cultural influences on the behaviors of people in crisis for whatever reason.

Inasmuch as suicide has occurred since the beginning of recorded history, a preventive model is more helpful than the tendency to treat suicide primarily as a result of mental illness. Suicide most often occurs during periods of socioeconomic and family turmoil, and in individual crisis situations. A preventive model should therefore be front and center with easily available treatment of disorders such as subclinical depression or substance abuse (see Chapters 3 and 7).

Nearly everyone has had contact with self-destructive people. Besides suicide and suicide attempts, some people slowly destroy themselves by excessive drinking or abuse of other drugs. Among primary care patients, some will have responded to a life crisis by a self-destructive act. Despite public education campaigns to dispel common myths about suicide, here are some key facts about suicide that everyone should pay attention to:

- Although people who commit suicide are usually in emotional turmoil, diagnosable mental illness is *not* the dominant factor in most suicides.
- Suicide cuts across class, race, age, and sex differences, while comfortable circumstances (e.g., good home and job) do not prevent suicide, as in "Why? He had everything going for him" following the suicide of a talented student.
- Although a significant number of people with sexual identity crisis commit suicide or make suicide attempts, they do so most often because of the prejudice, hatred, and sometimes violence they have endured from mainstream society.
- People who die by suicide almost invariably *talk about suicide or give clues and warnings about their intention* through their behavior, although the clues may not be recognized at the time.
- The majority of people who succeed in killing themselves have a history of previous suicide attempts. Ignoring this history may precipitate another attempt.
- Suicide is much too complex a process to occur as a result of a caring person asking a question about suicidal intent, as in this *misplaced fear*: "I'm afraid of putting the idea into his or her head."
- A person's mood or energy level is subjective and difficult to assess. People may kill themselves when depressed or following improvement; *frequent and repeated professional assessment* is therefore indicated, regardless of the level of depression.

Despite these facts, cultural taboos, and the strong feelings most people have about suicide, death and dying may inhibit the average person from learning more about self-destructive people. After a suicide, several feelings are common among survivors, including health care providers (HCPs) who offered medical services before a patient's death: *anxiety* that something we did or did not do caused the suicide; *relief*, which is not uncommon among family members or therapists who have exhausted themselves trying to help the suicidal person; or *guilt*, which often follows feelings of disgust or relief that the desperate person has died.

Understanding these feelings is crucial if we are to help distressed people find alternatives to suicide. But to do so on this sensitive issue, it is useful to consider the context of self-destructive behavior and how family and HCPs may have missed clues during an office visit.

Social Perspective

The frustration of some HCPs in working with self-destructive people can be traced, in part, to the socialization professionals receive in helping a sick person return to health. Success in their healing role depends partly on whether patients "behave" according to expectations of people in the "sick role"—originally defined from the study of physically ill persons.[3]

This "sick role" concept is unproblematic if applied to a patient's response to acute pain caused, for example, by a fracture or kidney stones. But if so-called social illnesses (e.g., sexually transmitted diseases, or STDs) do not fit the traditional sick role-helper model, think of this model's limitations if applied to a person who is self-destructive! Not only do suicidal people defeat the medical goal of fostering health and maintaining life, but self-injury appears to deliberately mock the natural instinct to live. In essence, a self-destructive person is requesting, directly or indirectly, a departure from the usual roles of patient and health service provider. Thus, if helping is limited to medical treatment when the problem is as *philosophical, religious, and social as it is medical*, the trouble that a doctor or nurse may encounter when treating suicidal persons is understandable. Our attention to these social and sick role concepts is particularly relevant for all concerned in a health care system that provides limited insurance coverage for "talk" therapies.

Psychological Perspective and Misplaced Rescue Fantasies

Role conflicts are complicated further if well-intentioned health providers have an unrecognized or excessive "need to be needed" and to save a self-destructive person. Besides denying the opportunity to "rescue" a patient, the suicidal person says, in effect, "I don't need you. How can you save me when I don't even want to save myself?" This is a very good question, considering what we know about the failure of medical treatment or psychotherapy if attempted without the client's consent and active collaboration.

The most complex manifestation of the social-psychological roots of conflict with suicidal people is in the *victim-rescuer-persecutor triangle* drawn from transactional analysis (see Chapter 3). Of all the phases of crisis work, most important here for all would-be helpers is sensitivity to the *universal human need for self-mastery*. We therefore need to control counterproductive rescue fantasies that can surface when we feel frustrated in our helping role. Not to do so could result in a vicious cycle that is exactly the opposite of our intentions:

- Our misguided rescue attempts are rejected.
- We feel frustrated in our helper role.
- We "persecute" the suicidal person for failing to cooperate.
- The suicidal person feels rejected.
- The helper feels like a victim.

Preventing and interrupting the victim-rescuer-persecutor cycle is one of the most challenging tasks in dealing with self-destructive people. Timely help is key here—offered in collaboration with the suicidal person and his or her significant others (see Chapter 3, Fig. 3.1).

Cross-Cultural Perspective

Suicide universally conveys the value that "death is preferred over life," and it has been part of the human condition from the beginning of time. However, deeply rooted belief systems will influence how and why suicide occurs and is interpreted in various societies.

Self-destructive behavior takes on added meaning when placed in a cultural-historical perspective. Views about it—whether it is honorable or shameful—have always varied. In the Judeo-Christian tradition, neither the Hebrew Bible nor the New Testament prohibits suicide. Jews (defenders of Masada) and Christians (martyrs) alike justified suicide in the face of military defeat or personal attack by pagans. Later, however, suicide took on the character of a sinful act. The religious standpoint is complemented now by legal and medical perspectives, with suicide today seen less as a moral offense than as a socially disgraceful act, a response to crisis, or a manifestation of psychiatric illness.

These social, psychological, and cultural facts of life are even more complex when considering the multiethnicity of North American, European, and other societies, and an emphasis on preserving one's unique cultural heritage. Dealing with feelings then (as in the case of George in Chapter 3) is a necessary first step toward helping people in suicidal crisis. Team relationships, peer support groups, and readily accessible consultation are also pivotal for successful care of self-destructive persons.

ETHICAL ISSUES: SUICIDE AND THE RIGHT TO DIE

Closely related to coping with feelings about self-destructive behavior is our position on the right to die and the degree of responsibility we have for the lives of others. Everyone should be familiar with these hotly debated topics:

- The right to die by suicide
- The right to physician-assisted suicide

- The right and the responsibility to prevent suicide
- The right to euthanasia and abortion (related topics)

Several ethical and legal questions have implications for suicidal persons, their family members, emergency medical teams, police, and human service providers. They provide an ethical basis for dealing with serious issues without either abandoning our own cherished beliefs or imposing them on others.

- How do we respond to a person's declaration: "I have the right to commit suicide, and you don't have the right to stop me"?
- If our own belief system forbids suicide, how might this belief influence our response to such a person?
- If a person commits suicide, whose responsibility is it?
- If we happen to believe the suicidal person alone is responsible, why do we often feel guilty after a suicide?
- What is the ethical basis for depriving a person of normal, individual rights by involuntary commitment to a mental health facility to prevent suicide?
- What do we do if someone close to us requests our assistance in committing suicide?

Opinions differ regarding the issue of responsibility to save others, the right to determine one's own death, and differentiating between adults and children in regard to rights and responsibilities. The *ethical* and *legal* aspects of certain issues must be distinguished. For example, many people believe that suicide is ethically acceptable in certain circumstances, but regardless of personal beliefs, it is illegal in the majority of the United States and in most other countries to assist another in the act of suicide. The passage in Oregon, Washington, Montana, and Vermont of measures allowing physician-assisted suicide is an exception to this rule, as is the case in several European countries. Other states are considering similar legislation or ballot initiatives. Family members and health care providers must consider the relevance of these debates in their everyday interaction with suicidal people and their ethically based attempts to be helpful. The following example illustrates some of the ethical questions.

EXAMPLE: JOHN—MENTAL HEALTH COMMITMENT

John, age 48, was diagnosed with ALS (Lou Gehrig's disease) and referred to psychiatric services when he became highly suicidal after learning about his wife's death in a car accident. He also had a substance abuse problem and went on a drinking binge after getting this additional shocking news. He was committed involuntarily to a psychiatric facility with the goal of preventing him from committing suicide. John found the hospital worse than anything he had experienced.

John had two very close friends and a small business of his own, but he had no contact with his friends while in the hospital. After 2 weeks, John begged to be discharged. He was no longer highly suicidal but was still depressed. He was discharged with antidepressant medication and instructed to return for a follow-up appointment in 1 week. John killed himself with sleeping pills (obtained from his primary care provider) and alcohol 2 days after discharge. The PCP and staff of the mental hospital did not understand how they had failed John.

John's eventual suicide illustrates the complexity of implementing mental health laws on behalf of suicidal people. First of all, the decision to commit a person must be based on a thorough suicide risk assessment. Second, even if John had been found to be a serious risk for suicide, involuntary hospitalization seemed to contribute to, rather than prevent, John's suicide. Hospitalization is indicated for suicidal people only when natural social network resources (such as John's friends) are not present.

Here are practical guidelines and responsibilities that family and healthcare providers (HCPs) need to consider regarding the rights of suicidal people: Each person has the final responsibility for his or her own life, including the right to live as one chooses or to end life. All health and emergency providers have a communal responsibility to prevent suicide when it appears to be against a person's own best interests—for example, when suffering from major depression without the benefit of treatment.

Responsibilities also include examining values and social practices that may inadvertently lead people to choose suicide only because they are socially disadvantaged and see no other way out. And if ethical arguments do not support legalized physician-assisted suicide, neither does an economic argument. Philosophers Emanuel and Battin[4] found that in the wealthy United States, total end-of-life health care expenditures would be reduced by only 0.07% if physician-assisted suicide were legalized. The choice of assisted suicide in these instances is not truly free. Our social responsibility does not require that we prevent a suicide at all costs. But we all need to recognize that misguided savior tactics can result in suicide if overbearing help is interpreted as *control*. However, HCPs have the additional responsibility to learn as much as they can about self-destructive people and advocate strongly to help a despairing patient such as John (and George, Chapters 2 and 3) find alternatives to suicide.

RECOGNIZING TYPICAL BEHAVIORS OF SELF-DESTRUCTIVE PEOPLE

To be understood is basic to the feeling that someone cares, that life is worth living. When someone responds to stress with a deliberate suicide attempt, those around the person are usually dismayed and ask *why*. The wide range of self-destructive acts adds to the observer's confusion, especially when considering the many overlapping features of self-destructive behavior. For example, Mary, age 50, has been destroying herself through alcohol abuse for 15 years, but she also takes an overdose of sleeping pills during an acute crisis.

The majority of adolescents who harm themselves have had serious personal, emotional, or behavioral problems. Volumes have been written about suicide—by philosophers, the clergy, psychiatrists and psychologists, nurses, and crisis specialists who have varied opinions regarding the process, meanings, morality, and reasons involved in self-destruction. The focus here is on the *meaning* of self-destructive behavior and the importance of understanding and reaching out to those in emotional pain.

Psychologist Edwin Shneidman,[5] founder of Suicidology as a specialty field, describes suicidal behavior as the "hurt, anguish, or ache that takes hold of the mind. It is intrinsically psychological; it is the... pain of negative emotions, such as guilt, shame, anguish, fear, panic, anger, loneliness, helplessness.... Suicide occurs when the *psychache* is deemed to be unbearable and when death is actively sought in order to stop the unceasing flow of intolerable consciousness... people reach the 'point of no return' in response to unendurable psychological pain".[6]

Self-Destructiveness: What Does It Include?

Our effectiveness in working with suicidal people requires knowledge of these aspects of self-destructive behavior:

- The range and complexity of self-destructive behavior
- Communication and the meaning of self-destructive behavior
- Ambivalence and its relevance to suicide prevention
- The importance of assessing for suicidal risk
- Sensitivity to ethical and cultural issues already noted as an aid to understanding, risk assessment, and appropriate intervention.

Self-destructive behavior includes any action by which a person emotionally, socially, and physically damages or ends his or her life. The spectrum of self-destructiveness includes biting nails, pulling hair, scratching, cutting one's wrist, swallowing toxic substances or harmful objects, smoking cigarettes, banging one's head, abusing alcohol and other drugs, driving recklessly, neglecting life-preserving measures such as taking insulin, attempting suicide, and committing suicide.[7]

At one end of the spectrum of self-destructiveness is Jane, who smokes but is in essentially good emotional and physical health. She knows the long-range effects of smoking and chooses to live her life in such a way that may in fact shorten it. However, on a risk assessment scale, Jane would hardly be regarded as suicidal. Smoking by Arthur, who has severe emphysema, is another matter. His behavior could be considered a slow form of deliberate self-destruction. At the other end of the spectrum is James, who plans to hang himself. Unless saved accidentally, James will most certainly die by his own hand.

Groups of Self-Destructive Persons

Everyone should be familiar with the four broad groups of self-destructive people:

1. *Those who commit suicide.* Suicide is a fatal act that is self-inflicted, *consciously intended*, and carried out with the knowledge that death is irreversible. This definition of suicide generally *excludes* young children because a child's conception of death as final develops around age 10. If full information is not available about the person's intentions, it is difficult to determine whether the act is suicidal or accidental. *Suicide is not an illness or an inherited disease*, as popular opinion and some professional practice seem to imply.
2. *Those who threaten suicide.* This group includes people who talk about suicide and whose suicidal plans may be either *very vague* or *highly specific*; some have made suicide attempts in the past; others have not. We should take all suicide threats seriously and consider them in relation to the person's intention and social circumstances.
3. *Those who make suicide attempts.* A suicide attempt is any nonfatal act of self-inflicted damage with self-destructive intention, however vague or inferred from behavior. Technically, the term *suicide attempt* should be reserved for those actions in which a person attempts to carry out the *intention* to die but for unanticipated reasons, such as failure of the method or an unplanned rescue, the attempt fails. Other self-destructive behavior can more accurately be defined as *self-injury*—a neutral term we should substitute for the term *suicide gesture*, which suggests that the behavior need not be taken seriously or that the person is "just seeking attention."

    Some suicidal persons are in a state of acute crisis—in contrast to some who are chronically self-destructive—and therefore experience a high degree of emotional turmoil. As discussed in Chapter 3 ("Decision Counseling"), such turmoil makes it difficult for a person to clarify his or her intentions, or it may interfere with making wise decisions about marriage, moving, and so on. Certainly, then, it is unwise to make an irrevocable decision such as suicide when in a state of emotional turmoil and crisis.

    The ambiguity arising from an acute crisis state should not be confused with a psychotic process, which may or may not be present. Despite issues of impulse control, in the large majority of instances self-destructive behavior is something that people *consciously and deliberately plan and execute*, as illustrated by George in Chapters 2 and 3.

4. *Those who are chronically self-destructive.* People in this group may habitually abuse alcohol or other drugs and are often diagnosed with personality disorders. Of special concern to HCPs whom the family or friends might engage are people who *deliberately* refuse to follow life-sustaining medical programs for conditions such as heart disease or diabetes. While these behaviors are not explicitly suicidal, individuals who engage in them may become overtly suicidal, thus complicating whatever medical problems already exist.

It is important to distinguish between self-destructive persons and those who engage in *self-mutilating activity* (for example, cutting, scraping, and bruising) that generally has no dire medical consequences, although some may end up killing themselves. Unlike suicidal behavior, self-mutilation typically does not involve an intent to die; rather, it is a way of coping and is usually employed by women. Many of these women are survivors of extreme childhood sexual abuse who have internalized their oppression.

THE PATH OR "HIGHWAY" TO SUICIDE

As described by sociologist Ronald Maris,[8] suicidal behavior can be viewed as a *highway* or continuum that begins with the first suicide threat or attempt and ends in suicide. As with any trip destined for a certain end point, we can always change our mind, take a different road, or turn around and come back. The highway to suicide can be viewed either as a short trip (acute crisis) or a long trip—chronic self-destructiveness extending for years or over a lifetime. But in either case, it suggests that suicide is a process involving:

- A person's beliefs about the meaning of life and death
- Availability of psychological and social resources
- Material and physical circumstances making self-destruction possible (for example, when a gun or pills are available or when a bedridden, helpless person is capable of self-destruction only through starvation)

The continuum concept is useful in understanding suicides that appear to result from impulsive action, as sometimes happens with adolescents. Even with adolescent suicides, though, examination and hindsight usually reveal alienation/isolation, an acute loss, developmental issues, family conflict, abuse, depression, self-doubt, and cynicism along life's path.

A destiny of suicide is not inevitable. Continuing down the highway to suicide depends on a variety of circumstances. People traveling this highway usually give clues to their distress, so *the suicide continuum or trip can be interrupted at any point*: after a first attempt, a fifth attempt, or as soon as clues are recognized. Much depends on available help and the suicidal person's ability to accept and use help. It is never too late to help a despairing person or to change one's mind about suicide.

Unfortunately, people who repeatedly injure themselves may be labeled and written off as manipulators or attention seekers. This usually means that family members and/or HCPs may conclude that a person who was serious about suicide would try something that "really did the job." Individuals who are labeled and ignored will probably continue to injure themselves with more serious medical consequences, signaling their increasing desperation for someone to hear and understand their cries for help.

They may also engage in the "no-lose game," which goes something like this: "If they (spouse, friend, family) find me, they care enough and therefore life is worth living. (I win by living.) If they don't find me, life isn't worth living. (I win by dying.)" In the no-lose game, the suicide method chosen is usually lethal but includes the possibility of rescue, such as swallowing pills. No-lose reasoning is ineffective in instances when one cannot reasonably expect rescue (for example, a family member rarely checks a person at 2 a.m.). It nevertheless indicates the person's extreme distress and illustrates the logic of the no-lose game.

Interrupting the continuum or path to suicide depends on understanding and responding compassionately to a person's clues along the highway to suicide that reveal psychic pain, distress, or despair, as described in the opening of this chapter. While the range of various self-destructive behaviors is very broad (e.g., substance abuse, failure to take medicine for diabetes or heart disease), the focus here is for family members, friends, close associates, and PCPs to *recognize the immediate and longer term danger of death by suicide* and do all we can to help suicidal persons obtain professional crisis care.

The Importance of Assessing Suicide Risk

Assessing suicide risk can be compared to diagnosing a cough before beginning treatment. Failure to assess the degree of suicide risk can result in the lack of referral for counseling after emergency medical treatment for self-injury, for example, wrist cutting or an overdose of pills. A preventable problem of guesswork about suicide risk is unnecessary hospitalization. It is inappropriate to hospitalize a suicidal person when the degree of suicide risk is very low and other sources of protection are available. A person who hopes, by a suicide attempt, to relieve isolation from family may feel even more isolated in a psychiatric hospital, as the earlier case of John illustrates. This is especially true when community and family intervention are indicated instead.

Sometimes health providers hospitalize suicidal people because of their own anxiety about suicide. Unresolved feelings of guilt and misplaced "rescue" fantasies usually precipitate such action. On the other hand, hospitals can provide relief of isolation and preventive intervention when social supports in the community are lacking. As with personal factors, we should not assume the presence or absence of social supports without a systematic psychosocial assessment (see Chapter 2).

Ambivalence: Weighing Life and Death

Suicidal people usually struggle with two irreconcilable wishes—the desire to live and the desire to die—that is, *ambivalence*. As long as the person is ambivalent about life and death, it is possible to help the individual consider choosing life over death. Suicide is not inevitable. Desperate people can change their minds if they find realistic alternatives to suicide.

Understanding ambivalence is basic to suicide prevention. Those who are no longer ambivalent do not usually come to an emergency service, see their HCP or pastor, or call crisis hotlines. An ambivalent person weighing life and death says, in effect, "If no one cares whether I live or die—not even my doctor!—I'd rather die than live." It also affirms the essential interpersonal and social nature of human beings described in sociologist Emile Durkheim's[9] classic work published over a century ago which raises this question: *If a person has no more meaningful attachments to a supportive family or community, why not die?* In short, during the period of ambivalence, it is potentially lifesaving to convey to a despairing person that *we care whether he or she lives or dies*, and thereby give the person a reason to choose life over death.

EXAMPLE: SALLY—RESPONDING TO HER CRY FOR HELP

Sally, age 16, made a suicide attempt by swallowing six sleeping pills. In medical terms, this was not a serious attempt. Although she contemplated death, she also wanted to live. She hoped that the suicide attempt would bring about some change in her miserable family life, so that she could avoid the last resort of suicide itself. Before her suicide attempt, Sally was having trouble in school, ran away from home once, experimented with drugs, and engaged in behavior that often brought disapproval from her parents.

All of these behaviors were Sally's way of saying, "Listen to me! Can't you see that I'm miserable, that I can't control myself, that I can't go on like this anymore?" Sally had been upset for several years by her parents' constant fighting and playing favorites with the children. Her father drank heavily and frequently was away from home. When Sally's school counselor recommended family counseling, the family refused out of shame. Sally's acting out was really a cry for help. After her suicide attempt, her parents accepted counseling. Sally's behavior improved generally, and she made no further suicide attempts.

Had Sally not obtained help, she probably would have continued down the highway to suicide. The usual pattern in such a case is that the attempts become medically more serious, the person becomes more desperate, and finally commits suicide. We can help the ambivalent person move in the direction of life through understanding and compassionate response to the *meaning* of the person's behavior.

DETECTING CLUES TO SUICIDE AND WHAT THEY MEAN

Listening and responding to emotional and behavioral clues leads to understanding as the foundation for risk assessment, decision, and action. In *suicide risk assessment* we ascertain the likelihood of suicide for a particular person. *Lethality assessment* refers to the degree of *physical* injury resulting from a particular self-destructive act. Clinical assessment tries to answer this question: What is the risk of death by suicide for *this individual* at *this time*, considering the person's life as a whole?

In considering this question, family, friends, and anyone concerned about the care of acutely distressed persons should be wary if offered a "rating scale" as a "first step" when seeking professional help—especially if this is *before* direct communication with an HCP. Such scales are primarily research tools and are too lengthy and time consuming in a crisis situation. A rating scale cannot substitute for an HCP's sensitive direct inquiry, for example: "Can you tell me what's happening to cause you so much pain?" Since a suicide attempt often signals a breakdown in communication with significant others, it is *unrealistic* to expect such a person to honestly answer a dozen or more rating scale questions about suicide while alone in the cold atmosphere of a clinic waiting room.

It is noteworthy that "patients-in-waiting" are routinely asked to complete medical history forms *before* seeing a health care provider. In such instances, everyone, therefore—the patient, family, and providers—would be better served by adding a few crisis-oriented questions to these standard "intake forms" used in clinics and doctor's offices (see Chapter 2, "Screening and Triage Questions"). So instead of completing a long research-designed questionnaire about suicide before seeing a live human being, patients and family should have access to information about suicide among the flyers regarding diabetes, heart problems, and so on that are routinely displayed in clinic waiting rooms. This is *particularly relevant* for those seeking primarily an antidepressant drug or tranquilizer while avoiding counseling, and perhaps using the drug later for a suicide attempt.

Besides the questionable use of valuable time in busy clinics, the problem with most lengthy scales is that they *do not exclude the nonsuicidal population*. For example, consider depression and its relationship to suicide: Among the millions of people diagnosed with depression, a significant percentage of them do not commit suicide, although approximately 60% who succeed in killing themselves have been diagnosed as depressed. This signals the *importance of treatment for depression*, especially for those expressing a profound degree of hopelessness. Of the 20 million or so persons with a depressive disorder, only 0.1% commit suicide. Similarly, the majority of people who commit suicide have made previous suicide attempts, yet eight out of ten people who attempt suicide never go on to commit suicide.[10,11] These statistics do not invite complacency; they simply indicate the *complexity of assessing suicide risk*, the limits of psychiatric diagnostic criteria, and the fact that *something changed* in favor of life for a particular person at risk—for example, *a cry for help was heard*.

MAJOR SIGNS REVEALING IMMEDIATE AND LONG-RANGE RISK OF SUICIDE

What we know about suicide risk is based on the study of *completed* suicides. Such research is among the most difficult of scientific studies, but the study of completed suicides has explained much about the challenges of risk assessment. This discussion of risk factors corresponds with the Best Practices Registry and the National Strategy for Suicide Prevention, a collaborative project of the Suicide Prevention Resource Center (SPRC) and the American Foundation for Suicide Prevention (AFSP), funded by the Substance Abuse and Mental Health Services Administration (SAMHSA).[12]

The *most reliable indicators* or signs of suicide risk distinguish people who commit suicide from the population at large and also from those who attempt but do not succeed in killing themselves. However, since there is not enough research to warrant general conclusions about suicide for different population groups, we should never be overconfident in applying signs to a suicidal person. It is *impossible to predict suicide in any absolute sense*. Therefore, the focus by HCPs should be on uncovering the *immediate* and *long-term* risk for a particular distressed person. The chaos of a crisis situation and an HCP's anxiety about suicide can be reduced by thoughtful attention to these general signposts. Family and significant others should be aware of these signs and whether HCPs have paid serious attention to them on behalf of their acutely distressed loved ones referred for professional help.

The classic signs of suicide risk have varied little over the years since Edwin Shneidman's 1960s inauguration of suicidology as a field of scientific clinical study. These principles for assessing suicide risk apply to *any* person in *any* setting contacted through *any* helping situation: telephone, primary care office, home, hospital, work site, jail, nursing home, school, or pastoral care. Assessment of the distressed person's emotional, cognitive, and behavioral functioning should be the focus, although a psychiatric disorder may be present in some instances. The following discussion is based on research in Western societies; suicide signs and methods vary in other cultural settings (see www. WHO–suicide rates across cultures). Sensitivity to these differences, however, is important in helping various immigrant and ethnic groups in distress in North America.

In their review of suicide risk factors, researchers Brown and Sheran[13] note, among other risk factors, the *particular significance* of the following four signs:

1. Has a specific, high-lethal plan for suicide with available means
2. Has a history of high-lethal attempts
3. Lacks both personality and social resources
4. Cannot communicate with available resources

Suicide Plan

The majority of persons who die by suicide deliberately planned to do so. *Without a high-lethal plan and available means* (e.g., gun or drugs), *suicide cannot occur.* People suspected of being suicidal should be asked several direct questions about their plan, keeping in mind these risk assessment criteria:

1. *Suicidal ideas.* "Are you so upset that you're thinking of suicide?" or "Are you thinking about hurting yourself?"
2. *Lethality of method.* "What are you thinking of doing?" or "What have you considered doing to harm yourself?"

    High-Lethal Methods
    - Gun
    - Hanging
    - Barbiturate and prescribed sleeping pills
    - Jumping
    - Drowning
    - Carbon monoxide poisoning
    - Aspirin (high dose) and acetaminophen (Tylenol)
    - Car crash
    - Exposure to extreme cold
    - Antidepressants (anyone who is prescribed antidepressant medication should expect an explanation of side effects and their possible misuse during acute crisis as a means of committing suicide)

    Low-Lethal Methods
    - Wrist cutting
    - Nonprescription drugs (excluding aspirin and acetaminophen [Tylenol])
    - Tranquilizers (antianxiety drugs)

The prescribing HCP should also *determine the person's knowledge about the lethality of the chosen method*. For example, a person who takes four or six tranquilizers with the mistaken belief that the dose is fatal is *alive more by accident than by intent*.

3. *Availability of means.* "Do you have a gun? Do you know how to use it? Do you have ammunition? Do you have pills?" Lives have often been saved by removing very lethal methods such as guns and sleeping pills. A highly suicidal person who calls a primary care office or crisis center is often making a final effort to get help, even while sitting next to a loaded gun or bottle of pills. Such an individual will welcome a direct, protective suggestion by an HCP or counselor, such as "Why don't you put the gun away?" or "How about you throw the pills out, and then let's talk about what's troubling you?" When friends and family are involved, they too should be directed to get rid of the weapon or pills. In disposing of lethal weapons, it is important to *engage the suicidal person actively in the process*, keeping in mind that power ploys can trigger rather than prevent suicide. If trust and rapport have been established with one's PCP, engaging the suicidal person is generally not difficult to do.

    Pharmacists may also have a preventive role here. For example, if a regular customer asks about a lethal dose of a sleep aid, the pharmacist might inquire about the person's support network, warn about possible dependency, or perhaps call the prescriber for suspected lethal use of the pills.

4. *Specificity of plan.* "Do you have a plan worked out for killing yourself?" "How do you plan to get the pills?" "How do you plan to get the gun?" A person who has a well-thought-out plan—including time, place, and circumstances—with an available high-lethal method is an *immediate and very high risk* for suicide. We should also determine whether any rescue possibilities are included in the plan—for example, "What time of day do you plan to do this?" or "Is there anyone else around at that time?"—and inquire about the person's intent. Some people *really do intend to die*; others intend to *bring about some change* that will help them avoid death and make life more livable—that is, a cry for help.

    While a specific plan is necessary to cause death, it is a less important sign of risk among people with a *history of impulsive behavior, especially adolescents*. We should also remember that for many persons, being "on the brink" and still deciding whether to live or die is a very scary place to be. In fact, most would welcome a message from anyone who cares enough to ask questions in a noncontrolling way as it conveys compassion that could make the difference between living or dying by suicide.

History of Suicide Attempts

In the US and Canadian adult population, suicide attempts occur 8–10 times more often than actual suicide. The rate among adolescents is about 50 attempts to every completed suicide. Among those who attempt suicide but do not go on to commit suicide, usually it is because some change occurs in their psychosocial world that makes life more desirable than death. However, the majority of people who kill themselves have made previous suicide attempts. A history of suicide attempts (65% of those who have completed suicide) is especially prominent among suicidal people who find that *self-destructive behavior is the most powerful means they have of communicating their distress to others.* Those who have made *previous high-lethal attempts are at greater risk* than those who have made low-lethal attempts.

Another historical indicator is a *change in method* of suicide attempt. A person who makes a high-lethal attempt after several less lethal attempts that elicited increasingly indifferent responses from significant others is a higher risk for suicide than one with a consistent pattern of low-lethal attempts, especially in the case of suicidal adolescents. Suicide attempts as a risk factor should also be considered in relation to depression. Longer episodes of depression (2–10 years) are more reliable for suicide prediction and underscore a pivotal point in suicide prevention work—the need to *reassess* for suicide risk.

It is also important to determine the outcome of previous suicide attempts—for example, "What happened after your last attempt? Did you plan any possibility of rescue, or were you rescued accidentally?" A person living alone who overdoses with sleeping pills and is rescued unexpectedly is alive more by accident than by intent. This person falls into a high-risk category for future suicide if there are other high-risk indicators as well. Suicide risk is also increased if the person has a negative perception of a psychiatric hospital or counseling experience, as the example of John reveals. This suggests great caution in employing mental health laws to hospitalize suicidal people against their will, and it underscores the pivotal role of a PCP if a patient reports that a mental health counseling referral is "just not working" for whatever reason.

Resources and Communication With Significant Others

Internal resources include strengths, problem-solving ability, and personality factors that help one cope with stress. *External resources* include a network of persons one can rely on routinely as well as during a crisis. *Communication* as a suicide sign includes (1) a person's explicit statement to others of intent to commit suicide and (2) the disruption of bonds between the suicidal person and significant others. People who finally commit suicide typically feel ignored or cut off from significant people around them, as dramatic murder-suicide events in schools and colleges affirm. This is extremely important in the case of adolescents, especially in instances of parent–child communication problems, and in preventable national tragedies of gun violence that involve killing others followed by the perpetrator's suicide (see Chapter 6).

Institutionalized racism and the unequal distribution of material resources in the United States appear to contribute to the rapidly increasing rate of suicide among minority groups. This is especially true among young (under 30) people who realize early in life that many doors are closed to them. Their rage and frustration eventually lead to despair, suicide, and other violent behavior.

Others may have apparent supportive resources, but serious depression and the conviction of their worthlessness prevent them from accepting and using such support. Adequate personality resources include the ability to be flexible and to accept mistakes and imperfections in oneself. Some people who kill themselves appear to have happy families, good jobs, and good health, but they may also have rigid role expectations imposed by culture, sexual identity, or socioeconomic status. Perceived role failure is usually gender specific—work failure for men and family or mate failure for women. Such rigidity in personality type is also revealed in a person's *tunnel vision* approach to problem solving: There is *only one solution* to a problem—*suicide*. Psychotherapy can help people develop more flexible approaches to problem solving.

Serious attention to these important signs by family, HCPs, and others concerned about suicide prevention leads to this risk assessment outcome: If a person has a *high-lethal plan, available means, no social support, and cannot communicate about despair and hopelessness*, the immediate and long-range risk for suicide *is very high* for this particular person—regardless of other factors. As already noted, *attempts at precise measurement on a scale are of little value* in the absence of *direct communication* with an acutely distressed person and his or her family. The risk *increases*, however, if other signs are also present:

- Recent loss of a significant relationship
- Physical illness
- Drinking and other drug abuse
- Physical isolation
- Unexplained change in behavior
- Depression
- Social problems
- Psychosis or obsessive-compulsive disorder
- Age, gender, race, marital status, sexual identity issues

Take *physical illness*, for example: National surveys highlight the fact that a large number of people with any problem seek out *first either a physician or pastor*. In the case of suicidal people, the visit may be their last attempt to find relief from distress. Thus, a primary care provider's failure to ascertain the suicide plan or to examine depression disguised by a complaint with no physical basis may lead to the practice of prescribing a psychotropic drug without a referral for counseling. An *acutely anxious or depressed person may interpret such a response as an invitation to commit suicide*. The possibility of suicide is even greater if a diagnosis affects the person's self-image and value system or demands a major switch in lifestyle—for example, AIDS, degenerative neurological conditions, heart disease, breast cancer, amputation of a limb, or cancer of the sex organs (see Chapters 3 and 7).

Or consider *depression*: As already discussed, although not all people who kill themselves show signs of depression, enough suicide victims are depressed to make this an important indicator of risk.[14] This is particularly true for the depressed person who feels worthless and is unable to reach out to others for help. Because most depressed people do not kill themselves and because a useful predictor must distinguish between the *general population* and those who make *suicide attempts*, we should refrain from declaring depression as a significant predictor of suicide. That said, *depression is a significant avenue for opening direct discussion of possible suicide plans*: "You seem really down. Are you so depressed that perhaps you've considered suicide?" Other disorders such as schizophrenia and obsessive-compulsive disorder may also increase suicide risk if appropriate treatment is lacking.[15,16]

Immediate Danger, Long-Range Risks, and Chronic Problems

A person might engage in several kinds of self-destructive behavior at the same time. For example, someone who chronically abuses alcohol may threaten, attempt, or commit suicide—all in one day. We should view these behaviors on this continuum: All are serious and important in terms of life and death. The difference is that for some the danger of death is *immediate*, whereas for others it is *long range*. Still others are at risk because of a high-risk lifestyle, chronic substance abuse, and neglect of medical care.

Distinguishing between immediate and long-range risk for suicide is not only a potential lifesaving measure but also is important for preventing or interrupting a vicious cycle of repeated self-injury. If immediate risk is high, and family or HCPs do not uncover it early on through direct empathic communication, a suicide can result. But if immediate risk is low, as in medically nonserious cases of wrist slashing or swallowing a few over-the-counter sleep aids, but we respond as though life were at stake and fail to ask about the *meaning* of this physical act, we run the risk of *reinforcing* self-destructive behavior. In effect, we say through our behavior, "Do something more serious (medically), and I'll pay attention to you." In reality, *medically nonserious self-injury is a life-and-death issue*—that is, if cries for help are repeatedly ignored, there is a high probability that eventually the person will accept the "invitation" to do something more serious and actually commit suicide.

Along with determining risk level (low, moderate, or high) we must also understand how ambivalence figures in a person's life-or-death decision making and the role of significant others who care whether a person chooses life over death—as in the no-lose game noted earlier.

WHAT TO DO: ESSENTIAL SERVICES FOR SELF-DESTRUCTIVE PERSONS

The US Department of Health and Human Services, Public Health Service, has published *National Strategy for Suicide Prevention: Goals and Objectives for Action* (2001).[17] Internationally, other countries have published similar national strategies. Family, friends, police, and bystanders should know what to do on behalf of persons on the brink of suicide. Three kinds of service should be available 24/7 for all at risk of killing themselves: (1) Emergency medical treatment, (2) Crisis intervention, and (3) Follow-up counseling or psychotherapy. In communities where these services are absent or inadequate, advocacy and citizen action are called for.

Emergency Medical Treatment

While health care providers are already knowledgeable about emergency medical treatment, unfortunately, this may be all that is received by some people at risk of suicide. Everyone should know that besides empathic listening to an acutely distressed person, if a suicide attempt is *medically nonserious*, the HCP's response *should not convey a life-and-death urgency*. A dramatic and misplaced medical response might reinforce self-destructive behavior while ignoring the underlying problems leading to the self-destructive act. For example, while suturing a slashed wrist, the physician, nurse, and a PCP should regard the physical injury neutrally, with an empathic tone and a focus on the *meaning* of self-injury: "You must have been pretty upset to do this to yourself. What did you hope would happen when you cut your wrists?" This can also set an example of how family members might respond to self-injury by a loved one. (See Chapter 3, Table 3.1, for an example.)

Crisis Intervention: Life-Saving Actions for Persons "On the Brink"

If a person whose suicide attempt is medically serious does not receive follow-up crisis counseling, the risk of suicide within a few months is very high. As already discussed, everyone concerned about a suicidal person should know that in a life-or-death crisis state, *prescribed drugs are one of the weapons used most frequently for suicide*. In agencies where mental health specialists are not available on-site in emergency services, staff should make every effort in safety planning to link the person and his or her family to a PCP who is careful to follow through with mental health referral and/or appropriate drug treatment (see Chapter 3).

In addition to the general crisis care strategies discussed in Chapter 3, family, friends, and others should be familiar with crisis counseling that typically is enacted by crisis specialists or mental health professionals:

1. *Relieve isolation.* If a highly suicidal person lives alone and there is no friend or supportive relative with whom the person can stay temporarily, hospitalization is probably the best course of action until the active crisis is over.
2. *Remove lethal weapons.* Guns and pills should be removed on advice by the counselor in active collaboration with the client, a relative, or a friend. If caring and concern are expressed and the person's sense of self-mastery and control is respected, he or she will usually surrender a weapon voluntarily, so that it is out of reach for easy or impulsive access during the acute crisis. While avoiding power tactics or engaging in the heated debate regarding gun control, all human service providers should calmly inform an acutely distressed person and the family of this sobering fact: *Suicide risk increases fivefold and homicide risk increases threefold when there is a gun in the home.*
3. *Encourage alternate expression of anger.* This means actively exploring with the individual other ways of expressing anger short of paying with one's life; for example, "I can see that you're very angry with her for leaving you. Can you think of a way to express your anger that would not cost you your life?" If anger at one's former partner, doctor, work supervisor, or counselor is connected to the suicide threat, an empathic but neutral response is called for: "Of course I'd feel bad, but not guilty. So I'd like to continue working with you around your illness even though you're disappointed right now with our progress."
4. *Avoid a final decision about suicide during crisis.* We should assure the suicidal person that the suicidal crisis—that is, seeing suicide as the *only* option—is a *temporary* state and try to persuade the person to avoid a decision about suicide until all other alternatives have been considered when past the pain of acute crisis.
5. *Beware of "no-suicide" contracts.* A cautionary note to upset clients who are asked to sign a "no-suicide" contract is in order here. The *no-suicide contract* is a technique used by some HCPs in which the client promises to refrain from self-harm between appointments and to contact the provider if contemplating self-harm. Since this controversial issue emerged in the suicidology literature, there is growing consensus on this point: Such contracts offer *neither special protection* against suicide *nor legal protection* for the therapist or other provider. No-suicide contracts may convey a *false sense of security to an anxious provider.* This is because any value the contract may have flows from the *quality of the therapeutic relationship*—ideally, one in which the provider conveys caring and concern about the client. In no way should a contract serve as a convenient substitute for the time spent in *empathic listening, crisis intervention and counseling, and careful planning with the despairing client* regarding therapeutic alternatives to suicide. Contracts may be no more than a mechanistic "quick fix" by time-pressured providers if not incorporated into an overall service plan as discussed here and in Chapters 2 and 3, including, for example, calling a hotline, or relieving isolation by asking a friend to join in a favorite recreation activity.[18,19]

6. *Reestablish social ties.* Restoring broken social bonds can be done through family crisis counseling sessions or finding satisfying substitutes for lost relationships. Active links to self-help groups such as Widow to Widow or Parents Without Partners clubs can be lifesaving.
7. *Relieve extreme anxiety and sleep loss—Psychotropic drug use.* A suicidal person who is extremely anxious and also has been unable to sleep for several days may become even more suicidal. To such a person, the world looks bleaker and death seems more desirable at 4:00 a.m. after endless nights of sleeplessness. A good night's sleep can temporarily reduce suicide risk and put the person in a better frame of mind to consider other ways of solving life's problems (see next section).

In such cases, psychotropic medication may be indicated on an emergency basis. But this should *never* be done for a highly suicidal person without daily crisis "check-in" by a concerned family member, friend, crisis counselor, or PCP. Without such concern, an extremely suicidal person *may interpret a drug prescription with delayed action as an invitation to commit suicide.* An antianxiety medication will usually suffice in these instances and thus improve sleep, as anxiety is typically the major cause of sleeplessness. Antidepressants, in contrast, are more dangerous as a potential suicide weapon. If medication is needed, the person should be given a *1- to 3-day supply at most*—always with a return appointment for crisis counseling.

PRECAUTIONS: PSYCHOTROPIC DRUG USE FOR SUICIDAL PERSONS

Primary care providers are already current on the general topic of psychotropic drugs. The focus here is a cautionary note to lay readers about the intersection between prescription drugs and suicidal danger, especially if prescribed by practitioners without specialty training in crisis care and psychopharmacology. Also, some clients may request or even "demand" a tranquilizer or antidepressant drug as a "quick fix" while ignoring recommendations for crisis counseling or psychotherapy to address underlying problems.

Antidepressants are not emergency drugs; however, these drugs may be used successfully for some suicidal persons who experience severe, recurring depression. Successful response to antidepressant therapy is highly variable, and debate about the use of psychotropic drugs continues. Thus, although some people respond favorably to antidepressant treatment, research and controversy continue regarding dosage and the success of such treatment in preventing suicide. Also, there is no compelling evidence that antidepressant treatment, even with safer psychotropic agents, has reduced suicidal risk, whereas the risk of overdosing on antidepressants is well established (see References and Further Reading).

The success of antidepressant drugs for persons with bipolar illness is significantly related to the timing of suicidal behavior, which occurs most often during the early course of the illness. Family members, clients seeking relief, and all HCPs should attend to these well-established results from decades of research: The greatest success of drug treatment occurs when used in *combination with psychotherapeutic approaches.* This principle is of the utmost importance when considering the use of psychotropic drugs for anyone, *especially adolescents* (see Chapters 3, 7, and 9).

Since antidepressant drugs are dangerous, they should be prescribed with extreme caution for suicidal persons—even when clients are explicitly advised of expected delays in symptom relief; for some drugs this maybe be up to 2 weeks.[20] When taken with alcohol, an overdose of drugs can easily cause death. People using these drugs can experience side effects, such as feelings of confusion, restlessness, or loss of control. Persons with symptoms of borderline personality disorder are prone to an increase in self-destructive behaviors while treated with antidepressants.

Another danger of suicide occurs after the person's depression lifts during drug treatment. This is especially true for someone who is so depressed and physically slowed down that there is insufficient energy to carry out a suicide plan. It is therefore critical to *use antidepressant drugs in combination with psychotherapy or psychiatric hospitalization for a depressed person who is highly suicidal,* especially if the individual is also socially and physically isolated.

EXAMPLE: JACK—DRUG TREATMENT FOR DEPRESSION

Jack, age 69, a widower living alone, had seen his PCP for bowel problems. He was also quite depressed. Even after complete examination and extensive tests, he was obsessed with the idea of cancer and was afraid he would die. Jack also had high blood pressure and emphysema. Months earlier, he had had prostate surgery. His family described him as a chronic complainer. The PCP gave him a prescription for an antidepressant drug and referred him to a local mental health clinic for counseling. Jack admitted to the crisis counselor that he had ideas of suicide, but he had no specific plan or history of attempts. After two counseling sessions, Jack killed himself by carbon monoxide poisoning. This suicide might have been prevented if Jack had agreed to psychiatric hospital treatment. But Jack could not be persuaded, as his past experience with court-ordered hospitalization was very traumatic for him.

A major issue in Jack's case—and indeed, for most people—is our basic human need for mastery and control over our own lives. Jack lived alone, and in the cultural milieu promoting "take pill, feel better," he probably expected to feel better immediately after taking the antidepressant, even though the delayed reaction of the drug had been explained. An alternative might have been to prescribe a drug to relieve his anxiety about cancer in combination with a plan to relieve isolation and gain some support by living with relatives for a couple of weeks.

In general, psychotropic drugs are indicated only if a person is too upset to be engaged in the process of problem solving during crisis (see later discussion and Chapter 3). Nonchemical means of inducing sleep should be encouraged. This assumes a thorough assessment and various psychosocial strategies before prescribing drugs. We should never forget that many suicide deaths in North America are caused by *prescribed* drugs. Sadly, Rogers'[21] account of drug abuse ("just what the doctor ordered") appears even more applicable today than decades ago.

Follow-Up Service for Suicidal People

Beyond crisis counseling and the careful use of psychotropic drugs, all self-destructive persons should have easy access to receive counseling or psychotherapy as an aid in solving the problems that led them to self-destructive behavior. Crisis counseling focuses on resolving situational problems, expressing feelings appropriately, and helping the person to change various behaviors causing discomfort, but without deep probing. Psychotherapy involves uncovering repressed feelings that have been denied expression for a long time. It may also involve changing deeply rooted and counterproductive patterns of behavior, such as an inability to communicate feelings or inflexible approaches to problem solving.

ILLUSTRATIONS: SUICIDE RISK LEVELS, SAFETY PLANNING, CRISIS CARE, AND FOLLOW-UP COUNSELING

Following are examples for planning crisis care and follow-up counseling for persons at low, moderate, or high risk of suicide. They also affirm this important point: There is *no such thing as absolute prediction of suicide*, and suicidology is not an exact science. But the Risk Assessment Tool (Table 4.1) helps us move beyond "guesswork" in showing suicide risk levels from Low, Moderate to High. It builds on the idea of a client or family worksheet, or a few key questions about danger added to routine medical history forms completed in clinic visits, as already noted.

Low-Risk Suicidal Behavior

This includes verbal threats of suicide with no specific plan or means of carrying out a plan. This category also includes self-injury by a person who knows that the effects of the method do not involve physical danger or clearly provides for rescue. Ambivalence in low-risk behavior tends more in the direction of life than death. Although the immediate risk of suicide is low, the risk of an attempt, a repeat attempt, and eventual suicide is high, depending on what happens after

Table 4.1 RISK ASSESSMENT TOOL: SUICIDE—LOW, MODERATE, AND HIGH LEVELS

Key to Risk Level	Danger to Self	Typical Indicators
1	No predictable risk of suicide now	Has no suicidal ideation or history of attempt, has satisfactory social support system, and is in close contact with significant others
2	Low risk of suicide now	Has suicidal ideation with low-lethal methods, no history of attempts or recent serious loss, has satisfactory support network, no alcohol problems, basically wants to live
3	Moderate risk of suicide now	Has suicidal ideation with high-lethal method but no specific plan or threats. Or has plan with low-lethal method, history of low-lethal attempts; for example, employed female, age 35, divorced, with tumultuous family history and reliance on psychotropic drugs for stress relief, is weighing the odds between life and death
4	High risk of suicide now	Has current high-lethal plan, obtainable means, history of previous attempts, is unable to communicate with a significant other; for example, female, age 50, living alone, with drinking history; or Black male, age 29, unemployed and has lost his lover, depressed and wants to die
5	Very high risk of suicide now	Has current high-lethal plan with available means, history of suicide attempts, is cut off from resources; for example, White male, over 40, physically ill and depressed, wife threatening divorce, is unemployed, or has received promotion and fears failure

the threat or attempt. The risk is increased if the person abuses alcohol and other drugs. Social and personal resources are present but problematic for people in this behavior group.

Gloria—Low Risk: #2, Assessment Tool

Gloria, age 42, took five sleeping pills at 5:00 p.m. with general knowledge of the drug's lethal capacity as a way to just "get away from it all" through sleep; she knew that five pills would not kill her. When her husband found her sleeping at 6:00 p.m. the next day, he had at least some awareness of her distress. Gloria is troubled by her marriage and has a limited social circle (her husband never liked any of her friends). She is employed part-time as a secretary. She really wants a divorce but is afraid she cannot easily make it on her own. Gloria also takes an antidepressant drug every day and limits her alcohol to a single glass of wine with dinner. Although troubled now, Gloria basically loves life. She has not made any other suicide attempts.

Suicide risk for Gloria: Her *immediate* risk of suicide is low. The risk of repeat suicide attempts is moderate to high, depending on what Gloria is able to do about her problem. For example, if she increases her alcohol consumption along with sleeping pills, her risk increases.

Emergency medical intervention: Medical treatment for Gloria is not indicated because pills are absorbed from the stomach into the bloodstream within 30 minutes. The dose of five sleeping pills is not lethal or extremely toxic. Other medical measures, such as dialysis, are therefore not indicated.

Crisis intervention: Crisis counseling should focus on the immediate situation related to Gloria's suicide attempt, decision about her marriage, and effectiveness of coping.

Follow-up service: In follow-up counseling, Gloria can examine her extreme dependency on her marriage, her personal insecurity, her limited social life, and her dependency on antidepressant drugs or alcohol as a means of problem solving. Gloria might also be linked to a women's support group that focuses on career counseling and the midlife transition faced by women.

Moderate-Risk Suicidal Behavior

This includes verbal threats with a plan and available means more specific and potentially more lethal than those involved in low-risk behavior. Also included are attempts in which the possibility of rescue is less certain. The chosen method, although it may result in temporary physical disability, is not fatal, regardless of whether there is rescue. Ambivalence is strong; life and death are seen more and more in an equally favorable light. The immediate risk for suicide is moderate. The risk for a repeat suicide attempt and eventual suicide is higher than for low-risk behavior if emotional pain is not relieved and no important life changes occur after the attempt or revelation of the suicide plan. The risk is significantly increased in the presence of chronic alcohol or other drug abuse.

Susan—Moderate Risk: # 3, Assessment Tool

Susan, an immigrant, age 19, came alone in a taxi to a local hospital emergency department. She had taken an overdose of her antidepressant prescription (three times the usual dose) a half hour earlier. Susan and her 3-year-old child, Debbie, live with her parents. She has never gotten along well with her parents, especially her mother. Before the birth of her child, Susan had a couple of short-lived jobs as a waitress. She dropped out of high school at age 16 and has experimented off and on with drugs. Since the age of 15, Susan had made four suicide attempts. She took overdoses of nonprescription drugs three times and cut her wrists once—attempts assessed as low lethality.

At the emergency department, Susan had her stomach pumped and was kept for observation for a couple of hours. She and the nurses knew one another from emergency medical visits after her other suicide attempts. She was discharged with a recommendation that she follow up with her PCP and seriously consider previous referrals for follow-up counseling. This emergency department did not have on-site crisis or psychiatric consultants. While there, Susan could sense the impatience and disgust of the staff. A man with a heart attack had come in around the same time. Susan felt that no one had the time or interest to talk with her. Twice before, Susan had refused referrals for counseling, so the nurses assumed that she was hopeless and did not really want help.

Suicide risk for Susan: Susan is not in immediate danger of suicide (risk rating: 3). She does not have a high-lethal plan and has no history of high-lethal attempts, although overdosing on a prescription antidepressant signals a change toward increased risk. Susan's overdose of *three times the prescribed dose* falls in the moderate-risk category. While Susan's personal coping ability is poor, she is not cut off from her family, despite their disturbed relationship, and has not suffered a serious personal loss. However, because there is no follow-up counseling or evidence of any changes in her troubled social situation, Susan is at risk of making more suicide attempts in the future which, if they are medically serious (e.g., a higher dose of drugs or slashing one's jugular vein), her risk of eventual suicide increases significantly. On the ambivalence scale, life and death may begin to look the same for Susan if her circumstances do not change.

Emergency medical intervention: Treatment for the overdose is stomach lavage.

Crisis intervention: Crisis counseling for Susan should include contacts with her parents and focus on the situational problems she faces: unemployment, conflicts with her parents, and dependence on her parents.

Follow-up service: Because Susan has had a chaotic life for a number of years, she could benefit from ongoing counseling or psychotherapy, if she so chooses. This might include her decision to continue her education and thereby improve her employment prospects. Family therapy may be indicated if she decides to remain in her parents' household. Group therapy is strongly recommended for Susan.

High-Risk Suicidal Behavior

This includes a threat or a suicide attempt that would *probably be fatal without accidental rescue and sophisticated medical or surgical intervention*, plus instances when a suicide attempt fails to end in death as intended, for example, in a *deliberate car crash*. Ambivalence in high-risk behavior tends more in the direction of death than life. The present and long-range risk of suicide is very high unless immediate help is available and accepted. Chronic self-destructive behavior such as substance abuse increases the risk even further.

Edward—Very High Risk: #5, Assessment Tool

Edward, age 41 and Caucasian, had just learned that his wife, Jane, decided to get a divorce. He threatened to kill himself with a gun or carbon monoxide on the day she filed for the divorce. Jane's divorce lawyer proposed that their country home and the twenty adjoining acres be turned over completely to Jane. Edward told his wife, neighbors, and a crisis counselor that his family and home were all he had to live for. Indeed, all Edward could afford after the divorce was the rental of a single shabby room. He and Jane have four children. Edward also has several concerned friends but does not feel he can turn to them, as he always kept his family matters to himself. Jane's decision to divorce Edward left him feeling like a complete failure. He has several guns and is a skilled hunter. A major factor in Jane's decision to divorce Edward was his chronic drinking problem. He had threatened to shoot himself 8 months earlier after a violent argument with Jane when he was drinking, and Jane kept urging him to get help from Alcoholics Anonymous.

Considering the most significant signs already noted, Edward's case reveals several strong signals of high risk:

1. He has a specific plan with an available high-lethal means: the gun.
2. He threatened suicide with a high-lethal method 8 months previously and is currently communicating his suicide plan.
3. He is threatened with a serious interpersonal loss and feels cut off from his most important social resources: his family and home.
4. He has a rigid expectation of himself, sees himself as a failure, and has a deep sense of shame about his failure as a husband and father.
5. His coping ability is poor, as he abuses alcohol and is reluctant to use his friends for support during a crisis.
6. He is also a high risk in terms of his age, sex, race, marital status, and history of alcohol abuse.

Suicide risk for Edward: Edward is in *immediate danger* of committing suicide—highest risk rating, #5. Even if he makes it through his present crisis, he is also a long-range risk for suicide because of his chronic self-destructive behavior—abuse of alcohol and threats of suicide by a readily available, high-lethal means.

Emergency medical intervention: None indicated currently. Depending on level of engagement in crisis counseling, Edward might benefit from an antianxiety drug for temporary stabilization, as discussed earlier.

Crisis intervention: Remove guns (and alcohol, if possible) or have wife or friend remove them *with* Edward's collaboration. Arrange to have Edward stay with a friend on the day his wife files for divorce. Try to get Edward to attend a self-help group, such as Alcoholics Anonymous, and urge him to rely on an Alcoholics Anonymous member for support during his crisis. Edward should have frequent crisis counseling sessions, including daily telephone check-in during the divorce crisis.

Follow-up service: Edward should have ongoing psychotherapy, individually and in a group, focusing on his alcohol dependency and rigid expectations of himself; therapy should focus on helping Edward find other satisfying relationships after loss of his wife by divorce.

HOW TO HELP FAMILY AND OTHER SURVIVORS OF SUICIDE

When a suicide occurs, it is almost always the occasion of a crisis for survivors. A "survivor" here refers to all those left behind by someone who commits suicide: family members, primary care provider, psychotherapist, friend, neighbor, and the entire community that grieves what might have been a preventable death.

The most immediately affected are usually family, the person's counselor and PCP, and other providers who did all they could to prevent the suicide. The anguish, grief, and possible guilt or relief felt by survivors is the usual province of mental health professionals. Primary care providers, however, if they have been attuned to family and psychosocial issues, will probably learn sooner or later about the suicide of a former patient. Given the deeply embedded feelings about death and dying felt by many, some survivors may present to PCPs with physical ailments with no observable or laboratory evidence of psychopathology. Typically, these ailments may mask unaddressed grief or the stress-related physical symptoms of persons caring for a chronically ill spouse or other family member who eventually dies. If the cause of death was suicide, such symptoms may be more serious.

Since even a psychotherapist may be unable to plumb the depths of despair that led to suicide, all the more so for a PCP who "after the fact" may recognize significant clues that were missed. Some survivors may feel misplaced guilt and a sense of responsibility for the suicide. They may experience a sense of relief if relationships were very strained or the person had attempted suicide many times and either could not or would not accept available help. Pediatric mental health professionals should be consulted for the special concerns of child and parent survivors.

To avoid guilt trips or a tendency to "scapegoat" (i.e., find someone to blame), or collude in silence about the suicide, the person's counselor or PCP should convene a post-suicide meeting with these three goals: (1) to ascertain who is best able to contact and offer support to the surviving family members; (2) to offer support to the PCP or counselor who treated the person; (3) to learn on behalf of others at potential risk by examining the entire situation for what clues might have been missed or how possible "system loopholes" may have short-changed the patient—in short, a helpful way for all to move forward following the tragedy of suicide.

Some survivors—even years after a suicide—have spent extraordinary energy trying to answer the question, Why? And while critical examination of treatment plans is helpful, we may never know the answer to this question in some cases. It is therefore important to remember that we are not gods, that suicide has been happening for many centuries, and that sometimes people commit suicide despite our best efforts to help them find alternatives.

REFERENCES, FURTHER READING, DISCUSSION GUIDE

REFERENCES

1. WHO. http://www.who.int/mentalhealth/prevention/suicide/suicideprevent/en/. Retrieved January 10, 2014.
2. American Association of Suicidology. Suicide Prevention Is Everyone's Business. http://www.int/mentahealth/prevention/suicide/. Retrieved January 10, 2014.
3. Parsons, T. (1951). Social structure and the dynamic process: The case of modern medical practice. In *The social system* (pp. 428–479). New York: Free Press.
4. Emanuel, E. J., & Battin, M. P. (1998). What are the potential cost savings from legalizing physician-assisted suicide? *New England Journal of Medicine, 339*(3), 167–172.
5. Shneidman, E. S. (1985). *Definition of suicide.* New York: Wiley.
6. Shneidman, E. S. (1987). At the point of no return. *Psychology Today, 21*(3), 54–58.
7. Farberow, N. L. (Ed.). (1980). *The many faces of death.* New York: McGraw-Hill.
8. Maris, R. W. (1981). *Pathways to suicide.* Baltimore, MD: Johns Hopkins University Press.
9. Durkheim, E. (1951). *Suicide* (2nd ed.). New York: Free Press. (Original work published 1897)
10. Motto, J. A. (1991). An integrated approach to estimating suicide risk. *Suicide & Life-Threatening Behavior, 21*(1), 74–89.
11. Beck, A. T., Steer, R. A., Beck, J. S., & Newman, C. F. (1993). Hopelessness, depression, suicidal ideation, and clinical diagnosis of depression. *Suicide & Life-Threatening Behavior, 23*(2), 120–129.
12. Best Practice Registry. National Strategy for Suicide Prevention. Suicide Prevention Resource Center. http://www.sprc.org/bpr. Retrieved January 10, 2014.
13. Brown, T. R., & Sheran, T. J. (1972). Suicide prediction: A review. *Suicide & Life-Threatening Behavior, 2,* 67–97.

14. Clark, D. C. (1999). Lifetime risk of suicide in major affective disorders. In D. Jacobs (Ed.), *Guide to suicide assessment and intervention* (pp. 270–286). San Francisco: Jossey Bass Publishers.
15. Tsange, M. T., Fleming, J. A., & Simpson, J. C. (1999). In D. Jacobs (Ed.), *Guide to suicide assessment and intervention* (pp. 287–299). San Francisco: Jossey Bass Publishers.
16. Weiss, R. D., & Hufford, M. (1999). Substance abuse and suicide. In D. Jacobs (Ed.), *Guide to suicide assessment and intervention* (pp. 300–310). San Francisco: Jossey Bass Publishers.
17. US Public Health Service. (1999). *Surgeon general's call to action to prevent suicide.* Washington, DC: Author.
18. Clark, D. C., & Kerkhof, A. J. F. M. (1993). No-suicide decisions and suicide contracts in therapy. *Crisis, 14*(3), 98–99.
19. Reid, W. J. (1998). Promises, promises: Don't rely on patients' no-suicide/no-violence "contracts." *Journal of Practical Psychiatry and Behavioral Health, 4*(5), 316–318.
20. Salzman, C. (1999). Treatment of the suicidal patient with psychotropic drugs and ECT. In D. Jacobs (Ed.), *Guide to suicide assessment and intervention* (pp. 372–382). San Francisco: Jossey Bass Publishers.
21. Rogers, M. J. (1971). Drug abuse: Just what the doctor ordered. *Psychology Today, 5,* 16–24.

FURTHER READING

Bongar, B., Maris, R. W., Berman, A. L., Litman, R. E., & Silverman, M. M. (1993). Inpatient standards of care and the suicidal patient: Part I: General clinical formulations and legal considerations. *Suicide & Life-Threatening Behavior, 23*(3), 245–256.

Boyd, J. H., & Moscicki, E. K. (1986). Firearms and youth suicide. *American Journal of Public Health, 76,* 1240–1242.

Cain, A. C. (1972). *Survivors of suicide.* Springfield, IL: Thomas.

Earley, P. (2006). *Crazy: A father's search through America's mental health madness.* New York: Berkley Books.

Evans, W. P., Owen, P., & Marsh, S. C. (2005). Environmental factors, locus of control, and adolescent suicide risk. *Child and Adolescent Social Work Journal, 22*(3-4), 301–319.

Everett, B., & Gallop, R. (2000). *The link between childhood trauma and mental illness: Effective interventions for mental health professionals.* Thousand Oaks, CA: Sage.

Fuller, J. (1997). Physician-assisted suicide: An unnecessary crisis. *America, 177*(2), 9–12.

Humphrey, D. (1992). Rational suicide among the elderly. *Suicide & Life-Threatening Behavior, 22*(1), 125–129.

Jamison, K. R. (2011). *The unquiet mind: A memoir of moods and madness.* New York: Random House, Vintage Books.

Leenaars, A. A., & Wenckstern, S. (1991). *Suicide prevention in schools.* Bristol, PA: Hemisphere.

Menninger, K. (1938). *Man against himself.* Orlando, FL: Harcourt Brace.

Pfeffer, C. R. (1986). *The suicidal child.* New York: Guilford Press.

Remafedi, G. (Ed.). (1994). *Death by denial: Studies of gay and lesbian teenagers.* Boston: Alyson.

Richman, J. (1992). A rational approach to rational suicide. *Suicide & Life-Threatening Behavior, 22*(1), 130–141.

Samuels, D. (May 2007). Let's die together. *The Atlantic,* 92–98.

Stephens, B. J. (1985). Suicidal women and their relationships with husbands, boyfriends, and lovers. *Suicide & Life-Threatening Behavior, 15*(2), 77–90.

Webb, N. D. (1986). Before and after suicide: A preventive outreach program for colleges. *Suicide & Life-Threatening Behavior, 16*(4), 469–480.

Zito, J. M., Safer, D. J., dosReis, S., Gardner, J. F., Boles, M., & Lynch, F. (2000). Trends in the prescribing of psychotropic medications to preschoolers. *Journal of the American Medical Association, 283*(8), 1025–1030.

DISCUSSION GUIDE

1. Everyone has some general knowledge about suicide. After reading this chapter, arrange a discussion with two or three persons concerned about the topic. Compare your current knowledge with that of others and the "Facts and Feelings" about self-destructive persons. For example, frustration, fear, the possible rewards of "being there" for a despairing person, and so on.

2. With a small group, explore the ethical issues regarding suicide and the "right to die." Do you agree or disagree? Why or why not?

3. Consider examples from your own and others' experience about the usefulness of knowing major signs of immediate and/or long-range risk of suicide. How did this knowledge help you in a suicidal crisis situation?

4. If a suicide occurred in your family or close network of friends, in retrospect, what clues might you have missed among the classic signs of distress that typically are present among people considering suicide? For example, what did he or she say? What behaviors revealed increasing desperation on the path to suicide?

5. If you or someone you know lost a loved one to suicide, what was the quality of crisis counseling and follow-up care available to you or the person's family survivors? If it was less than satisfying, consider what you and others might do about this.

6. From reading this chapter and the standards of care for suicidal persons—whether as a lay person or health care provider—how would you assess the adequacy of crisis care and suicide prevention services in your community, for example, 24/7 availability. If inadequate, what actions might you take to remedy this situation?

CHAPTER 5

Victimization by Violence, Sexual Assault, and Emotional Abuse

Healing from the crisis of victimization by violence or verbal abuse

CHAPTER OUTLINE

Key Facts and Issues About Violence and Victimization   116
Violence as a Human Rights Violation   118
Violence by Women and Among Sexual Identity Minority Groups   119
Violence In and Beyond the Family   122
The Complexity of Violence and Abusive Behavior   123
Recognizing Risk and Future Danger Levels of Victimization   129
Tools for Identifying Immediate and Future Danger   131
Triage Questions: Screening for Victimization and Life-Threatening Behaviors   131
Crisis Care and Follow-Up Counseling for Survivors of Violence and Abuse   134
Mandatory Reporting by Emergency and Primary Care Providers   135
Example: Woman Abused by Intimate Partner   137
References, Further Reading, Discussion Guide   139

It was a cold snowy windswept day as Melinda, age 18, drove alone to visit her family for the holidays. When her car broke down, she turned on the caution lights, hoping someone would stop to help as she waited inside the car. Melinda's cell phone did not work in the isolated region. Within 10 minutes a driver, Erin, stopped. He assessed the situation and declared that her car was "dead" and would need to be towed for repair. Melinda accepted Erin's offer of a ride through small towns to the nearest station, but once in his car, Erin demanded her home address. Erin's helpful attitude turned threatening, as Melinda grew fearful, weighing the odds of protecting herself on her home turf vs. freezing to death on the lonely highway. She chose going home, where Erin raped her. Sobbing through the night, Melinda blamed herself for her "stupidity" in not insisting that he drop her off at a service station. With the help of a rape crisis counselor, Melinda was referred to a group healing session for sexual assault victims and finally stopped blaming herself for the crime, as she also learned various cautions for preventing rape.

Victimization by violence knows few national, ethnic, religious, or other boundaries. Media reports from local and international arenas alert us daily of more sad news about violence—this, despite civil rights legislation, victim advocacy, and violence prevention efforts by volunteers and professional health and mental health providers. Abuse and violence often originate from bias based on gender, race, religion, disability, and/or sexual identity. Immigrants and refugees may be particularly vulnerable because of social isolation, language barriers, racism, and fear of deportation if they seek help.

This chapter addresses violence and abuse from the perspective of victim-survivors. It should be considered in tandem with Chapter 6, which features the urgency of recognizing potentially dangerous persons at home, at work, or elsewhere. Together, these chapters show the interconnections between individual victim-survivors of violence and the broader sociocultural, human rights, and public health perspectives on this painful topic. Since victimization occurs across the life span from childhood through old age, the focus here is for would-be victims and their families to recognize early on any life-threatening danger, its prevention, and crisis care regardless of violence type or age of victim-survivors. Readers are alerted to References and Further Reading for in-depth coverage of *particular* kinds of victimization, for example, sexual assault and elder abuse. This chapter highlights what everyone can do at home, at work, and on the street for safety from attack and, if threatened or abused, the importance of seeking life-saving linkages and follow-up counseling with crisis and trauma specialists.

KEY FACTS AND ISSUES ABOUT VIOLENCE AND VICTIMIZATION

Statistically, most violence worldwide is perpetrated against women of all ages, children (girls and boys), and other men by heterosexual males. Contrary to widely held fears of attack by strangers, the majority of victims know their abusers. Some women abuse or kill their male partners;[1] and mothers physically abuse children in numbers approximately equal to that of abusive fathers, stepfathers, and/or boyfriends. This figure is misleading, however, when considering that mothers typically are the primary caretakers of children, and most spend more time with them than fathers do.

Facts from government and other sources highlight the urgency of prevention and crisis care of persons victimized by violence or abuse[2,3,4]:

- Around 25% of couples are violent with each other (United States).
- At least 25% of pregnant women have a current or past history of abuse (United States and Canada); about 40% experience the first violent incident when pregnant.
- Battering is the most common cause of injury to women worldwide; in the United States, the incidence exceeds accidents, muggings, and stranger rape combined.
- Battering and abuse are primary reasons why many women and children are homeless (United States).
- Between 60% and 70% of runaways and 98% of child prostitutes have a history of childhood sexual and/or physical abuse.
- Significant numbers of homicides (40% in Canada) are in family relationships; in the United States most domestic homicides are by men killing women, with others by women killing men, usually after years of abuse. Killings of women out of jealousy and male ownership or family "honor" still occur across cultures.
- Violence within relationships tends to escalate in severity and frequency over time without early preventive intervention.
- About 50% of boy victims become abusive later, underscoring the fact that later violence is not "inevitable" and early "learned behavior" can be replaced with nonabusive responses to stress.
- Significant numbers of children witness violence, with special services available for such children in major metropolitan areas across continents.
- Living in a violent home is now considered a form of child abuse.
- Over 1 million children under age 16 are brought into the international sex trade per year.
- Most violence is committed by heterosexual men against children of both sexes, women, and other men—homophobia not withstanding.
- Rates of violence by girls and women are increasing, reflecting in part the power of male examples and violence-tinged media influences (United States and Canada).
- A majority of rape victims know their attackers; for example, shocking numbers of sexual assaults are committed against military personnel by peers and supervisors.
- Millions of adult and child rape victims have been attacked as the centuries-old "spoils of war" practice and the breakdown of civil order.

Health professionals were among the last groups to get on board responding to violence as a public health issue—after survivors themselves, their advocates, and the legal/criminal justice professions. National surveys of nursing schools in the United States and Canada reveal that nurses' formal preparation did not adequately prepare them to identify, treat, and care for survivors of sexual abuse and violence.[5,6]

These key "facts" about violence are useful for every person potentially at risk, and for health care providers as a "reality check" with their patients—people already injured or vulnerable to abuse—who keep hoping and believing, for example, that "He promised he'd never do it again"... "I think he's going to change if I'm patient enough"... "I just know it [the violence] will stop if we both stop drinking" or, in the case of sexually abused teens, "I'll just run away as soon as I have a chance."

VIOLENCE AS A HUMAN RIGHTS VIOLATION

The United Nations has defined violence as a human rights issue, has convened international meetings on the topic, and the United Nations Decade for Women conferences have featured numerous workshops on the worldwide problem of violence against women. The last UN conference was held in Beijing, China, in 1995, with 36,000 women attending, including government representatives from all UN member nations. It is noteworthy that such UN conferences were convened at 10-year intervals over a few decades, but *not repeated since the 1995 Beijing Conference* despite widely published shocking examples of gender-based violence worldwide, although other work continues to address the issue. Every 2 years in recent decades the World Health Organization (WHO) sponsors the World Conference on Injury Prevention and Safety Promotion—mostly recently in New Zealand (2012) and London (2010).

The UN convention on eliminating all forms of discrimination against women situates violence in a human rights framework. The WHO report at the 2010 London conference summarized many disturbing facts and recommendations about such violence in general, and the related issue of perpetrators of violence. The UN and WHO documents published from international conferences reveal continuing facts and recommendations for action around the worldwide scourge of violence[7,8]:

- The persistence and unacceptability of all forms of violence against women
- Strengthening the political commitment and joint efforts of all stakeholders to prevent and eliminate violence against women
- Identifying ways and means to ensure more sustained and effective implementation of state obligations to address all forms of violence against women
- Increasing state accountability
- Violence against women is severe and pervasive throughout the world.
- Many women are subjected to sexual, psychological, and emotional violence by an intimate partner.
- More than 130 million girls have been subjected to female gender mutilation/cutting.
- Women experience sexual harassment throughout their lives.

- The majority of the hundreds of thousands of people trafficked annually are women and children.
- Violence against women in armed conflict frequently includes sexual violence.
- Women who are subject to violence are more likely to suffer physical, mental, and reproductive health problems.
- Domestic violence and rape account for 5% of the total disease burden for women aged 15–44 in developing countries.
- Violence before or during pregnancy has serious health consequences for mother and child.
- Women who have experienced violence are at higher risk of contracting HIV.
- Violence against women may prevent them from full economic participation and hinder employment opportunities.
- Girls who have experienced violence are less likely to complete their education.
- The direct costs of violence against women are extremely high.

These points underscore the fact that interpersonal violence is not *just* a "women's issue"; rather, it is a global human rights issue that is capturing the increased attention of world leaders, executives of corporations who see the economic toll of violence among employees, and religious leaders, most of whom no longer condone abuse of wives as grounds for maintaining marital bonds at the expense of victims. A human rights perspective emphasizes the accountability of perpetrators and opportunities for learning nonviolent approaches to interpersonal conflict, appropriate health and social services for victim-survivors, and principles of restorative justice. This includes eliminating the abuse of power at the highest levels, as in state-sponsored violence, and a platform of prevention at all levels.

VIOLENCE BY WOMEN AND AMONG SEXUAL IDENTITY MINORITY GROUPS

While women are the predominant group afflicted by sexual assault and intimate partner violence, the principles and crisis care discussed in this chapter also apply to women's abuse of their male partners and to violence among lesbian, gay, bisexual, and transgendered persons.[9] The failure to acknowledge women's violence is equivalent to viewing women as less than moral beings, just as excusing male violence implies that men are less than moral beings. Women, like men, should be held accountable for their behavior.

While national survey data reveal roughly equal incidence of male and female violence in the United States, the *context* of female violence needs more attention: Female violence is primarily in self-defense, and their attacks generally are not as dangerous or physically injurious as those of men. In addition, when women kill their mates, it is usually after years of abuse, and they do so less frequently than men kill their wives.[1] Considering also the fact that at least 25% of pregnant women have a current or past history of being battered, the contrast is even more dramatic especially as revealed in emergency settings where most victims are female. In addition, abused men typically have much more freedom to leave because of their socioeconomic advantage in society and relative freedom from child care.

Differences in physical strength between most men and women also play a role: The majority of men are physically more capable of inflicting injury than are women. But linguistically, since some women are more articulate than their male partners, their verbal abuse may inflict long-lasting wounds while essentially going unpunished. Men who are abused by their partners should nevertheless receive the same medical care and social support as recommended for women.

The pattern of injustice and violence used primarily in self-defense should be kept in mind in trials of women who kill abusive husbands. Rather than medicalizing the woman's case by using a contrived insanity plea, women should have a fair trial on self-defense grounds when evidence points in that direction. The suggestion that abuse of male partners is more rampant than woman battering covers up the roots of violence against women in traditional social structures and the low socioeconomic status of women that allows violence to flourish worldwide, as documented by PAHO/WHO.[8]

Prevention and intervention strategies for abused heterosexual partners apply to those in gay, lesbian, bisexual, or transgendered (GLBT) relationships.[9] The stigma of GLBT identity is added to the stigma of domestic violence. Asking for help necessitates "outing" oneself to law enforcement officers, health care providers, and so on, who may or may not be tolerant of "alternative lifestyles." The threat of an intimate partner outing one's mate if he or she reveals abuse or attempts to leave the relationship can be a *powerful tool of control*. Possible consequences of losing child custody/visitation, job, and family alienation are serious deterrents to such revelations.

Another disadvantage for GLBT victim-survivors is that few, if any, resources such as shelters are available for them. And despite national progress toward GLBT rights, additional burdens are rooted in the bias and social isolation faced by many of these couples; individuals in these relationships usually rely more heavily than others on their partners for emotional support and companionship. The excessive dependency in any intimate relationship may be the source of additional stressors in the interpersonal context of abuse. In addition, gay men are more vulnerable than lesbian women or heterosexual men to violence from strangers or associates who are motivated explicitly by antigay bias or homophobia.

The extraordinary stress experienced by couples in alternative lifestyles is compounded by stereotypes and the bias that keeps them isolated in the first place. One such stereotype is that all lesbians are feminists, and because a battering lesbian partner has violated the feminist agenda of nonviolence, she may thereby be judged as less deserving of help. Another stereotype is that women become lesbians because they have been victims of sexual abuse. In reality, not all lesbian women are feminists, and some feminists are just as homophobic as others are. In fact, many women have been sexually abused as children; most of them are heterosexual. Finally, because lesbian, gay, bisexual, and transgendered people are members of a larger cultural community, why would they be exempt from having absorbed the pervasive message of *violence as a control strategy and a solution to conflict resolution*? Their disadvantaged social position may result in greater sensitivity to issues of abuse generally, but they face even greater odds in avoiding violence than the general population.

Considered from a human rights perspective, appropriate service for victims in alternative lifestyles, demands that HPCs, friends, and others examine attitudes that can prevent battered lesbian, gay, bisexual, or transgendered partners from disclosing their plight and receiving needed help. In general, the legacy of victim blaming experienced by battered women is exacerbated among those in sexual identity minority groups. Major cities in Canada and the United States now have publicly established groups addressing violence among these minority groups, for example, the Violence Recovery Program at the Fenway Community Health Center in Boston. State and provincial offices for victim assistance can provide information about local services for these groups (see www.healthcaresaboutIVP.org).

And so the challenge remains: How do we make progress on this key human rights issue? A good start is education about values and cross-cultural exchange for prevention and successful intervention efforts worldwide. Key in this effort is challenging the widespread belief that some people have the right to control others or to devalue certain members of society and thus justify violence. A fundamental premise for addressing this human rights issue is this: Put a philosophy of *caring* at the center of family interaction and professional collaboration, and commit ourselves to continuing education on this urgent topic.[10,11,12] (See Chapter 3 for essential skills.)

Framing violence in a human rights perspective aids in stopping the victim blaming that may occur even among some victim-survivors (e.g., the case of Melinda) who blame themselves for what happened. It also puts a break on "cultural relativism," that is, explaining interpersonal violence as "just a part of *their* culture" and thereby excusing *us* from action that would defend everyone's basic human right to safety, while holding abusers of that right accountable. This means saying something like this to a victim-survivor: "No matter what [your husband or wife] might have said, what happened to you is *not right and it's not your fault.*"

In general, there is progress in correctly defining violence as a human rights issue, and we have moved on from an earlier time of denial, victim blaming, and excusing perpetrators. Violence is now widely framed as an abuse of one's basic right to safety and freedom from injury involving psychological, sociological, and feminist interpretations. In this book, violence is viewed predominantly as a *social phenomenon*, a means of exerting *power* and *control* that has far-reaching effects on personal, family, and public health worldwide. The term *family violence* is therefore avoided here, as it may obscure the fact that most perpetrators in families are men, and most victims are children and women of all ages regardless of marital status.

In the United States, the US Surgeon General's Workshop on Violence and Public Health in 1985[3] emphasized the fact that victims' needs, treatment of assailants, and violence prevention should command much greater attention from health and social service professionals than it had until recently. A significant recommendation from this interdisciplinary government conference was that all publicly licensed professionals (physicians, nurses, social workers, psychologists) should be trained and *examined* on the topic of violence and victimization as a condition of licensure. Since then, there has been progress on many fronts (for example, the 1999 American Association of Colleges of Nursing position paper[5] noted that teaching about violence is *essential* for graduation). But despite the key role of health care providers (HCPs) in prevention and care of victim-survivors, many cite limited coverage of the topic in their degree programs.

VIOLENCE IN AND BEYOND THE FAMILY

The historical neglect of victimization and its prevention and treatment in primary care and other settings underscores the value placed on family privacy and the myth that the family is a haven of love and security. This pattern of neglect also points to several related issues:

- Social values regarding children, how they should be disciplined, and who should care for them
- Social and cultural devaluation of women and their problems worldwide
- A social and economic system in which many elderly citizens often have no worthwhile place
- A social climate with little tolerance for minority group sexual identity
- A legal system in which it is difficult to consider the rights of victims without compromising the rights of the accused
- A knowledge system that historically has interpreted these problems in private, *individual* terms rather than in *public health and social context*

Victims and Survivors

The term "victim-survivor" includes a variety of persons regardless of relationship to assailant—family member, intimate partner, therapist, coworker, acquaintance, stranger, patient/client. "Victim-survivor" is intended to explicitly acknowledge one's victimization but also convey an abused person's *potential for growth, development, and empowerment*; that is, a status beyond the dependency implied by "victim."

An emphasis on growth beyond "victimhood" to "survivor" status is important, especially in situations in which some individuals, under criminal trial for violent acts, use their history of victimization as grounds for "temporary insanity" pleas to be excused for their violent behavior. Certainly, persons deeply wounded by abuse deserve an appropriate social and health care response. But while responding with compassion, it is crucial to acknowledge human beings' inherent freedom, resilience, and their capacity to rise beyond tragic circumstances—*particularly if they receive social support*. These points apply regardless of the gender of either the assailant or survivor.

Current international attention to the abuse and victimization of women and children is due primarily to the work of survivors themselves, community-based and criminal justice activists, and women's studies scholars, with health professionals joining later. The insights and practice protocols of these pioneers are fundamental in developing complementary programs in health and social service agencies which traditionally have underserved victim-survivors of abuse.[11,12]

Many volumes across health, mental health, and criminal justice disciplines cite the complexity of violence and abuse. Here the focus is on the important role of family, friends, neighbors, and primary care providers (PCPs) who are key players in early detection, prevention, and obtaining crisis care from police and trauma specialists. The terms *violence* and *abuse* are used interchangeably. *Perpetrator* is used to convey the importance of one's accountability for violent or abusive behavior, and the necessary collaboration between medical and legal/criminal justice sectors concerned with the rights of both victim-survivors and perpetrators.

THE COMPLEXITY OF VIOLENCE AND ABUSIVE BEHAVIOR

Explaining violence in simplistic or psychiatric/medical language is short-sighted and revealed in some common but misguided sentiments that (1) "only a sick man could beat his wife"; (2) child abuse is a syndrome calling for "treatment" of disturbed parents; (3) a "crazed madman" was responsible (and by implication, therefore not accountable) for highly publicized terrorist attacks; (4) "temporary insanity" sometimes excuses murder (even though juries are becoming more skeptical about this plea—influenced, perhaps, by research findings and widespread public knowledge about the topic); and (5) women who kill their abusers are victims of the "battered woman syndrome."

Psychiatric and Biomedical Influences on Violent Behavior

Public debate about biomedical approaches to social problems is increasing. We now know that describing violent persons and their victims in predominantly *individual* terms or a psychiatric framework is at best incomplete and at worst does little to address the *roots* of violence.

The view here expands on the Crisis Paradigm (Chapters 1 and 2): crises stemming from violence should be treated with a *tandem* approach, that is, considering *both individual and sociocultural factors* to explain violence. A person in crisis because of violence will experience much of what also occurs during crisis from other sources. And similar help, such as listening, social support, and decision counseling, applies as well. But shortchanging the sociocultural origins of violence can hinder important prevention efforts, crisis care, and the follow-up counseling designed to avoid implicitly blaming the victim. For victim-survivors of violence, attaching a psychiatric diagnosis such as Posttraumatic Stress Disorder (PTSD) may compound the problem rather than contribute to its solution.

The Underpinnings of Violent and Abusive Behavior

There is no single "cause" of interpersonal violence. Rather, examining complex, interrelated *reasons* can help us understand why some individuals are violent and others are not. Psychological, cultural, and socioeconomic factors are often present together, forming the *context* in which *violence as a means of control* seems to thrive. Children, many seniors, and often wives are economically dependent on their caretakers and in most cases are physically weaker than their abusers. Caretakers of children and older people are often stressed psychologically by difficult behaviors and the lack of social and financial resources to ease the burdens of caretaking. In cases of woman battering and sex-role stereotyping, psychological and economic factors intersect at both ends of the social class continuum: Poor women are less able to survive on their own, and some women who earn more than their husbands are more vulnerable to attack in a non-egalitarian marriage.

Example: Richard

A young mother with four children felt overwhelmed trying to care for her 5-year-old hyperactive child, Richard. The woman's husband was employed as a hospital maintenance worker but found it difficult to support the family. The family could not obtain public assistance, although their income was just above the level to qualify for food stamps. The mother, losing patience with Richard, spanked him for misbehavior. By evening, Richard was even more hyperactive, so the mother sometimes put him to bed without feeding him. The father and mother mutually approved of this form of disciplining Richard. A neighbor reported the parents of suspected abuse after observing the mother chase and verbally abuse Richard on the street, with a strap poised to spank him.

Violence toward others, then, is one way a person can respond to stress and attempt to resolve a personal or family crisis at the same time. For example, a person with low self-esteem who is threatened by the suspected infidelity of a spouse may react with violence, although this is not inevitable. Rather, violence is *chosen*, although it may be influenced by behavior such as the abuse of alcohol and other drugs. Violent behavior typically is *intended to control another person* and often is influenced by the social, political, legal, and belief and knowledge systems of the violent person's cultural community. The element of choice implies *defining violence as a moral act—* that is, while anger and impulsivity may play a role, violence is *social action* engaged in by human beings who by nature are rational and conscious. Through socialization and legal constraints, humans become accountable for their actions in various situations, while violence may be excused on grounds such as self-defense.

However, a person's consciousness may be clouded and responsibility mitigated by social and cultural factors rooted in history. For example, under certain circumstances, a violent person may be excused from facing the social consequences of his or her behavior, as in cases of self-defense or serious mental illness. This does not mean that every violent act is a sign of a psychiatric disorder (e.g., borderline personality disorder or PTSD) and that the perpetrator should therefore be "treated"—which might shortchange or dismiss his or her accountability. Nor does it mean that violence can be excused on grounds of racial or economic discrimination; this would suggest that the moral stature of socially disadvantaged groups is below the accepted standard of responsible behavior. Given the poverty, unemployment, and other tragic results of social inequalities endured by many people—mostly racial minority groups—perhaps in no other instance is the *tandem approach* to crisis intervention more relevant: Violent *individuals* are held accountable for their behavior, while the political and socioeconomic *context* in which much violence occurs is also addressed. Thus, an individual can be held accountable and be restrained or rehabilitated, while we also address sociocultural issues that contribute to a victim's vulnerability and the perpetrator's choice of aggressive behaviors in the first place.

The Moral Context vs. Adversarial "Either/Or" Approach to Understanding Violence

Attention to perpetrators and why they injure or kill people closest to them forms part of a comprehensive program to reduce violence. Some would argue that programs for perpetrators deflect from the more urgent need of refuge for victims. Violence is a major public health problem as well as a criminal justice issue.

At worst, an either-or position damages both victim-survivors and assailants; at best, it constitutes empty polemics, whereas a both-and approach is more fruitful. It is therefore not a question of whether we (1) *either* provide refuge and care for battered women and children *or* provide treatment programs for their abusers, (2) *either* hold parents accountable for the violent and abusive behavior of their children *or* offer parent effectiveness training and social and financial support to parents unduly burdened with the task of parenting, or (3) *either* teach inner-city youth anger management skills *or* address the sociocultural and economic roots of their anger.

Essentially, either-or debates are adversarial and reflect the *power and control* component of violence itself. These counterproductive arguments have surfaced anew just as progress has appeared in respect to understanding male violence. These principles apply regardless of gender, race, ethnicity, religion, or sexual identity. They also invite critique of the growing tendency toward "medicalizing" violence and victimhood but also serve as a caution against interpreting everyday life stressors in a biomedical or psychiatric framework.

Accordingly, victim-survivors and their families seeking help should routinely consider whether HCPs' responses include *not just medical treatment of injury* but also attend to the moral, social-psychological, and legal dimensions of victimization and abuse: *Violence is an infraction of society's rules regarding people, their relationships, and their property.* It is complex and intertwined with sociocultural, political, medical, and psychological factors touching its immediate and chronic aftermath.

Functioning members of a society normally know a group's cultural rules and the consequences when violating them. Persons lacking such knowledge might be publicly excused and receive treatment instead of punishment on grounds of circumstances that alter one's normal liability for rule infractions. A moral society requires restitution to individual victims from those not excused, and would design a criminal justice system that prevents crime rather than laying the foundation for further crime by inhumane punishment. A truly moral approach to violence would also avoid or reform practices that discriminate on the basis of race, gender, class, or sexual identity, practices that create a climate in which crime flourishes with the implicit support of society.

Victim Blaming

One major result of health professionals' acceptance (until recently) of mainstream values about violence is the blaming of victims for their plight, a legacy embedded in the psyches and attitudes of abused clients as well as their caretakers.

One incest survivor asked: "Am I guilty for loving my father? It was up to my dad to draw the line...He was the adult in control."

The all too common self-blame and depression among victims are rooted in society's assigning accountability for violence to victims rather than their assailants. A battered woman's query: "How can I please my husband? I did everything he demanded" varies only slightly from the question: "What did you do to provoke him?" In other words, victims tend to blame themselves because others have first blamed them. Such victim blaming implies, for example, that to stop intimate partner violence and/or escape death itself, a victim succumbs to being a fugitive, with continued responsibility for children, while her assailant escapes and goes on with life as usual. Victim blaming is increasingly being challenged through dramatic media exposure, but it continues in the general arena of clinical and legal discourse.

Recent mandatory arrest laws are a new twist on the tradition among Native American people in the United States: If a man battered his wife, *he* had to leave, *he* could not marry again, lead or take part in a war party or hunt, or own a pipe. And Canadian men's "National White Ribbon Campaign" illustrates that intimate partner abuse is not merely a women's issue but a community responsibility.

A "downward spiral" (Fig. 5.1) springs from culture and rigidly defined social roles and illustrates what happens if the victim-blaming process is not interrupted at its source or as soon as possible: If it is the individual victim-survivor against society, and values and policies about accountability for violence are not addressed, a victim-survivor typically will suppress the emotional pain of abuse and violence, with self-blame and depression easily following. Unless this downward spiral is interrupted—preferably through grassroots prevention efforts, societal change strategies, and holding perpetrators accountable—psychiatric disorders, further violence, and even suicide or murder may result.

The sad process of victim blaming is influenced by "medicalization," that is, the tendency to interpret life's problems—whether medical or not—in a medical framework. Applied to violence, this means ascribing a psychiatric diagnosis to the victim (e.g., depression or borderline personality disorder in *DSM* nomenclature) and excusing the assailant (e.g., temporary insanity), thus alleging psychopathology and obscuring the sociopolitical roots of the problem.

The *Diagnostic and Statistical Manual of Mental Illness* (*DSM*), now in its fifth edition, while controversial and scientifically questionable, is nevertheless widely accepted even by nonmedical clinicians as the bible of psychiatry.[13,14,15]

A *DSM* diagnosis also may mean "adding insult to injury" from the original violence by treating it as evidence of psychopathology, which may be cited as grounds to excuse accountability for violence and abuse. This misguided approach benefits neither victim nor perpetrator—and loses an opportunity for perpetrators to learn nonviolent responses to life stressors. On the positive side, as a result of widespread political activism from many progressive groups, diagnoses such as "rapism" and "homosexuality" no longer appear in the ever-expanding roster of diagnosable mental "illness".[16]

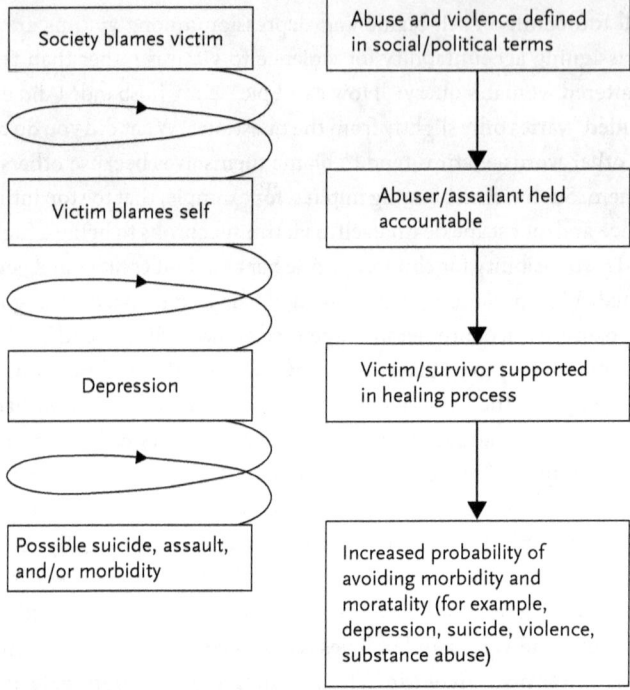

Figure 5.1 Abuse, the Downward Spiral, and Alternate Path
Primary prevention is ideal, but intervention at *secondary* and *tertiary* levels can also prevent morbidity and save lives.

Client Experience and Empowerment as Base

Health services and education on behalf of victim-survivors are grounded in the realities and complexities of the victimization experience. As a battered woman stated in response to the question of what health providers and others might do to help: "Come to a shelter…listen to our stories…learn how to be with us…we don't expect you to do it for us, but just be there to help when we finally decide to leave." This means that HCPs, family, friends, and neighbors must immerse themselves—at least vicariously—in the unique and tragic world of victimization as a way to lend a helping hand. Key to survivors' empowerment is partnering with them and recognizing that they are in charge of their healing and do not expect to be rescued. It also requires personal attention to self-care as a means of avoiding burnout and cynicism when facing the challenges of violence prevention and victim-survivor care.

This overview assumes a continuum between what happens between family members and intimates and the larger sociocultural milieu. It lays the foundation of what every citizen should know about the crisis of victimization—whether by sexual assault, physical punishment, intimate partner violence, and verbal abuse across the life cycle of childhood, adulthood, and old Age:

- Prevention
- Intervention during crisis
- Follow-up service (psychosocial care and psychotherapeutic treatment)

Each of these topics is important, but here the focus is on what victim-survivors, their families, and friends should expect from professionals when injured physically and psychologically by violence, sexual assault, or verbal abuse. This includes especially PCPs and in some cases, the expertise of trauma and mental health specialists. It means that PCPs, family, and friends need to recognize a "cry for help" and ambivalence around a "life or death" decision following acute trauma from assault.

Example: Collene

Collene, age 15, had never told anyone about her father's repeated visits to her room, where he sexually abused her over a 4-year period. Collene did not tell her mother because she thought her mother already knew and approved of what was happening. She looked forward to leaving home and marrying her boyfriend, age 19. One night, Collene's boyfriend raped her; afterward she went into the bathroom and took 20 of her mother's sleeping pills. If her mother had not heard her crying and taken her to the hospital for emergency treatment, Collene would have died.

When these basic services are minimal or not easily accessible, there is danger that victim-survivors in crisis may spiral downward toward chronic mental health disorders, suicide, or even retaliatory violence, as discussed earlier and in Chapter 2. Interrupting the downward spiral typically requires specialized counseling for both victim-survivors and perpetrators. But without first steps in homes, communities, and primary care, further abuse and life-threatening danger may be the unfortunate (but preventable) result (see Crisis Paradigm, Chapter 1).

RECOGNIZING RISK AND FUTURE DANGER LEVELS OF VICTIMIZATION

Everyone concerned about victimization and the care of survivors should be on alert about what service to expect from various HCPs at entry points to the health and social service system. This includes familiarity with the questions about possible victimization trauma that should be part of routine medical "intake" forms in clinics and doctors' offices (see Chapter 2).

As a result of client and professional advocacy over several decades, protocols for such assessments are now mandated by health care accreditation bodies such as JCAHO. Anyone concerned about the adequacy or standard of treatment received should take note of whether an agency's accreditation status is current and publicly posted in waiting rooms and elsewhere.

Creating a Climate for Revealing Danger and Level of Injury

A first step for HCPs in victim-survivor care is creating a supportive climate for client disclosure and ascertaining the degree of injury and its psychological aftermath. This is because victim-survivors may be reluctant to report abuse if they sense the climate is unreceptive for disclosure or that the provider is too busy to listen. Creating such a climate enhances the prospects of positive outcomes in survivor care and treatment. And it highlights what everyone needs to know and realistically expect from professional providers.

- *Beware of a judgmental attitude.* Many victim-survivors already feel judged and/or blame themselves for the abuse. Even before learning all the facts of a particular situation, attitudes have a way of speaking louder than words; for example, most people know how it feels to receive a verbal "I'm sorry" or "condolence" wish that does not match the giver's unspoken "cold" attitude.
- *Create a space for privacy and time to listen.* Survivors recognize the heavy demands and interruptions most HCPs face, and like others they will patiently wait their turn in the face of an emergency situation; but being left in a room alone for 20 minutes or longer with no explanation is anxiety provoking and unconducive to disclosure.
- *Be convinced of the importance of your own role and that of HCPs.* While not expecting "rescue," for some survivors, a PCP often is the first person in the health care system with whom they truthfully share their plight.
- *Whether a victim, family member, or HCP, examine personal values regarding violence, and deal with a possible history of victimization in one's own life* (as in "wounded healer") that has been long buried but which may surface in unexpected ways when confronted with the treatment needs (and/or lack thereof) of an abused patient. Such a "wounded healer" may feel a need to "close down" out of self-protection or fall into a misdirected "rescue" trap and have empowerment issues (see Chapter 3, Victim, Rescuer, Persecutor triangle).
- *Be ready to talk directly and empathically about the violence.* Using a structured protocol is helpful, as discussed next.

TOOLS FOR IDENTIFYING IMMEDIATE AND FUTURE DANGER

In Chapter 2, a Triage Tool was introduced as a foundation for risk-to-life (suicide, victimization, assault/homicide) screening questions to incorporate into all intake questionnaires across health care settings. The importance of these questions in all health and social service settings cannot be overemphasized. That is, if there is immediate risk to life (by suicide or violence), other diagnostic questions should take second place.

The term "triage" is a familiar one to all health professionals, although not always equally applied if the imminent danger of suicide or homicide is compared, say, with the typical urgency of treating a heart attack or stroke. These "triage" questions are replicated here from Chapter 2 for easy reference by readers focused on victim-survivor care and serve as a baseline for assessing level of trauma from victimization.

TRIAGE QUESTIONS: SCREENING FOR VICTIMIZATION AND LIFE-THREATENING BEHAVIORS

1. Have you been troubled or injured by any kind of abuse or violence? (for example, hit by partner, forced sex)

   Yes____ No____ Not sure____ Refused____
   If yes, check one of the following:
   By someone in your family____ By an acquaintance or stranger____
   Describe:

2. If yes, has something like this ever happened before?

   Yes____ No____ If yes, when? _____
   Describe:

3. Do you have anyone you can turn to or rely on now to protect you from possible further injury?

   Yes____ No____ If yes, who? _____

4. Do you feel so bad now that you have thought of hurting yourself/suicide?

   Yes____ No____ If yes, what have you thought about doing? _____
   Describe:

5. Are you so angry about what's happened that you have considered hurting someone else?

   Yes____ No____ Describe:

These triage questions *asked on admission across all health care settings* lay the foundation for more detailed assessment of someone victimized by violence or abuse. Table 5.1 presents a Victimization Assessment Tool that builds on information from Triage Questions. It complements the tool for suicide risk (Chapter 4) and the Assault/Homicide Tool in Chapter 6. These tools highlight the *life and death levels of danger during crisis*—toward oneself and others. Together, they underscore the most urgent facets of comprehensive crisis care discussed in Chapters 2 and 3, and the importance of teamwork and lay/professional collaboration on violence and abuse issues. As in suicide risk assessment, *there is no such thing as absolute prediction of violence toward others.*

Table 5.1 VICTIMIZATION ASSESSMENT TOOL

Key to Risk	Level of Victimization	Typical Indicators
1.	No experience of physical violence or abuse	No memory of violence recently or in the past.
2.	Experience of abuse/ violence with minor physical and/or emotional trauma	Currently, verbal arguments that occasionally escalate to pushing and shoving or mild slapping. History *may* include past victimization that is no longer problematic or for which a solution is in process.
3.	Experience of abuse/ violence with moderate physical and/or emotional trauma	Abused several times a month in recent years, resulting in moderate trauma/emotional distress (for example, bruises, no threat to life, no weapons). History *may* include past victimization that is still somewhat problematic (for example, a sexual abuse incident/overture by a parent or stepparent over 2 years ago)
4.	Experience of abuse/violence with severe physical and/or emotional trauma	Violently attacked (e.g., rape) or physically abused in recent years, resulting in physical injury requiring medical treatment. Threats to kill, no guns. History *may* include serious victimization (e.g., periodic battering, incest, or other abuse requiring medical and/or psychological treatment).
5.	Life-threatening or prolonged violence/abuse with very severe physical and/or emotional trauma	Recent or current life-threatening physical abuse, potentially lethal assault or threats with available deadly weapons. History may include severe abuse requiring medical treatment, frequent or ongoing sexual abuse, recent rape at gun/knifepoint, other physical attack requiring extensive medical treatment.

These three tools also illustrate the interrelationship between violence, victimization, and suicide, which, if missed in primary care and other entry points, may shortchange the specialized follow-up counseling indicated for all victim-survivors and perpetrators of violence. In general, people may find it uncomfortable to ask direct questions about suicide and violence. But the key point here is the *context* for asking sensitive questions, that is, the doctor–patient, parent–child, or friend–friend *relationship*. Such questions can uncover a person's loss of hope and help. They *signal that the primary problem is severe emotional trauma from victimization or verbal abuse*. As one battered woman said: *"I've healed from the physical wounds but will never forget what he said to me."* The triage questions, noted earlier, suggest that such routine inquiry could prevent suicide or murder as desperate responses to victimization trauma.

These assessment tools or variations thereof are part and parcel of the formal training of physicians, nurses, social workers, and clinical psychologists in required courses on emergency medicine and psychiatric/mental health care. But lay readers should be familiar with them while "taking stock" and evaluating the kind of treatment they or family members receive in crisis situations across various health care settings. As one survivor said to a sympathetic friend: "After keeping secret the incest and my husband's terrible treatment for so many years, it was such a relief when that really nice doctor doing a regular physical exam asked me directly if I'd ever been abused... sure is different from the old days of shame and hoping the memory of it would somehow just go away!"

As discussed in Chapter 2, *no crisis assessment is complete without ascertaining the life-threatening risk of suicide, and trauma from victimization and assault.* Research among female suicidal teenagers and adults reveals significant relationships between self-destructive behaviors and histories of childhood sexual abuse and intimate partner violence.[17,18] Work with battered women, for example, has uncovered the repeated revelation by survivors seeking help: "No one asked".[19] As the study by Sugg and Inui[20] suggests, physicians, nurses, and others have moved beyond their traditional fear of opening Pandora's Box by inquiring about abuse.

Screening in primary care protocols for intimate partner or other abuse is now common in many US and Canadian health care agencies. Yet such screening is often obscured in a check-off medical history form where it can easily be overlooked in direct interview, especially by PCPs who are unprepared to explore further if the client checked "yes" about abuse or safety in a routine intake questionnaire. On the other hand, lengthy screening tools may be counterproductive in busy emergency and primary care settings. Most important beyond screening and immediate safety measures is *assuring referral and follow-up to crisis counselors* based on information obtained from the Triage and risk assessment tools. Trauma counselors may use more in-depth diagnostic tools that are beyond the time boundaries and ordinary expertise of PCPs and the lay reader. An exception to this general pattern might be pediatricians, midwives, and OB/GYN providers who, besides their specialty expertise, function as PCPs and know some of their clients over many years. Information from a Triage tool should be an *essential component of all medical records*.

CRISIS CARE AND FOLLOW-UP COUNSELING FOR SURVIVORS OF VIOLENCE AND ABUSE

Identification of victimization status and danger level should be followed by in-depth assessment (preferably by mental health professionals with backgrounds in victimology who are also sensitive to gender issues). This will uncover the extent of a victim-survivor's trauma. Emergency departments already have established protocols (including mandatory reporting) for treatment of various victims, for example, rape, child witnesses of violence, and others which ideally include the follow-up roles of PCPs and trauma specialists.

Victim/survivors, their family, and friends should be alert to important techniques that HCPs employ in these and related situations: (1) withhold judgment, (2) offer an empathic, supportive response, (3) assist the victim-survivor with safety planning, and (4) provide information—a card or brochure with the numbers of hotlines, support groups, and counseling services. This seemingly small response is central, for example, to an abused woman's eventual decision to leave a violent relationship.

Key here is the empowerment a victim-survivor experiences in just knowing that others respect her decision, even if it is to stay in the violent relationship for the time being. Survivors also need explicit recognition from providers that ultimately it is *their* decision that makes the difference and they can take credit for the decision. Because abused persons often feel powerless and un-respected, if HCPs convey the message that they are in charge of their lives, such a message may serve as a premise for their eventual action, even if they currently are not ready for more than medical treatment. Linkage to specialty follow-up services, therefore, cannot be over-emphasized. The Victimization Assessment Tool is helpful here, not only for HCPs, but for family, friends and survivors themselves for gaining insight about immediate danger and personal history of victimization by violence and abuse.

Crisis Care Essentials

In addition to the general crisis intervention strategies discussed in Chapter 3, the following techniques are pivotal for victim-survivors whether the injury and abuse is from rape, intimate partner battering, an attack from a stranger, or in the case of frail elders, a family member or caretaker. Everyone concerned can use these points as markers of what to reasonably expect from HCPs attending to victim-survivors.

- Assure the abused or threatened person of safety and protection through available resources, for example, police, child and adult protective services.
- In explicit language, assure the victim-survivor that she or he is not to blame for another person's violent behavior.
- Reassure the victim-survivor that one's feelings and reactions to the assault are normal, not a sign of mental illness.
- Inform the person of legal rights and what this realistically means; for example, a rape victim's right to file charges along with the prospect of what might ensue from an assailant's defense attorney, such as implicitly "blaming the victim"; or the legal responsibility of health providers to report intimate partner, child, and elder abuse.
- Keep in mind the centrality of power dynamics and the person's need to regain a sense of control over one's life.
- While offering empathy and support, refrain from making decisions for the person.
- Provide emergency and other easy-to-understand information, including realistic means of avoiding life-threatening danger. Primary care settings should have this kind of information available to all clients in waiting areas.
- Link the person to specialized self-help groups.

The preventive, crisis, and follow-up aspects of helping victim-survivors should be considered with a view to their *vital connectedness*. This triple approach to the problem may not only help end the pain and terror of persons who are attacked but may also remove the negative consequences of violence for children, women, men, and the entire society.

MANDATORY REPORTING BY EMERGENCY AND PRIMARY CARE PROVIDERS

The required reporting of violence applies to PCPs, police officers, and others. But it also raises the controversial question of mandatory reporting of domestic violence (as is required in *all* cases of child and elder abuse or neglect). Such mandatory reporting laws for abused adults vary across states. For current information about mandatory reporting, see www.futureswithoutviolence.org or use the toll-free phone number 1-888-RX-ABUSE.

Central to reporting controversy is the issue of empowerment as expressed by female emergency department patients. Nearly half of non-English-speaking patients have opposed mandatory reporting on grounds of protecting autonomy and sociopolitical factors such as fear of deportation. Mandatory reporting might also be counterproductive in providing a "quick fix" or loophole for emergency department health professionals who may overlook linking abused women to crisis and follow-up mental health services—as in, "I've reported it, so it's now someone else's responsibility."

Also important is assuring abused persons that they are not responsible for their victimization, no matter what the person who battered them says to the contrary (see Fig. 5.1). Even when used in self-defense, retaliatory violence often escalates rather than decreases the violence. The adage "Violence begets violence" applies here. In addition, we should not assume that victim-survivors (female or male) are routinely in need of psychotherapy, as this could add a psychiatric label to an already heavy burden. If the person is suicidal, the principles and techniques discussed in Chapter 4 apply.

As primary caretakers of children, once an abused woman is treated for physical trauma and resolves the dilemma of what to do next, she may be faced with the crises of finding emergency housing, caring for children, and obtaining money. If a community does not have a "safe home" network or emergency shelter, if she cannot stay with relatives and has no money, she may have little choice but to return to the violent situation. In such instances, crisis workers and PCPs should assist her in developing a survival plan that includes, for example, having a bag packed and getting a key to a friend's house in case of acute danger. We also need to remember that in rural isolated communities worldwide, secure shelters may be nonexistent, or that a woman needing protection is expected to rely on kinship or tribal networks.[21,22]

When a woman decides to leave, up-to-date abuse prevention laws in the United States require police to accompany her to her home to get her children, legal documents, and whatever possessions she can bring to an emergency housing situation. Almost invariably, when a woman is battered, her children are affected as well. An important element of helping a mother in crisis, as well as her children, is the availability of child care services and attention to housing and other problems. The children are often highly anxious and in need of a stable, calming influence as well as appropriate physical outlets and nonviolent discipline. Pediatric PCPs caring for children—either physically and/or sexually abused or as witnesses to violence—need firm linkages for referrals to child psychiatric specialists.

Survivors of intimate partner violence say they do not expect us to rescue them. Rather, they want us to listen to their terror and dilemmas, and offer support as they seek safety, healing, and a life without violence. Because calling the police and emergency medical resources is a routine step for many, putting them in touch with specialized crisis workers is the *first and most important thing emergency personnel and HCPs can do* after providing medical treatment and safety planning.

Two factors, however, may impede the accomplishment of this task: Some victim-survivors may not acknowledge the cause of their physical injuries, or they provide a cover-up story. There are several reasons for this: (1) a battered woman may have been threatened by her mate with a more severe beating if she reveals the beating; (2) she may simply not be ready to leave for her own reasons; (3) she may sense the judgmental or unsympathetic attitude of a physician or nurse and therefore not confide the truth. Because of social isolation, prejudice, and fear of deportation, immigrant minority and refugee women who are abused usually face additional impediments to receiving help.[23]

Sensitivity to these factors will help PCPs to interpret a woman's evasiveness about her injuries and recognize the implausibility of a cover-up story; for example: "When we see women with injuries like this, it's often because somebody hurt them." Besides physical injuries, a battered woman will show other signals of distress and may present with aches and pains or vague symptoms not traceable to specific medical causes. PCPs who use the Triage and risk assessment tools offered here can more accurately identify and appropriately respond to a battered woman in crisis.[24] As is true with suicidal persons, *direct questioning* in the context of a trusting relationship usually results in the person's relief to know that someone is caring and sensitive enough to discern one's distress and ask the right questions. These principles and sensitive inquiries also apply in instances of elder abuse by family members or others on whom a frail older person is dependent for care and protection. For example, a frail victim-survivor may fear further abuse if she or he confides in a supervising visiting nurse. As in the case of child abuse, reporting to Adult Protective Services is mandatory.

While structured counseling sessions are not usually the role of PCPs, the following example illustrates how such might proceed with a victim of intimate partner violence. It shows that providers must pay serious attention to the multiple psychological and social problems often connected to violence and abuse, as discussed in Chapter 3. While this example highlights risks of victimization based on gender and immigrant status, the principles apply to similar issues such as ethnicity, sexual identity, poverty, or other factors that negatively affect reporting and crisis care around violence and abuse—in short, the care that victim-survivors deserve regardless of their individual circumstances.

EXAMPLE: WOMAN ABUSED BY INTIMATE PARTNER

Sandra Le Claire is a 22-year-old woman currently separated from her abusive husband of 5 years. She came to the United States from a war-torn country, where French was her second language after her native tongue; Sandra is now learning English. She is the mother of two small children, ages 2 and 5. She does volunteer work and is in the process of applying for public assistance. Her husband has been her sole source of financial support, and since their separation 9 months ago, his support has been sporadic at best. Sandra presented with cuts and bruises about her face and across her chest and two black eyes, which were swollen shut—all as a result of a beating by her husband. On previous emergency department visits for minor injuries she was referred to her PCP, but she never followed through because of threats by her husband. Sandra says the current beating was the culmination of an argument over her husband's lack of financial support to her and her children. She has never been willing to press charges against her husband out of fear, as he has threatened to kill her; nor has she ever retaliated with violence herself. She has been drinking more frequently and heavily and is becoming increasingly depressed and despondent about her situation. Sandra has suicidal ideation but denies having a specific plan, although in the past she has thought about taking an overdose of Tylenol when upset with her husband. She says her children have not witnessed any of the abusive episodes.

Sandra became pregnant at age 16 after moving to the United States with her parents, and quit high school to get married. She grew up in poverty, the youngest of five children with an alcoholic father and a born-again, church-going mother. Sandra viewed her marriage as a way out.

Although her father worked steadily, he did not earn enough money to support both his family and his drinking. Her mother did not believe in divorce. She raised the children and largely ignored her husband's drinking, sustaining many beatings herself at his hands. Though Sandra is supported by her mother, who helps her with child care, she does not feel understood. Her mother believes God will provide. She tells Sandra it is just a phase that men go through and that things will improve for Sandra, as they have for her, since Sandra's father has grown less violent over the years. Sandra is not sure she can wait. Since English is her third language, Sandra has problems with getting financial aid because she cannot complete the forms. Her abusive husband is also a drinker. Sandra had no drinking problem prior to abuse.

Using the Comprehensive Mental Health Assessment (CMHA) and the Service Contract framework presented in Chapter 3, the major problems and issues Sandra faces are illustrated and rated for danger and safety levels in Table 5.2 (see www.crisisprograms.org for complete Record System). This example illustrates primary attention to danger and safety issues in a situation like Sandra's—that is, items # 20, 13, and 14 from the CMHA assessment tool. Based on risk levels on a rating scale of 1 (low stress/very high functioning) to 5 (high stress/very low functioning)—it illustrates life-saving intervention strategies for Sandra, based on high risk levels and requiring serious attention by professionals and family members.

This example highlights appropriate intervention by PCPs based on level of danger from abuse or violence. It can also serve as a standard for lay readers to evaluate the kind of care that should be available to all victim-survivors of violence or abuse.

Table 5.2 SERVICE CONTRACT: A BATTERING SITUATION (EXCERPT)

Item # CMHA Scale	Problem/Issue Specification		Strategies/Techniques (Planned Actions of Client and Health Provider)
20.	Safety—self (5)	Husband threatened to kill her	*Explore* (a) shelter option (b) changing locks (c) restraining order (d) feelings regarding use of these options
13.	Violence/abuse experienced (4)	Does not seem clear about extent of danger	*Provide information about* (a) shelter number and admission process (brochures/cards) (b) emergency phone number
14.	Injury to self (3)	Suicidal ideation/ no specific or past attempts	*Discuss/listen* to feelings of hopelessness and reluctance to confide in close friend.

Stress rating code: 1 = low stress; 5 = high stress.

REFERENCES, FURTHER READING, DISCUSSION GUIDE

REFERENCES

1. Hoff, L. A., & Brown, L. (2014) *Violent women and girls: Abused, acculturated, mentally ill, accountable?* (research and publication in process).
2. WHO (2010). *Injuries and violence—The facts.* Department of Violence and Injury Prevention and Disability. Geneva, Switzerland: Author.
3. US Surgeon General. (1986). *Surgeon General's workshop on violence and public health: Report.* Washington, DC: US Department of Health and Human Services.
4. Centre for Public Health. (2010). *Safety first: Stories and key figures on violence, injuries and their prevention.* Liverpool, UK: John Moores University.
5. American Association of Colleges of Nursing. (1999). *Position paper: Violence as a public health problem.* Washington, DC: Author.
6. Woodtli, A., & Breslin, E. (2002). Violence-related content in the nursing curriculum: A follow-up national survey. *Journal of Nursing Education, 41*(8), 340–348.
7. WHO (2010). *Preventing intimate partner and sexual violence against women: Taking action and generating evidence.* Geneva, Switzerland: Author.
8. PAHO/WHO (2003). *Violence against women: The health sector responds.* Washington, DC: Author.
9. Renzetti, C. M. (1992). *Violent betrayal: Partner abuse in lesbian relationships.* Thousand Oaks, CA: Sage.
10. United Nations. (1996). *The Beijing declaration and the platform for action.* New York: Author.
11. WHO (2010). *Violence prevention: An invitation to intersectoral action.* World Conference on Injury Prevention and Safety Promotion. London: Author.

12. Hoff, L. A., & Bell, M. (2010). Comprehensive service issues: Health and criminal justice interface. In L. A. Hoff, *Violence and abuse issues: Cross-cultural perspectives for health and social services* (pp. 209–230). London: Routledge.
13. Becker, D. (2013). Chapter 6: Post traumatic stress disorder and the war for mental health. In *One nation under stress: The trouble with stress as an idea* (pp. 148–181). New York: Oxford University Press.
14. McHugh, P. R. (2001). The DSM: Gaps and essences. *Psychiatric Research Report*, 17(2-3, 14–15).
15. McNally, R. J. (2011). *What is mental illness?* Cambridge, MA, New York and London, England. The Belknap Press of Harvard University Press.
16. Watters, E. (2010). *Crazy like us: The globalization of the American Psyche*. New York: Free Press.
17. Herman, J. (1992). *Trauma and recovery: The aftermath of violence*. New York: Basic Books.
18. Everett, B., & Gallop, R. (2000). *Linking childhood trauma and mental illness: Theory and practice for direct service practitioners*. Thousand Oaks, CA: Sage.
19. Hoff, L. A. (1990). *Battered women as survivors*. London: Routledge.
20. Sugg, N. K., & Inui, T. (1992). Primary care physicians' response to domestic violence: Opening Pandora's box. *Journal of the American Medical Association, 267*(23), 3157–3160.
21. Hoff, L. A. (2010). *Violence and abuse issues: Cross-cultural perspectives for health and social services*. London and New York: Routledge.
22. Saylors, K., & Daliparthy, N. (2006). Violence against native women in substance abuse treatment. *American Indian and Alaska Native Mental Health Research: The Journal of the National Center, 13*(1), 32–51.
23. Hoff, L. A. (2010). Oppression, abuse, and enslavement of indigenous people across continents; and Torture and trafficking survivors, and abuse of immigrants. In L. A. Hoff, *Violence and abuse issues: Cross cultural perspectives for health and social services* (pp. 115–148). London and New York: Routledge.
24. Hoff, L. A., and Morgan, B. D. (2012). Crisis care basics in primary care. In *Psychiatric and mental health essentials in primary care* (pp. 49–63). London and New York: Routledge.

FURTHER READING

Bell, C. C., Jenkins, E. J., Kpo, W., & Rhodes, H. (1994). Response of emergency rooms to victims of interpersonal violence. *Hospital and Community Psychiatry, 45*(2), 142–146.

Bennett, L. (2012). *Dynamic psychotherapy with adult survivors*. Lanham, MD: Jason Aronson.

Bograd, M. (1984). Family systems approaches to wife battering: A feminist critique. *American Journal of Orthopsychiatry, 54*(4), 558–568.

Brendtro, L. K., Brokenleg, M., & Van Bockern, S. (1990). *Reclaiming youth at risk*. Bloomington, IN: National Educational Service.

Brown, J. C., & Bohn, C. R. (1989). *Christianity, patriarchy, and abuse: A feminist critique*. New York: Pilgrim Press.

Brownmiller, S. (1975). *Against our will*. New York: Simon & Schuster.

Buzawa, E. S., & Buzawa, C. G. (1996). *Domestic violence: The criminal justice response*. Thousand Oaks, CA: Sage.

Counts, D. A. (1987). Female suicide and wife abuse: A cross-cultural perspective. *Suicide & Life-Threatening Behavior, 17*(3), 194–204.

Dangor, Z., Hoff, L. A., & Scott, R. (1998). Woman abuse in South Africa: An exploratory study. *Violence against Women: An International Interdisciplinary Journal, 4*(2), 125–152.

Dobash, R. E., & Dobash, R. P. (Eds.) (1998). *Rethinking violence against women.* Thousand Oaks, CA: Sage.

Eyre, J., & Eyre, R. (1993). *Teaching your children values.* New York: Simon & Schuster.

Figley, C. R., & Nash, W. P. (Eds.). (2005). *Combat stress injury.* New York: Routledge.

Finkelhor, D. (1984). *Child sexual abuse: New theory and research.* New York: Free Press.

Greven, P. (1990). *Spare the child: The religious roots of punishment and the psychological impact of physical abuse.* New York: Knopf.

Groves, B. M., Zuckerman, B., Marans, S., & Cohen, D. (1993). Silent victims: Children who witness violence. *Journal of the American Medical Association, 269*(2), 262–264.

Hoff, L. A. (1990). *Battered women as survivors.* London: Routledge.

Hoff, L. A., & Rosenbaum, L. (1994). A victimization assessment tool: Instrument development and clinical implications. *Journal of Advanced Nursing, 20*(4), 627–634.

Lerner, H. L. (2005). *The dance of anger: A woman's guide to changing the patterns of intimate relationships.* New York: Harper.

Levy, B. (1991). *Dating violence: Young women in danger.* Seattle: Seal Press.

London School of Hygiene and Tropical Medicine. (2003). *The health risks and consequences of trafficking in women and adolescents.* London: Author.

Mawby, R. I., & Walklate, S. (1994). *Critical victimology.* London: Sage.

McEvoy, A., & Erickson, E. (1994). *Abused children: The educator's guide to prevention and intervention.* Holmes Beach, FL: Learning Publications.

McNally, R. (2011). *What is mental illness?* Cambridge, MA: Belknap Press of Harvard University Press.

Powers, J., & Jaklitsch, B. (1989). *Understanding survivors of abuse: Stories of homeless and runaway adolescents.* San Francisco: New Lexington Press.

Russell, D. E. H. (1986). *Secret trauma: Incest in the lives of girls and women.* New York: Basic Books.

Ryan, W. (1971). *Blaming the victim.* New York: Vintage Books.

Stark, E., & Flitcraft, A. (1996). *Women at risk: Domestic violence and women's health.* Thousand Oaks, CA: Sage.

Thornhill, R., & Palmer, C. (2000). *A natural history of rape.* Cambridge, MA: MIT Press.

US Surgeon General. (1986). Surgeon General's workshop on violence and public health: Report. Washington, DC: US Department of Health and Human Services.

Wiehe, V. R. (1998). *Understanding family violence: Treating and preventing partner, child, sibling, and elder abuse.* Thousand Oaks, CA: Sage.

Yllo, K., & Bograd, M. (Eds.). (1987). *Feminist perspectives on wife abuse.* Thousand Oaks, CA: Sage.

DISCUSSION GUIDE

1. Considering the facts about violence and victimization, discuss with your family or friends the safety or increased danger you experience in your community. If generally more safe than dangerous, how do you explain the situation? If more dangerous, what do you think are the reasons, and what can you do about it?

2. Have you or someone close to you been victimized by violence, sexual assault, or verbal abuse? If yes, how has this affected your daily life and sense of safety? For example, do you feel constantly "on alert" lest it happen again? Was there any evidence of self-blame or victim blaming in this instance? Consider with your family and friends what you can routinely do to prevent physical attack or sexual assault on the street or at home.
3. If you have children, what can you do to balance keeping them safe while avoiding either overprotection or misguided trust that "nothing like this could happen in our great neighborhood"?
4. If you or a loved one was assaulted, was the treatment and care received helpful in the healing process or, to the best of your knowledge, substandard?
5. Considering the different levels of danger or violence, why is this an important part of maintaining safety at home without turning yourself into a "police officer" on constant alert or organizing your whole life around self-protection?
6. Discuss with family or close friends the pros and cons of mandatory reporting of violence. Do you agree or disagree with this policy? Why do some people fail to report? What are the advantages and possible disadvantages or dangers of reporting by some victimized persons?

CHAPTER 6

The Violent and Abusive Person

Preventing Violence Is Everybody's Business

Violence and abuse: A major health and social issue **worldwide**

CHAPTER OUTLINE

Key Facts and Issues   144
Violence Defined: Individual and Public Health Perspectives   146
Violence, Values, and Culture   148
Violence and Learned Behavior   151
Youth Violence and Prevention   152
Assessment of Dangerousness, Assault, and Homicide Risk   155
Tools to Assess Assault Injury and Homicide Risk   157
Violence and Abuse in the Workplace and Forensic Psychiatry   159
Example: Connie—Violence and Psychiatric Disorder   160
Crisis Intervention With Assailants and Those Threatening Violence   161
Programs for Violent Men   163
Signposts of Restorative Justice   164
Primary Prevention of Violence and Antisocial Behavior   165
References, Further Reading, Discussion Guide   167

Eric, age 28, was employed but distressed over interpersonal relationships on the job. He came to a group therapy session, and shortly after the session began, Eric got up and swung his clenched fists, first at one of the therapists. Then he swung at other clients, while making threatening statements. Eric had apparently had something to drink, as the smell of alcohol was on his breath. But while swinging his fists at people, he seemed very controlled and came just an inch or so from their noses. The therapists and other clients were unable to persuade Eric to stop his violent, threatening behavior and therefore called the police. Eric was taken to the nearby jail. The senior therapist meanwhile, feeling overwhelmed with guilt about her client being in jail, reviewed the mental health laws to ascertain grounds for having Eric transferred from jail to a mental health facility. She reported the incident to the executive director (a psychiatrist) and explored with him the idea of having Eric committed for treatment. The psychiatrist replied, "Treated for what? Threatening you and the other clients?" The therapist revised some of her traditional ideas about "treating" people for violent behavior while holding them accountable for it was something of an afterthought.

This example highlights not only "gender" influences on violent behavior but also issues of accountability, mental disorders, and the intersection of criminal justice and psychiatric services affecting perpetrators of violence and abuse. While men and boys are the perpetrators of most violence worldwide, the rates of violence by girls and women is increasing—in one respect, a perverse side effect of women's greater "freedom"—in this case, to engage in the same abusive behaviors as men. This chapter addresses many urgent but unresolved issues regarding violence in communities across cultures that continue to surface.

KEY FACTS AND ISSUES

In recent decades, many professional, governmental, and lay groups have devoted major efforts to end the plague of violence still occurring across the globe—in the Americas, Europe, Asia, and Africa. Yet sobering stories from victim-survivors and their advocates show that much work is still to be done. Following are issues and practices that demand attention from health and social service professionals, community advocates, and everyone concerned about the physical, social, and psychological wounds inflicted by violence and abuse, and what we can do toward healing.[1]

Facts and Some Questionable Practices

1. In some schools, teachers abuse children physically and mentally under the guise of "discipline."
2. Health care services in many countries are unequally available and various segments of service are fragmented or poorly coordinated. More "one-stop health service centers" are needed to insure that life-saving information is easily available to actual and potential victims.[2]
3. In some cultures, traditional healers and elders play a significant role in resolving marital and family disputes. Respect for these traditions and

collaboration with lay and other healers is in the best interests of both victim-survivors and perpetrators needing services.
4. Members of societies with strong patriarchal values tend to deny the existence of child sexual abuse, treat women as subordinates, and often blame the victim regardless of evidence about the perpetrator. Across cultures worldwide, some women are raped or killed in an effort to maintain traditional male power, honor, and control.[3]
5. Gender sensitivity training should be part of all health sciences programs.
6. The law or cultural values are sometimes used to maintain male dominance, and in many instances violence-related disputes and charges drag on in courts for years.
7. Some countries have no national, regional, or local system of secure refuges for victims terrorized or threatened with their life at home. And indeed, even if such refuges existed, women in extremely isolated rural areas might be reluctant to use them at the cost of future isolation from the extended family network that might result.
8. Across cultures, despite laws and public education programs, there is a tendency to excuse perpetrators on grounds of psychopathology and/or their own histories of abuse as children.[4]
9. While recognizing the importance of focusing on the needs of victim-survivors rather than their assailants, violence prevention programs for abusers must be included. While exasperated advocates may suggest: "Put them in prison and throw away the key," this is not a realistic response, first because all human beings have basic rights, and second, because violence prevention programs globally emphasize accountability for one's behavior and opportunities to learn nonviolent responses to conflict.[5] At the primary prevention level, all would-be parents should be prepared to avoid sex role stereotyping in child rearing—a deeply embedded practice signifying the power of a patriarchal value system that upholds male superiority and aggressive behavior.[6]
10. In societies that have only begun to address violence and abuse issues, concerned persons might ask: "Where do we start?"

This question gets at the pivotal purpose of this chapter: to explore key issues and provide a framework for understanding and preventing violence. It offers basic principles and examples from diverse sources that professionals and laypersons alike can consider without having to "reinvent the wheel". Through Internet and distance learning options, we can develop new partnerships and make a difference worldwide. A key theme here is to move beyond academic and practice "turf wars" and our "shock" following still another example of violence and terrorism, and affirm the belief that "we are all in this together."

Since we mostly agree on issues that really matter, the best outcome for all is to work toward common goals. Put another way, we really do need one another on this urgent topic. But since violence and its outcomes are affected by personal and deeply embedded values, awareness of our own values and relationships is important because of how they may influence our work with both victims and perpetrators. Most significant here is recognition that *violence is basically an abuse of power*. To paraphrase sociologist C. Wright Mills,[7] this chapter clearly and explicitly is sensitive to social justice issues and our role in making the world a better place.

VIOLENCE DEFINED: INDIVIDUAL AND PUBLIC HEALTH PERSPECTIVES

Although influenced by cultural, psychological, and political factors, *violence is a social act*, although it usually includes physical assault. At its most basic, interpersonal violence is not merely an instinct-driven response. Rather, it is primarily the chosen action of human beings who *may* be mentally deranged and therefore excusable, but who generally know a society's rules regarding right and wrong behavior—a universal value governing societies across the globe over the ages.

It is critical to define these layers of violence: What is "interpersonal," and what is "violence"? Violence constitutes behavior for which the perpetrator is *accountable* to the moral community. This definition is important because it goes deep into various aspects of both individual and institutional levels and the problem of victim blaming.

Historically, violence has sometimes been excused as a "cultural norm"; the term "cultural relativism" describes such a misplaced attribution (see section on "Violence, Values, and Culture"). Another interpretation defines violence as an inevitable outcome of aggressive instincts or as an expectable result of mental illness and therefore excusable. Some of these traditional definitions are still alive and used to explain violence. In Boston, Massachusetts, for example, despite progress in judicial education and reform, public controversy raged for weeks around a judge's sentence of probation instead of jail time for an offender who admitted kidnapping and attempting to rape a child; the explanation offered was that some people act out in an "aberrant way" in stressful situations.

Violence is now widely interpreted in psycho-sociocultural and feminist terms, that is, as a predominantly social phenomenon with far-reaching effects on personal and public health worldwide. That is the position taken in this book. In this framework, violence—in most instances—constitutes behavior learned in a milieu permeated with social inequalities based on age, gender, race, ethnicity, and sexual identity. In a cultural context, everyday life is filled with images of violence and physical force portrayed as the dominant modes of conflict resolution, with fewer depictions of *accountability* for violence.

Violence consists of exerting physical force and power over another—usually with the intent of *controlling, disempowering, and/or injuring the other*. Though violent abuse has serious implications for physical and mental health, it is not in itself a medical phenomenon except in the few instances in which a person is found to be "insane"—a legal term designating a person's mental incapacity (and therefore excusability) while behaving violently. Nor is violence merely a criminal justice phenomenon. Rather, it crosses legal, ethical, and health care domains, and society's major institutions, thus rendering it a complex issue with moral, sociocultural, political, and personal ramifications.

Physical violence is almost invariably accompanied by verbal abuse. For example, regular verbal threats of abuse or killing cause no immediate *physical* trauma, but they clearly strike terror and fear for one's life in the heart of the intended victim. We all need to recognize the damaging effects of verbal abuse generally, its frequency during conflict between intimate partners, the particular traumas of racial or ethnic slurs, and the taunting of lesbian, gay, and transgendered people or those with disabilities. Such verbal abuse is rooted in bias, fear, and/or hatred and is often followed by threats or acts of physical violence. Persistent psychological abuse, even without physical attack, can devastate a person emotionally and lead to serious health problems. Also, verbal abuse usually precedes physical abuse. However, in order not to underestimate the life-threatening nature of some violence, it is important to distinguish verbal insults, for example in a dating relationship, from sexual or other life-threatening assault at knife or gunpoint.

The terms "abuse" and "violence" are used interchangeably in this book, although abuse—especially sexual—does not always entail physical injury. For example, an incest victim, after several years of abuse, may have no visible injuries, but most surely she or he is deeply "violated" and almost invariably suffers severe emotional trauma. As battered women often say: "It is easier to heal from the physical wounds than the emotional ones," though the two are linked. Without satisfactory healing of such deep-seated emotional wounds, serious physical and mental health problems are often the unfortunate result. One way many cope with the trauma of abuse is by dependence on psychotropic drugs, especially in the absence of appropriate support at crisis points, and follow-up counseling or psychotherapy (see Chapter 3).

We have moved from defining violence as a private matter, a family problem, a medical illness, or a cultural norm, to a view of violence as a *social act and public health issue worldwide*. A human rights perspective directed to the global epidemic of violence is pivotal in the United Nations (1996) report on the Beijing Women's conference and platform for action[8] (see Chapters 3 and 5).

In most communities worldwide, one's greatest risk of attack is from family members. However, the term "family violence" obscures the reality that most perpetrators within the family are heterosexual men, and most victims are women of all ages and children. "Family violence" also shortchanges the sociocultural roots of abuse, which extend beyond the family to deeply embedded cultural values and traditional social arrangements which particularly disempower women and children. "Family violence" also excludes some major forms of violence: physical and sexual assault by an acquaintance or stranger; sexual exploitation by therapists and other professionals; rape as the spoils of war; and the traffic of women and children in the international sex trade arena. Socialization in child rearing, education, youth culture, employment practices, and family ideology are all central in defining interpersonal violence more broadly (see Chapter 5, "Violence In and Beyond the Family").

VIOLENCE, VALUES, AND CULTURE

Cross-culturally there is wide variation in ideas about interpersonal violence and the roles of men and women. Professionals, like other members of a cultural community, are informed by deeply embedded beliefs, myths, and traditions concerning women, marriage, the family, and violence. As a result, despite claims of neutrality and objectivity, victim-survivors, their families, and assailants need to recognize value-laden approaches in health service protocols on behalf of victim-survivors and assailants.

It is useful, therefore, to consider some key concepts that underpin our understanding of violence and its effects on diverse groups. *Ethnicity* is tied to the notion of shared origin and culture. In multicultural societies such as the United States and Canada, ethnic identities can shift and change based on power distribution and factors like language, skin color, religion, or country of origin, while some groups may define themselves as *bicultural* within a dominant culture of a particular society. If we do not know another's cultural heritage, we should explore it with sensitivity and a nonjudgmental attitude. *Ethnocentrism* is the emotional attitude that one's own ethnic group, nation, or culture is superior to that of others. Exaggerated ethnocentrism can lead to prejudice, bias, violence, and discrimination toward others based on their ethnic or religious identity, for example, "Jews are greedy," "Blacks are lazy," "Mexicans are dirty," or "Muslims are religious fanatics." Such *stereotyping* refers to an unvarying pattern of thinking and pigeonholing a person or group in a box that disallows for individuality, critical judgment, and basic respect for people different from oneself—thus putting a damper on positive care outcomes.

Cultural relativism is also important as we assess care and treatment of victim-survivors and assailants. First, it requires that instead of prejudging others, we should consider various actions, beliefs, or traits within their cultural *context* in order to better understand them. Cultural relativism presents particular difficulties with respect to violence. That is, some cultural practices may be harmful to physical and emotional health and welfare by allowing outsiders to ignore or dismiss certain human rights violations such as woman battering as "relative" to particular cultures, as in the expression, "That's just part of their culture," which in effect defies the principle of everyone's right to safety and freedom from injury or abuse.

A dramatic and controversial example illustrating cultural relativism is female genital mutilation (FGM), which, in one folk language, is called *tahara*, or "purity," implying that girls and women who have not undergone this procedure are "impure." In some cultures, female genital mutilation is a rite of passage. However, the term FGM is controversial; for example, out of cultural context, its meaning is obscured. In this book the World Health Organization (WHO) definition is offered: FGM is a human rights violation. WHO has urged abolishing the ritual because of its harmful effects on women's reproductive health and sexual expression.[9]

In a related vein, the importance of female virginity and marital fidelity is upheld by the custom of "honor killings" carried out by the "offended" husband or male family member. Though legally forbidden in most societies and not approved by Islamic religious tradition, honor killings continue with minimal punishment for perpetrators. These killings occur mostly in the Middle East, although three such killings have been reported in the American states of Georgia, New York, and Texas and in Canada. The instances for honor killings include when a woman engages in extramarital sex, has been raped, or has engaged in any action viewed as a violation of chastity norms. She is thus labeled as "unclean" and thereby brings disgrace to a family's "honor"—judgments used by male relatives to justify killing her.

At the heart of these killings is the double standard regarding male and female sexual expression. In essence, the cultural value of "purity" is typically attached to women but not men, and it is by no means limited to Islamic societies. In Christianity, this double standard dates back many centuries to a time when illiteracy was common and major moral teaching was done through preaching and art forms. For example, in an architectural gem of a church in Italy—resplendent with sculptures and mosaics—all the martyrs (Christianity's most honorable form of death) are depicted as male, while all the virgins are depicted as female. This is not to say that male martyrs perhaps were also virgins, or that some female virgins were also martyrs, but the bias favoring male status is clear.

The power of symbols for conveying values enduring over many centuries to the current era is illustrated in this question about the widespread contemporary acceptance of male promiscuity: If men are not expected to control pre-marital sexual expression to the same extent prescribed for women, but still desire a "virgin" bride, where are all the virgins supposed to come from? Clearly, this "double standard" crosses religious and male/female boundaries, as indicated in this quip by a contemporary American Jewish woman (age 29, in a society where the majority of both men and women willingly "lose" their virginity before age 19): She was "saving" her virginity until she found a Jewish husband. When her friend asked whether her betrothed was also a virgin, she laughed, saying, "Somebody has to know what they're doing!" Acceptance of male dominance is also evident among contemporary American brides who are "given away" to the groom by their father, apparently with no awareness of this custom's origin in the ancient cultural norm of the "patriarch" (owner of wives, children, animals, and the estate) transferring ownership of his daughter to another male. Tolstoy's[10] classic *Anna Karenina* reveals patriarchal values and the tragic result of Anna's extramarital love, including her suicide.

The double standard and male ownership of women reverberates across generations to the present era. Contemporary women threatened with their lives by abusive partners are familiar with this declaration of "ownership": "If I can't have you, nobody can," while current news stories about murders of female partners frequently cite male jealousy and murderous rage because of a woman's choice to divorce and/or find a new partner.

The double standard and cultural norm excuse for indifference to violence is also revealed in language, for example: "Boys will be boys" and this statement excusing promiscuity or even rape, "Once a man is aroused, he cannot stop himself"—a demeaning judgment suggesting men's inability to control sexual expression, and thereby implying male moral stature as inferior to that accorded women. Here is another example of language revealing beliefs: After noting repeated episodes of violence against a Native woman, the frustrated observer says, "That's the way they are…What can you do?" Such a remark fails to connect personal trauma to the tragic political oppression and forced social isolation endured by aboriginal people. Such thinking that reveals cultural relativism also obscures the reality of *pre-reservation* life among the Lakota Sioux, for example, when wife beating was rare, even a taboo—a violation of harmony, moderation, and the deeply embedded Sioux value of equality between adult men and women.[11]

In a similar vein, most adults in Western societies believe it is impossible to rear a child without at some point using physical discipline, despite research documenting the negative results of this approach to child rearing. Children in traditional cultures are not just the responsibility of their parents; they are considered the responsibility of the clan, the entire community—their care is not confined to individual parents whose parenting abilities vary.

Additionally, some people still believe that women who are raped have somehow "asked for it." As one victim-survivor said: "Some don't believe the survivor's reality…that is one of the worst things they can do." Unfortunately, the legacy of disbelieving victims is still alive. This is particularly dangerous in the case of innocent children who most often cannot defend themselves. In some treatment settings, survivors may face double jeopardy in that traditional psychiatric theories may distort the reality of sexual abuse. For example, the primary problem of abuse may be obscured under a diagnosis of borderline personality disorder. Such a diagnosis effectively discredits victim-survivors who are brave enough to disclose a victimization history during psychiatric assessment and treatment, and affirms the widespread power of biomedical models and psychiatric labeling.

Another deeply embedded value concerns the centuries-old acceptance of rape (and its rare prosecution) as the "spoils of war." Only recently has this crime been addressed in the UN-sponsored World Court war crimes tribunal at The Hague as an international example of a violation of human rights.

VIOLENCE AND LEARNED BEHAVIOR

The incidence of violence by girls and women in both heterosexual and lesbian relationships is increasing. This suggests that women may adopt the aggressive behaviors traditionally engaged in by men. It also describes violence as "learned behavior," equally available to boys and girls, men and women.

The position taken in this book is to explain increasing rates of female violence as a complex relationship between these factors: (a) acculturation and learned behavior; (b) retaliation in response to abuse; (c) psychiatric disorders intertwined with histories of abuse; (d) and women and girls as moral beings and accountable for their behavior in a bias-free justice system. Key here is that persons inclined to violence can *learn nonviolent approaches* to conflict resolution, traditionally the domain of women. In other words, while conflict is endemic to the human condition, violence is not. This important point lends a note of optimism to an otherwise grim subject and strengthens major themes of this chapter:

- Boys and girls, and women and men can learn nonviolent as well as violent responses to stress and conflict.
- Families, friends, and neighbors are typically the earliest observers of antisocial and abusive or violent behavior.
- Health professionals (and students aspiring thereto) can learn compassion and crisis intervention with victims and assailants.
- Human service providers learn about shared responsibility among disciplines (e.g., police, crisis counselors) and can teach clients and the public about violence prevention.
- Health care and other workers can learn nonviolent responses when they themselves are abused in work settings.
- Everyone concerned can emphasize community-focused responses to victim-survivors and perpetrators.

Conflict Resolution, Gender Roles, and Male Liberation

Social conflict analysis, bias based on gender, and male violence against women uncovers inequality between men and women not only in a social context but also politically and economically. From a "power" perspective, such inequality reveals women as a "minority" group, while men benefit from the unequal relationship, which is perpetuated by sexist ideology. Put bluntly, much violence originates in gender inequality. Allocation of rigid gender roles, which in fact continues to legitimize male violence and male aggression against women worldwide, is something that everyone everywhere needs to be concerned about.

Interestingly, historical observation shows a gradual weakening of the men's liberation movement in the 1970s and 1980s. Consequently, on one hand, the progressive wing of men's liberation formed a pro-feminist movement, which addressed gender relations and power. On the other hand, the conservative wing maintained their antifeminist view founded upon rigid sex roles. However, a fuller concept of humanity and characteristics such as strong and weak, and active and passive are not the province of only one sex. While progress has been made on this front, social and economic inequalities based on gender persist across cultures. In the United States, for example, while some women have done very well financially, the overall wage differential is roughly the same as decades ago.[12]

YOUTH VIOLENCE AND PREVENTION

Aggressive, antisocial, and violent behavior among children and adolescents is gaining international attention. Overall crime rates in the United States and Western Europe have declined sharply for several years, while dramatic shootings by school children have captured international attention. Bullying and mobbing—usually child-on-child aggression—continue to create terror in schools and have even been associated with suicide.

Cultural Climate and Other Roots of Youth Violence

Youth violence has moved parents, legislators, and others to deep soul-searching about the cultural climate and other factors that have spawned these tragedies. Key among these are inconsistent discipline, abuse, alcohol, and troubled parent–child relationships. Without vigilance, raising boys according to the cultural ideal of being active, aggressive, and independent can unwittingly lead to violence by some when family and other supports are weak. Schools may inadvertently collude in rewarding boys' aggressiveness by "going the extra mile" with attention and resources for the nation's future male leaders.

Given the cultural norms, perhaps the most surprising thing is that there is not more violence. In their classic work, educators and youth workers Brendtro, Brokenleg, and Van Bockern[13] trace the discouragement and alienation of youth at risk to four ecological hazards:

1. *Destructive relationships*, as experienced by the rejected or unclaimed child, hungry for love but unable to trust, expecting to be hurt again
2. *Climates of futility*, as encountered by the insecure youngster, crippled by feelings of inadequacy and a fear of failure
3. *Learned irresponsibility*, as seen in the youth whose sense of powerlessness may be masked by indifference or defiant, rebellious behavior
4. *Loss of purpose*, as portrayed by a generation of self-centered youth, desperately searching for meaning in a world of confusing values

These hazards are intertwined with contemporary parenting and family life—among poor families, inadequate time and resources for effective parenting; among some privileged families, excessive material indulgence and permissiveness that leave a child with few boundaries and skills to control behavior and a vacuum around life's larger meaning beyond consumerism.

In the United States, in view of such factors as racism, the powerful gun lobby, and the pauperization of mothers who are raising children alone in an inequitable labor market, not only must teachers, parents, and peers influence antisocial children, but policy makers, church leaders, and all who care about the future of humanity must look "upstream" to discover why children are lost to violence and despair. In a study of violence and recurrent trauma among young Black men, Rich and Grey[14] present a model with positive prospects of interrupting the "Code of the Street" as the pathway to repeated injuries by violence. Marian Wright Edelman,[15] citing a survey commissioned by the Children's Defense Fund and the Black Community Crusade, said: "This poll confirms what black leaders already know—that we have a major black child crisis, the worst since slavery."

In response to the crisis of youth violence that is primarily sociocultural in origin, will we invent yet another medicalized explanation like "urban stress syndrome" to excuse assailants and neglect victims? Or will we examine social environments we have created or allowed to fester as a plague that threatens the lives of all who dwell there? Many youthful offenders have had no support in healing from childhood trauma. Our homes and schools have untold numbers of child witnesses of violence. Will people make a connection between values, the proliferation of guns, and the shocking increase of children killing children—and others? A hopeful example addressing this question is "Sandy Hook Promise" founded by Kathy and Ian Hockley, the grieving parents of their son killed in the Newtown massacre. Their work highlights the power of individual and community action addressing this and similar tragedies.[16]

Of course, this is not an either-or dichotomy. Mitigating circumstances must be considered in judging individual cases, but excusing violent youth action does nothing to facilitate their growth and resiliency potential when supported through crisis. While facing the enormous challenge of youth violence, it is crucial to remember that we are *influenced* by our past, not *determined* by it. Further, with social support, some violent youth who have endured almost unimaginable cruelty have lived to tell their stories of endurance and survival.

Clearly, youth violence cuts across class, race, and gender boundaries. Despite continued disparity in educational and other resources between racial minority groups and the white majority, it is noteworthy that in the vast majority of school shooting tragedies, the assailants were white boys from a range of socioeconomic classes. These highly publicized instances of youth violence tend to obscure the statistical decline in youth crime rates, including school-based violence, over the past several years. But nonstatistical examination of these dramatic examples of youth violence reveals interrelated influences. In many instances, social alienation, bullying and harassment by classmates, and mental health problems were evident but not attended to with preventive crisis care measures—especially recognizing and responding to the meaning of supposedly "idle" verbal threats or unusual behaviors.

Protective influences on child resilience include extended family support networks, family connectedness, and family religious beliefs. Also key is fostering a school and community that cares for and values children, sets high expectations for all, and invites active school and community participation. Perhaps most important is parental modeling of nonviolent responses to stress, avoiding harsh discipline on the one hand or overindulgence on the other (e.g., lavishing a child with gifts in place of quality time spent with the child). In short, we should offer families, schools, and communities what at-risk youth may otherwise seek in violent street gangs. For young persons lacking parental support, other caring adults can fill some of the gaps. "Comeback" stories reveal that some youth, despite horrific childhoods of abuse and neglect, can thrive and reach rewarding adulthood if even *just ONE adult truly cares* what happens to them. Together, we can assist alienated young people to change the dangerous path they are on.

Crisis Prevention and Intervention Programs

Despite the grim picture of youth violence, the tide may be turning; crisis intervention and anger management programs are being developed in many schools and special treatment settings for disturbed youth. Ecological approaches include the active involvement of parents and the entire community to provide safety and a hopeful future for its most vulnerable citizens. There are many models of effective intervention with troubled youth, and many professionals and others are skilled at using them.

In their hope-inspiring book, *Reclaiming Youth at Risk*, Brendtro, Brokenleg, and Van Bockern[13] draw on values of a traditional Native society of North America, the Lakota Sioux, in their application of the medicine wheel, with its four spokes depicting *belonging, mastery, independence, and generosity*. To many Native peoples, the number four has sacred meaning. They see the person standing in a circle (a symbol of life) surrounded by the four directions—the requisites for a child to feel whole, competent, and cherished as a member of the community.

The tradition in which the entire community assumes responsibility for its children is highlighted by a widely publicized case of tribal justice. Two 17-year-old boys of the Tlingit Nation in Alaska, who were convicted of robbing and beating a man, were turned over to their village by a judge in Washington State. Village elders meted out justice in the form of a year to 18-month exile on Alaska's uninhabited islands. The intent was for the boys to reflect on their behavior, observe the power of natural beauty, and emulate the basic skills taught by their elders—something offenders rarely learn in a locked cell. David Blumenkrantz,[17] founder of the Center for Advancement of Youth, Family, and Community Service in Connecticut, features such learning from elders in the Rite of Passage Experience (ROPE) sessions conducted internationally. The community-based session focuses on initiating children into a culture of civility and compassion. This means more attention to how we are raising our children vs raising their test scores.

A central theme in these programs is that *controlling, authoritarian responses by adults to aggressive youth behavior are part of the problem*, not the solution. This is because much of youth violence springs from a history of abuse, neglect, and behaviors that control rather than nurture, direct, and foster growth through love and consistent nonviolent discipline. Inconsistent discipline—or conflicting messages from parents and other adults—leaves children confused, directionless, and anxious. Many young people act out aggressively because they feel disempowered and alienated in a society that does not meet their needs. But as frightening as youth aggression and other violence can be, it is crucial to remember a major theme in this book: *Violence begets violence.*

Certainly, at-risk youth can learn and benefit from nonviolent responses to conflict situations. But if they see no hope of escape from racism and a neglected social milieu, their individual tactics to avoid violence may be very short lived. The greater challenge, then, is in the primary prevention domain of changing the socioeconomic and other factors—including a cultural climate glorifying violence—that severely shortchange young people, a nation's most precious resource (see Crisis Paradigm in Chapter 1, Fig. 1.1, Boxes 3 and 4).

ASSESSMENT OF DANGEROUSNESS, ASSAULT, AND HOMICIDE RISK

As in the case of suicide risk assessment, there is *no absolute prediction of homicide risk*. The topic itself is highly controversial. Researcher Monahan,[18] for example, cites three criticisms regarding prediction in forensic work:

1. It is empirically impossible to predict violent behavior.
2. If such activity could be forecast and averted, it would, as a matter of policy, violate the civil liberties of those whose activity is predicted.
3. Even if accurate prediction were possible without violating civil liberties, psychiatrists and psychologists should decline to do it, since it is a social control activity at variance with their professional helping role.

Whereas prediction of violence is an issue in professional forensic work, *assessment of dangerousness and violence potential* can be a *matter of life or death* at home, in schools, at work, and in clinical settings. Assessment of risk for dangerousness, assault, and homicide is a central part of police officers' and health and crisis workers' jobs. And the average citizen is always calculating safety maneuvers when in known risk areas. This is not the same as making an official prediction of risk as part of the court-requested psychiatric or psychological examination of persons who are detained for crimes and who plead insanity. Although assessment of dangerousness is far from an exact science, health and social service workers do not have to rely *only* on their experience or guesswork. Nor should family and close associates rely on "guesswork" instead of drawing on evidence as presented here from crisis, psychiatric, and criminal justice theory and knowledge gained through skilled communication with persons and their families at risk either as victims or perpetrators of violence.[19]

Criteria and Dynamics in Risk Assessment

Based on Monahan's pioneering research, risk assessment criteria include:

1. *Statistics*—for example, men between the ages of 18 and 34 commit a much higher percentage of violent crimes than older men or women of any age. Statistical indicators, however, should be viewed with the same caution as in suicide risk assessment.
2. *Personality factors*, including motivation, aggression, inhibition, and habit. For example, once a person adopts the habit of responding to upsets by verbal threats and physical force, it lays a foundation for further, potentially lethal violence.
3. *Situational factors*, such as availability of a weapon or behavior of an unwitting potential victim.
4. *The interaction* between these variables.

Researcher H. Toch,[20] writing about violent men, claims that the *interaction* factor (in several stages) is a *crucial one influencing violence*. First, the potential victim is classified as an object or a potential threat—essentially, a *dehumanization* process. Based on this classification, some action follows, after which the potential victim may make a self-protective move. Whether or not violence occurs depends on the interaction of such variables and the effectiveness of the victim's self-protection. It is also influenced by the would-be attacker's interpretation of the intended victim's resistance as an "ego" threat demanding retaliation. *Establishing a bond*, therefore, between a victim and assailant or terrorist can counteract dehumanization and thus serve to prevent an attack, although that strategy should not be relied on in all cases. This is the basis for a widely held principle in crisis intervention and hostage negotiation: *Time* and keeping *communication* channels open—rather than precipitous action, taunts, or threats—can benefit the negotiator and save the lives of victims, terrorists, and suicidal persons. Communication is also central to health care providers who are threatened at work by their patients or disgruntled family members (see Chapter 3).

Clearly, assessing danger is no simple matter, but lives can be saved by taking seriously the fact that *only potentially dangerous people make threats of assault or homicide*. A careful read of newspaper accounts of murders reveals almost invariably the assailant's verbal and other cues that were *either ignored or misinterpreted as not being serious*. These accounts underscore how important it is for family members and others to know how to respond to threats of harm without escalating potential danger by impulsive action. For example: "Brian, I know you're upset about what Aron did to you, but you say you could kill him?...Please, let's talk about this, OK?"

Responding with compassion and concern to strong words like "kill" can potentially make the difference between life and death, especially if it is followed up with a telephone call to a crisis hotline for further assessment and next steps. In short, everyone needs to be alert to cues such as an angry outburst and agitation. And we should always inquire about the meaning of verbal threats that too many times are dismissed by family, friends, and sometimes even professional colleagues. Health and social service providers need to routinely educate their clients and the general public about this safety issue.

TOOLS TO ASSESS ASSAULT INJURY AND HOMICIDE RISK

When the indicators of dangerousness described in Table 6.1 (developed and tested in the 1970s—see Chapter 2) were introduced for routine use in community mental health clinics, staff were astounded at how many clients were entertaining violent fantasies. But crisis workers also noted the *clients' openness to receiving help in dealing with their anger and violent impulses*. These findings apply to three major categories of abusive and violent behavior: (1) the international increase in violence and antisocial behavior among young people; (2) violence and abuse in the workplace; and (3) programs for men who batter and emotionally abuse their women partners.

Besides their usefulness in standard criminal justice and police work, the criteria for assessing the degree of danger and risk of assault apply in a number of situations:

1. In crisis, emergency, mental health, and forensic services
2. In primary care settings
3. In workplace settings where people are threatened with violence or being taken hostage, or are stalked at home
4. In all domestic disputes

While acknowledging that violent people can learn to resolve conflict nonviolently, *past violent behavior* is still a powerful indicator of future behavior. And as the triage questions in Chapter 5 indicate, routine screening for assault and homicide potential is gender neutral. Health care professionals (HCPs) must therefore communicate with an abused woman, for example, about her own potential and possible plans for assaulting or killing her assailant in retaliation for abuse.[21,22]

Also, while a history of mental illness may be an important factor in assessing danger, the rates of violence by mentally ill persons is within the range of rates among the general population.[23] However, violence by mentally disturbed people is often apparent in the "revolving door" scenario presented in Chapter 1, patients' rights and access to guns. On the other hand, from media accounts, patchy access to 24/7 crisis care and psychiatric treatment appears to play a role in high-profile homicide cases at school and in the workplace.[24] And so, to learn from history, it seems relevant to revisit the insights of scholars like C. Wright. Mills[7] and Erich Fromm[25] regarding the complex roots of violence and the importance of routine danger assessment by health and social service workers.

Translated into everyday safety concerns, at home and elsewhere, the following criteria are helpful as guidelines to assess for risk of assault or homicide:

- History of homicidal threats
- History of assault
- Current homicidal threats and plan, including on the Internet
- Possession or easy availability of lethal weapons
- Use or abuse of alcohol or other drugs
- Conflict in significant social or clinical relationships—for example, infidelity, threat of divorce, labor-management disputes, authoritarian approaches to mentally ill patients
- Threats of suicide following homicide

Application of Criteria: An Assessment Tool

Assessing for dangerousness, assault, and homicide risk is aided by use of an assessment tool, Table 6.1, excerpted from the Comprehensive Mental Health Assessment tool introduced in Chapter 2.

Table 6.1 ASSAULT AND HOMICIDAL DANGER ASSESSMENT TOOL

Key to Danger	Immediate Dangerousness to Others	Typical Indicators
1.	No predictable risk of assault or homicide	Has no assaultive or homicidal ideation, urges, or history of same; basically satisfactory support system; social drinker only
2.	Low risk of assault or homicide	Has occasional assault or homicidal ideation (including paranoid ideas) with some urges to kill; no history of impulsive acts or homicidal attempts; occasional drinking bouts and angry verbal outbursts; basically satisfactory support system
3.	Moderate risk of assault or homicide	Has frequent homicidal ideation and urges to kill but no specific plan; history of impulsive acting out and verbal outbursts while drinking, on other drugs, or otherwise; stormy relationship with significant others with periodic high-tension arguments
4.	High risk of homicide	Has homicidal plan; obtainable means; history of substance abuse; frequent acting out against others, but no homicide attempts; stormy relationships and much verbal fighting with significant others, with occasional assaults
5.	Very high risk of homicide	Has current high-lethal plan; available means; history of homicide attempts or impulsive acting out, plus feels a strong urge to control and "get even" with a significant other; history of serious substance abuse; also with possible high-lethal suicide risk

VIOLENCE AND ABUSE IN THE WORKPLACE AND FORENSIC PSYCHIATRY

One of the first principles in everyone's workplace is safety—for ourselves, our clients, significant others, and the general public. Moving from the global to everyday work life, violence as an occupational health hazard has gained public attention. Police officers, health, mental health, crisis, and other workers make up a special category of victims.

The potential danger from clients and/or abuse by one's colleagues (lateral violence) embroils us in the controversial relationship between crime and mental illness (forensic psychiatry). Despite numerous debates on this topic, the distinctions between crime and mental illness overlap with relevance to life crises and the safety of HCPs, police, security personnel, and other workers often caught in the middle. With greater skills in applying risk assessment knowledge in the workplace, many injuries from violence might be avoided, since mentally ill persons are probably no more violent than they were in the past, and their rates of violence are comparable to those of the general public.[23]

While some people who commit crimes are mentally ill, therefore entitling them to leniency before the law, many insanity pleas leave much room for doubt. Insanity is a *legal*, not a mental health, concept. Difficulties with this issue in the United States are complicated by a criminal justice system that often denies a decent standard of treatment to criminals. The humanitarian impulse of most people is to spare even a violent person an experience that seems beyond the deserts of the crime.

It is paradoxical, then, that the tendency to only *treat* a person, rather than also holding him or her responsible for violent behavior, exists in concert with the movement to assert the rights of mentally ill patients. We cannot have it both ways. One cannot, on the one hand, exercise the freedom to reject treatment and hospitalization for behavioral disorders and, on the other hand, plead temporary insanity when one then fails to control violent impulses and commits a crime (or, in psychiatric and primary care settings, assaults a staff member who may or may not press criminal charges). The following example illustrates this point, as well as the need for mental health and health professionals to examine their misplaced guilt feelings when they hold clients accountable for their violent behavior.

EXAMPLE: CONNIE—VIOLENCE AND PSYCHIATRIC DISORDER

Connie, age 51, was being treated in a private psychiatric facility for a drinking problem and depression following a divorce. A mental status examination revealed that Connie was mentally competent and not suffering from delusions or other thought disorders, though she was very angry about her husband's decision to divorce her because of her drinking problem. When Connie, therefore, decided to check out of the residential treatment facility against medical advice, there was no basis for confining her involuntarily, according to any interpretation of the state's mental health laws. A discharge planning conference was held, at which follow-up therapy sessions were arranged through a special program for alcoholic women. Connie failed to keep her counseling appointments. One week after leaving the psychiatric unit, Connie attempted to demolish her former husband's car by crashing her own car into it. She endangered the lives of other people by driving on sidewalks, where pedestrians successfully managed to escape her fury. Connie was arrested and taken to jail. While the judge preferred committing Connie to the psychiatric unit where she had been treated, testimony by a mental health professional supported this decision: Mental status examination and Connie's intact physical capacity provided no basis on which to keep her from being a further menace to society by psychiatric vs criminal justice containment. Connie was furious with her counselor for not offering psychiatric grounds for avoiding a jail term.

This example suggests spillovers of violence from home to workplace, as well as using alcohol as an excuse from accountability for violent behavior. A biomedical versus public health response to workplace violence may help perpetuate the problem if the larger social ramifications of the issue remain unaddressed. Obviously, this takes us well beyond an injured health care worker's responsibility. Yet safety in one's workplace and our common humanity in a violent society demand such a two-pronged approach to this serious issue.

Too often the signs of impending assault or homicide are either not recognized or are ignored until it is too late, as documented in widely publicized massacres at schools and worksites. It is important to note that murder does not occur in a cultural or social vacuum; it does not "just happen." Typically, it is *deliberately planned*, although impulse may play a part.

Fortunately, the days of assaulted health workers having to absorb their injury and emotional trauma as "part of the job" appear to be coming to an end. Research has uncovered the relationship of workplace injury to gender, race, and class factors, as well as to the work environment itself—for example, inadequate staffing and lack of structured supervisor support.[26] Guidelines from the US Occupational Safety & Health Administration and labor union action are promising trends in redressing the neglect of many victimized workers who have been on their own trying to recover from the trauma of such mostly preventable violence. Posttrauma support programs for injured workers are also gaining attention.

CRISIS INTERVENTION WITH ASSAILANTS AND THOSE THREATENING VIOLENCE

All of the principles of crisis intervention (see Chapter 3) apply to the violent or potentially violent person at home, in school or prison, and the workplace to help ensure safety of self and others. Following is a summary of these principles applied to aggressive, antisocial, or violent people:

1. Keep communication lines open. As long as a person is communicating, violence usually does not occur.
2. Facilitate communication between an angry family member, disgruntled employee or patient, for example, and the person against whom he or she is threatening violence. While hospital security personnel have designated crisis intervention roles, the premature engagement of a security officer may backfire if excessive physical force is used to gain control of a potentially

dangerous situation. Remembering the principle that "violence begets more violence," when physical containment is indicated, humane and respectful behavior is fundamental to safety.

3. Develop specific plans—*with* the dangerous person—for nonviolent expression of anger, such as time-out, jogging, punching a pillow, or calling a hotline, whether at home, on the street, at work, or in a psychiatric or substance abuse treatment unit.
4. Communicate by telephone or behind closed doors whenever possible when dealing with an armed person, especially until rapport is established and the person's anxiety subsides. This includes applying the risk assessment criteria as in Table 6.1.
5. If dangerous weapons are involved, collaborate with police for their removal whenever possible; implement emergency policies and procedures for appropriate application of force by a security officer or police, and by mobilizing a team effort to warn fellow workers. *Failure to work in teams can be life threatening.*
6. At work, insist on administrative support and emergency backup help; *refuse any assignment that requires working alone in high-risk settings*—for example, psychiatric wards, crisis outreach visits, or community-based homes for discharged psychiatric patients. If home visits are indicated, obtain information about potential danger whenever possible via telephone and team consultation *before* arriving at home premises.
7. Make hotline numbers and emergency call buttons readily available.
8. Examine and discuss with colleagues the social and institutional factors influencing violent behavior—for example, harsh authoritarian approaches to employee relations, which may trigger revenge and violence by an upset patient or a disgruntled worker; failure to help disturbed persons seek professional help as an alternative to violence; and rigid structures and rules for geriatric and psychiatric patients.
9. Warn potential victims of homicide, based on risk assessment and the principles of the Tarasoff case from the University of California.[27] A general guideline for warning potential victims is a rating of "moderate—# 3, or "high—# 4 or 5" on the Risk Assessment Tool (Table 6.1).
10. Remember that a *violent person who is also threatening suicide is a greater risk for homicide*, in that accountability for violence is thus eliminated.
11. Conduct follow-up of every threat or incidence of violence, and engage in social and political activity to prevent violence.

Several factors, however, may become obstacles to crisis intervention with violent persons: (1) the sense of contempt or loathing one may feel toward a criminal or patient who has threatened a health or social service worker, (2) the fear of the prisoner or other person threatening violence, and (3) the need to work within the physical and social constraints of a detention setting or workplace where one does not anticipate interaction with disturbed or violent persons. People working in these settings, therefore, must be keenly aware of crisis intervention principles to prevent violence and deal with crises in a variety of threatening or dangerous situations.

PROGRAMS FOR VIOLENT MEN

Newspaper accounts reveal that restraining orders have not prevented the murders of women by their intimate partners and other victims. In fact, work and advocacy with abused women reveals that they are perhaps in greatest danger after filing a restraining order, particularly in cases in which the woman's partner feels that he owns her and is now confronted with an external force threatening his need to control her. This reminds us of the need for caution in persuading a woman to seek court protection. It also supports trusting the woman's own judgment of the man's potential for violence, and attention to the contextual factors that may infuriate him to the point of violence.

Moving beyond the debate about whether perpetrators should receive treatment or serve time in jail, the both-and approach discussed in Chapter 5 should generally be the norm, even when the women who have been battered—especially those intent on salvaging their relationship and marriage—just want the violence to stop, by whatever means. To carry out this approach, the health and criminal justice aspects of domestic violence must be synchronized, culturally sensitive, and include systematic follow-up through probationary and court systems.[28,29] In a public health and crisis prevention framework, any program for abusive men must include three facets:

1. The need to assess and reassess their potential for further assault or homicide, as suggested in Table 6.1.
2. The importance of holding the perpetrator accountable for violent behavior, regardless of mental pathology and any excuses, such as the woman's behavior provoked her partner to violence.
3. A focus on the *roots* of the problem and on *power and control* over one's partner, not just "anger management," since anger is a "trigger" not typically used except against the intimate partner.

These program elements imply regular supportive contact by a PCP or crisis counselor with the woman who was abused and is possibly still at risk, particularly if she has filed a restraining order and in instances when men present themes of jealousy, desperation, and ownership of their partner.

Court-mandated counseling has led to a proliferation and variety of programs for violent men.[5] Among all of them, accountability and victim safety are central, regardless of competing perspectives. Evaluation outcomes reveal that the longest, most comprehensive program demonstrated the lowest reassault rate. For example, a 9-month program of weekly group counseling also includes an extensive clinical evaluation, substance abuse treatment, individual psychotherapy for emotional and mental problems, and casework with women partners. Since effective programs are designed to confront and diffuse power and control dynamics, a short "anger management" approach can be dangerous—especially to the abused spouse—if led by someone without knowledge and expertise about this core feature of violence. Comprehensive programs move well beyond the simple "hope and trust" that a violent partner will change that some abused women may rely on.

In most programs for men who batter, group counseling is the preferred mode, usually including other men who have been violent in the past but are no longer violent, and led by a male/female team. This approach builds on the premise that violence is not inevitable but is learned and reinforced through parenting practices and its pervasiveness in the sociocultural milieu. Abused women and others who believe couples counseling is the answer to stopping violence should note that *this highly controversial approach tends to obscure violence as the primary problem.* This is because it implies a counselor's "neutrality" in regard to criminal behavior. If couples counseling is used, safety, ownership of responsibility for violence, and a *prior* intention of reconciliation must first be established.

Although programs for violent men and refuges for victims must be supported, these secondary and tertiary measures would be much less costly in financial and human terms if primary prevention and "restorative justice" were more valued and promoted. Primary care providers serving the families and children of prisoners also need to pay special attention to the medical ramifications of chronic social and economic stress traceable to prolonged imprisonment of a spouse or parent.

SIGNPOSTS OF RESTORATIVE JUSTICE

The mandatory minimum drug sentencing laws of 1986 have played a major role in the imprisonment of young black males and the 400% increase of incarcerated women in the United States. This law, the widening gap between the privileged and the disadvantaged, and policies emanating from the legacy of slavery and racism in the United States, contribute to the counterproductivity of punitive versus rehabilitative measures.

Instead of a criminal justice system emanating from revenge and punishment, as in "three strikes and you're out," which often does not fit the crime, let us consider the principles and Signposts of Restorative Justice. Citing values of the Mennonite community, Zehr and Mika[30] state, "Crime wounds....Justice heals." We are working toward restorative justice when we:

1. focus on the *harms* of wrongdoing more than the rules that have been broken;
2. show equal concern and commitment to *victims and offenders*, involving both in the process of justice;
3. work toward the restoration of *victims*, empowering them and responding to their needs as they see them;
4. support *offenders* while encouraging them to understand, accept, and carry out their obligations;
5. recognize that while *obligations* may be difficult for offenders, they should not be intended as harms and they must be achievable;
6. provide opportunities for *dialogue*, direct or indirect, between victims and offenders as appropriate;
7. involve and empower the affected *community* through the justice process, and increase its capacity to recognize and respond to community bases of crime;
8. encourage *collaboration* and *reintegration* rather than coercion and isolation;
9. give attention to the *unintended consequences* of our actions and programs; and
10. show *respect* to all parties, including victims, offenders, and justice colleagues.
(Reprinted with permission from the Mennonite Central Committee)

These principles mirror the basic social justice teachings of civilized societies and major religions worldwide. They poignantly represent contemporary rejection of the sad historical chronicle of centuries of wars, torture, and racial and other discrimination enacted in the name of religion. In response to terror and other crimes against humanity, personal responses of revenge against and hatred of abusers (vs. understanding, compassion, and forgiveness) do nothing for the healing process of those injured. Instead, such "get even" approaches spurn the very idea of social justice and the important fact that "violence begets more violence" (see Chapter 8, "Disasters of Human Origin").

PRIMARY PREVENTION OF VIOLENCE AND ANTISOCIAL BEHAVIOR

So long as loopholes exist in the criminal justice system's response to interpersonal violence such as battering, refuges are no less than lifesaving for many women at risk. Similarly, residential treatment programs for out-of-control youth are necessary. But the very fact that an entire system of residential programs for battered women has been established speaks to the tendency, especially in the United States, toward *reactive* rather than *preventive* approaches. History reveals that all societies establish rules for how to treat deviant members.

The fruits of such reactive policy recommendations are underscored by a study in 29 cities documenting that the lives saved by the shelter system are mostly those of men—that is, murders are prevented because women receive help through hotline, shelter, and legal services before reaching the point of using deadly force against their abusers.[31] However, if the male partners do not receive help, they are more likely to kill the women. In other words, refuges for abused women are just that—an emergency resource, not primary prevention. But moving beyond emergency measures will yield limited results without the community-wide endeavors such as in the following arenas.

Personal and Social-Psychological Strategies

When sincerely addressing the issue, individuals may become overwhelmed by the pervasiveness of violence and withdraw out of a sense of helplessness, self-protection, burnout, or what is sometimes referred to as *vicarious traumatization*—that is, internalizing the psychic pain that victimized patients share with empathic providers. It is important therefore that HCPs and clients at risk focus on selected actions and obtainable goals, including, for example:

1. Adopting nonviolent language in everyday social interaction
2. Using nonviolent ways of disciplining children; attending parent effectiveness training groups to assist with difficult child-rearing challenges
3. Providing all workers with violence prevention information and emergency protocols, including how to recognize and respond humanely to an upset or disgruntled client or coworker with antisocial tendencies
4. Remembering that since violence and victimization are deeply rooted in sociocultural, economic, and political context, individual efforts *alone*—while necessary—are not sufficient to address the problem.

Sociopolitical Strategies

These strategies are most successful when combined with personal and social-psychological approaches because people need grounding in information and self-confidence in order to stand firm against obstacles in the political arena.

1. *Educating the public through schools, community organizations, and churches.* For example: How many people who have attended church, synagogue, or mosque, for example, have heard a sermon condemning violence against women and children or have sponsored programs to explicitly address such issues?
2. *Contacting legislators and organizing for a change in laws that may be outdated or otherwise do not address the issues local people face.* In the United States, for example, this includes addressing the powerful gun lobby or the high rate of

incarceration among African American youth as opposed to Caucasian youth for comparable offenses.
3. *Using advocacy and systematic organizing around racial and economic justice.* This includes seeking equality in educational opportunities and addressing the media influence on violence.

Professional Strategies

In the United States, the Surgeon General's report (US Department of Health and Human Services, 1986)[32] recommended that all licensed professionals be required to study and pass examination questions in violence prevention and the treatment of various victims of violence. As a complement to this public policy statement, HCPs and their teachers can exert leadership and advocacy within their own groups for curriculum and in-service program development to systematically address this topic.

At present, such educational endeavors are incidental at best. The American Association of Colleges of Nursing[33] produced a position paper underscoring the need for inclusion of violence content in all nursing education programs, but later surveys revealed remaining gaps in nursing education programs.[34] Similar programs have been developed for medical and criminal justice professionals in North America and other countries.

The vast knowledge already available to professionals must be combined with personal strategies in order to:

- Widely disseminate new knowledge about this poignant topic to the public.
- Change the values and attitudes that have served as fertile soil for nurturing and normalizing violent and antisocial behavior.
- Support broad prevention policies and programs of social institutions through the political process necessary to bring about needed change.

Together, personal, psychological, sociopolitical, and professional strategies can do much and make a difference in ending the worldwide plague of violence, abuse, and preventable suffering.

REFERENCES, FURTHER READING, DISCUSSION GUIDE

REFERENCES
1. WHO (2010). *Injuries and violence—The facts.* Department of Violence and Injury Prevention and Disability. Geneva, Switzerland: Author.
2. WHO (2010). *Violence prevention: An invitation to intersectoral action.* World Conference on Injury Prevention and Safety Promotion. London: Author.

3. Husseini, R. (2009). *Murder in the name of honor.* Oxford, England: One World Oxford.
4. Adams, D. (2007). *Why do they kill? Men who murder their intimate partners.* Nashville, TN: Vanderbilt University Press.
5. Edleson, J. L., & Tolman, R. M. (1992). *Intervention for men who batter: An ecological approach.* Thousand Oaks, CA: Sage.
6. Brown, J. C., & Bohn, C. R. (1989). *Christianity, patriarchy, and abuse: A feminist critique.* New York: Pilgrim Press.
7. Mills, C. W. (1959). *The sociological imagination.* Oxford, UK: Oxford University Press.
8. United Nations. (1996). *The Beijing declaration and the platform for action.* New York.
9. PAHO/WHO (2003). *Violence against women: The health sector responds.* Washington, DC: Author.
10. Tolstoy, L. *Anna Karenina.* Amazon. Penguin Classics.
11. Hoff, L. A. (2010). Oppression, abuse, and enslavement of indigenous people across continents. In *Violence and abuse issues: Cross-cultural perspectives for health and social services* (pp. 115–133). London: Routledge.
12. Rivers, C., & Barnett, R. (2013). *The new soft war on women: How the myth of female ascendance is huring women, men, and our economy.* Amazon. Tarcher/Penguin imprint.
13. Brendtro, L. K., Brokenleg, M., & Van Bockern, S. (1990). *Reclaiming youth at risk: Our hope for the future.* Bloomington, IN: National Educational Service.
14. Rich, J. A., & Grey, C. M. (2005). Pathways to recurrent trauma among young Black men: Traumatic stress, substance use, and the "Code of the Street." *American Journal of Public Health, 95*(5), 816–824.
15. Edelman, M. W. (1994). Poll finds pervasive fear in blacks over violence and their children. *Boston Globe,* p. 6.
16. Sandy Hook Promise. Retrieved on January 10, 2014 from http://www.sandyhook.org.
17. Blumenkrantz, D. G., & Goldstein, M. (2014). *In search of self: Exploring undergraduate identity development.* San Francisco: Jossey-Bass.
18. Monahan, J. (1981). *Predicting violent behavior: An assessment of clinical techniques.* Thousand Oaks, CA: Sage.
19. Hoff, L. A., & Bell, M. (2010). Chapter 13: Comprehensive service issues: Health and criminal justice interface (pp. 209–230). In *Violence and abuse issues: Cross-cultural perspectives for health and social services* (pp. 115–133). London: Routledge.
20. Toch, H. (1969). *Violent men.* Hawthorne, NY: Aldine de Gruyter.
21. Brown, A. (1980). *When battered women kill.* New York: Free Press.
22. Chesney-Lind, M. (1997). *The female offender: Girls, women, and crime.* Thousand Oaks, CA: Sage.
23. Friedman, R. A. (2006). Violence and mental illness—How strong is the link? *New England Journal of Medicine, 355*(20), 2064–2066.
24. Galizzi, M., Miesmaa, P., & Slatin, C. (2010). Injured workers' underreporting in the health care industry. A study integrating qualitative and quantitative data. *Industrial Relations.*
25. Fromm, E. (1973). *The anatomy of human destructiveness.* New York: Holt, Rinehart and Winston.
26. Hoff, L. A. (2010). Implementation issues: Personal/professional victimization. In *Violence and abuse issues: Cross-cultural perspectives for health and social services* (pp. 191–208). London: Routledge
27. Tarosoff v. The Regents of the University of California. (1976). 551 P.2d 334.

28. Seck, M., & Hoff, L. A. (2010). Chapter 10: Perpetrators of abuse and violence: Individuals and state (pp. 149–168). In *Violence and abuse issues: Cross-cultural perspectives for health and social services* (pp. 149–168). London: Routledge
29. Hoff, L. A., & Bell, M. (2010). Chapter 13: Comprehensive service issues: Health and criminal justice interface. In L. A. Hoff *Violence and abuse issues: Cross-cultural perspectives for health and social services* (pp. 209–230).
30. Zegr, H., & Mika, H. (1997). *Restorative justice signposts*. Akron, PA: Mennonite Central Committee.
31. Masters, B. A. (1999, March 13). Women's shelters save mostly men. *Boston Globe*, p. A3.
32. US Department of Health and Human Services. (1986). *Surgeon General's workshop on violence and public health: Report*. Washington, DC: Author.
33. American Association of Colleges of Nursing. (1999). *Position paper: Violence as a public health problem*. Washington, DC: Author.
34. Woodtli, A., & Breslin, E. (2002). Violence-related content in the nursing curriculum: A follow-up national survey. *Journal of Nursing Education, 41*(8), 340–348.

FURTHER READING

Arnetz, J. E., & Arnetz, B. B. (2001). Violence towards health care staff and possible effects on the quality of patient care. *Social Science and Medicine, 52*, 417–427.

Bennett, L., & Piet, M. (1999). Standards for batterer intervention programs: In whose interests? *Violence Against Women, 5*(1), 6–24.

Blumenkrantz, D. *ROPE: Rite of Passage Experience*. Hartford, CT and internationally.

Bograd, M., & Mederos, F. (1999). Battering and couples therapy: Universal screening and selection of treatment modality. *Journal of Marital and Family Therapy, 25*(3), 291–312.

Browne, A. (1989). *When battered women kill*. New York: Free Press.

Dobash, R. E., & Dobash, R. P. (Eds.) (1998). *Rethinking violence against women*. Thousand Oaks, CA: Sage.

Holinger, P. C, Offer, D., Barter, J. T., & Bell, C. C. (1994). *Suicide and homicide among adolescents*. New York: Guilford Press.

Meloy, R. (1992). *Violent attachments*. Northvale, NJ: Aronson.

Mendel, M. P. (1994). *The male survivor*. Thousand Oaks, CA: Sage.

Monahan, J., & Steadman, H. J. (Eds.). (1994). *Violence and mental disorder: Developments in risk assessment*. Chicago: University of Chicago Press.

Morgenstern, H. (1997). Editorial: Gun availability and violent death. *American Journal of Public Health, 87*(6), 899–900.

Pence, E., & Paymar, M. (1986). *Power and control: Tactics of men who batter*. Duluth: Minnesota Program Development.

Rodriguez, M. A., McLoughlin, E., Hah, G., & Campbell, J. C. (2001). Mandatory reporting of domestic violence injuries to the police: What do emergency department patients think? *Journal of the American Medical Association, 286*(5), 580–583.

Rynearson, E. K. (Ed.). (2006). *Violent death: Resilience and intervention beyond the crisis*. New York: Routledge.

Stark, E., Flitcraft, A., & Frazier, W. (1979). Medicine and patriarchal violence: The social construction of a "private" event. *International Journal of Health Services, 9*, 461–493.

Tavris, C. (1983). *Anatomy of anger*. New York: Simon & Shuster.

Webster, D. W, Vernick, J. S., Ludwig, J., & Lester, K. J. (1997). Flawed gun policy research could endanger public safety. *American Journal of Public Health, 87* (6), 918–921.

Wright, M. A., Wintemute, G. J., & Rivara, E. P. (1999). Effectiveness of denial of handgun purchase to persons believed to be at high risk for firearm violence. *American Journal of Public Health, 89*(1), 88–90.

DISCUSSION GUIDE

1. Do you agree or disagree about the role of culture and learned behavior to explain the continuing tragedy of violence worldwide?
2. Try to recall an instance of violence or abuse in your family or neighborhood. What clues were present that you and others may have responded to or missed? If you responded: What did you say, or who did you call? And what was the response you received?
3. If your community does not have an active neighborhood watch group, consider with family or friends what steps you might take to organize one. If such a group already exists, discuss how active it is in community-based violence prevention and explore how it might collaborate with the closest police protection service.
4. Convene a discussion group to consider principles of "restorative justice" and its merits compared with some punitive measures that may incite revenge and further violence.
5. With family and close friends, consider the intersection between observable antisocial behavior and dangerous assault, and your role in possible violence prevention efforts.

PART III

Crises Arising From Unexpected Stressful Events and Life Cycle Passages

Part III

CHAPTER 7

Threats to Health Status From a Serious Illness or Accident

Connecting the dots between serious medical events and emotional crisis

CHAPTER OUTLINE

Example: Michael and Maria French   174
Crisis Care in Diverse Health Care Settings   175
Example: Angela—Suicidal Adolescent   179
Crisis Response of People in Health Status Transition   180
Essential Elements of Successful Crisis Resolution   182
Preventive Intervention   184
Example: Interview With Maria French   185
Crises Regarding Surgery   186
Example: Alex—A Preventable Suicidal Response to Multiple Stressors   187
Children Having Surgery   187
Crisis and Chronic Illness: HIV and AIDS   188
Examples: Daniel and Sophia—Living With AIDS or Addiction   189
Caretakers of People With Serious Illness: Support and Self-Care   196
Crisis Care of People With Addictions and Eating Disorders   197
Example: Emma—Substance Abuse and Crisis   198
Interplay Between Crisis, Family Troubles, and Chronic Mental Health Problems   200
Example: Ruth—Child Abuse, Divorce, and Self-Destructive Behavior   200
The Crisis of Dementia, Alzheimer's Disease, and Institutional Placement   201
References, Further Reading, Discussion Guide   203

Many have said that if their health is intact, they can endure almost anything else. This is because a deterioration in health status is hazardous in itself and potentially life threatening, while poor health leaves people more vulnerable to other stressful events.

To avoid a crisis state, we need a sense of physical and emotional well-being, an image of ourselves that flows from general acceptance of our physical attributes and some control over basic life functions and activities of daily living. These aspects of life are acutely threatened by illness, accidents, surgery, physical or mental handicap, and abuse of alcohol and other drugs. Still, we can avoid a florid crisis experience if supported by family, friends, and health workers, and we have necessary assistance regardless of financial status. Self-defeating outcomes such as suicide, assault or homicide, mental illness, and depression can also be avoided if appropriate treatment and emotional support are available when experiencing threats to health.

Centuries ago, Hippocrates said that it is more important to "know the man who has the disease than the disease the man has." So let us consider Michael and Maria French and what we need to know about helping them through a serious illness.

EXAMPLE: MICHAEL AND MARIA FRENCH

Michael French, age 55, had suffered from prostate cancer for several years. During the past year, he was forced to retire from his supervisory job in a factory. The cancer spread to his bladder and colon, causing continuous pain as well as urinary-control problems. Michael became very depressed and highly dependent on his wife, Maria, age 51. Stress for both of them increased. Michael began to suspect Maria of infidelity.

Now Maria needed to go to the hospital for a hysterectomy. The operation was scheduled, but her husband vigorously protested her leaving him. At the last minute, Maria repeatedly canceled the surgery. Finally, her doctor pressed her to go through with the operation.

Along with the ordinary fears of anyone facing a major operation, Maria was very worried about her husband's condition when she visited him at the hospital. However, she was too embarrassed by Michael's accusations of infidelity to discuss her fears with the nurses or doctor. Because Maria did not look sick to Michael, he felt she was abandoning him unnecessarily. To a good friend, he raged that he would kill her when she came home. He dismissed their tenants without notice and changed the locks on the doors. Maria and Michael were now in a crisis, a period of *danger*—and of *opportunity*.

Like Michael and Maria, many distressed people talk with trusted friends or relatives but never seek professional help. When they do seek such help, their *first* visit often is to physicians or clergy, *not* mental health professionals. People in emotional crisis related to illness, injury, surgery, or handicap rarely come to the attention of crisis specialists or mental health workers in the acute crisis stage. This pattern underscores the pivotal role in crisis care played by friends and relatives, and by general health providers such as physicians and nurses. Also, in the front lines are police, rescue teams, firefighters, and Travelers Aid caseworkers who are often the first to confront a person injured or in emotional shock from an accident, violent attack, or fire.

Maria and Michael were fortunate. Their friend, afraid of Michael in his wildly emotional state, contacted Maria in the hospital and also called a local community health nurse who had been making biweekly visits to supervise Michael's medication. The nurse in turn called a nearby crisis clinic.

This chapter addresses crisis care in *general* health care situations, such as Maria's and Michael's, or from physical intactness and handicap. The strategies apply in personal contact with friends and relatives; in doctors' offices; emergency, intensive care, and other hospital departments; primary care settings; and prenatal clinics—virtually all health and human service settings, including long-term care facilities. Stories here illustrate the important mind/body connections when confronted with a physical illness, regardless of a particular diagnosis—especially if the illness is life threatening.

Physical illnesses or accidents are often the beginning of a series of problems for an individual and that person's family. A potentially fatal illness can incite the same sense of dread and loss that death itself implies. Besides fear of death, a person's self-image is threatened by serious physical alteration resulting from surgical amputation of a limb, scars from an accident or extensive burns, or HIV/AIDS. If injury and illness result from a preventable disaster, positive crisis resolution is especially challenging to avoid despair, revenge, or violence.

People with sexually transmitted diseases (STDs) are also particularly crisis prone; shame, revulsion, ignorance, and fear about such diseases can precipitate marriage breakups, suicidal tendencies, social isolation, self-loathing, and depression. And if a person realizes that an STD may be a forerunner of AIDS and was caused by having unprotected sex, the potential for crisis is increased. This is also true when HIV is transmitted through rape.

CRISIS CARE IN DIVERSE HEALTH CARE SETTINGS

Crisis situations demanding response are as diverse as the people experiencing them. Everyone in health-related distress or crisis needs to know about the numerous opportunities health practitioners have for assisting people experiencing threats to health, life, and self-image from illness, accidents, and related problems.

Crisis and Emergency Medical Care

While all human service workers have a responsibility for such assistance, those in emergency and acute-care settings are strategically positioned to influence the outcome of high-risk crisis situations. The nature of emergency and acute-care settings, with a focus on lifesaving procedures, may require putting the emotional facets of crisis such as intense fear on the back burner temporarily, while focusing on emergency medical procedures. If life is at stake, no one would place the expression of feelings, however intense these may be, before lifesaving measures.

Yet because of the tense atmosphere of emergency medical scenes, it is important to remember that emotional needs do not disappear when physical needs take on life-and-death importance. An appropriate attitude and sensitivity to clients' emotional needs must accompany necessary lifesaving procedures. A team approach accomplishes this best; the strain on nurses, physicians, and emergency medical technicians would be enormous without teamwork. Staff burnout in these settings is often very high in any case, while the lack of teamwork and staff support, the inappropriate placement of personnel in high-risk work, or the lack of training in crisis intervention frequently contributes to such burnout and its impact on patient care.

In cases of cardiac arrest at hospitals, emergency medical work occurs in concert with crisis intervention. This includes attention to family members who may get lost in the shuffle of a medical emergency situation. Patients and their families should therefore be familiar with the key aspects of the crisis care process (discussed in detail in Chapters 2 and 3) that should be applied on their behalf in emergency medical, primary care, and institutional settings:

1. Identification of persons at risk through routine inquiry on initial contact— for example, "What happened?"
2. Level I assessment (triage) for (a) physical and emotional trauma and (b) risk to life— "Have you thought about hurting yourself or someone else?"
3. Empathic, supportive response—"I'm so sorry for what you've been through."
4. Safety planning (if assessment reveals risk to life)— "We want to do everything possible for your health and safety."
5. Linkage, effective referral for Level II assessment, and follow-up— to family: "It's very important that you follow through with counseling when we're sure your son is stable after treating the overdose."

Thus, for example, if questions about suicide and violence toward others are not raised, it could mean lapse in a hospital's accreditation requirements regarding such routine risk assessment in general medical settings. Inadequate assessment can result in a person rejecting a referral for crisis counseling, physical refuge, Alcoholics Anonymous, or other service following emergency medical treatment (for example, after a suicide attempt, rape, battering, or crisis related to drinking). Successful referrals are often influenced by the health care worker's attitude and recognition of the complexity of these situations. In short, health practitioners in emergency settings are not usually expected to assist people through *all* phases of crisis resolution. Effective crisis care, however, does require routine attention to the emotional aspects of events threatening health and life, offering support, and linking people to reliable sources for further assistance. Thus, for example, keeping an anxious patient informed of time constraints and other facts in a busy emergency center may prevent violent or abusive outbursts by an impatient family member demanding, "What's taking so long?"

Crisis Care in Primary Health Care Settings

Although mental health and crisis care are often cited in health reform policy statements, a mind-body split is still evident as many general health practitioners hesitate to deal with emotional issues, citing psychological discomfort or lack of time. Understandably, most nonpsychiatric physicians and nurses do not think of themselves as psychotherapists, yet the psychosocial facet of treatment and care is a given whether the primary health problem is physical or emotional. Likewise, people seeing primary care providers for a medical problem appreciate receiving attention to the emotional facets of their illness or accident, while they do not expect psychotherapy from them. However, the misperception of crisis intervention as "therapy" may partially explain the reluctance of some general health practitioners to incorporate crisis care into routine health care practice.

The increasing emphasis on primary care and concerns about the escalation of health care costs underscore the inclusion of crisis intervention as an essential element of comprehensive health care. As the book's Crisis Paradigm illustrates, prevention is less costly than treatment. But crisis and quick-fix drug approaches should not be used *as financially expedient* substitutes for the longer term care and rehabilitation that some problems require. In many primary care situations, risk assessment, social support, and a referral to a peer support or self-help group will do, as discussed in Chapters 2 and 3.

For example, one woman said that her physical and emotional recovery after a mastectomy might have been much more precarious if a nurse had not comforted her when she broke down crying the first time she looked in the mirror. This was the beginning of her grief work around the loss of her breast. The surgical nurse, who was not a psychotherapist, simply understood and responded to the crisis dimensions of the woman's transition in health status and potentially her self-image. People with cancer or another life-threatening illness often say that the shared strength from a support group is what keeps them going as they struggle with the side effects of treatment and, for some, the reality of their final loss.

Crisis Care in Hospitals and Nursing Homes

If an acutely or chronically ill person also needs hospital or nursing home care, the potential for other crises looms for the individual and his or her family. Hospitals and other institutions can be considered as subcultures in which the longest term occupants—the staff—know the procedures and rules that prevent chaos and help them do their jobs. The sick person, however, especially one who has never been hospitalized, may experience culture shock, a condition that can occur when the comfort of familiar things is suddenly missing.

In extreme cases, a person in culture shock feels too surprised or numbed by a new culture's unfamiliarity to proceed with managing everyday life tasks. Without support in an institutional environment a person's usually successful response to life's ups and downs may be weakened. Hospitalization can feel like being stranded in a foreign country without knowing the local language or customs. Add the fear of the unknown regarding the outcome of treatments, and it is easy to understand why some patients lash out at staff in what may appear to be unreasonable outbursts or manifest other classic signs of crisis. Even in transitional or long-term care placements, attention to these issues, especially upon admission, can avoid much pain for both client and staff.

Someone who feels unready for hospital discharge may also be at risk of a crisis response. In an era of escalating health care costs, timely discharge may seem cost-efficient. But premature discharge does not save money and may eventually cost more through readmission—or it may result in a family caretaker crisis or an extreme response such as suicide (see Chapter 1, the "Revolving Door").

In some instances, people's illnesses and the stress of hospitalization are complicated further by negligence, mishandling, or unethical medical practice. When this occurs, in addition to the original illness, the patient (or survivor) must contend with the personal damage inflicted by the very people he or she trusted.

Crisis Intervention in Psychiatric and Residential Settings

As noted in Chapters 2 and 3, admission to a psychiatric facility is often a sign that crises have not been constructively resolved at various points along the way. Whenever possible, crisis hostels and other alternatives to psychiatric hospitalization should be used if a person cannot be helped in the home environment. Although psychiatric service is intended to relieve acute breakdowns or stress situations, as in general medical care, rigid authoritarian approaches can create another kind of crisis.

EXAMPLE: ANGELA—SUICIDAL ADOLESCENT

Angela, age 18, highly suicidal, upset, and dependent on her family, was admitted to the psychiatric service of a private hospital on the advice of a psychiatrist whom the mother had called a few hours earlier. Angela and her mother arrived at the hospital at 3:00 p.m. The admitting nurse stayed with them until 3:30 p.m., when she was scheduled to go off duty. Angela was just beginning to calm down but became very upset again when the nurse left. The nurses were unable to reach the physician to obtain a prescription for tranquilizing medication. Meanwhile, visiting hours ended and Angela's mother was asked to leave. At this point, Angela became even more upset. The nurse on the evening shift was unable to quiet or console her. By the time an order for tranquilizing medication arrived, Angela's behavior had become uncontrollable, and she was placed in a high-security room, as she became more suicidal. During the process of administering the medication, Angela screamed that she wanted to see her mother. After being told her mother was no longer in the unit, she became more upset; Angela struck and injured the attending nurse and was then placed in four-point restraints.

This example shows that the rules and regulations of the hospital (now much more relaxed) and absence of an efficient call system to obtain doctor's orders for emergency medication contributed to Angela's crisis state, which reached the point of panic. In general, seclusion and physical restraint (whether in emergency or other hospital departments) are perceived as a form of punishment; therefore, they should be avoided except when assessment reveals a high risk of violence toward staff or others. This is because physical or psychotropic drug restraint threatens a person's basic need for self-mastery and control. As a trainer on violence against health care workers observed (in the year 2010) a near automatic application of physical restraints on an emotionally upset patient who was not violent, he asked the nurse: "Have you tried talking with this patient?"

Families of acutely disturbed people should recognize that the principles of crisis intervention already discussed apply in mental institutions and residential settings. Goals in institutional settings include helping people to (1) express their feelings, (2) understand their situation and develop new ways of problem solving, and (3) reestablish themselves with family and community resources. The staff in residential facilities should examine their programs and routines to determine whether people become even more upset than they were originally as a result of the rules, thus defeating the purpose of the residential program.

For example, most psychiatric facilities routinely search patients on admission for dangerous articles, contraband, and anything that might be used as a weapon. Considering the frequency of attacks on staff serving vulnerable and recovering psychiatric patients, such searches seem reasonable. They should not, however, be done without a full explanation to the patient as to the reasons.

The constraints of managed care in the United States may account for many violent outbursts by psychiatric patients. This may include the excessive use of chemical restraint as a substitute for longer psychotherapeutic approaches not covered by insurance. Such system-produced crisis episodes are compounded if staff use rigid authoritarian approaches—in essence, engaging in power struggles with persons already feeling disempowered and vulnerable. Instead, the ideal is skilled crisis prevention strategies that are primarily interpersonal. Once health care and other human service workers adapt to the culture of bureaucratic mini-societies, they can easily forget that others may experience "culture shock" when entering them—not unlike the shock an anthropologist or tourist might feel when entering a foreign country.

CRISIS RESPONSE OF PEOPLE IN HEALTH STATUS TRANSITION

To better understand the responses of those who are in pain, are ill, or are hospitalized, relatives, friends, and those who work with them must address certain questions:

- How do sick and hospitalized people feel?
- How do they perceive their illness and its relationship to their beliefs and lifestyle?
- How do they manage being in the "sick role"?

The person whose physical integrity, self-image, and social freedom are threatened or damaged by these hazards to health shows many of the usual signs of a crisis state, as discussed in Chapter 2. Because a majority of distressed people present first in health clinics, emergency departments, or offices of primary care providers, all health care workers should recognize their pivotal role in detecting and preventing a full-blown crisis in these settings. And because—even before this—many of these same people present in their friends' living rooms, their neighbors' kitchens, or their pastors' studies—all observers play a pivotal role in convincing their distressed friends, neighbors, or parishioners to seek help.

So let us review what everyone should know when a person's usual health status is threatened or lost—keeping in mind *differences between the emotional pain of crisis and a serious psychiatric illness* and the ideal of a preventive holistic response to acutely distressed persons. Thus, for example, instead of concluding a patient encounter with a psychiatric diagnosis such as generalized anxiety disorder (GAD) in the biomedical paradigm, providers, family, and friends should assume that the presenting symptoms signal *emotional pain* (from loss, threat, abuse, and so on)—not necessarily a "disorder"—and proceed with comments such as "You seem to be very upset. Can you tell me what's happening?" To the client requesting a tranquilizing prescription: "Of course I can write you a prescription; that will help you feel less anxious, but it won't really solve whatever is troubling you. I think I'd be helping you more if we talked a bit before giving you a tranquilizer to see if maybe a referral for counseling would be the most helpful." This approach avoids attaching a psychiatric diagnosis to essentially *normal* responses to life's ups and downs and sometimes to life-threatening events. (See Chapter 3 for responsible use of psychotropic drugs during crisis.)

Classical Crisis Manifestations Related to Health Status Transition

Whether at home or already consulting your doctor about threats to health, it is helpful to know the typical signs of impending crisis when dealing with such threats and the impairment or loss of everyday functioning and self-care. This implies attention to signals of acute distress in oneself or someone we care about; that is, physical, emotional, cognitive, and behavior changes in one's *usual* self.

1. *Biophysical response.* Besides enduring the pain and discomfort from the disease or injury itself, the person losing health and bodily integrity suffers many of the biophysical symptoms experienced after the loss of a loved one (see "Loss, Grief, and Bereavement" in Chapter 3).
2. *Feelings.* After an amputation or a diagnosis such as heart disease, AIDS, diabetes, or cancer, people respond with a variety of feelings:
   - Shock and anger: "Why me?"
   - Helplessness and hopelessness in regard to future normal functioning: "What's left for me now?"
   - Shame about the obvious scar, handicap, or reduced physical ability and about dependence on others: "What will my husband think?"
   - Anxiety about the welfare of spouse or children who depend on them: "How will they manage at home without me?"
   - Losing a sense of bodily integrity and goals the person hoped to achieve before the illness, accident, or trauma from abuse: "I don't think I'll ever feel right again."
   - Doubt of acceptance by others: "No one will want to be around me this way."
   - Fear of death, which may have been narrowly escaped in an accident or a violent attack by one's partner, or which now must be faced, in the case of cancer: "It was almost the end" or "This is the end."
   - Fear that one's sex life is over after diagnosis of prostate cancer: "Am I condemned to lead a celibate life now?"

3. *Thoughts and perceptions.* The fears raised by a serious illness, an accident, or a changed image from the trauma of abuse or from a surgical operation usually color a person's understanding of the event itself and how it will affect the future. For example, a young woman with diabetes assumed that she would be cut off from her cocktail party circuit, which she felt was necessary in her high executive position. She lacked knowledge about how social obligations might be synchronized with diabetes.

    A person with heart disease may foresee spending the future as an invalid; the reality is that he or she must change only the manner and range of performance. The woman with a mastectomy may perceive that all men will reject her because of the bodily alteration; in reality only some men would do so. A woman who does not have a secure relationship with a man before a mastectomy may experience rejection; we can help such a woman consider the value of a relationship with a man who accepts her primarily for her body. Women with stable relationships are seldom rejected by their husbands or lovers following a mastectomy.

4. *Behavior.* People who are ill or suffering from the physical effects of an accident, surgery, or other trauma typically endure additional stress. First, hospitalization enforces a routine of dependency, which may be necessary when people are weak, but the routine also keeps the hospital running according to established rules. However, rigidity in such rules may defeat the purpose for which hospitals exist: quality care of patients. A patient's fears, anger, and lack of knowledge about illness, hospital routines, and expectations can elicit the worst behavior from someone who is otherwise cooperative and likable. Rules and regulations governing visitors to these settings present a further hazard to people already in a difficult situation. The environment of an intensive care unit—the tubes, lights, and electrical gadgets—is a constant reminder to patients and family members of proximity to death.

    Understanding and sensitivity to cultural and other differences in response to illness, pain, and hospitalization are essential. All should recognize that across cultures, people vary in their attitudes about pain and how to respond during illness or hospitalization.

ESSENTIAL ELEMENTS OF SUCCESSFUL CRISIS RESOLUTION

Overall, professionals, family, and others familiar with the common signs of impending crisis can do much to relieve unnecessary stress and harmful outcomes of the illness and hospital experience. A person in crisis from sudden illness needs an opportunity to do the following:

- Express feelings such as fear about its threat to normal functioning
- Gain an understanding of the illness, what it means in terms of his or her values, what limitations it imposes, and what to expect in the future

- Learn that high anxiety is not unusual when facing the unknown and possibly negative or dangerous results of a medical exam and diagnostic tests
- Communicate with family members

Maria and Michael French (continued)

In the case of the French couple introduced at the beginning of this chapter, the community health nurse called by the family friend contacted a nearby crisis clinic. Here is the kind of care everyone in a medical or health related crisis should receive—whether at home, in a clinic, or hospital.

First, the crisis counselor called Maria in the hospital to talk about her concerns and to determine whether Michael had any history of violence or whether guns were available (See. Chapter 6). Michael's accusations of infidelity—which Maria said were unfounded—may have been related to his concern about his forced dependency and to feelings of inadequacy, as he had cancer of the sex gland.

The crisis counselor then called Michael and let him know that the counselor, Maria, and the neighbors were all concerned about him. Michael accepted an appointment for a home visit by the counselor within the next few hours. He expressed his fears that people were trying to take advantage of him during his wife's absence—his stated reason for dismissing the tenants and changing the locks. Further exploration revealed that he felt inadequate to handle household matters and the tenants' everyday requests, which Maria usually managed.

Michael agreed to the counselor's recommendation for a medical-psychiatric-neurological evaluation to determine whether his cancer might have spread to his brain. The counselor explained that brain tumors can contribute to acute emotional upsets or paranoid ideation such as Michael was experiencing.

As Michael had no independent means of visiting Maria in the hospital, the counselor arranged for such a visit. The counselor also scheduled a joint counseling session between Michael and Maria after they had had a chance to visit. This session revealed that Michael and Maria each had serious concerns about the welfare of the other. In their two telephone conversations during Maria's stay in the hospital, Michael and Maria had been unable to express their fears and concerns. The joint counseling session was the highlight in successful resolution of their crisis. Michael's threat to kill Maria was a once-in-a-lifetime occurrence, triggered by his unexpressed anger at her for "leaving him" and for the troubles he had experienced during her absence.

When Maria returned from the hospital, the crisis counselor arranged a joint session at the French home. This session included the two of them, the community health nurse, and the friend who had made the original calls. Such "social network" sessions (typically conducted by a medical social worker) are designed to avoid having patients "fall through the cracks" in situations that involve multiple players (see Chapter 9, "Social Network and Group Approaches to Crisis Care"). For the French family, this conference had several positive results:

- It calmed the friend's fears for Michael.
- It broadened everyone's understanding of the reactions people can have to the stress of illness and hospitalizations.
- The community health nurse agreed to enlist further home health services to relieve Maria's increasingly demanding role of nurse to her husband.
- Michael and Maria agreed to several additional counseling sessions to explore ways in which Michael's excessive dependency on his wife could be reduced.

Michael and Maria had never discussed openly the feelings they both had about Michael's progressive cancer. In future sessions, the French couple dealt with ways they could resume social contacts with their children and friends, whom they had cut off almost completely.

PREVENTIVE INTERVENTION

Family and friends confronting a loved one's serious or life-threatening illness can benefit from the French family example and how to prevent negative crisis outcomes in such instances, and what they should reasonably expect from health care professionals. This example reveals at least three earlier points at which crisis intervention should have been available to Michael and Maria French:

1. At the time Michael received his diagnosis of cancer
2. When Michael was forced to retire
3. Each time Maria delayed her operation, as well as at the point of Maria's hospitalization

In each of these instances, nurses and physicians were in key positions to help the French couple through the hazardous events of Michael's illness and Maria's operation. Sessions with the crisis counselor confirmed the fact that the French couple, like many people facing illness, received little or no attention regarding the fears and social ramifications of their illnesses and hospitalization.

When Maria expressed to the community nurse her original concern about Michael's early retirement, the nurse might have extended her 10-minute visits, thus allowing time for Maria to express her concerns. For example, the nurse could have said, "Maria, you seem really concerned about your husband being home all the time. Can we talk about what's bothering you?" Or the nurse might have made a mental health referral after observing Michael's increasing depression.

The gynecologist attending to Maria's health problems could have explored the reason for her repeated cancellations of the scheduled surgery, saying, "Mrs. French, you've cancelled the surgery appointment three times now. There must be some serious reason for this, as you know that the operation is necessary. Let's talk about what's at the bottom of this." Such a conversation might have led to a social service referral.

The nurse attending Maria before her operation, as well as the community health nurse visiting the home, might have picked up on Maria's concerns about the effect of her absence on Michael. Such a response requires listening skills and awareness of psychological cues given by people in distress. The nurse could then have explained the hospital resources, such as social services or pastoral care—ways of helping Maria explore the problem further.

EXAMPLE: INTERVIEW WITH MARIA FRENCH

HOSPITAL NURSE: Mrs. French, you've been very quiet, and you seem tense. You said before that you're not particularly worried about the operation, but I wonder if something else is bothering you.

MARIA: Well, I wish my husband were here, but I know he can't be.

NURSE: Can you tell me more about that?

MARIA: He's got cancer and isn't supposed to drive. I hated leaving him by himself.

NURSE: How about talking with him by phone?

MARIA: I've done that, but all we talk about is the weather and things that don't matter. I'm afraid if I tell him how worried I am about him, he'll think I'm putting him down.

NURSE: Mrs. French, I understand what you're saying. A lot of people feel that way. But you know there's really no substitute for telling people honestly how we feel, especially those close to us.

MARIA: Maybe you're right. I could try but I'd want to be really careful about what I say. There's been a lot of tension between us lately.

NURSE: Why don't you start by letting him know that you wish he could be here with you and that you hope things are OK with him at home. (Pause) You said there's been a lot of tension. Do you have anyone you can talk to about the things that are bothering you?

MARIA: No, not really.

NURSE: You must feel pretty alone. You know, we have counseling services here in the hospital that could be very useful for you and your husband. I could put you in touch with someone, if you like.

In this brief interaction about Maria's surgery—a potentially hazardous event—the nurse has (1) helped Maria express her fears openly, (2) conveyed her own understanding of Maria's fears, (3) helped Maria put her fears about not communicating with her husband in a more realistic perspective, (4) offered direct assistance in putting Maria in touch with the person most important to her at this time, and (5) made available the resources for obtaining counseling service if Maria so desires.

This type of intervention should be available to everyone with a serious illness or who experiences the traumatic effects of an operation, burns, or an accident. Putting people in touch with self-help groups is another important means of reducing the hazards of illness and hospitalization. Such groups exist for nearly every kind of illness or operation a person can have: heart disease, leukemia, diabetes, mastectomy, amputation, and others. Many hospitals also hold teaching and discussion groups among patients while still in the hospital—an excellent forum in which people can air feelings with others who have similar problems, gain a better understanding of an illness or operation and how it will affect their lives, and establish contacts with people who may provide lasting social support.

CRISES REGARDING SURGERY

Maria's surgery was necessary and important, but it came at a bad time. Another set of issues arises from unnecessary surgery. Although unnecessary elective surgery is under scrutiny for ethical and cost-containment reasons, cosmetic surgery (mostly on women) is a booming business in affluent societies despite highly controversial results such as disfigurement and immune system breakdown.

The issue of surgery as a crisis point is particularly poignant in the case of mastectomy. Increasingly, women who have had mastectomies are referred to self-help groups such as Reach for Recovery, which offer emotional support during this crisis-prone period. However, in many communities, advocacy is needed to obtain such referrals. As the rate of breast cancer steadily grows and research begins to examine possible environmental causes such as contamination of the food chain by pesticides, it is important to link this personal traumatic event with broader social concerns.

Men having surgery on sex organs also need supportive communication and accurate information. Although radical surgery (prostatectomy) has increased dramatically in recent years, there is little evidence that this surgery saves lives, whereas there is evidence of incontinence and impotence following the operation. Since prostate cancer grows very slowly, most older men with the disease die of other causes. The crisis for men having such surgery is heavily tinged by the threat to male potency and self-image that is signaled by cancer or surgery affecting sex organs. The hazards of such a diagnosis are compounded because many males have been socialized not to cry or express feelings readily. If doctors and nurses appear too busy for discussion of these sensitive and emotion-tinged topics, at the very least they should provide appropriate referrals to social and psychological services for help with crises stemming from threats to health and bodily integrity.

EXAMPLE: ALEX—A PREVENTABLE SUICIDAL RESPONSE TO MULTIPLE STRESSORS

A 47-year-old accountant, Alex was under a lot of stress. His wife of 15 years had recently told him that she wanted a divorce. He was coping and had discussed the impending divorce with a crisis counselor in his community. But when his physician diagnosed his cancer of the testicle, the added stress was more than he could handle.

Alex's physician noted his distress but simply told him to check into the county hospital's psychiatric unit 30 miles away if he continued to feel upset. Even though the physician did not know that Alex was already seeing a crisis counselor in the community, if he had no time to listen to Alex, he should have made a local referral. It is not unusual for local crisis specialty services to go unused if effective linkages with health and other front-line professionals are lacking.

Instead of going to the distant county hospital, Alex went home, told his wife what the physician had said, and shot himself in his front yard—an unexpectedly tragic outcome that might perhaps have been averted through appropriate crisis care.

CHILDREN HAVING SURGERY

If illness, surgery, and hospitalization are occasions of crisis for most adults, they are even more so for children and their parents. Professionals with special training in child development now work in child life departments of many hospitals. They arrange preadmission tours and listen to children's questions and worries. These worries can be quite diverse—and perhaps unexpected.

- Sam, age 4, has been told by his doctor that a hole will have to be made in his stomach to make him well again. Because the doctor neglected to mention that the hole will also be stitched up again, Sam worries that "the things inside me will fall out."
- Cindy, age 9, sees an intravenous bottle and tubes being wheeled to her bedside. She had once seen the same apparatus attached to her cousin Jeffrey, who later died. As the needle is being inserted, she wonders whether she is as sick as Jeffrey was.

- Ken, a junior high school football player, is confined to a traction frame. Unable to dress or wash himself each morning, he suffers acute embarrassment in front of the nurses.
- Darryn, a 7-year old immigrant child with cerebral palsy and in state protective custody, was in a hospital for leg surgery. In the foreign environment of the hospital, strung up in traction, immobile, and in pain, he became hysterical when the surgical staff came in for rounds. The night before he had been watching the TV drama "Roots" and saw images of the Ku Klux Klan hanging Blacks. The medical team coming in en masse in white uniforms caused him to panic.

If a child is going to the hospital, child life workers offer the following advice to parents:

- Accept the fact of the hospitalization
- Be honest with your child
- Prepare yourself; for example, find out about procedures
- Prepare your child, for example, through preadmission get-acquainted tours
- Whenever possible, stay with your child

CRISIS AND CHRONIC ILLNESS: HIV AND AIDS

"Working with Ted changed my life. I'll never be the same." [*hospice volunteer*]

"It's humiliating to be so dependent on people. I want to kill myself." [*23-year-old man with Kaposi's sarcoma, dying of AIDS*]

"The nurses really want to be here [in a hospital AIDS unit]. Lance never has any appetite, but he forced himself to eat one of the chocolate chip cookies I made because, he said, 'You made it just for me.' I almost cried, there was such a bond there." [*psychiatric liaison nurse*]

"I can't move my legs at night, but if I touch even one person, then maybe it will help them be good to my boy, who lost his mother to this horrible disease." [*woman dying of AIDS*]

These statements from people with acquired immunodeficiency syndrome (AIDS) and those who help them dramatize the *opportunity* and the *danger* of a crisis that more than many others may symbolize a much larger crisis of the modern world—the persistent and growing inequalities that leave the poor, people of color, women, and culturally marginalized groups disproportionately at risk for AIDS, an illness that typifies life crises as a whole and cuts across the ramifications of crises: loss, grief, and mourning; suicide by despairing people with the disease; antigay violence; social network support; family and community crises; status changes in health, residence, and occupation; and finally, life cycle transitions and death.

Although AIDS is a complex multifaceted illness, here the focus is on the perspective of people living with AIDS and those who help them, keeping in mind the link between personal pain and sociocultural issues that leave them disempowered and vulnerable. The crisis care examples discussed here apply to any serious illness traceable to poverty or values about treatment embedded in social inequalities and cultural norms that leave some groups severely disadvantaged in the context of health care as a *basic human right*. Thus, while HIV/AIDS is highly treatable and early death is often avoided in wealthy Western countries, this is not the case for millions of disadvantaged poor people worldwide. The examples of Daniel and Sophia highlight the *danger* and *opportunity* of crisis when health is threatened.

EXAMPLES: DANIEL AND SOPHIA—LIVING WITH AIDS OR ADDICTION

Daniel is a 38-year-old bisexual man who has been diagnosed with AIDS and lived for 18 months in a hospice managed by a local AIDS Action Committee (AAC). Pneumocystis pneumonia was the occasion for Daniel's several hospitalizations. He is down from his usual 185 pounds to 130, has periodic bouts of nausea and diarrhea, and has some neurological involvement affecting his gait. Once a successful health care worker and artist, Daniel lost his human service job because of federal cuts in domestic programs and could not find another. Getting AIDS further reduced his employability. This left him without a paid job, supporting himself through Social Security disability payments, and availability of food stamps.

Daniel says that "When I left the hospital, I had no money, no job, no apartment. I'm still struggling with the VA for the benefits coming to me. If it weren't for AAC, I would have been out on the street. With the trouble I've had getting care, especially an awful case worker, I got a dose of what the elderly and the homeless go through. You know, I say 'forget your cure.' What would I ever want to come back [from death] for? Homelessness? Poverty? I have no regrets. I used to be seen as a pillar of strength, then people saw me as sick and no longer there for them, but slowly they're coming back. So I don't have a regular job anymore, but now I'm a teacher and counselor [helping other people with AIDS], and I work three hours volunteering at a local men's shelter. I also do liaison work at the hospital where I was a patient. Yes, I get weak, but now I do what I can when I can and as much as I can. There's not the same pressure as before. As long as I don't set expectations, there's no disappointment."

Sophia, age 30, has a 4-year-old son whom she placed with relatives as an infant because she could not care for him properly as long as she was addicted to drugs. She suffers from night sweats, thrush, shingles, chronic fatigue, abscesses, a platelet disorder, and central nervous system involvement, including seizures and memory loss. Through her 12 years of addiction, Sophia worked as a waitress and a prostitute to support her drug habit. "It's hard to realize that all the things I dreamed about if I was drug free can't be now because of AIDS. I thought having a baby would help me get my act together. I was wrong, but I would never hurt my son. I don't take pride in too many things I've done, but I spared Mickey by putting him in a stable environment. I'm not sorry I had Mickey because he's what keeps me going now. If it weren't for him, I probably would have killed myself already. I'm not through doing what has to be done—helping other drug users and letting my son know me better. And I do a lot of talks for doctors and nurses about AIDS."

Her eyes shine with pride when she talks about her son. "Mickey and I spend every weekend together. I'm making some videos for him, so he will remember who I was and how much I love him. He knows to say no to drugs. Behind every addict, you know, there is a child, a lover. It's people's responsibility to set aside their biases, to take care. I have my problems, but at least I can care for someone else's pain, maybe because I've been close to pain. Some say they should lock up prostitutes, but don't tell me it's my fault that a man rides around in his Mercedes-Benz looking for sex instead of being faithful to his wife. I have wonderful friends. When the memory problems get worse, I'll give one of them power of attorney because my family judges me very harshly, and if I left it to them, they would put out all the people who care about me when I'm dying. None of my family come to see me when I'm in the hospital. It's sad. I've spent half my life finding myself, and now I'm going to die, but I have an opportunity to plan my time and get closure, and that's good."

Daniel and Sophia are at peace. Both are doing meaningful work. At his young age, Daniel feels he has accomplished much of his life's work and does not seem to be afraid of death. When asked whether he would commit suicide if his symptoms included a new crisis point, dementia, he said, "No. It could be tough, though, because I've always been very independent and self-sufficient." As Daniel's neurological symptoms progressed, his struggle to remain at peace intensified. He also was stressed by the fact that some of his friends could not face the reality of his approaching death, but instead of expressing their pain and impending loss, they either avoided him or made fleeting visits, stating they "didn't have time" to talk. Daniel's occasional angry outbursts toward his friends may also be displacements of the anger he feels about dying, anger that is difficult to express because it implies a contradiction to his "caretaker" and "nice guy" self-image. Sophia readily expresses her sadness and pain but says her work is not done yet, so she keeps going and no longer feels like killing herself.

How did Daniel and Sophia arrive at the peace and acceptance they experienced in spite of constant physical pain and the knowledge that they were dying? By what process did Daniel win his "fight" to get where he is? How did Sophia come to manage her ultimate life crisis in a constructive manner and finally give up her addiction to drugs? The Crisis Paradigm (introduced in Chapter 1) illustrates the process of dealing with the crisis of a life-threatening illness and how people can capitalize on the opportunity of a tragic unanticipated event to arrive at positive resolution and avoid the danger inherent in crisis. The following discussion elaborates on the paradigm, using the AIDS crisis experience and illustrations from the lives of Sophia and Daniel. It shows what people with AIDS have in common with others, such as victims of violence or human-made disaster, whose crises originate primarily from the sociocultural milieu (see www.crisisprograms.org, Crisis Paradigm and HIV/AIDS).

Crisis Origins

A diagnosis of HIV/AIDS is an unanticipated, traumatic event of overwhelming proportions. Individuals, of course, can modify behaviors such as drug use or unprotected sex that place them at greater risk. But education in risk-reduction behaviors must be combined with economic and other change, with special attention to the intertwined origins of the problem.

Only a few years ago, death was the almost certain prediction of an illness like AIDS, and it still is for those uninsured or too poor to afford the expensive treatment and support services for living with AIDS—an increasingly available option for people in wealthy countries. Progress in the United States and Canada with civil rights of the gay community has also alleviated the additional stress affecting sexual minority individuals who are not "out" or whose communities are unfriendly or openly hostile toward such groups.

Similar prevention and treatment challenges apply to the international opium trade and life-threatening heroin addiction. As the Crisis Paradigm shows, the intersecting origins of crisis for people with HIV-AIDS or addiction may apply to the diagnosis of any serious illness in which stigma or poverty plays a key role, for example, STDs—sexually transmitted disease.

The events that often follow diagnosis of a life-threatening illness or addiction—loss of job, home, friends, and sometimes family—are closely tied to sociocultural origins and differ from losses such as temporary homelessness due to a fire or the unexpected death of a loved one from an illness that is not stigmatized.

Personal Crisis Manifestations

People afflicted with AIDS will experience most of the common emotional responses to a traumatic life event. Anger springs not simply from being stricken by the ultimate misfortune of facing an untimely death but also from unfair or violent treatment by a society with limited tolerance for anyone who is different or is judged as receiving deserved punishment for a deviant lifestyle. Anxiety is felt not only for their own health and welfare but also for their lovers or previous partners whom they may have infected. *Survivor guilt*, as noted for some disaster survivors in Chapter 8, may also surface for those who have lost partners and loved ones to AIDS. Some may also feel guilt or shame over their gay lifestyle, having internalized societal homophobia. Sophia says, for example, "I can't take pride in too many things I've done," but she does not wallow in guilt, nor is she ashamed of being a lesbian even though her family condemns her for it.

Denial of the medical facts and the need for behavioral change, especially if accompanied by free-floating anger at being infected, may result in irresponsible sexual behavior and the risk of infecting others. When Sophia learned that cleaning her needles with bleach or practicing safer sex could have prevented her infection, she expressed regrets that she may have infected others, but if she did, it was out of ignorance, not malice. In general, the most ethical approach is to inform a sex partner of one's infection and addiction status. Crisis counseling is clearly indicated for persons who act out their anger by placing others at risk. Sexual decision making is a complex process often not amenable to a simplistic, "just say no" approach. Sadness over loss of health and impending death is compounded by fear of losing friends or lovers and lack of the support necessary to face early death.

Anxiety's usual interference in cognitive functioning during crisis may be exacerbated with AIDS because of the fear of dementia. For example, normal forgetting may be interpreted as a first sign. AIDS dementia complex may sometimes be the only sign of AIDS. Sophia clearly planned for this possibility by arranging for a friend to act with power of attorney on her behalf. In the case of Charlie, another person dying with AIDS, flashes of awareness and clarity pierced his general comatose state, so that he could convey his wish not to be kept alive with heroic measures.

In general, the emotional and biophysical stress responses common during any life crisis are exaggerated here because of sociocultural facets of the crisis that are usually beyond the control of an individual to manage alone. In addition, the physical toll that AIDS or addiction exacts usually includes drastic energy reduction, which in turn increases stress because of inability to engage in physical stress-reduction activities.

Aids to Positive Crisis Resolution

Despite Daniel's spirit of independence, he recognized his need for support and accepted it. He said that the hospital nurses were wonderful and that friends and his overall attitude helped the most. Daniel also said that he was greatly strengthened by helping his friends face death, an experience also common among many people with cancer or other serious illness.

What about Sophia? Precisely what did she have or receive that assisted her along the path of constructive coping with AIDS? Sophia tells of being hospitalized for abscesses, violating hospital rules by shooting up drugs on the ward, and leaving the hospital only to collapse shortly afterward. She knew that without treatment she would probably die, but having a drug fix at the time seemed more important. Later she checked back into the hospital and was confronted by the head nurse, who said, "You ruined my day. I can help you, but here are the rules. Are you willing to keep them?" Sophia said, "You know, that nurse did me a real favor. She was furious with me and I don't blame her, but instead of burying her anger, she confronted me and I could tell that she did it because she cared."

These responses highlight the point repeatedly made by people with AIDS and others facing a life-threatening illness: *They are not victims and do not want to be treated as victims.* For those of us less ready for death than Daniel was, it is important to remember that emotional healing from life's traumatic events requires the individual in crisis to make sense out of the experience and to process it within his or her personal meaning system. For example, when Daniel's immune system became weaker and weaker, he was advised to discontinue volunteer work at the men's shelter to protect himself from further infections. He then replaced his on-site volunteering with a monthly monetary donation out of his meager welfare funds.

Similarly, Sophia found meaning in her suffering and a reason to keep going for the sake of her child as well as for the influence she had on the drug problem and the help she gave health professionals learning about AIDS and addiction. Her lifelong proximity to suffering and pain apparently heightened her sensitivity to the needs and pain of others. Assistance to Daniel, Sophia, and many like them during crisis is available primarily through local support groups that provide housing and hospice care as well as neighborhood people who help as needed with mowing the lawn, keeping the sidewalks clear, and tending the garden. With this kind of assistance, people like Daniel and others in a hospice house are able to live a normal life in the community and face their impending deaths with greater comfort than institutional care would provide.

The crisis care strategies that helped Daniel correspond to the interrelated origins of his crisis which together led to his growth and development, for example, resolving with his ex-wife old issues around his bisexuality. No longer rushed and overworked, he felt needed and wanted by homeless men and others and had a healthy circle of friends, including a cadre of mental health professionals who enjoyed chatting with him. While maintaining as much independence as possible, he did not hesitate to ask for needed help. Daniel said that AIDS forced him to take a "closer, more intense look at life, so now I'm more ready to leave it"—the *opportunity* of crisis.

For Sophia, in addition to her educational work with health professionals and the importance of being there for her son as long as possible, she said, "There's a reason for this. I went on the radio and made $53,000 for the AIDS Action Committee. It makes it meaningful. I feel robbed by this disease and my drug habit, but it's an opportunity to plan my time and get closure, and that's good."

Avoiding Negative Crisis Outcomes

For Jesse, one of Daniel's friends with AIDS, things did not go as well, at least temporarily. Jesse had Kaposi's sarcoma. His skin was dying; he was being eaten away. Jesse also had neurological involvement and some beginning symptoms of dementia. He found it humiliating to have people do things for him that he was used to doing for himself. Daniel helped out by putting reminders up around the house to compensate for Jesse's growing mental impairment. One day, Jesse declared to Daniel that he just could not go on any more: "I want to kill myself." Daniel's response was, "Jess, no matter how bad this hits us, let's face it together. I'm in pain, too. You know where I'm at. Let's share it. You're strong. Look at what you've done for others." Jesse did not commit suicide but died in the hospital a few weeks later.

Suicide and Ethical Issues

As we examine the interchange between Daniel and Jesse, it is clear that Daniel did not simply talk Jesse out of suicide. First of all, the issue of suicide for people dying of AIDS or another chronic illness raises all the ethical issues discussed in Chapter 4. In the case of AIDS, it might be easier for people to favor "rational suicide" than in other crisis situations. Many would therefore argue for the right of people dying with AIDS to commit suicide rather than suffer the horrors of physical and mental deterioration. However, Daniel, Sophia, and many like them tell us that life can be meaningful and worthwhile in spite of great suffering. If those afflicted with a life-threatening illness experience insult added to injury through scorn and violence and then decide to commit suicide, those of us left can well ask whether such suicides, even those considered to be rational, could be traced to our failure to respond to them with the necessary, nonjudgmental care.

If a person with a terminal illness requests assistance in committing suicide, the caretaker or friend must not only be familiar with ethical and legal issues regarding suicide but should consider hidden messages as well. One of those messages may be the inability or unwillingness to tolerate chronic severe pain. Most people dying of cancer do not wish to kill themselves. But perhaps the greatest challenge for supporters of dying people is to help create a milieu that will make suicide an unnecessary choice. This includes providing adequate pain medication and information about nonpharmacological treatment of chronic pain. An appropriate environment and care, either at home or in a hospice house, would underscore the love and caring that help dying people put their material affairs in order; say good-bye to lovers and family after reconciliation and, it is hoped, healing; and be recognized and valued for their place on this earth and thus be ready for life's final stage (see Chapter 9).

Women and Children With AIDS

Sophia and Daniel illustrate commonalities among people with AIDS: shock, anger, loss, and mourning a shortened life. But women, whether sick with AIDS or as caretakers, face several special issues. For example, because of cultural messages regarding body image, women may experience greater stress around appearance as they deteriorate physically. Women have the additional stress of worrying about becoming pregnant and possibly transmitting the virus to their offspring. Fortunately, having her child infected with the AIDS virus was not one of Sophia's many stressors. Women who are HIV positive generally are advised not to become pregnant. However, although there is support for a sperm-washing procedure for men who wish to have children, there is no corollary support for women with the same desire. Women's continued inequality has major implications for risk not only of contracting AIDS from their male partners demanding sex but also of violence if they urge the use of condoms.

If women with AIDS are also, like Sophia, intravenous drug users (the largest group of US women with AIDS) and fail to prevent pregnancy, their ability to take care of a child will be even more limited because the problems connected with drug use are added to the debilitating effects of AIDS. Sophia's foresight in this area (and access to resources not available to many poor women) moved her to place her child with a stable family when she was unable to overcome her addiction.

A woman whose child has AIDS will probably feel guilty and angry whether she does or does not have AIDS herself. The millions of orphans in AIDS-devastated countries underscore the double burden of illness and caretaking as AIDS affects women.

Lesbian women, although in the lowest risk group for AIDS, are nevertheless at risk for the same reasons other women are. Sophia, for example, traces her infection to dirty needles to support her drug habit, not to her lesbian status. Lesbian women are affected by the crisis in other ways as well. As significant others for gay men, some lesbians will suffer the loss of friendships through the deaths of these men. They are similarly affected by antigay discrimination and violence. Lesbians are also concerned if they are considering artificial or self-insemination. Finally, lesbians in the United States are among the majority of AIDS caretakers.

The tragedy of AIDS is even more poignant with respect to children. While an adult with AIDS can come to terms with the inevitability of death and work through the crisis, including its implications for previous and future sexual behavior, children with AIDS obviously cannot. This implies an additional challenge for people with AIDS to prevent pregnancy and for caretakers to treat and care for children with AIDS with extraordinary compassion.

Similarly poignant and tragic is the fear of HIV infection following rape. Although this double crisis also affects male victims of rape, the majority of rape victims are women. The emotional trauma for such victims is overwhelming, particularly in the face of continuing public attitudes of blaming the crime of rape on its victims and prosecuting very few assailants. If these attitudes prevail, rape victims may continue to blame themselves not only for the rape but also for contracting AIDS; in addition, they must face all that any other person with AIDS confronts in an untimely death.

CARETAKERS OF PEOPLE WITH SERIOUS ILLNESS: SUPPORT AND SELF-CARE

We have seen that Daniel and Sophia have come through health crises to the point of peace and acceptance of eventual death with the help of natural and formal crisis care. But sick people who lack such resources may not face life's final passage to death with peace, fulfillment, and the comfort of family and friends without extraordinary assistance from various caretakers.

Caring for others whose needs are very great exacts serious emotional and physical health tolls on family and friends. In hospitals as well, women provide most of the care for the acutely ill and dying; in addition, they face the stress of overwork because of fiscal constraints and health reform measures that leave nurses and low-wage workers vulnerable. So now, as typical in the past, the cost of caring is borne disproportionately by women, regardless of sexual orientation.

The extraordinary stressors and potential crises caretakers must deal with include: danger of needle stick infection for nurses and physicians; stigmatization due to association with devalued members of society; confrontation with issues of sexual identity; one's own risk of illness and death; assuming power-of-attorney roles; dealing with suicide issues; and finally, simple overload from association with the depths of pain and tragedy surrounding people with an illness like AIDS, their families, and lovers. Providing ongoing support for all crisis workers and family members helps to prevent burnout, compassion fatigue, and the eventual loss of needed staff. Among families as well, the ability to care for a dying loved one varies, requiring that professionals provide what families may not be able to. Caring for a dying person includes the need for a comprehensive system of respite service for families offering care at home, in addition to skilled home nursing assistance (see Chapter 9).

Physical and Mental Handicap and Crisis Vulnerability

Living with or caring for a person with significant handicaps is a specialty topic beyond the scope of this book, except for noting that any person with a handicap is more vulnerable than others to additional stressors, trauma, and potential crises. For example, physical limitations may prevent some handicapped people from protecting themselves in cases of domestic dispute, rape, or robbery. Lack of access to public transportation and buildings affects mobility for some people. Others cannot take care of their own financial security and social security for a healthy self-image.

Another vulnerability of people with mental handicaps is that their grief following the loss of a loved one often goes unnoticed (see Chapter 3, "Loss, Grief, and Bereavement"). The alienation and feelings of powerlessness associated with such vulnerability can also lead to unhealthy coping, such as excessive drinking.

CRISIS CARE OF PEOPLE WITH ADDICTIONS AND EATING DISORDERS

The abuse of alcohol, other drugs, or food is not a crisis in itself. One common view of these problems is that they are diseases. Substance abuse problems may also be negative outcomes of earlier crises that left the abusers with greater vulnerability to future crisis episodes; that is, when people were in crisis at earlier points in their lives, they lacked the social support and personal strength to resolve the crisis in a more constructive manner. In either case, the person who abuses substances is engaging in a chronic form of self-destructive behavior (see Chapter 4).

The abuse of food by excess eating is sometimes accompanied by bulimia—compulsive gorging followed by self-induced vomiting to avoid weight gain. This is related to excess dieting, which may result in anorexia nervosa, a life-threatening condition of severe weight loss. Because eating disorders are most common among young women, they are increasingly linked to female identity issues and the pressure on young women to conform to cultural images of women's roles and body size.[1,2] Crises arising from these chronic problems and preventive intervention can bring about lasting change in the tendency to abuse food.

People abusing food, drugs, and alcohol commonly avoid getting help for their problem until another crisis occurs as a result of the addiction itself. Frequently, a crisis takes the form of a family fight, eviction from an apartment, loss of a job, or trouble with the law. Depending on the attitude and skill of friends and family and other helpers at such times, later crises may be the occasion of a turning point. The example of Anita illustrates this point. Over many years, Anita was abused physically and verbally by her husband. Her way of coping with the abuse was by overeating to the point of gaining over a hundred pounds. When her husband threatened her life, she finally left the violent marriage and sought refuge in a shelter for abused women. This crisis was a turning point, leading Anita to seek help for her compulsive overeating in Overeaters Anonymous, a peer support group similar to Alcoholics Anonymous.

Chronic Self-Destructive Behavior and Crisis Intervention

Partly because of negative attitudes toward self-destructive people, the opportunity to break free of addictions and a self-destructive lifestyle is often missed. Taking advantage of available crisis services can greatly reduce the sense of defeat experienced by substance abusers and those around them alike. Crisis care principles that apply especially to people dependent on alcohol or other drugs include the following:

1. Crisis represents a turning point—in this case, a turning away from drugs or food as a means of coping with stress. Users might reach a turning point in their lives through constructive interaction with health and social service workers.
2. In crisis care, we avoid doing things *for* rather than *with* people. Proposed solutions to problems are mutually agreed on by the person in crisis and the people who are helping. The substance-dependent person will often act helpless and try to get people to do things for him or her unnecessarily, thus increasing dependency even more. While expressing concern, family and other would-be helpers should avoid falling into this rescue trap (see Chapter 3, Fig. 3.1, the Victim-Rescuer-Persecutor Triangle).
3. Basic social attachments that have been disrupted must be reinstated or a substitute found to help avoid further crises and more self-destructive behavior. Usually, people who abuse drugs, alcohol, and food are more isolated than most.
4. For all of these reasons, social network intervention (see Chapter 9) is particularly helpful in assisting a person during repeated crisis episodes traceable to unresolved chronic problems. Although other approaches often yield little progress, clinicians skilled in network techniques point to impressive results.

Failure to observe these points leads to greater unhealthy dependency on alcohol or other drugs; the increasing frustration of family, friends, and practitioners who are trying to help; and vulnerability to crisis episodes. These crisis intervention techniques should be available at home, in hospitals, transition facilities, primary care offices, and in police and rescue services—wherever the substance-dependent person is in crisis. Such crisis care—as *opportunity*—would be a first step for many persons toward a life free of these harmful addictions.

EXAMPLE: EMMA—SUBSTANCE ABUSE AND CRISIS

Emma started drinking heavily at about age 27. When she was 35, her husband divorced her after repeatedly pleading that she do something about her drinking problem. He also obtained custody of their two children. Emma was sufficiently shocked by this turn of events to give up drinking. She joined Alcoholics Anonymous and remarried at age 37. She hurried into this second marriage primarily because she wanted another child. A year later, her child was born.

A year after that, Emma began drinking again and was threatened with divorce by her second husband. Emma made superficial attempts to stop drinking and began substituting an antianxiety prescription drug when she felt anxious or depressed. Her second husband divorced her 6 months later. This time, Emma retained custody of her child, though it was a close fight.

Emma took a job, was fired, went on welfare assistance, and began spending a lot of time in bars. This time, a friend was there to help. On her friend's urging, Emma finally decided to seek help for her alcohol and tranquilizer dependency. She gave up drinking but continued a heavy use of the antianxiety drug, sometimes taking as many as six a day. Emma was inconsistent in carrying out plans to reorganize her life to include less dependence on drugs and more constructive social outlets.

One day, a neighbor reported to the child protection agency that she believed Emma was neglecting her child and should be investigated. The child protection worker learned that Emma indeed had few social contacts outside the bars and occasionally left her 2-year-old child unattended. Emma was allowed to maintain temporary custody of her child with regular home visits by a caseworker to supervise her parenting activity.

The threat of losing her third child was a sufficient crisis to act as a turning point for Emma. The caseworker urged Emma to seek continued help with her problems from her counselor. Emma finally gave up her dependency on drugs, developed a more satisfying social life, and returned to work. She also made plans for another marriage, this time being more selective in her choice of a partner and less desperately dependent on a man for security.

The crisis of losing her children as a result of chronic dependence on alcohol and drugs led Emma to give up her self-destructive lifestyle. Two divorces resulting from her drug dependency were not enough to make her change. In fact, Emma did not seek available counseling on either of these occasions. She said she was ashamed to ask for help and in any case did not think she could afford it. Other people abusing drugs and alcohol seek help and make changes after other types of crisis: serious financial or job failures, threats of imprisonment, or brushes with death such as delirium tremens (DTs)—a sign of advanced alcoholism—bleeding ulcers, liver damage, or near-fatal suicide attempts.

Emma's case also illustrates the damaging effects of alcoholism on children. According to the National Institute on Alcoholism and Alcohol Abuse, millions of US minors living at home have at least one alcoholic parent. Besides the daily stresses and crises experienced by these children, many become alcohol dependent themselves. High school and college students in the United States engage in binge drinking at alarming rates.

The increasing availability of crisis services and follow-up treatment programs should result in earlier choices toward growth rather than self-destruction for substance-dependent people. There are also increasing numbers of self-help groups for adult children of alcoholics that can be contacted through local Alcoholics Anonymous branches. (See Chapter 3 for the *most serious drug abuse* problem: the overuse of prescription drugs, especially in the absence of 24/7 crisis care and counseling.) M. J. Rogers[3] wrote in 1971: "Drug abuse: Just what the doctor ordered"; unfortunately, this continues unabated decades later.

INTERPLAY BETWEEN CRISIS, FAMILY TROUBLES, AND CHRONIC MENTAL HEALTH PROBLEMS

The story of Ruth illustrates further the complex interplay between acute crisis, abuse, and chronic social problems: beatings as a child, feelings of rejection, a troubled marriage, suicide attempts, depression, death of a husband by suicide, and alcohol dependence. It also highlights how crisis care can be the occasion for a turning point in a chronically troubled life.

EXAMPLE: RUTH—CHILD ABUSE, DIVORCE, AND SELF-DESTRUCTIVE BEHAVIOR

Ruth recalls: "I called the crisis center because I was afraid I'd attempt to take my life again. All my suicide attempts stemmed from feeling rejected, especially by my father. He picked on me and favored my older sister. I couldn't do anything right. Once I stole some money from my mother's purse, so I could buy a gift for my friend (now I think I was trying to buy friendship). My father beat me so that my hands were bleeding; then he made me show my hands to my mother. My mother cried when he beat me, but I guess she was afraid to stop him. When my father was dying, he asked me to forgive him. I said I did, but I guess I didn't, not really.

"I dropped out of school after tenth grade and got a job in a stockroom and later worked as a bookkeeper. I got married when I was nineteen. Our first five years were beautiful. We had three boys. I loved my husband very much and waited on him hand and foot. We bought a home, and he helped finish it. During the second five years, he started changing and got involved with another woman. My family and everyone knew, but I kept denying it. Then he left for about four months. I made a suicide attempt by turning on all the gas. I didn't really want to die; I just wanted him to stop seeing the other woman and come back to me. He came to pick me up at the hospital, and two weeks later I went over to his girlfriend's house and beat her up. I could have gotten in trouble with the law for that, but she didn't press charges.

"After that, we tried to patch things up for about four months, but it didn't work. Then I started seeing other men. We had lots of arguments. I threatened divorce and he threatened to kill himself, but I didn't believe him. One night, he sat in his car and wouldn't come in to go to bed when I asked him. At 7:00 a.m., my oldest son reported finding dad dead in his car. I thought it was my fault. Even today, I still blame myself. His parents also blamed me. My father was still alive then, and he and my mother stood by me. After my husband's death, I made another suicide attempt. I was in and out of the hospital several times, but nothing seemed to help in those days.

"Three years after my first husband's death, I remarried. We argued and fought, and again I felt rejected. When I was afraid of taking an overdose of aspirin, I called the crisis center and was referred to the local crisis and counseling center near my home. I can't say enough good things about how my counselor, Jim, helped me. After all those years of being in and out of hospitals and several suicide attempts, I'm so glad I finally found the help I needed all this time.

"I don't think I'd ever attempt suicide again. I still struggle with the problem of feeling rejected, which I think is the worst thing in the world to go through. Even though I feel I'm on the horizon of something much better, I still have my down days and have to watch that I don't drink too much. But I don't think I'd ever let myself get as down and out as I've been in the past. I've seen that real help is available when I need it."

THE CRISIS OF DEMENTIA, ALZHEIMER'S DISEASE, AND INSTITUTIONAL PLACEMENT

Among acute and chronic medical conditions that portend personal and family crises, one of the most heart-rending is the onset of dementia, usually requiring institutional care in later stages. The complexity of institutional placement and the family's pain and anxiety are exponentially increased in instances of dementia, particularly Alzheimer's disease (AD), especially when the common tendency toward denial is paramount in its early stages. Some refer to AD—the risk of which increases with age—as the cruelest of diseases because serious cognitive impairment ultimately destroys a person's functioning as a whole human being.

Losing one's ability for self-care and managing activities of daily living, while also aware in early stages that it is happening and is beyond one's control, can be a truly terrifying and sometimes life-threatening experience. As one highly educated psychologist tearfully said to her friends during diagnostic workups: "I feel like I'm losing my soul." At a later point when dealing with her anger at having a court-appointed guardian to manage her affairs, she said: "I want to kill him and then myself." While this woman's life was in danger from wandering off in front of running cars, by this time in development of the disease, she in fact would have been incapable of the planning necessary for committing either murder or suicide.

Families of persons with AD should avail themselves of the many support and technical sources needed—in some cases, over years. Also, guidance from a professional geriatric care manager—if available and affordable—typically includes legal and gerontological nursing specialists. The lack of such help increases vulnerability to crisis and adds to the growing evidence of increasing morbidity and mortality rates among family caretakers of a spouse with AD or other dementias.

Nursing staff sensitive to crisis surrounding admission to a nursing care facility—whether for AD or other reasons—are in a key position to prevent some negative outcomes. The newly admitted resident, along with the family, should be provided ample opportunity to express feelings associated with the event. Family members persuaded to be honest with the resident about the situation and not deny reality will feel less guilty and more able to maintain the social contact needed by the resident. Staff should actively reach out to family members, inviting them to participate in planning for their parent's or relative's needs in the nursing care facility. This will greatly relieve the stress experienced by an older person during the crisis of admission and adjustment. It will also reduce staff crises. When families are not included in the planning and have no opportunity to express their own feelings about the placement, they often handle their stress by blaming the nursing staff for poor care. This is a desperate means of managing their own guilt as well as the older person's complaints about the placement.

Besides the crisis of admission, other crises can be prevented when nursing care facilities have these typical services: (1) activity programs in keeping with the age and sociocultural values of the residents, (2) programs involving the residents in outside community events, and (3) special family programs. Unfortunately, the quality of nursing care facilities frequently reflects a society's devaluation of older people. Funding is often inadequate, which prevents employment of sufficient professional staff.[4]

This chapter and its stories underscore the centrality of health for a happy and productive life. It also shows how health care, a major domain of all societies worldwide, is complexly related to other domains—the family, government, the economy, religion, and the arts. When individuals experience serious threats to health and lack the kind of preventive intervention described here, the negative results for the affected individual and his or her family, typically extend to the entire community—for example, in extra costs of chronic illnesses, labor shortages, and tragedies such as suicide and violence toward others. Workers in long-term care facilities (especially nursing assistants) are next after police and firefighters on rates of injury or death on the job.[5]

The systematic inclusion of crisis care across diverse settings is therefore a value to society and all its members that cannot be overstated. Everyone should recognize health care—and one of its major components, crisis care—as a *basic human right*, not just a privilege for only the lucky few.

REFERENCES, FURTHER READING, DISCUSSION GUIDE

REFERENCES
1. The Boston Women's Health Book Collective. (2011 rev.) *Our bodies, ourselves.* New York: Simon & Shuster.
2. Watters, E. (2010). *Crazy like us: The globalization of the American psyche.* New York: Free Press.
3. Rogers, M. J. (1971). Drug abuse: Just what the doctor ordered. *Psychology Today, 5,* 16–24.
4. Melillo, K, & Houde, S. (2011). *Geropsychiatric and mental health nursing* (2nd ed.). Chapters 2 and 3 (pp. 31–51) and Chapters 11, 12, 13, and 14 (pp. 253–334). Sudbury, MA: Jones & Bartlett Learning.
5. Mawn, B., Siqueira, E., Koren, A, Slatin, C., Melillo, K., Pearce, C., & Hoff, L. A. (2010). Health disparities among health care workers. *Qualitative Health Research, 20*(1), 68–80. Thousand Oaks, CA: Sage.

FURTHER READING
Chopra, D. (1990). *Quantum healing: Exploring the frontiers of mind/body medicine.* New York: Bantam Books.
Fadiman, A. (1997). *The spirit catches you and then you fall down.* New York: Farrer, Straus and Giroux.
Gawande, A. (2011, January). The hot spotters: Can we lower medical costs by giving the neediest patients better care? *The New Yorker,* 41–51.
Hoff, L. A., & Morgan, B. (2011). *Psychiatric and mental health essentials in primary care.* London: Routledge.
Sobo, E. J., & Loustaunau, M. O. (2002). *The cultural context of health, illness, and medicine.* (2nd ed.). Santa Barbara, CA: Praeger.
Sontag, S. (1978). *Illness as metaphor.* New York: Farrar, Straus & Giroux.
Weil, A. (2004). *Natural health, natural medicine: The complete guide to wellness.* Boston: Houghton Mifflin.

DISCUSSION GUIDE
1. Recall from your own experience, or that of another, a visit to a primary care provider (PCP) for a medical ailment that followed several months of extraordinary stress (e.g., financial problems, death in the family) and consider these questions: (a) Did you feel comfortable discussing with the PCP the mind/body connections or social facets of your medical problem? (b) If not, what was the reason? Did the PCP not have enough time, or did the PCP seem interested only in the medical ailment and quickly prescribe an antianxiety drug? (c) Depending on the outcome of a clinic visit such as this, would you continue with this PCP or seek out someone else? Why or why not?
2. Think of a friend, family member, or acquaintance who responds to life stressors by dependence on drugs or alcohol. You have observed this on more than one occasion. After reading this chapter, consider how you might approach this person and/or convince him or her to seek professional help.

3. An aging family member often expresses fear of being stricken with Alzheimer's disease and her intention to kill herself before it happens. Although there is yet no cure for this devastating disease, review for yourself and others what dietary and lifestyle measures can aid in the prevention of Alzheimer's.
4. If you or someone you know appears close to crisis or burnout in caring for a chronically ill family member, consider what self-care actions can be helpful in this kind of situation without feeling "guilty" about not doing enough.

CHAPTER 8

Loss of Job, Home, and Financial Security

Coping with accidental and preventable loss of essentials in everyday life

CHAPTER OUTLINE

Threats to Job, Home, and Financial Security   206
Example: Angie—Fear of Success   208
Paid and Unpaid Work   209
Challenges of the Poor and Young Adults Toward Occupational
    Security   211
Work Disruption: From the Local to Global Scene   212
Example: Russell and Jenny Owens—Medical and Marital Problems   214
Retirement Preparation—Anticipated or Forced?   215
Residential Change and Threats to Security at Home   216
Example: Noreen Anderson—Social Isolation   219
Example: A Cambodian Genocide Survivor   220
Homelessness and Vulnerability to Violence   221
Job and Home Loss Following Disaster   224
Critical Incident Stress Debriefing (CISD): Crisis Care Values and
    Cautions   227
Disasters of Human Origins   228
Comparing Disasters From Natural and Human Origins   229
Preventing Posttraumatic Stress Disorder—PTSD   230
Making Meaning out of Loss: Accidental or Intentional Violence   232
Human Resilience and Learning From Disaster   233
Communication and Listening as Emotional Crisis Prevention   236
References, Further Reading, Discussion Guide   239

Basic human needs include success in our ascribed and achieved social roles and a secure, stable dwelling place. Meeting these needs implies the following:

- The ability and opportunity to be creative and productive in a way that is meaningful to us and accepted by others.
- Membership in a supportive community that values our presence and contribution.
- Enough material supplies to maintain self-sufficiency and protection from the elements.

Just as a serious change in health status threatens a person's self-image, so does the ability to be self-supportive. Underscoring the interacting relationship between health, occupational, and general social security, people who rely only on an employer for health insurance may remain in unfulfilling jobs that can literally make them sick. In the United States, losing one's job typically means losing health insurance as well, thus adding to stress, fear, and insecurity about the future. In turn, these additional stressors affect a person's health status and ability to function at precisely the time of greatest need.

When occupation-based stress intersects with domestic demands or turmoil, depression is not uncommon. This includes stress from overwork by people who cannot afford to build regular leisure time into their lives. Persons who occupy multiple roles are typically more resilient than others. But if something goes wrong in the maze of responsibilities, "workaholics" can more easily be disillusioned and plunge into depression, having placed "all their eggs in one basket"—work. Job security means security at home, since housing for most is their major source of social security. An extreme response to job loss is a dismissed employee's violence against or even murder of the employer and others (see Chapter 6, "Violence and Abuse in the Workplace and Forensic Psychiatry").

THREATS TO JOB, HOME, AND FINANCIAL SECURITY

Intertwined hazards around occupational and residential security are increased among persons with a history of mental illness, for victims of violence, and for persons forced out of home and country because of war or ethnic cleansing. Typically, we look forward to the comfort and security of returning home safely after a day's work, a vacation, or a business trip. When threatened at home or work, a person's security can change dramatically by moves from

- Home to street
- A secure job to unemployment lines or poverty

- A sense of self-sufficiency to unexpected dependency
- Financial security to uncertainty about where the next meal is coming from or where the next night will be spent: On someone's couch? In a welfare hotel? A shelter? The mean streets? Another country?

Losing a job and security at home are not only stressful but also can lead to acute crisis without necessary support. People suffering occupational and housing losses need to mourn these painful losses, some of which are life threatening. The expression "going postal" refers to a crisis situation like this: During a national economic recession a postal worker, age 45, father of four children, the only source of family income with a stable record of employment, is given written notice of termination with no discussion. He angrily leaves the worksite, goes home for his gun, returns to the post office, kills the supervisor who fired him, and then kills himself.

This angry worker might not have responded with such violence if more humane personnel and labor relations policies had required a face-to-face discussion before sending such a blunt paper notice—regardless of the reason for abrupt dismissal. Working people need the hope that comes from advocacy, immediate access to crisis care (as in 24-hour hotlines), and social change to alleviate conditions that deprive people of jobs and homes and perpetuate the widening gap between the world's rich and poor.

Promotion, Success, and Economic Security

Promotion and success at work usually are not hazardous or the occasions of crisis. But for some, promotion can be the last straw that could lead to suicide. Such a vulnerable person promoted to a prestigious position may feel incapable of performing as expected in the new role. A promotion with increased responsibility and change in relationships among peers (e.g., resentment by peers of the promoted person's higher rank and pay) can also be a crisis point.

The combination of losing familiar supportive relationships at work and the challenge of unfamiliar work may be too much to handle. A person's vulnerability to crisis in these circumstances is affected by several factors:

1. The general openness of communication in the company or agency
2. The person's ability to discuss questions and fears with a trusted confidant; for example, a worker expressing worries about self-confidence or performance fears that this might jeopardize a promotion
3. The person's perception of self and performance expectations in a given role—especially difficult for perfectionists or young adults looking for a compatible and secure place in the work world.

The Success Neurosis and Gender Roles

A crisis stemming from promotion has also been called the *success neurosis*, especially among persons who view themselves as second-rate or occupy second-best positions. If their work has been primarily that of housewife and mother, they may fear failure and become immobilized when other opportunities arise.

Crises associated with promotion and success are usually "quiet" crises. Typically, workers in this situation are not acutely upset but feel generally anxious and depressed, are bewildered about being depressed, and feel disappointed in not measuring up to their own expectations. Their lack of self-confidence, rigid expectations of themselves, and deep fear of failure may lead to consideration of suicide in the event of actual failure.

Anxiety, depression, and suicidal thoughts may move a person in this kind of crisis to seek help. Usually, several crisis counseling sessions are sufficient for the person to

- Express underlying fears, insecurity, and disappointment with self
- Gain a realistic perspective on his or her abilities
- Grow in self-confidence and self-acceptance
- Use family and friends to discuss feelings and concerns openly rather than viewing such expressions as another failure

EXAMPLE: ANGIE—FEAR OF SUCCESS

Angie, age 37, had been doing volunteer work with the mental health association in her community. One of her special projects was helping handicapped people run a confection stand for local Parks and Recreation Department events. Because of the high quality of her work—which she could only acknowledge self-consciously—her friends urged her to open and manage her own coffeehouse. She finally did so, and the project was a glowing success. Angie suddenly found herself in the limelight, a situation she had not anticipated. She could not believe it would last. After a few months, she began feeling tense and depressed and thought vaguely about suicide. She talked with her physician about her problem and was referred to a psychotherapist for help.

Short-term crisis counseling with someone like Angie may reveal deeper problems of low self-esteem, rigid role expectations, inflexible behavior patterns, and habitual reluctance to communicate feelings of distress. Psychotherapy should be offered and encouraged, as suicide risk may increase if other crisis situations arise. But in addition to crisis counseling, we need to examine the social and economic inequalities that may leave women at greater risk of failing in their career aspirations. For example, executive women (unlike executive men) who want to avoid being derailed from the career ladder typically must jump through two hoops: traditional masculine behavior and traditional feminine behavior. This is a new version of the old adage "Women must be twice as good to get half as far." One consequence of such stress might be an obsession with work, to the detriment of a healthy balance between work and other activities. Although women have made progress in traditionally male-dominated professions—for example, law, medicine, and engineering—they are vulnerable to the same gender-based harassment and abuse as women in traditionally female-dominated professions such as nursing. Finally, despite their high professional status, they shoulder the same dual burden that most women carry: They still do the bulk of unpaid domestic work and child care.

PAID AND UNPAID WORK

Worldwide, in labor statistics jargon, *work* is defined as paid work. In Africa, for example, 60% to 80% of agricultural work is done by women, though it is not included in official labor force counts.

Economist Marilyn Waring[1] traces work-related crises to cultural values and the tradition that men do *public* work and are paid well for it, while women do *private* work and are paid little or not at all. As Waring notes, if women's work "counted," official labor statistics and potentially the entire social landscape could be transformed.

When women do work outside the home, the majority do so in traditionally female jobs, such as nursing, child care, and clerical work. Because most women today work outside the home for economic, psychological, and social survival, the points of stress and potential crises are numerous as long as traditional values prevail. For example, au pair Louise Woodward cared for an infant whose parents were physicians and financially secure. The infant died under her care and she was charged with the infant's death and tried for murder. The internationally publicized trial revealed the persistence of values regarding parenting, gender, and work outside the home. In this case, only the mother worked part-time in order to be more available for parenting; yet it was only the *mother* who was publicly vilified for not setting her career aside so she could be at home full-time and eliminate the need for an au pair.

For many women, the cost of caring is very high and will get higher as the number of seniors and people with AIDS increases, unless men assume more equal responsibility for the caring work of society. Crisis counseling or therapy is indicated for individual men and women struggling with these issues. The long-term results, however, will be limited without more attention to change around gender-based inequalities, as suggested by Sheryl Sandberg[2] and others.

Institutional Barriers to Promotion and Economic Security

Aside from regressive cultural values about men, women, and work, institutional barriers to promotion affect millions of workers, especially ethnic minorities and poor women. Globalization has led to ever-widening gaps between the rich and traditionally disadvantaged groups. These social problems can lead to homelessness, child neglect, marital discord, bitterness, withdrawal from the mainstream of social life, substance abuse, suicide, and violence. The "feminization of poverty" is rooted partly in different results of divorce for women and men: The postdivorce poverty of most women reflects the burden of single parenting and sometimes minimal financial support from the children's father, a situation more pronounced in cases of domestic violence.

Despite some exceptions to this pattern and instances of divorce settlements unfair to men, this situation is dramatized by the fact that within a year of divorce, the standard of living for most women decreases significantly and for men it increases. Racial minorities comprise the largest percentage of poor women and children. Labor statistics show that women with children in the United States still earn less than men doing comparable jobs despite the Equal Pay Act passed in 1965. Offering psychotherapy or crisis counseling alone for disadvantaged workers without job training, day care, and advocacy for adequate housing misrepresents the social and cultural origins of work-related hazards traceable to race, class, and gender bias in the workplace. Even many in the business community are recognizing that continued wage disparities hurt not only the individuals affected but also business as a whole.

In sum, women probably will not achieve equality in the paid workforce until men do an equal share of society's unpaid—but nevertheless very necessary—work. Statistics compiled for the 1985 United Nations Decade for Women Conference in Nairobi, Kenya, revealed that women do two thirds of the world's work (not counting unpaid child care), earn one tenth of the world's income, and own less than one hundredth of the world's property.

One serious, even damaging result of these inequalities is the intergenerational welfare dependency for some recipients. Women's work in rearing children alone, often following abuse and because some divorced fathers do not pay child support, is not ideal either for families or the larger community. The related matter of teen pregnancy is not just a racial minority issue; it also reflects poverty and the increasing unwillingness of teens to defer sexual activity, an issue that crosses racial boundaries.

According to a study by the Educational Testing Service, most welfare recipients lack the education and training needed to escape poverty, but work-first programs generally do not provide such training. Another reason for prolonged welfare dependency in the United States is the lack of affordable child care for poor mothers, while the role of fathers in parenting is virtually unchanged from traditional patterns. As Robert Kuttner[3] asks, "When was the last time you read an article about the stresses of being a working father?" But when fathers do their share in child care, they often suffer more negative repercussions than women do in the workplace, thereby reinforcing the traditional value that child care is really just "women's work."

The Louise Woodward example reveals the perverse irony or double standard regarding women's work and welfare reform: The mother, a physician with a comfortable income from her own and her husband's professional work, is expected to stay home full-time to ensure proper child care; whereas poor mothers—many on welfare because of abuse—are expected to work outside the home whether or not child care is available. The hazards of these practices for the education and healthy development of children are great. As pioneer child and family advocate Jonathan Kozol[4] notes: This neglect of the nation's greatest resource—its children—means that future generations will pay the ultimate price. A similar double standard shows up in other work-related policies, for example, little organized effort to reform policies of tax credits to corporations that expand to cheap labor markets such as Bangladesh; subsidies to wealthy agribusiness originally intended for small farmers; tax-supported outlays to sports clubs and their wealthy players; tax rebates on mortgages for those lucky enough to own a home; and so forth.

CHALLENGES OF THE POOR AND YOUNG ADULTS TOWARD OCCUPATIONAL SECURITY

Despite the grim results of some regressive US social policies affecting children, youth, and the society's communal health, there are some very effective, nonpunitive welfare reform efforts in the United States. In Wyoming, for example, the 65% reduction in its welfare caseload is the result of a people-to-people small-town approach and caseworkers offering support instead of threat. Caseloads were reduced, and guidelines replaced rigid rules. Recipients are assured of continued benefits so long as they actively pursue a job, classes in preparing for a job, and opportunities for job training with the aim of "work eventually" instead of "work first."

This issue of welfare and *workfare* is especially urgent because of its connection to the hopelessness and apathy of chronically poor people. When the usually booming US economy takes a downturn, groups at the economic bottom who are mostly untouched during the "good times" are even worse off in the "bad times." A major reason for their fate through both boom and bust economic cycles is that their education in many substandard schools has not prepared them to command a living-wage job in the era of high technology and a globalized economy. The significant dropout rates in US high schools exacerbates risks for future occupational security.

This situation may only worsen without progress toward equality of educational advantage, especially in large inner-city school systems, and where poverty is rampant, as on American Indian reservations. In such a climate, despair and violence flourish. Perhaps in no instance is the link between personal crisis and socioeconomic and cultural factors more dramatically illustrated. The tandem approach to prevent violence (see Chapter 6) applies here: Assist individuals through traumatic life events like joblessness and unemployment (often based on race and class status), *hold them accountable for violence* and child supervision, and *simultaneously* engage them and others to address the roots of their plight (see Crisis Paradigm, Chapter 1, Fig. 1.1, Box 3).

Young people's transition to adulthood and economic self-sufficiency is more difficult and complicated than in the past. Traditionally, the launch into responsible adulthood was through

- mastering a trade or studying for a profession,
- assuming direction of a family business,
- committing to a life partner and raising a family, or
- in other ways contributing to societal needs.

Those broad patterns still hold for most. But moving from childhood to adulthood is now a more protracted, difficult, and complex mixture of continuing dependency on parents stretching into the twenties and beyond for financial help and a place to live between jobs. Yet not all parents (e.g., the "sandwich" generation caring for parents and securing their own retirement security) have the resources to offer these supports. Still others face even greater demands because their children have physical, mental, or behavioral problems.

Following the 1992 Los Angeles riots, Bondi Gabrel, an ethnic minority owner of an apartment complex in that riot-torn community, could have abandoned his damaged building. Instead, he *employed* gang members and provided leadership options and a vision of another lifestyle. So instead of vandalizing property, gang members were paid to guard it. When chosen as *person of the week* by a national television network, Mr. Gabrel said, "This is what happens when you invest in people.... We haven't asked for enough." This example shows that the death and life of an urban neighborhood depend on multifaceted approaches that should be widely replicated.

WORK DISRUPTION: FROM THE LOCAL TO GLOBAL SCENE

Just as promotion, success, or disadvantaged status can be a source of crisis or threat to health, so can disruption or change in work role, especially for a person accustomed to a lifetime of job security. The depression of inner-city neighborhoods is connected to global economic changes and the widespread loss of manufacturing jobs, which had been the mainstay of security for many who are now desperate.

Ethnic minority and immigrant groups are the most affected by the loss of US manufacturing jobs, many of which have been transferred to poor countries with cheaper labor and looser laws protecting both workers and the environment. Many of these workers have little choice except for low-paying service jobs with few benefits and little chance of advancement. Globally, the gap between rich and poor is widening, with reports of exploited and cheaply paid workers (mostly very young women escaping rural poverty) in repetitive and grueling manufacturing jobs. These conditions hark back to conditions over a century ago in the Merrimack Valley cotton mills of Massachusetts and other New England states. These mills thrived off cotton extracted by Southern slave labor and heralded beginnings of the American industrial revolution.

Western society's attitude toward work, especially in the United States, includes a tendency to value and respect people in proportion to how much money they earn and social status derived from earnings, as in the embedded cultural value, "You're worth what you earn." This value system helps fuel welfare reform debate and the suspicion by the "haves" that the "have-nots" are responsible for their misfortune and could remedy it if they simply tried harder. Such judgments do not account for the complex relationship between most unemployment situations and either global economics or discrimination based on race, gender, age, disability, or ill health. Usually, unemployed or underemployed persons in a changing economy are deeply regretful of their position and struggle continually to correct it. These complexities and troubles are even more serious among recent immigrants, many of whom have few rights and legal protections and often live in fear of deportation if they make their plight known, or if undocumented, are subject to government raids. Unemployment, then—or the threat of it—whether by firing, layoff, or because of a personal problem like illness, is frequently the occasion of emotional crisis, including violent responses like suicide or murder. While unemployed people must act on their misfortune, they will be much more empowered to do so if not blamed for their plight.

Regardless of the reasons, a person in crisis because of unemployment usually needs a great deal of support. If unemployment originates from personal sources, social support and individual crisis intervention are indicated. However, if someone is unemployed because of economic recession or discrimination, he or she can avoid feeling hopeless and powerless if help is available from groups devoted to changing the underlying sources of work disruption. This includes policy changes that would prevent corporations—primarily from profit motives—from simply closing US plants, laying off hundreds of employees, and moving to a country where labor is cheaper without consideration of the workers who have built their lives around the company. In Germany, for example, workers in an automobile manufacturing plant decided on a 4-day workweek so that *none* lost their jobs. Routine protests during meetings of the World Trade Organization, the World Bank, the International Monetary Fund, and the Organization of American States suggest a new era of social change as activists clash with police to demonstrate for fairness to workers and for environmental protection in the face of global trade policies and agreements.

For most of us, our success hinges on meaningful work that is personally satisfying and valued by the community. For example, a 55-year-old man in a middle-management position forced into premature retirement may begin to drink or attempt suicide in response to the crisis of job disruption. These and other work-related crises are within the common province of personnel directors, occupational physicians and nurses, or anyone the person turns to in distress.

EXAMPLE: RUSSELL AND JENNY OWENS—MEDICAL AND MARITAL PROBLEMS

Russell Owens, age 52, was a civil engineer employed for 20 years as a research consultant in a large industrial corporation. When he lost his job because of a surplus of engineers with his qualifications, he tried without success to find other employment, even at lower pay. Family financial needs forced his wife, Jenny, age 47, to seek full-time employment as a biology instructor; she had previously been employed only part-time. Jenny was grateful for this opportunity to advance herself professionally. She always regretted the fact that she had never tried to excel at a job. Gradually, Jenny became resentful of having to support herself, her husband, and their 16-year-old daughter, Gwen, in addition to assuming major responsibility for household tasks. Although Russell did some of the housework in addition to running errands and handling emergencies, he sensed that his work was not up to Jenny's expectations. This was very stressful for Russell, adding pain in his marital relationship beyond the sense of failure and inadequacy he already felt from his job loss.

Russell also found it difficult to follow Jenny's advice to seek help with his depression and increasing dependence on alcohol. The strain in their marital relationship increased. Jenny eventually divorced Russell, and he committed suicide.

This tragic example highlights the importance of preventive intervention. Russell's drinking problem and eventual suicide might have been avoided if immediate help had been available to him at the crisis points of job loss and threat of divorce. Counseling might also have resulted in a constructive resolution of Jenny's resentment of Russell concerning the housework.

Rural and Urban Occupational Transitions

Similar dynamics are apparent in the farm and fishing occupations. These workers face not only a threat to their source of livelihood but also to their way of life. Many of these crises originate in policies favoring unbridled corporate accumulations and profits at the expense of individual farm families. For example, federal price supports for farm products are cut back because of a "surplus." Yet in New England, where hundreds of Vermont dairy families have been driven off their farms, there is no milk surplus. Rather, the large amounts of milk at issue are from huge corporate farms in California.

It is ironic that in a country of immigrants who fled Europe and prized the opportunity to earn an honest living on the land, people are now in crisis because public policy favors government subsidies to large agribusiness rather than small farmers. No doubt the suicides, alcoholism, violence, and family conflicts arising from these policies will continue unless grassroots efforts and public policy reverse the conditions causing so much pain and despair among the nation's rural citizens, for example, Farm Aid Rural Management in Bismarck, North Dakota, and the Kitchen Table Alliance in Ontario. These groups have offered support, advocacy, crisis prevention, and referral for distressed workers and their families.

Although the farm and fishing crisis in North America has abated, similar disruption of a way of life is now occurring in fishing communities worldwide. In poor countries, millions of rural dwellers flock to shantytowns near water, only to continue their grim struggle for survival, often with additional threats of violence in crowded slums or death from tidal waves, as in the Southeast Asian tsunami. Prevention of suicide, violence, and substance abuse in these communities depends on government and international agencies attention to the roots of this work issue and its long-term dangers.

RETIREMENT PREPARATION—ANTICIPATED OR FORCED?

Some people look forward to retirement. Others dread it. For many people, retirement signifies loss of status, a reduced standard of living, and a feeling of being discarded by society—especially if one is forced to retire early due to illness or other disability. Fortunately, retirement patterns are changing as more older persons consider retirement as the continuation, not the end, of a fulfilling life.

Attitudes toward retirement and whether it is pleasant or an occasion of crisis depend on the situation retired *to* and one's lifestyle. Here are key questions we can ask about ourselves and those who may be at risk around retirement:

1. Does the retiree have satisfying interests or hobbies outside of work? If work has not been balanced with other life issues, preretirement planning is very important for an overworked person.
2. Does the person have a special retirement project in mind, such as a literature class, carpentry, or cooking? For people of means, Road Scholar offers many such programs.
3. Does the person have a safe and comfortable place to live? This is highly influenced by the job issues already noted.

4. Does the person have enough retirement income to manage without excessive dependence?
5. Is the person in reasonably good health and able to manage without hardship?
6. Has the person been well adjusted socially and emotionally before retirement?

Even if a retired person's circumstances are favorable in these areas, retirement can still be stressful. We live in a youth-oriented society, and retirement signals that one is nearing old age; after that, death approaches.

For many, retirement is not an occasion for crisis. They may be self-employed and simply keep working at perhaps a reduced pace with a healthy attitude toward life in each development phase, including old age. One view of the life cycle suggests three phases: *learning, earning, and returning*. So instead of just retiring, we have an opportunity to return wisdom and other values to society and to have something returned to us after years of learning, earning, and caring for others.

Crisis-prone retirees should have the assistance offered to anyone experiencing a loss. They need the opportunity to grieve the loss of their former status, explore new ways of feeling useful, and eventually accept their changed roles.

RESIDENTIAL CHANGE AND THREATS TO SECURITY AT HOME

Moves across country or to a different continent require leaving familiar surroundings and friends for a place with many unknowns. Even though someone in transit may have many problems at home, at least he or she knows what the problems are. Pulling up stakes and starting over can be an exciting venture, an occasion for joy and gaining a new lease on life, or a source of deep distress and an occasion for crisis. On scales ranking life stressors, moving ranks right after death of a loved one for stress level.

Anticipated Moves

Consider the young woman who grew up in the country and moves to the city for the first time. She asks herself, Will I find a job? Will I be able to make friends? Will I be unbearably lonely? Will I be safe? Or the career person looking for opportunities wonders, Will things be any better there? How will I manage not seeing my family and friends very often? And last, consider the war refugee or immigrant, who worries, How will those foreigners accept me? Will I be able to learn the language so I can get along? Who will help me if things go wrong? What if I want to come back and don't have the money? These questions are more urgent for some would-be immigrants, as nations tighten their borders and entry rules for people intending no harm, but only seeking a job and better life for themselves and their children.

These are a few of the many questions and potential problems faced by people who hope a move will improve their situation. Even so, moving typically is a very stressful occasion. It takes courage to leave familiar territory, even when the move would free one from many negative situations. So no matter what motivated the move, and despite hoping for better things to come, typical during this transition state is a sense of loss—of close associations with friends or relatives and the security and familiarity of place—even if moving to much better circumstances. The feeling of loss might even include depression and perhaps feelings of guilt about leaving friends and relatives. Recognizing and expressing these feelings, and keeping an open relationship with friends left behind, can be helpful in preventing a moving-related crisis and free one up to enjoy new opportunities.

People who look forward to a move are vulnerable to other crises. Once at their destination, the situation may not work out as anticipated: The new job may be less enjoyable than the old one; the escape from a violent city to a farm may seem less secure than expected; new friends may be hard to find; and envisioned job opportunities may not exist.

Social isolation and the inability to establish and maintain satisfying social attachments in a new environment can leave a person vulnerable to crises and even suicide. Elderly people, for example, who move to a group residential setting have a much improved chance of adjusting well to the change and perceiving it as a challenge if (1) they had a choice in relocation, (2) relocation was predictable and understandable within their meaning system, and (3) they received necessary social support. In the Co- Housing movement, diversity by age is an important goal, so they reserve some units (for example, five households out of twenty-five) for persons 55 and older. A planned move of this sort for people who dread living in housing complexes only for old people could do much to avoid a crisis during this major life transition.

Unanticipated Moves

The potential for crisis is even greater for those who do not want to move but are forced to. For example:

- The family uprooted to an unknown place because of a job transfer
- Inner-city dwellers—especially older people—dislocated because of urban renewal and being priced out of the housing market
- Victims of disaster moving from a destroyed community
- People evicted because of unpaid rent
- Mentally ill patients discharged to the community without adequate shelter and social support
- Abused women and their children who are forced to leave their homes to avoid beatings or death

- Political or war refugees who must leave their homelands
- Migrant farm workers who must move each year in the hope of earning a marginal subsistence

Refugees

Globally, refugees typically lose family members and property, and face dramatic cultural differences, tripled social burdens, or isolation. Thousands of teenagers either have no home "safety net," run away from home, or are simply "on the move." Some young people run away because of physical or sexual abuse, or because they have come out as gay, lesbian, bisexual, or transgendered and are rejected by their families. Often they lack housing, food, and money; are exploited sexually or feel forced into prostitution; may succumb to substance abuse; and in extreme cases are killed by police for petty stealing and vagrancy.

War refugees who are crowded into camps in neighboring countries face similar hazards—unsanitary conditions, indifference, brutality, and even rape by soldiers and officials. As if these prices of civil and ethnic strife were not enough, some refugees face grim prospects for immigration, depending on race and political considerations of a prospective host country. In the United States, for example, these hazards can be traced to immigration quotas negotiated between Congress and the Immigration and Naturalization Service. International debates and advocacy continue in an effort to protect vulnerable refugees fleeing from war or persecution.

Refugees also include groups who are relocated by their own governments. Some of the most dramatic historic examples of such forced relocation and its long-term damaging effects are the destruction of Boston's West End in the 1950s and the 1953 dispatching of 85 Inuit people from northern Quebec to the High Arctic. These families were wrenched apart and endured extreme hardship and deprivation while still seeking justice, as are South Africans after apartheid. Finally, ordinary travelers en route from one place to another lose money or belongings or are attacked.

Despite its crisis potential, moving can also be an occasion for growth through success in facing new challenges. Although highly mobile families may have fewer deep friendships, the family unit may feel closer and stronger through successful coping in diverse circumstances. Counseling people with emotional problems related to relocation typically includes four phases in coping with a move: (1) decision making—the less a person contributes to the decision, the more potential for trouble; (2) preparation—mastering the many details preceding a move; (3) separation from the old community—including acceptance of the sadness and loss involved; and (4) reinvestment—through engagement in the new community. These phases are akin to grief work and the rites of passage (see Chapters 3 and 9).

EXAMPLE: NOREEN ANDERSON—SOCIAL ISOLATION

Noreen Anderson, age 61, was confined to her apartment with a serious muscle disease. She was forced to retire at age 58 and had felt lonely and isolated since then. She did not have family in the area but did have many friends. However, they gradually stopped visiting her after she had been confined for a year. Now her apartment building was being converted to condominiums that she could not afford. Everyone in the building had moved out except Noreen, who was unable to move without help. Fortunately, Noreen's phone was not disconnected. She called various social service agencies for help and was finally referred to a local crisis center.

An outreach crisis counselor went to Noreen's apartment. She expedited an application through a federal housing agency supporting Noreen's move to a senior citizens' housing project. The counselor also engaged an interfaith volunteer agency to help Noreen pack and processed a request for immediate physical supplies through Catholic Charities. Noreen was grateful for the help she received after her several desperate telephone calls, but by this time she was depressed and suicidal. The crisis counselor saw her in her new apartment in the senior citizens' housing project for several counseling sessions. She helped Noreen get in touch with old friends again and encouraged regular visits with the friends. A number of Retired Senior Citizen Volunteers also visited Noreen, which helped relieve her isolation and loneliness. Noreen was no longer suicidal at the termination of the counseling sessions.

International Institute and Other Support of Refugees

Crisis hotlines, agencies like the International Institute and Travelers Aid in all major cities and airports, and easy clinic access in one's new country or community can do much to support immigrants, refugees, and stranded youth who are upset, fearful, or at risk of suicide or violent attack.

The International Institute and special refugee groups are pivotal in helping people in crisis related to immigration. The institute's unique contribution is crisis work with refugees and immigrants who do not know the local language. Inability to speak a country's language can be the source of acute crises related to housing, employment, health, welfare, and legal matters. Multilingual Institute workers assist refugees and immigrants in these essential life areas. Not knowing the local language can even result in mistaken arrest of a refugee as the confused person anxiously tries to find housing, transportation, and other services in an unfamiliar place.

There is an International Institute or comparable agency in nearly all metropolitan areas, where most refugees and immigrants first settle. Smooth referrals for health and social service are critical for preventing crises among immigrants.

The language crisis is so acute for some immigrants that they may be mistakenly judged psychotic and taken to a mental hospital, or they may have to rely inappropriately on their own children for translation. Intervention by a multilingual person is a critical part of care in such cases. Unfortunately, this important social service agency has low visibility in the community and may not be linked adequately with 24-hour crisis services. Such linkages should be routine as health and crisis services become more comprehensive and cosmopolitan.

The actual and potential crises of immigrants and refugees have become more visible as ethnic conflict and international tensions have grown. People persecuted or sought out for their public protest against injustice seek refuge and political asylum in friendly countries with greater frequency. Cooperation between private and public agencies for these people is paramount to avoid unnecessary distress and crisis. In addition to legal, housing, language, and immediate survival issues, refugees typically experience the emotional pain of losing their homeland. No matter how they may have been treated, most of us have a strong attachment to our country of birth. Whether this bond is broken voluntarily or by threat to life, refugees need compassionate listeners as they mourn their loss and find substitutes for what was left behind. They also should not have to endure prolonged detention in substandard facilities, which the United Nations defines as a denial of basic human rights.

EXAMPLE: A CAMBODIAN GENOCIDE SURVIVOR

Sarong Ty, age 57, is an immigrant living in Massachusetts. Ms. Sarong was seen in a local Cambodian-directed multiservice Health Center for her trouble with insomnia, secondary to intrusive thoughts and nightmares. As a survivor of the Cambodian genocide, she arrived in the United States with her children and settled in a Cambodian immigrant community in Massachusetts.

Sarong was the oldest of five girls born to farmers in a remote province of Cambodia. She was 31 when the Khmer Rouge overthrew the Lon Nol government in Cambodia. She and her family lived in a refugee camp for 6 years. Her father died of malaria in 1975; her mother died of starvation more than a decade later. Married at age 20, Sarong's husband had left her for another woman while in the refugee camp. They had eight children, two of whom are incarcerated in Massachusetts for street crime and domestic violence. As sole provider of her eight children, Sarong is unemployed, receives public welfare assistance, and is now raising her 7-year-old grandson whose mother is involved with the drug culture.

Sarong's chief complaint on intake at the Community Health Center was "not having enough money to pay for food, rent, and getting by month to month." At 77 pounds, she is frail and reports eating one meal a day consisting mostly of rice. Her mood was sad, lonely, and angry. She denied alcohol or drug use in past or present, but she attended the Addiction Treatment Program for socialization and information about how to protect her grandson from drugs and to help her daughter-in-law. Sarong has classic symptoms of post traumatic stress disorder (PTSD) and grieves the loss of her country and extended family. To ease her sorrow, she uses the traditional healing method of coining. She is illiterate in her own language and practices Buddhist meditation.

Let us consider what Sarong has in common with others experiencing crisis and what is unique about her situation. First, the *commonalities*:

1. Sarong's pain of loss (one of the most common themes of emotional crisis)—loss of her family, country, and husband
2. The physical health and social consequences of abuse and torture, in her case by the Khmer Rouge, and Sarong's relocation and extra parenting burden in an adopted new country
3. The similarities of her plight with Nazi Holocaust, Bosnian, Rwandan, Kenyan, and Sudanese survivors of genocide, massacres, and ethnic cleansing
4. Intergenerational and cross-cultural conflict in child-rearing practice, minus a marital partner and usual social supports for child rearing
5. Sarong's parenting of grandchildren because her adult children are incarcerated or suffering from addiction or other disabilities

What is *unique* about Sarong's experience? And what are the implications for practice? Sarong's suffering epitomizes the depth of psychological trauma and its impact on physical health as a survivor of torture and genocide by the government of one's own country. (This is unique among Western-raised people in crisis, but not among similar survivors of torture and ethnic cleansing, and refugees fleeing from war-torn countries springing from age-old religious and interethnic strife.) A lesson from Sarong's suffering is awareness that PTSD results from traumatic events that are well beyond the range of more ordinary or "normal" life crises, or because timely crisis care and social support were lacking at the time of the initial traumatic experience (see "Preventing Post Traumatic Stress Disorder").

One way that refugees and immigrants cope with their loss is to preserve their customs, art, language, ritual celebrations, and food habits. These practices provide immigrants with the security that comes from association with their familiar cultural heritage. Sensitivity of neighbors and agency personnel to immigrants' cultural values can go a long way in helping refugees feel at home. In contrast, members of host countries need particular sensitivity regarding a practice like female genital mutilation, which some immigrants wish to continue (see Chapter 5 regarding this cultural issue and what the World Health Organization defines as a human rights violation).

HOMELESSNESS AND VULNERABILITY TO VIOLENCE

Some people live in cardboard boxes, ride the subway all night long, or stay in doorways of public buildings until they are asked or ordered by police to move. Some sleep on steel grates to catch steam heat from below. Some abused women and their children move from shelter to shelter, staying the limit at each because battering may not fit the city's criteria of eligibility for emergency housing; one mother of three finally bought a tent and camped in a city park.

Besides having no secure place to stay, homeless people are frequent victims of rape or robbery of their few possessions; homeless youth are often victims of child prostitution; among the elderly homeless, some are disabled, some are deaf or blind, and some have symptoms of Alzheimer's disease. Contrary to popular perception, a good percentage of homeless persons hold low-paying jobs that do not provide enough income to pay inflated rental prices. Many are victims of eviction when apartments are converted to condominiums for upwardly mobile, mostly white professionals. At no time since the Great Depression have homeless people represented such a cross-section of a wealthy Western society. The plight of homelessness in the United States was starkly visible in New Orleans after Hurricane Katrina. Overnight, working men and women—never before without a roof over their heads—found themselves sleeping under the stars in Depression-era conditions while political and business leaders squabbled with nonprofit agencies about housing for the poor and disabled who suffered the greatest impact.

Among industrialized nations, the most visible and the highest numbers of homeless people are in the United States. As the problem continues over decades, many worry that homelessness will become institutionalized as a permanent feature of social life. How can we explain homelessness in a country as wealthy as the United States? Several factors contribute to the crisis of homelessness and the health and social problems that follow: (1) the growing inequalities between rich and poor; (2) in the United States, the lack of a national health program that includes sufficient coverage for crisis and mental health services; and (3) the continuing bias against mentally ill persons and the resulting inadequate transitional housing and support services to prevent homelessness.

But the problem is by no means limited to the United States. Worldwide recession and the continuing stigma of mental illness occur cross-culturally, as Ethan Watters[4] writes in *Crazy Like Us*. Perhaps most alarming of all is the fact that homeless people include families with children. For these families, getting to work or school is a maze of buses and subway rides, taking as long as 2 hours one way, while they await their turn for transfer from temporary housing in a motel to placement in affordable housing that is all too scarce.

Homelessness strips people of their self-respect, denies them basic human rights, and blights the future of a nation's greatest resource: children. The crisis of homelessness in the United States is due primarily to the severe cuts in federal funds to build or rehabilitate low-income housing and (in some communities) to an overpriced real estate market that may be free of obligation to include low- and moderate-income housing in their building ventures.

Skyrocketing housing costs in cities like New York, San Francisco, London, and Boston have also resulted in the average family in smaller cities spending as much as two thirds of their income on housing. This trend contrasts sharply to the former US bank affordability standard of around 35% of income for housing. Child and family advocate Jonathan Kozol[5] found from his months with homeless people in one of New York's welfare hotels that the city spends $1,900 per month for a family of four—basically, supporting enormous profits for a modernized poorhouse. Kozol's informants wondered why so much money was spent on such hotels rather than designated for rent support in regular housing. Unfortunately, questions regarding basic human rights and fair distribution of resources are more relevant than ever.

These problems are even more dramatic for mentally ill persons, as Pete Earley[6] writes about the saga of his son who landed in prison for lack of available treatment for bipolar disorder—basically, a failed deinstitutionalization program and inadequate community planning.

It would seem a foregone conclusion that what homeless people need most is a home—a hallmark of the American dream. Yet despite the crisis of affordable housing in large US cities, major responses to this crisis have been biomedically focused (that is, case management and "treatment" of the "disordered" homeless). Rather, homelessness is primarily a *social* problem with enormous potential for acute crisis. It requires a policy response that would address inequality around jobs and housing that fuels homelessness. Progress on the homeless crisis demands a "both-and," not "either-or" approach—especially around the pattern of discharging psychiatric patients to shelters or the street because of inadequate mental health services (see "revolving door" in Chapter 1).

One of the most tragic examples of failing to address the problems fueling homelessness is the 1999 deaths of six firefighters in Worcester, Massachusetts. Significantly, these deaths occurred from the firefighters' attempt to *rescue a homeless couple living in an abandoned warehouse.* The homeless young couple, expecting a child, were charged with manslaughter and prosecuted because they failed to report the fire that started from their tipped-over candle during a domestic fight. As the Crisis Paradigm shows, a crisis deeply rooted in social problems demands sociopolitical response in addition to rescue of individuals in danger.

How then can we turn the tide of the grave threat to the basic need for secure housing? What do we do for people who have no place to sleep or who are at risk of dying from exposure to the elements despite affluence all around them in the richest country in the world? People often react with embarrassment or discomfort around a homeless person who appears on a doorstep or begs for spare change. But regardless of how charitably people respond to individual appeals for help, the crisis of homelessness in a humane, democratic society entails more than goodwill or charity. Although there is still a tendency to blame the victim, as Ryan's[7] classic book expounds, people do not choose to be poor or homeless.

Increasingly, grassroots groups and health and governmental agencies are trying to interrupt the vicious cycle of individuals and families forced to navigate between the streets and homeless shelters. Primary prevention addresses not only the harmful health effects of inadequate housing but also the societal and ethical responsibility to meet the shelter needs of everyone, including the most disadvantaged. Attorney Bret Thiele[8] of the Center on Housing rights and Evictions (COHRE) in Geneva, Switzerland notes, that housing rights are embedded in international law and various UN Conventions such as the Universal Declaration of Human Rights and the Convention on the Rights of the Child.

Another hopeful and empowering example of moving beyond shelter and stopgap measures is the first federally funded farm in Cape Cod, Massachusetts. The farm is staffed by residents with histories of chronic homelessness. Each has a private room with shared dining and bathroom facilities—reminiscent of the single-room-occupancy living quarters that were plentiful in most cities before gentrification and cutbacks in government housing assistance. Residents must work 35 hours per week at the farm or in neighboring businesses, pay about 25% of their income to rent, commit to teaching newly acquired skills to at least one new arrival, try to get a high school diploma if they do not have one, and abide by the strict rules of no alcohol or drugs.

At the national level, a similar approach called "Housing First" is gathering momentum across the usually partisan ideological landscape. It is aimed at *ending* homelessness, not merely managing it. A 1999 Congress endorsed the idea by requiring that HUD (US Department of Housing and Urban Development) allocate at least one third of its homelessness funding toward permanent housing for chronically homeless and disabled persons.

JOB AND HOME LOSS FOLLOWING DISASTER

The basics of crisis care from other losses and in earlier chapters apply to all victim-survivors of disaster—whether from natural or human origins

Help During Impact, Recoil, and Postrauma Phases

Experience with victim-survivors of disaster laid the foundation for crisis care following other stressful life events: the impact, recoil, and posttrauma phases. Table 8.1 illustrates the kind of help needed and who is best suited to offer it during these phases of a disaster; it also suggests the possible outcomes for victim-survivors if help is not available in each of the three phases.

Table 8.1 ASSISTANCE DURING THREE PHASES OF NATURAL DISASTER

	Help Needed	Help Provided by	Possible Outcome If Help Unavailable
Phase I: Impact	Information on source and degree of danger Escape and rescue from immediate source of danger	Communication network: radio, TV, public address system Community rescue resources: police and fire departments, Red Cross, National Guard	Physical injury or death
Phase II: Recoil	Shelter, food, drink, clothing, medical care	Red Cross Salvation Army Voluntary agencies such as colleges to be converted to mass shelters Local health and welfare agencies Mental health and social service agencies skilled in crisis intervention Pastoral counselors State and federal assistance for all of the above services	Physical injury Delayed grief reactions Later emotional or mental disturbance
Phase III: Posttrauma	Physical reconstruction Social reestablishment Psychological support concerning aftereffects of the event itself; bereavement counseling concerning loss of loved ones, home, and personal property	State and federal resources for physical reconstruction Social welfare agencies Crisis and mental health services Pastoral counselors	Financial hardship Social instability Long-lasting mental, emotional, or physical health problems

Crisis Intervention and Follow-Up Service

Crisis care of disaster survivors should be embedded in the natural context of practical problem solving, not in a formal counseling framework, or a quick CISD formula (see later). During and after a disaster, people need an opportunity to

- Share the experience at their own pace and express their feelings of fear, panic, loss, and grief
- Become fully aware and accepting of what has happened to them
- Resume activity and begin reconstructing their lives with the social, physical, and emotional resources available

Assisting victims through the crisis, we should

- Listen with concern and empathy; ease the way for the victims to tell their tragic story, weep, and express feelings of anger, loss, frustration, and despair
- Help survivors accept the reality of what has happened a little bit at a time—for example, simply staying with them during the initial stages of shock and denial, accompanying them to the scene of the tragedy, and offering support when they are faced with the full impact of their loss
- Assist victims in making contact with relatives, friends, and other resources needed to begin the process of social and physical reconstruction—for example, make telephone calls to locate relatives, accompany them to apply for financial aid, and provide information about social and mental health agencies for follow-up services

In group settings where large numbers are housed and offered emergency care, panic-stricken survivors should be separated from the rest and given individual attention to avoid the contagion of panic reactions. Assigning these survivors simple, physical tasks helps them move toward constructive action. Anything that helps victims feel valued as individuals is important. But despite massive efforts to help disaster survivors, among some who live through the experience, lifelong emotional scars may be left—depending on age, predisaster emotional stability, and so forth. Crisis and bereavement counseling can at least reduce some negative effects and should be available to all victims (see Chapter 3).

Typically, a disaster-struck community cannot meet all of the physical, social, and emotional needs of disaster victims. Wide recognition of this fact is evident in the outpouring of volunteer and government assistance to stricken communities. In most disasters, the need is too great for the local community to act alone, especially because some of its own human service workers (police officers, nurses, clergy, and counselors) will themselves be among the disaster victims. Since the United Nations declared the 1990s as the International Decade for Natural Disaster Reduction, many nations have established standard recovery and assistance programs (for example, in the United States, Federal Emergency Management Assistance, or FEMA) in disaster-struck communities, although these government programs vary according to a country's wealth.

As in other crisis situations, individual responses and the needs of natural disaster victims vary according to psychological, economic, and social circumstances. Some natural disaster victims interpret these tragedies as acts of God, or fate, or bad luck—and thus beyond anyone's control. Emotional coping can then occur through grief work, followed by action to rebuild lives. Survivors' interpretation of these crises as *natural and beyond their control* is the basis for their hope despite enormous suffering. It is the reason they can rise from the rubble and begin a new life; it lets them move beyond the emotional pain and gain new strength from the experience. This element of disaster response and recovery constitutes the *greatest distinction* between natural disasters and those occurring from human indifference, neglect, or design.

CRITICAL INCIDENT STRESS DEBRIEFING (CISD): CRISIS CARE VALUES AND CAUTIONS

Firefighters, police, and health professionals have long engaged in "debriefing" with colleagues following critical events such as suicide or murder to ascertain success, failure, and what can be learned for future practice. Now this routine assessment has evolved for disaster survivors into a structured critical incident stress debriefing (CISD). A cautionary note here is for every disaster survivor who may feel pressured into such ritualized group work. This is because in normal grief work and crisis care after loss, it is important not to pathologize what is essentially a normal response to an event typically beyond the range most people experience. Especially important here is that some survivors might interpret structured debriefing as a sign they are going crazy.

In contrast to the basics of crisis care long-known from crisis theory pioneers like Tyhurst,[9] Caplan,[10] and others (see Chapter 1), the highly ritualized CISD process casts the *basics of crisis care* into a very formal structure to elicit feelings following serious trauma. Formally trained psychotherapists and specialists in victim care know about the potential damage of prematurely eliciting expression of deep psychological trauma without appropriate follow-up and support. Some survivors may not want to divulge to a well-intentioned stranger their feelings of shame and rage about a traumatic event, a fact that varies cross-culturally.

Another reason for caution about CISD is the secondary trauma ("vicarious traumatization") that some CISD participants might experience from hearing others' graphic descriptions. A related cautionary note concerns the personality characteristics of some emergency personnel conducting CISD sessions, for example, a high need for control, a need for immediate gratification, and a strong need to be needed (see Chapter 3, Fig. 3.1, Victim-Rescuer-Persecutor Triangle).

Researcher Jeffery Mitchell's[11] adaptation of CISD in its subset, Critical Incident Stress Management (CISM), draws on a theme from medical practice.

That is, "managing" diabetes or heart disease, for example, is one thing, but in crisis care, active participation by the person in crisis is pivotal to positive crisis resolution. "Management" suggests control and taking charge, but it means little without the active collaboration of those "managed"—as corporate and other leaders have experienced.

DISASTERS OF HUMAN ORIGINS

Nature's potential for violence seems small beside the destructive possibilities of disaster caused by human beings.

Survivors of State-Sponsored Neglect and Preventable Harm

In Bhopal, India, a gas leak at a chemical plant killed 2,000 and disabled tens of thousands more. In Bangladesh, over a thousand deaths occurred from collapse of a clothing manufacturing building. Besides the 300 dead and 10,000 evacuated from the Chernobyl nuclear accident in the former Soviet Union, radioactive fallout affected people and animals thousands of miles away, and illness and death from the accident are still being counted, even as the plant is finally being dismantled. The explosion of a fertilizer plant in West, Texas, killed hundreds. Survivors of the underground gold mine explosion near Yellowknife in the Northwest Territories, Canada, cite the tragedy as proof of the need for reform of labor-management relations. Famines in Ethiopia, Mozambique, and Somalia, though apparently "natural," can also be traced to human origins. Ethnic cleansing and tribal wars in the former Yugoslavia, Rwanda, and Kenya are the most recent human-made disasters creating incalculable misery and loss of life. The systematic slaughter of people in Rwanda is being compared with the Nazi Holocaust and Cambodian genocide in the war crimes category. *Environmental racism*, a term applied to placing toxic waste dumps in communities where ethnic minority groups live, and in poor countries, surely takes its toll—with cleanup and restitution yet to occur in many places.

The human potential for both good and evil seems limited only by the technology we create. For example, a child can be saved through a liver transplant; amputated limbs can be replaced; energy from the sun can be collected and stored; but technology also made it possible for the Nazis to perform inhuman experiments on Jews and others in concentration camps, and for most of the population of Hiroshima and Nagasaki to be destroyed. While many enjoy the benefits of scientific knowledge, others suffer. For example, in the United States, the Love Canal disaster was a prototype for the 1980 Superfund Law enacted by Congress as the public health response to hazardous waste sites—the human origins of preventable disasters. Yet the amount of money spent in the United

States for prevention of disasters from faulty buildings and lax safety regulations pales, for example, compared to the $10 billion per month spent on the Iraq war.

Preventive public health measures like massive safe water campaigns prevented epidemics among the Asian tsunami refugees. Oxfam[12] and other international aid providers (some already established in the infrastructure) and church relief groups cite this effort as a "story of aid done right."

"Aid done right" also points to questions about the assumptions of some Western mental health disaster practitioners—one, the belief that it helps to talk about our problems, and another, respect of cultural differences in response to crisis. The tsunami volunteers (most of whom were survivors themselves) agreed that it was helpful to talk about the event. But they also had concerns about burdening others with their accounts. Societies vary in beliefs and policies that influence who gets help and who does not. They also differ about the value of "talking" to outsiders about their crisis experience. Typically, well-intentioned volunteers from other areas of the world can stay for only short periods of time and then must leave, perhaps without exit or follow-up plans. These issues are central to success when working with victim-survivors from other cultures who have different worldviews and value systems.

What Lois Gibbs,[13] a Love Canal, New York, resident turned activist, wrote a quarter century ago applies poignantly to the long-term fallout from Hurricane Katrina and other survivors of preventable disasters:

> We need your support and your help to end the suffering of men, women, and especially children of Love Canal. We have lost our constitutional rights of life, liberty and the pursuit of happiness. Justice for all but not Love Canal Victims.
>
> We cannot live at Love Canal—we cannot leave Love Canal.

COMPARING DISASTERS FROM NATURAL AND HUMAN ORIGINS

The disastrous effects of violence from natural and human sources can be described in both personal and social terms. Although people have moved back to Love Canal, this highly publicized disaster holds lessons for other communities still struggling against toxic waste and development issues. For example, the Hurricane Katrina disaster has been linked to the deliberate building plans on wetlands; left in their natural flood protection role instead of building on them might have spared the hurricane's worst damage.

The postdisaster work of Psychiatrist Robert J. Lifton[14] and social worker Eric Olson is classic in depicting survivors' psychological recovery, depending on whether the disaster's origins are natural (as in "act of God") or human-made, and therefore preventable. In Buffalo Creek, West Virginia, a mining corporation carelessly dumped coal waste, which formed artificial dams that eventually broke and caused dozens of deaths. Buffalo Creek residents knew that the dam was considered dangerous and that the mining corporation had neglected to correct the problem. When loved ones, homes, and the natural environment were destroyed, survivors concluded that the mining company regarded them as less than human. In fact, one of the excuses offered by the company for not correcting their dangerous waste disposal method was that fish would be harmed by alternative methods. The survivors' feelings of devaluation were confirmed by their knowledge of the coal company's proposal of hasty and inadequate financial settlements. The physical damage to the community was never repaired, either by the company or through outside assistance. Residents are constantly reminded of the disaster. The collapse of a clothing factory in Bangladesh decades later suggests a failure to learn from and take preventive action in similar disasters worldwide, as in the Bangladesh tragedy.

Unlike the Rapid City, South Dakota natural disaster from torrential rain, after which the community recovered fully, survivors of the Buffalo Creek, West Virginia mining disaster did not respond to the disaster with community rejuvenation borne of the tragedy. Lifton and Olson attribute this tremendously different response to the disaster's *human (rather than natural) origin*. Even though the mining company was forced to pay $13.5 million in a psychic damage suit, Buffalo Creek residents said they and their community could never be healed. Considering genetic, health, and material damage such as that suffered by Love Canal residents, monetary compensation becomes practically meaningless. Money cannot repair such losses. *Prevention of* and *learning from* such tragic neglect seem the only reasonable responses.

The reactions of Buffalo Creek and Love Canal survivors are similar to those observed among survivors, including children, of Hiroshima, the Nazi Holocaust, and other wars. Survivors of planned disaster—including thousands of civilian deaths and displacement from their communities during war and political conflicts as in Syria decades later—feel that their humanity has been violated. Their psyches are bombarded to such a degree that their capacity for recovery may be permanently damaged.

PREVENTING POSTTRAUMATIC STRESS DISORDER—PTSD

Emotional recovery from traumatic stress requires the ability to incorporate events into one's meaning system and to maintain at least a perception of control. If a situation seems beyond one's control, self-blame may be used as a way to cope with the event.

And so, if the origin of trauma or prolonged distress is external—for example, exposure to occupational hazards, displacement to refugee camps during war, or disasters traced to negligence—it is important that victims recognize their true sources rather than blame themselves. Interpreting a person's anger and demand for compensation as a "dependency conflict" or in other psychopathological terms is a form of blaming the victim. Instead, traumatized people should be linked to self-help and advocacy groups. This helps channel their anger into constructive action for necessary change—for example, improved workplace safety standards, antiwar activism, and group action regarding toxic waste (see Crisis Paradigm). This is not to say that individual problems do not play a role in some injury claims. But such problems should not be used to hide the fact that dangerous exposures to harmful chemicals reduce some people to joblessness, ill health, and poverty.

Many of these ideas are relevant to the popular application of PTSD to the aftermath of many stressful events. PTSD is a controversial and much-published concept describing a *chronic* condition that may occur *months or years* after an original trauma that falls outside the normal range of life events, such as during a war or in a concentration camp, or from terrorist bombings. Some of its features are similar to other chronic conditions like clinical depression, panic disorder, and alcoholism. PTSD contrasts with the relatively short crisis response time after distressful life events.

It is significant that PTSD as a psychiatric diagnosis was added to the *Diagnostic and Statistical Manual of Mental Disorders* (the *DSM*) around the period of tumultuous post-Vietnam controversies. That is, veterans of this war suffered injuries not only on the battlefield but on return home were abused by anti-Vietnam war protesters, leaving them feeling devalued for their military service. Such treatment of veterans demands social action and more widely available crisis care, not adding a psychiatric "disorder" label to distressed veterans' histories. After all, and unfortunately, widespread bias against mental illness and its treatment is still alive and well.

More likely, PTSD may be a too-late substitute for crisis care that perhaps was missing on the front lines of combat or immediately on return home—not months later when the PTSD label might be avoided. Its increasing prevalence as a psychiatric diagnosis in the aftermath of *any* stressful life event is a dramatic example of "pathologizing" and "medicalizing" everyday stressful life events. It may also signify the absence of crisis care and grief work for *all traumatized people close to the time a distressful life event occurs* and the importance of *preventing* abuse, trauma, and war in the first place.

Despite these conceptual issues regarding PTSD, it is wise and humane to provide all combat veterans what they need (without a psychiatric label) when suffering from what should be considered a "normal" response after exposure to the extraordinary horrors of war—experiences falling well beyond the ordinary range of the average person's life. Social work professor Dana Becker[15] offers an in-depth history and analysis of PTSD in clinical practice.

MAKING MEANING OUT OF LOSS: ACCIDENTAL OR INTENTIONAL VIOLENCE

The world knows about the atomic bombs dropped in Japan, the Nazi Holocaust, the Cambodian genocide, and the mass murders and rapes in Rwanda and Darfur. War and environmental pollution are planned disasters that bring about physical, social, and emotional destruction of immeasurable proportions.

Responses to war trauma and terrorist attacks in the global community are similar to the impact, recoil, and posttrauma experienced by other disaster survivors. The responses vary according to episode—that is, brief, long-term, repeated, and prolonged exposure. An extreme and powerful threat overwhelms peoples' usual coping mechanism and sense of safety and security. All affected by terrorism typically assess their old values and beliefs about themselves, the world around them, spirituality, and human nature. In this process, people either integrate the experience into their existing values and beliefs or accommodate and develop new ones. Those who cannot integrate or accommodate will most likely experience physical and psychological symptoms that may be unexplainable. Terrorism and grief reactions are connected and similar, but uniquely different and distinct.

Outcomes of terrorism are affected by personal, predisposing, and protective factors affecting the grief and recovery process: (1) disequilibrium—the immediate aftermath; (2) denial—outward adjustment; (3) and integration—or coming to terms with what happened. As with other terrorist attacks, after the 2013 Patriots Day bombing of the Boston Marathon, there were thousands of national and international outpourings of grief and support for the dead and injured. As a reminder of family and community love, and the urgency of terrorist prevention across continents, a memorial was created in the historic heart of Boston, where hundreds of gifts were placed and are now preserved in the city's archives.

Maintaining or regaining health (*salutogenesis*) and avoiding illness (*pathogenesis*) are greater challenges when the crisis originates from sociocultural sources—in this case, disasters of human origin (see Fig. 1.1, Crisis Paradigm, in Chapter 1). This is because the emotional healing process requires, among other things, that people answer for themselves the question, "Why did this happen to me?" If the answer is, "It was fate," "It was God's will," or "That's life; some bad things just happen," people can more easily recover and rebuild their lives, especially with social support. But if the answer can be traced to one's gender, race, sexual identity, or other prejudice; to neglect or hatred from individuals, groups, or corporations (as in environmental pollution); to ethnic cleansing; or to any other human origin, the persons affected must receive a message of caring and compensation to counteract the devastating effects of such criminal actions.

Medical sociologist Aaron Antonovsky,[16] from his study of Holocaust survivors, writes that when compassion and caring are absent, a person's sense of coherence, including *comprehensibility, meaningfulness,* and *manageability* (pp. 17–19) is shaken. The survivor tends to absorb the blame and devaluation implied by others' neglect or outright damage. This process is similar to the "downward spiral" to depression and other dangerous outcomes discussed in Chapter 5 (Fig. 5.1), which can occur when survivors of violence are blamed for their plight. Follow-up service for *individual* survivors of disasters of human origin includes particular attention to the *meaning* of these traumas in cross-cultural perspective, such as the Boston Marathon and other memorials illustrate.

Those meanings are often associated with social and political action, especially prevention efforts that can benefit other people. Working with survivors of the September 11, 2001 attack, researchers Ai et al.,[17] emphasize spirituality as a coping tool, and how working with clients of different religious beliefs helps them use their value systems to recover from traumatic violence. Inspiring examples of international collaboration and making meaning out of human-made disasters include:

- A group of Boston women raised funds to build and staff schools for girls after the Rwanda genocide.
- Physician Paul Farmer's leadership to provide surviving Rwandans medical and related services, including mentoring American medical students in delivering cross-cultural health care.
- A Boston woman who lost a family member in the 9/11 attack found meaning in using her survivor funds to build a school for girls in Afghanistan.
- Tulane University students fanned out across New Orleans to assist with the unfinished work of rebuilding after Hurricane Katrina and aligning the lessons from Katrina with their formal courses.

HUMAN RESILIENCE AND LEARNING FROM DISASTER

Vietnam veterans are still trying to rebuild their lives after a generation of being made scapegoats for a nation's guilt and shame about a war they were not personally responsible for starting. Many Iraq veterans have embarked on a similar journey. Holocaust survivors have formed awareness groups as resources for support and the preservation of history. Atomic bomb survivors say their sacrifice was worthwhile if only the bomb is never used again. First Nations people are fighting for their cultural survival as well as against the destruction of the environment, which in their worldview they define as a crime against the harmony that should exist between nature and human beings. Lois Gibbs's story about the Love Canal tragedy moved a nation to awareness of similar hazards in numerous other communities. Not unlike the parent survivors of teenage suicide, these survivors search for meaning in their suffering by sharing the pain and tragedy of their lives to benefit others. The survivors of human malice, greed, and prejudice tell us something about ourselves, our world, and the way we relate to one another and the environment.

Yet more than a hundred years after the American Civil War, over a half century after the Holocaust, and decades after the Vietnam War, we still have

- Racially motivated violence and institutionalized racism across the United States
- Crimes with apparent anti-Semitic and other ethnic, religious, and political motives, from Boston to London, Madrid, Bosnia, Haiti, Rwanda, and the Middle East
- A systematic attempt to declare the Holocaust a "myth"
- Repeated famines in African countries that can be traced to war and to the widening gap between the haves and have-nots of the world
- An international nuclear capacity continuing apace for destruction more than 1 million times the power of the atomic bomb dropped on Hiroshima

To meet the challenges of these potentially destructive forces, there are now national and international debates about nuclear proliferation, regional wars, and the arms trade unparalleled in human history about their importance to our ultimate survival. But the social, political, religious, and psychological ramifications of national and international crises and chronic problems are complex, controversial, and passionately debated. People are deeply divided, for example, in their views about

- Whether or how ethnic cleansing should be stopped
- What the division of government spending should be between domestic and defense needs
- Whether the environmental crisis is as serious as some claim.

These issues will probably be argued for a long time. The following facts remain nevertheless:

- Many crises can be traced to social, economic, and political factors of local and global origins.
- Children are pressing their teachers for answers about crime and environmental threat.
- Fear about nuclear accidents and environmental pollution has increased since the Chernobyl disaster.
- Effective crisis care cannot occur without considering the sociocultural context of the crisis.

Sociologist C. Wright Mills[18] declared decades ago the imperative that individual and public crises be understood in terms of their human meaning. Public issues should be debated and acted on, not abstractly, but in terms of their impact on each of us—you, me, our families and friends, and others. Not only is there a dynamic interplay between public and private life, but in both realms our sensitivity and listening to others' perceptions and value systems regarding controversial issues can foster cooperation and prevent conflict.

Each person's unique perception of traumatic events is central to understanding and resolving a crisis. Without communication, we cannot understand another's interpretation of an event or issue; or we may become a hindrance to constructive crisis resolution. The differences in interpretations of personal, social, and political problems are as diverse as community members themselves. Without question, *communication* is critical to uncovering these interpretations, understanding people in crisis, and assuring appropriate care. As psychiatrist Norris Hansell[19] notes, a person shares a traumatic experience through emotional display, behavior, and verbal communication—"crisis plumage." Responses are often embedded in cultural differences. If there is no caring and supportive listener, the chances of a constructive crisis outcome are diminished.

But while listening is *necessary*, it is *not sufficient* if the crisis originates from unfair or divisive sociocultural issues. Social and political actions are therefore pivotal to a positive crisis outcome if the origin of the crisis is social and political (see Fig. 1.1 in Chapter 1, Crisis Paradigm, Box 3, right circle). Individuals seriously traumatized from sociopolitical sources are more real than the casualty figures reported on the evening news make them seem.

- Richard, a refugee from Rwanda with recurrent nightmares, is someone's husband, father, son, and brother. He is 48 years old and lives on Locust Street in a town of 45,000 people.
- Shigeko is an atomic bomb survivor who has had 26 operations on her face and lips and is glad that she is alive and that her son is not ashamed of her appearance.
- Jane, age 5, lives near a hazardous waste site and has toxic hepatitis.

People like these and many others tend to get lost in statements of "statistically significant" incidences (of cancer, deformed children, or other medical problems), scientific jargon, and "investigative procedures" for determining whether corrective action is in order. This kind of generalizing typically does not apply to real people. The abstractness, along with the grossness of the figures—10 million victims of the Holocaust, nearly 500,000 dead from atomic bomb blasts—contributes to denial and psychic numbing for the average person. The numbers, the destruction, and the sheer horror are unimaginable for most of us. To defend ourselves against the terror, we may deny and try to convince ourselves that there is nothing we personally can do about these global issues.

Although the Cold War is officially over, we have stockpiles of nuclear arms sufficient to destroy the planet several times over, and additional nations are testing nuclear devices even as the United Nations Security Council debates how to deal with one regional crisis after another in which thousands of innocent civilians (many of them children) are slaughtered or wounded by warring factions. As psychiatrists Apfel and Simon[20] (p. 72) note, "If we decide it is the responsibility of the enemy's leadership to take care of its own children, then we can more easily go ahead with our bombing program. If we decide children anywhere in the world are also our children, we can less easily bomb. We distance ourselves and say that children who are far away are not our children, and if they suffer it is because their leaders and their parents are irresponsible." In the spirit of violence prevention we can learn from Sara Ruddick's[21] thesis regarding "maternal practice": It is reasonable to suggest that if men and women shared equally in the everyday tasks of caring for children and learned the conflict resolution tactics demanded by nonviolent parenting, they would insist that more resources be spent to promote peace and conserve lives and resources than the many millions presently spent on war and destruction.

From a safe distance, it is relatively easy to think of our enemies as less than human and therefore worthy of destruction. As in our attitudes toward homeless persons, deinstitutionalized psychiatric patients, and unwed mothers, our enemies seem distant; they belong to groups and are the responsibility of the state or church. When we objectify persons like this, we do not have to think of them as someone's sister, brother, child, father, mother, or friend.

Our worst enemies are people like ourselves: They eat; sleep; make love; bear children; feel pain, fear, and anger; communicate with one another; bury their dead; and eventually die. Statistics and machines will never be a substitute for human interaction, just as rating scales can aid but not displace clinical judgment in evaluating individual suicide risk. As Albert Einstein said, "Peace cannot be kept by force. It can only be achieved by understanding."

COMMUNICATION AND LISTENING AS EMOTIONAL CRISIS PREVENTION

In a particular crisis situation any of us may encounter, if we do not *communicate*, for example, with a suicidal person, we will not understand why death is preferable to life for that individual, and we therefore may be ineffective in preventing suicide. If we take the time to *talk* with and *listen* to a person in crisis, we are less likely to suggest or request a drug as a crisis response. Similarly, in the national and international arena, if we keep communication open and foster diplomatic action to handle crises, there is less likelihood of using physical force to solve problems. Human communication, then, is the key to our survival—as individuals and as a world community.

Our ethnocentrism (as in "our culture is best") is often so strong, and greed and power motives often so disguised, that the average person may find it difficult to think of disasters of human design as a form of violence. Victims of disasters and other traumas of human origin, however, feel *violated*. They have experienced directly the destruction of their health, their children, their homes, their sense of security, their country, their hopes for the future, and their sense of wholeness and worth in the human community.

In many ways, the poignant testimonies and tragic lives of the victims of ethnic, class, religious, and political conflicts speak for themselves. Still, two of the most painful aspects of their crises are that they feel ignored and often cannot receive even material compensation for their enormous losses. People suffering from these policies feel denied. A hopeful sign of policy change is the vital international response to the Asian tsunami, the Philippines hurricane, and other horrific disasters, while some countries have reduced the debt burden of disaster-struck poor countries. Another hopeful sign is advocacy for forgiving these debts altogether, in that most of it originated in global economic policies developed with the major advantage going to rich countries.

If we have not listened, or remained silent when we should have spoken, convinced that we have nothing to say about public issues, perhaps we should reexamine what Nobel Peace Prize recipient Albert Schweitzer said in 1954: "Whether we secure a lasting peace will depend upon the direction taken by individuals—and, therefore, by the nations whom those individuals collectively compose." Survival is too serious to be confined to partisan politics, the government, or liberal versus conservative debates. Every citizen—and certainly crisis workers we rely on when in acute distress—should pay attention to the critical issues confronting the human race. Therapist-claimed "neutrality" about these issues will not do in cases of crisis originating in sociocultural and political sources. From much experience with various victims, we have learned that people traumatized by violence need *explicit public acknowledgment* that *what happened to them is wrong.*

When confronted with the enormity and horror of disaster from human sources, denial is understandable. Although we may feel helpless and powerless, in fact, we are not. The opinions of officials and professionals are not necessarily wiser or more lifesaving than those of ordinary citizens. Lois Gibbs story, *Love Canal: My Story*, emphasizes the fact that as an average citizen with limited education and almost no funds, she was able to fight city hall and the White House and win. Every country has someone or many like Lois Gibbs, who, in the face of unnecessary and preventable suffering, join with others to make a difference for themselves, their families, and the world.

Murray Levine,[22] a community psychologist, wrote, in his introduction to Gibbs's story (pp. xii–xviii), reasons why her story and others like it should be told; he also illustrated crisis and preventive responses to a disaster of human origins:

1. Lois Gibbs is in many respects a typical American woman—a mother of two children and a housewife. In response to crisis and challenge, she courageously "transcended herself and became far more than she had been."

2. Her story informs us of the relationship between citizens and their government and shows that the government's decisions about a problem are not necessarily in the interests of ordinary people whose lives are threatened by these decisions.
3. Lois Gibbs's story is one of "inner meanings and feelings of humans," a story that "provides a necessary and powerful antidote to the moral illness of those cynics and their professional robots who speak the inhuman language of benefit-cost ratios, who speak of the threat of congenital deformities or cancers as acceptable risks."

The differences, then, between disasters of natural and human origin are striking: the uncontrolled, violent forces of nature (fire, water, wind, and temperature), destructive as they are, appear minuscule in comparison with disasters from human sources. The possible crisis outcomes for the victims are also markedly different, with enormous implications for prevention. We see that technology has been a double-edged sword, sometimes the cause of disaster, sometimes the cure. Through technology and public health planning, much has been done to harness some of the destructive potential of nature. Natural disaster-control technology, land management policies, and resources for aid to victims should now be shared more widely in disaster-prone areas of the world. But when it comes to disaster from human sources, we have been much less successful in directing and controlling conflict and indifference toward the health and welfare of others. This is unfortunate but not hopeless. Violence is not inevitable. Rather, it results from *our choices, action, and inaction* (see Fig. 1.1 in Chapter 1, Crisis Paradigm, Box 3, right circle).

In understanding people in crisis (see Chapters 1 and 2) the emphasis was on examining crisis origins. Regarding disasters of human origin, our examination leads us to the *most pressing social, political, and economic questions facing humankind*. After hearing the voices of survivors of nuclear bombs, chemical spills, concentration camps, genocides, or still another war or ethnic cleansing, we should pay acute attention and question the social and political choices that led to these disasters. Our questions about these crises should be asked in tandem with assuring that individuals in crisis receive the care they need *when in crisis—not just years later for preventable chronic problems*. Without it, we may conclude that helping victims of human-made disasters is a hopeless exercise. Frustration, loss of effectiveness, and burnout may replace the understanding, sensitivity, and problem-solving ability everyone in crisis deserves.

Coming full circle, and keeping our gaze on both the risks and growth potential of living through disaster, let us consider this: Among the many origins of personal crisis, human-made disaster presents not only the greatest *danger* across cultures but also the greatest *opportunity* to make a difference for individuals, families, communities, and whole nations affected by such devastating and preventable crises.

REFERENCES, FURTHER READING, DISCUSSION GUIDE

REFERENCES
1. Waring, M. (1990). *If women counted: A new feminist economics*. San Francisco: Harper San Francisco.
2. Sandberg, S. (2013). *Lean in: Women, work and the will to lead*. New York: Alfred A. Knopf.
3. Kuttner, R. (2000, February 2). The hidden failure of welfare reform. *Boston Sunday Globe*, p. C7.
4. Watters, E. (2010), *Crazy like us: The globalization of the American Psyche*. New York: Free Press.
5. Kozol, J. (2000). *Ordinary resurrections: Children in the years of hope*. New York: Crown.
6. Earley, P. (2006). *Crazy: A father's search through America's mental health madness*. New York: Berkley Books.
7. Ryan, W. (1971). *Blaming the victim*. New York: Vintage Books.
8. Thiele, B. (2002). The human right to adequate housing: A tool for promoting and protecting individual and community health. *American Journal of Public Health, 92*(5), 712–715.
9. Tyhurst, J. S. (1957b). The role of transition states—including disasters—in mental illness. In *Symposium on preventive and social psychiatry*. Washington, DC: Walter Reed Army Institute of Research and the National Research Council.
10. Caplan, G. (1964). *Principles of preventive psychiatry*. New York: Basic Books.
11. Mitchell, J. (2003). Major misconceptions in crisis intervention. *International Journal of Emergency Mental Health, 5*(4), 185–197.
12. Oxfam America. (2006, Winter). A story of aid done right. *Oxfam Exchange, 6*(1), 14. Author.
13. Gibbs, L. (1982). *Love Canal: My story*. Albany: State University of New York Press. Foreword by Murray Levine.
14. Lifton, R. J., & Olson, E. (1976). The human meaning of total disaster: The Buffalo Creek experience. *Psychiatry, 39*, 1–18.
15. Becker, D. (2013). *One nation under stress: The trouble with stress as an idea*. New York: Oxford University Press.
16. Antonovsky, A. (1980). *Health, stress, and coping*. San Francisco: Jossey-Bass.
17. Ai, A. L., Cascio, T., Santangelo, L. K., & Evans-Campell, T. (2005). Hope, meaning, and growth following the September 11, 2001, terrorist attacks. *Journal of Interpersonal Violence, 20*(5), 523–548.
18. Mills, C. W. (1959). *The sociological imagination*. Oxford, UK: Oxford University Press.
19. Hansell, N. (1976). *The person in distress*. New York: Human Sciences Press.
20. Apfel, R. J., & Simon, B. (Eds.). (1994b). *Minefields in the heart: Mental life of children of war and communal violence*. New Haven, CT: Yale University Press.
21. Ruddick, S. (1989). *Maternal thinking: Toward a politics of peace*. Boston: Beacon Press.
22. Levine, M. (See Gibbs, 1982, *Love Canal: My story*.)

FURTHER READING
Gans, H. J. (1962). *The urban villagers*. New York: Free Press.
Jencks, C. (1994). *The homeless*. Cambridge, MA: Harvard University Press.

Lifton, R. J. (1993). *The protean self: Human resilience in an age of fragmentation*. New York: Basic Books.
Mitchell, J. (2003). Major misconceptions in crisis intervention. *International Journal of Emergency Mental Health*, 5(4), 185–197.
Reverby, S. (1987). *Ordered to care*. Cambridge, UK: Cambridge University Press.
Schor, J. B. (1993). *The overworked American: The unexpected decline of leisure*. New York: Basic Books.
Sidel, R. (1996). *Women and children last: The plight of poor women in affluent America*. New York: Penguin Books.
Sommers, T., & Shields, L. (1987). *Women take care: The consequences of caregiving in today's society*. Gainesville, FL: Triad.

DISCUSSION GUIDE

1. Although divulging one's income is a sensitive issue for many, try to ascertain any unfair labor and salary issues you may suspect in your workplace. If you think there is any unlawful inequality based on gender or race, for example, consider with a trusted coworker or friend how you might address this problem without threat of losing your job.
2. If you (or someone you know) experienced homelessness following a disaster, what kind of crisis care was available? If a disaster worker conducted critical incident stress debriefing (CISD) with you, was it helpful, or did it perhaps feel intrusive after such a traumatic experience? Were emergency workers attentive to the guidelines offered in this chapter regarding CISD?
3. After reading this chapter, convene a small discussion group to consider what we each can do to prevent disasters originating from neglect and/or substandard buildings, for example, and what we can learn from the catastrophic losses of war and other intentional violence.
4. Given the many heart-rending stories of disaster and violence around the globe, discuss self-care with family and friends, and how we can avoid "compassion fatigue" as we try to be helpful.

CHAPTER 9

Life Cycle Changes, Loss and Growth

From Birth to Death

Navigating and growing through challenges across the life cycle

CHAPTER OUTLINE

Challenges and Rewards Through the Life Cycle   242
Ritual as an Aid to Healthy Development and Happiness   243
Comparing Traditional, Questionable or Damaging, and Growth-Promoting Rituals   246
Birth and Parenthood   249
Example: Lorraine and Family—Mourning the Death of a Child   251
Physically and Mentally Handicapped Persons   258
Parenting a Handicapped Child   259
Example: Mona Anderson and Family—Down Syndrome   260
Adolescence and Young Adulthood: Danger and Opportunity   262
Example: Robert—A Gay Haitian Youth   264
Families and Communities in Crisis   266
Example: The Page Family and Crisis Counseling   269
Intimate Relationships: Beginnings and Endings   271
Example: Helen—Divorce   274
Chronic Problems and Crisis Vulnerability: Boundaries and Distinctions   276
Social Network and Group Approaches to Crisis Care   277
Example: Alice—Excerpt From Networking Session   280
Example: Ramona—Networking in a Shelter for Abused Women   282
Middle-Age Turning Points: Growth, Sadness, or Decline?   283
Growing Older: Challenges, Risks, and Joy   285
Attitudes Toward Seniors   285

Services for Elderly People   286
Example: Anton Carlton—Home Care   287
Death: The Final Passage   289
The Hospice Movement   293
References, Further Reading, Discussion Guide   295

How do we handle challenges and loss as we move through life cycle changes from birth to death? What is necessary for avoiding acute crisis during passage from childhood to increasing responsibilities as adults? What do these passages mean for people from diverse cultures or societies in which poverty, ethnic bias, or gender bias leaves whole groups of people particularly vulnerable to crisis? Worldwide, people can benefit from information and examples that help people navigate the natural changes we encounter from birth to death, and those unanticipated stressful or traumatic events that complicate challenges and loss over the life course.

CHALLENGES AND REWARDS THROUGH THE LIFE CYCLE

Anthropologists and psychoanalysts have referred to human development transition states as *life crises*. In anthropology, "crisis" refers to a highly significant, anticipated event or phase in the life cycle that marks one's passage to a new social status, with expected changes, rights, and duties. Traditionally, these status changes are accompanied by rituals (such as puberty and marriage rites) meant to assist individuals in their new role and what to expect in their family and the community. The rituals also can buffer the stress and challenges of these potentially *critical*, though *normal*, life events. In traditional societies, families and the entire community, led by "ritual experts," are intensely involved in the life passages to help buffer the challenges of new roles as community members. A contemporary version of this tradition is the rites of passage experience (ROPE) conducted by the Center for Advancement of Youth, Family, and Community Service in Connecticut, and internationally[1] (see Chapter 6, "Youth Violence and Prevention"). This *anthropological* concept of life crisis corresponds roughly to the anticipated crises discussed in clinical literature and this book's Crisis Paradigm (see Fig. 1.1 in Chapter 1) and other chapters.

    Crisis in its *clinical* meaning flows from social psychiatry and public health. It emphasizes the sudden onset and brief duration of acute emotional upsets in response to identifiable traumatic events. In this sense, adolescence, marriage, giving birth, and entering middle age are *not* clinical crises except in extraordinary circumstances; for example, an expected infant is stillborn or born with a serious or life-threatening medical condition. Such an unanticipated traumatic event during transition to parenthood has the *potential* for activating an *acute emotional upset* in the clinical sense. *Turning points* like this involve social and psychological challenges for successfully navigating life cycle changes and expected tasks. For example

- Changing one's social role from single to married, plus parenthood
- Changing one's self-image, such as young to middle aged, healthy to sick
- Gathering material and social resources to support a new family member

As turning points in human development, these life challenges and their potential for a "clinical" crisis state fit the classic definition of *crisis* as a period of both danger and opportunity. They also highlight the importance of the social, cultural, and material resources necessary for individuals to avoid acute emotional upsets. Another connection between the anthropological and clinical definitions of *crisis* is the fact that acutely upset individuals, as members of cultural communities, do not exist in a social vacuum. They are therefore influenced by social expectations of how to behave and by values guiding their interpretation of expected and unexpected life events, which figure strongly in the way one resolves a particular emotional crisis.

- Thus, if it is unclear *who* a person is, *what* the person is expected to do, or *how* the person fits into familiar social arrangements based on cultural values, he or she may experience unusual stress during life cycle changes. Confusion about one's role can create so much stress that a person with conflicting or changed roles may withdraw from social interaction and an unsupportive social arrangement to reduce anxiety-provoking encounters. For example, if pregnant teenage girls sense that they are expected to drop out of high school, they are more likely to be poorly educated, unemployed, and dependent on welfare and to marry early, which enhances their potential for future crises.
- If widowed people sense that they are a threat to social groups of married people, they may feel cut off from social support and thereby increase their risk of emotional crisis around traumatic events.
- If children of parents feuding about divorce are not allowed to see their grandparents, they may ask, Who is my family? The deprived grandparent may ask, What have I done wrong that they treat me like this?

RITUAL AS AN AID TO HEALTHY DEVELOPMENT AND HAPPINESS

An important means of reducing stress and minimizing the chaos associated with role ambiguity is the constructive use of ritual. A dramatic difference between traditional and urban or industrialized societies is the relative importance of ritual and the separation between the sacred and the profane. Industrialization across cultures typically includes increased secularism and a decrease in sacred ceremonialism.

In his classic work *Rites of Passage*, anthropologist van Gennep[2] distinguished three phases in the ceremonies associated with life cycle change: rites of separation (prominent in funeral ceremonies), rites of transition (important in initiation and pregnancy), and rites of incorporation (prominent in marriage). A complete schema of rites of passage theoretically includes all three phases. For example, a widow is *separated* from her husband by death; she occupies a *liminal* (transitional) status for a time, and finally is *reincorporated* into a new marriage relationship.

These rites are protective during potentially hazardous life passages, times that may be dangerous to a person who feels unsupported by the community. As anthropologist LaFontaine[3] notes: Ritual thus makes public what is private, makes social what is personal, and gives the individual new knowledge and strength. For example,

- A person who loses a loved one needs a public occasion to mourn.
- Persons who are intimate and cohabiting desire social approval (typically through marriage).
- A dying person who is anointed has new knowledge of the imminence of death and greater strength to accept death.
- A divorced person needs community support following a failed marriage, including, perhaps, a ritual for public recognition and acceptance of a new role.

Rites of passage vary historically and across cultures. Until recently, it was generally assumed that rites of passage are relatively unimportant in modern societies: Public and private spheres of activity and social roles (worker, parent, or political leader) are more clearly separated than in traditional societies and hence in less need of ritual support. However, Kimball, in the foreword to van Gennep's work, notes that there is no evidence that people in a secular urban world have less need for ritualized expression during transition states—as marriage and funeral rituals readily show. Some contemporary discarding of ritual can reflect a move toward greater freedom of the individual. But ritual can be a powerful, controlling, and sometimes dangerous way to maintain the status quo in traditional and contemporary societies.

Less ritual thus implies more personal freedom. So while some rituals protect the individual during stressful transitions, they have a social purpose as well. For example, anthropologist Spencer's[4] research with the traditional Samburu of Kenya, a polygynous gerontocracy (society ruled by elders) kept young men in a marginal position relative to the larger society and forbade them to marry until around age 30, an institution known as *moranhood*. This ritual preserved the concentration of power and wives among the older men.

Another ritual under scrutiny is female genital mutilation FGM, which affects millions of women and girls, mostly in African, Far Eastern, and Middle Eastern countries. Sometimes referred to as female circumcision, unlike male circumcision, the operation (categorized in four types) damages or destroys a woman's normal sexual response and can cause life-threatening physical complications (see Chapter 1, "Diverse Approaches to Crisis"). Novelist Alice Walker's[5] fictionalized account, *Possessing the Secret of Joy*, has made the practice and its context of gender-based oppression widely visible in the Western world. The World Health Organization, the United Nations, Canada, and the United States have declared the practice illegal. The Nigerian Nurses and Midwives Association, Somali immigrant physicians, and other groups worldwide advocate for elimination of the practice and the education of health professionals in how to deal sensitively with women presenting their daughters for the ritual in Western medical settings. However, as with teen pregnancy and similar issues, this culturally embedded practice is complex, controversial, and intricately tied to socioeconomic and educational equity for women worldwide.

A contemporary negative ritual is the heavy drinking, and sometimes hazing, associated with admission to college campus clubs—a practice under increasing scrutiny over past decades. Despite legal restrictions and US college campus efforts to control the purchase and use of alcohol, binge drinking is indulged in by thousands of young people. In a contemporary twist on traditional rites of passage, these young people (not unlike their Samburu brothers or Somali sisters) feel pressured to drink in order to "belong" in a new environment without the usual supports of family and neighborhood. Wherever these destructive rituals occur, students have poorer grades, reduced career motivation, and increased dropout rates—all challenges for school and parents' groups to create positive rituals for students under stress, who have a powerful need to belong.

Women and Marriage Across Cultures

Contemporary women worldwide typically view marriage and especially the ritual of the wedding day as high points in their lives, with some judging themselves as failures if they cannot marry and retain a husband. Caught up in the emotional high of the wedding ritual, with dreams of "living happily ever after," the average bride is unconscious of the social significance of the waning ritual of being "given away" by her father and relinquishing her own name to assume that of her husband. Some women willingly interrupt or delay careers to support their families through unpaid and devalued household work. Many are happy and secure in their role and testify that their dreams have come true.

Millions, however, are battered, as the marriage license seems to have been transformed for some into a "hitting license," as sociologists Straus, Gelles, and Steinmetz[6] found in their national survey of US families. Some women feel trapped and become convenient objects of violence or find themselves poor and rearing their children alone. Many women are left behind for younger women, especially during middle age, when women may be considered "over the hill" whereas men become more "distinguished." Often this occurs after women have sacrificed education and career opportunities in order to fulfill the social expectation of building a stable home. Among teenage mothers in the United States, their typical financial inequality is tied to the absence of marriage and a two-parent structured family life for nurturing children toward responsible adulthood.

Ritual, then, can serve to maintain social equilibrium, including expectations of behaving according to accepted roles. However, traditional social roles that are reinforced through the negative use of ritual can exact a considerable price from certain individuals—for example, more heart disease and suicides for men, social isolation or death for adolescents by suicide, and battering or poverty for women. The consideration of ritual here reveals a continuum between traditional and contemporary rites of passage, and it suggests that people in all times and places need ritual. But what kinds of rituals are needed, and under what circumstances should they take place? How can ritual be helpful for the individual in transition as well as for society?

COMPARING TRADITIONAL, QUESTIONABLE OR DAMAGING, AND GROWTH-PROMOTING RITUALS

Ritual holds a paradoxical place in a secularized society. On the one hand, it is viewed as a sign of an earlier stage of social evolution. On the other hand, certain rituals are retained without critical examination of their expression in contemporary life. In modern life, three approaches to ritual are observed: (1) ritual is often denied any relevance; (2) some of its most oppressive and destructive aspects are recycled from ancient tradition to include the abuse of alcohol, guns, or cars and medical technology to prolong life; (3) when ritual is observed, it is highly individualized, as in the rite of psychotherapy, in which the "50-minute session" and other practices are observed. Such rituals are complemented by medicalization and its focus on individuals rather than groups in modern urban societies.

These interpretations of ritual, however, are in the process of change. Meaningless and destructive rituals are being dropped entirely or are being questioned. For example, many women today retain their last names after marriage, and *both* parents of the bride *and* groom (rather than only the father of the bride) participate in the marriage ceremony. Similarly, with cultural awareness, barbaric rituals, oppression, and violence are no longer seen as the province of any one society, traditional or modern. Looking the other way in the face of human rights violations with a shrug—"Oh, that's just their culture" (i.e., *cultural relativism*)—is no longer acceptable.

Everyone concerned with healthy development from birth to death should consider the place of ritual and its potential power to prevent crisis for persons facing the challenges of life's major turning points. They will also benefit by knowing what to expect from professionals for crisis prevention during these periods of turmoil and vulnerability. Whether critical life passages also become occasions of emotional crisis will depend on

1. What the individual does to prepare for anticipated transitions
2. The nature and extent of social support available during turning points
3. The occurrence of unanticipated hazardous events (such as fire, accident, illness, or loss of job) during life transition phases, when vulnerability is usually greater
4. The creativity of primary care providers and crisis workers in helping individuals and families develop positive contemporary rites of passage where there are few or none.

In our families and communities, we can examine and compare the strengths and potential hazards of rites of passage over the life cycle. The goal is to strengthen positive rituals and end very harmful ones, such as binge drinking and gang initiation.

Traditional Rites

Traditional rites include:

- Birth: *Traditionally* attended by family and/or a midwife in a natural squatting position. Death risk is high if there are complications. *Unexamined or medicalized* birth typically includes ultrasound, drugs, and placement of mother in a horizontal position. *Emerging positive rituals* include natural birth aided by husband or friends, coaching at home or a birthing center, and attended by a midwife with medical backup available for special at-risk cases.
- Puberty/Adolescence rites: *Traditionally*, a period of learning from elders the rules, traditions, and responsibilities of initiation into adult roles. In contemporary cultures, *positive* rituals include religious rites such as Bar Mitzvah, confirmation, or *Quincianara* in Spanish-speaking groups. Obtaining a driver's license has the potential for positive ritual regarding safe driving, along with education and support groups such as ROPE[1] in Connecticut and internationally, regarding responsible driving, sexual behavior, and duties of parenthood. Very *questionable* and potentially *dangerous* rites are binge drinking on college campuses and initiation into gang culture.
- Intimate Relationships—Beginnings and Endings: Traditionally and currently, these include betrothal, bridal showers, stag parties, an egalitarian marriage ceremony, consciousness-raising groups regarding equality in spousal roles, divorce ceremonies, and support groups for the divorced and for parents without partners.

- Middle Age: Generally not ritualized, although at this phase, individuals may experience an increase in social value and respect by the community. On the *questionable* side, postmenopausal women may be regarded as asexual and devalued, while men past youth become more "distinguished." *Positive* rituals might include education and support groups for midlife challenges, such as for partners to redefine marriage (or other committed relationships) to avoid "empty nest" and other midlife stressors or crisis.
- Old Age: Also generally not ritualized; *traditionally,* older persons may experience increased social value and respect. *Questionable* at this time is forced retirement (sometimes referred to as "redundancy") or unwanted institutional placement for care. *Positive* action includes policies to support elderly people at home, respite services for caretakers, senior citizen programs such as part-time or shared jobs, and opportunities to contribute as a volunteer.
- Death: *Traditionally*, over centuries and across cultures, burial and other rituals feature celebrating a person's life. In Western cultures, the funeral director is the main "ritual expert" often in collaboration with a religious representative. *Questionable* practice in Western cultures is prolongation of life with sophisticated medical intervention (in absence of a living will and sometimes against family wishes) when medical prognosis reveals that death is imminent. *Positive* rituals include support groups for grief work, and widow-to-widow and other self-help groups for survivors.

These life cycle transitions highlight the dynamic relationship between the individual, family, and society. For example, adolescents who choose marriage or parenthood even though they are not ready for those responsibilities may become liabilities to society and typically face more complex problems later. But the reason they are personally unfit as parents might be traced to inadequate support from adults during this stressful period. Some legislators and schools favor requiring psychoeducation courses as a condition for a marriage license. Many church groups have required such courses for decades. These contemporary rituals are an attempt to increase marital happiness and prevent the often negative results of divorce, especially for children.

Crisis care pioneer Naomi Golan[7] describes the specific tasks to be accomplished by individuals and families during transition states. They include "material-arrangemental" tasks (exploring resources and choices in the new role) and "psychosocial" or "affective tasks" (dealing with feelings of loss and longing for the past). These tasks during life cycle change resemble the emotional, cognitive, and behavioral element of effective crisis coping (see Chapter 3). But our successful coping with loss and stressful changes greatly depends on the social and cultural setting. If a society is poor in supportive rituals, if familiar and secure routines and supports in an old role are not replaced, and if there is little attention to social support needs, even the strongest individuals may be unnecessarily scarred during passage through life's stages.

The challenge of moving on to a new stage of development or role may become a threat: *"Will I succeed or fail?" "What will people think if I fail?" "No, I don't think I can face having this baby—not without the help of its father." "Life just isn't worth living if I can't keep on working. I'm worth more dead than alive."* Keeping in mind the value of *positive* rites of passage and their relationship to stress and crisis in modern society, let's consider the *dangers* and *opportunities* of these normal passages from birth to death. And note that during these passages for oneself and family members, crisis counselors and mental health professionals can be thought of as contemporary "ritual experts" (see Fig. 1.1 in Chapter 1, Crisis Paradigm, Box 3, lower circle).

BIRTH AND PARENTHOOD

Parenthood places continual demands on a person from the time of conception until at least the child's eighteenth birthday. Parents must adjust to include an additional member in the family, a process especially difficult for first-time parents, even when they joyfully assume the role of parenthood and willingly regard children as a welcomed responsibility. The unique pleasure and challenge of bearing and nurturing a child through childhood into adult life usually outweighs the ordinary problems of parenthood.

Some parents fall into their role unwillingly or use it to escape less tolerable roles. Consider, for example, the adolescent who seeks relief from a disturbed family home and uses pregnancy as an avenue of escape or the couple who may have more children than they can properly care for emotionally, physically, and financially. Some women still view themselves as having no other significant role than that of mother and wife. Others do not limit their pregnancies because of religious beliefs forbidding artificial contraception. Still others lack the knowledge and means to limit their pregnancies. Unwanted children and their parents are more crisis prone than others. Emotional, social, and material poverty are important contributors to their crisis vulnerability.

All parents, whether or not their children were wanted, are under stress and strain in their parental role. Parenthood requires a constant giving of self. Except for the joy of self-fulfillment and watching a child grow and develop, the parent–child relationship is essentially nonreciprocal. Infants, toddlers, and young children need continuous care and supervision. In their natural state of dependency, they give only the needy love of a child who says, in effect, "I am helpless without you. Take care of me. Protect me."

Some children, in fact, not only are dependent and needy but also for various reasons are a source of great distress and grief to their parents. Their difficult behaviors, such as trouble at school or drug abuse, often signal trouble in the parents' marriage or in the entire family system. Sometimes parents try to deal with these troubles by themselves, struggling for a long time with whatever resources they have. Often they are ashamed to acknowledge a problem with the child and instead view any problem as a reflection of their own failure. Still other parents may lack help from child and family resources, either because the resources do not exist or because they cannot afford them.

Chronic problems of parenthood often persist until a crisis occurs and finally forces parents to seek outside help. Common problems include a child's getting into trouble with the law, running away from home, becoming pregnant during adolescence, truancy, being expelled from school, or making a suicide attempt.

Parents often seem surprised when these problems occur, but a closer look may reveal signs of trouble that were formerly unobserved or ignored. Teachers, recreation directors, pastors, truant officers, and guidance counselors who are sensitive to the needs of children and adolescents can help prevent some of these crises. They should urge parents to participate in a family counseling program *early*, at the first sign of a problem. It is important for counselors and parents to keep in mind that even if preventive programs are lacking, it is never too late to act. An acute crisis situation provides, once again, the opportunity for parents and child to move in the direction of growth and development and for the parents to fulfill their needs for generatively.

Common Crisis Points for Parents

Over the course of parenting, many experience these common crisis points.

Death of a Child

Upon death of a child, crisis often occurs not only because of the parents' excruciating loss but also because the death requires parents to reorder their expectations about the normal progression of life to death—that parents usually precede their children in death. Thus, the loss of a child (including an adult child) is like no other death experience. Some claim it is felt more acutely than loss of a spouse. It is also keenly painful to accept the fact that death has cut off the child's passage through life. Besides being a profound loss, the death of a child threatens the parents' perception of parenthood and the normal life cycle. And if the child's death was by suicide, the parents' painful loss is even more acute (see Chapter 4, "How to Help Family and Other Survivors of Suicide").

The sudden death of an infant is known as *crib death*. The exact cause of these deaths is still unknown, hence the medical designation of sudden infant death syndrome (SIDS). With no warning signs, the parents or a babysitter will find the infant dead in its crib. They bring the infant to the hospital emergency department in a desperate, futile hope of reviving it. The parents or caregivers have fears and guilt that they may somehow have caused the death. The fact that emergency service staff may seem suspicious or appear to blame the parents complicates this crisis. Indeed, the emergency staff must rule out the possibility of child battering, which they cannot do without examination.

Whether or not the child was battered, emergency personnel should withhold judgment. Parents in either case are in crisis and need understanding and support. Those in crisis over SIDS should be offered the opportunity to express their grief in private and with the support of a nurse. Hospital chaplains can often assist during this time and should be called in accordance with the parents' wishes. Parents should also be given information about sleeping position and self-help groups of other parents whose infants died suddenly in their cribs.

Today, in wealthy societies, most health care providers and many parents are aware of correct sleeping position after the 50-year rate increase in SIDS was closely examined; it had been widely assumed that the exact cause of these deaths was unknown. Now, researchers Hogberg and Bergstrom[8] in Sweden and other Western countries have uncovered the *prone* (lying on the stomach) sleeping position as the *missing risk factor* in all previous research aimed at finding a cause of SIDS. It turns out that the 50-year rise in SIDS rates corresponded with the widespread medical advice against the *supine* position (infant lying face up) to prevent swallowing vomitus or the turned-from-side-to-side position—advice popularized by Dr. Spock's and other baby books in the 1960s, 1970s, and 1980s. With the drop in SIDS rates in the mid-1990s, after a gradual *shift from prone to supine* positions, the study authors refer to SIDS as an "iatrogenic" tragedy that is, showing that the misdirected infant care advice was targeted to and accepted by whole populations.

The most widely known and used group for parents regarding SIDS death is the Sudden Infant Death Syndrome Foundation, a national organization with chapters in all states and major cities. The program includes support from other parents, counseling from maternal-child nurse specialists, education through films, and a speakers' bureau with medical and lay experts on the topic. All parents should be advised by health care providers about the *safest sleeping position: face up*. Yet, even with revised information regarding infant sleeping position, not all infant deaths can be prevented, as Lorraine's loss of her child shows.

EXAMPLE: LORRAINE AND FAMILY—MOURNING THE DEATH OF A CHILD

Lorraine explains: "I can't begin to tell you what my life was like before Doris at our counseling center helped me. Six months ago, my second child, Deborah, only 2 months old, died from crib death. When she stopped breathing at home, I called the rescue squad. They resuscitated her and took her to the hospital. Deborah was kept in the intensive care unit for 2 months. Finally, the hospital and doctor insisted that we take her home. When we did, she died the very same day. I was completely grief stricken, especially since I am 41 years old and had waited so long to have a second child. Our other child, David, is 7. I just couldn't accept the fact that Deborah was dead. My husband and the doctors kept telling me to face reality, but I kept insisting on an answer from the pediatrician as to why Deborah had died. I began having chest pains and problems breathing. Several times, my husband called the ambulance and had me taken to the hospital for elaborate heart tests. My doctor told me there was nothing physically wrong with me.

"I went home and things got worse. My husband became impatient and annoyed. I worried day and night about doing something wrong with David and eventually causing his death. The school principal finally called me to say that David was having problems at school. I realized I was being overprotective, but I couldn't help myself. The school recommended that we go to a child guidance clinic with David. I resisted and went back instead to my pediatrician and insisted once again on knowing the cause of Deborah's death. The pediatrician was apparently tired of my demands and recommended that I see a psychiatrist. I felt he was probably right but also felt we couldn't afford a psychiatrist; we had spent so much money on medical and hospital bills during the past year. I became so depressed that suicide began to seem like my only way out. One night, after an attack of chest pain and a crying spell, I was so desperate that I called the suicide prevention center. The counselor referred me to the local counseling center, where I saw Doris.

"With Doris's help, I discovered that I was suffering from a delayed grief reaction. Through several counseling sessions, I was able to truly mourn the loss of my child, which I had not really done through all those months of trying to be brave, as my doctor and husband wanted me to be. Doris and I included my husband in some of the sessions. On her recommendation, I finally joined a group of other parents whose infants had died of crib death. I began to understand my fear of causing David's probable death and could finally let go of my overprotectiveness of him."

Although crib death has special features, the death of children in other ways is also traumatic and requires similar support and opportunities for grief work. A self-help group such as Compassionate Friends offers friendship and understanding to bereaved parents after the death of a child, whether by illness, murder, accident, or suicide.

Miscarried or Stillborn Child

The response of a mother at this crisis point is similar to that of a mother giving birth to a handicapped child: anger, loss, guilt, and questioning. Mothers may ask, "Why did this have to happen to me? What did I do wrong? What did I do to deserve this?" Most important in this crisis for parents as a first step in grieving their acute loss is open acknowledgement of the loss—usually through the sensitive and compassionate *disclosure of facts* by medical personnel. Such honest disclosure helps to allay any misplaced tendencies toward self-blame or parental neglect. And since burial of the stillborn child follows soon, clergy representing religion-affiliated parents serve as primary facilitators of the grieving process. Besides hospital polices regarding the disposition of remains, referrals to grief counselors should be made available to bereaved parents.

The discomfort that some health professionals still feel with death and loss is compounded by ethical issues in cases of miscarriage. An insensitive remark such as *"You* can always try again," fails to consider the mother's bonding with the unborn life or that she may not want to try again. A mother needs to mourn this loss within the framework of the meaning the pregnancy had for her and her family.

Similarly, women who have an abortion need to grieve the loss, regardless of the moral and religious conflicts that may accompany the event. Despite continued public controversy over abortion, for most women faced with an unwanted pregnancy, abortion is rarely a matter of good versus evil, but rather the lesser of two evils in the face of daunting odds. In either case, social support and opportunity to grieve, not blame, are indicated in such pregnancy-related crises.

Illness or Behavior Problems of a Child

Similar social support is needed by parents whose children are seriously ill, have had a serious accident, or are dying. The modern, relaxed visiting regulations in most hospital wards for children have reduced this crisis possibility for both parents and child. Parents are encouraged to participate in their child's care, so that the child feels less isolated and anxious about separation from parents, and the parents feel less threatened about their child's welfare. When behavioral problems are the issue, parents, teachers, and health providers should note the cautions and dangers of using psychoactive drugs as a first-level response (see Chapter 2, Child Screening Checklist; Chapter 3, "Prescription Drugs"

Divorce and Single Parenthood

The rate of divorce in North America is around 50%. The parent who gains custody of the children has the major responsibility of child rearing, at least until remarriage; the other parent may experience loss of the children, which is more acute if the divorced parents live in different cities or a foreign country. If the loss is accompanied by a sense of relief, guilt usually follows. To assuage guilt, the relieved parent may inappropriately shower the children with material gifts or accuse the other parent of being too strict, inattentive, or uncaring. This crisis point of parenthood can be anticipated whenever the divorce itself is a crisis for either parent. Divorce counseling can help avoid future crises.

The increase of no-fault divorce laws and attention to the needs of children in divorce settlements also can help prevent crises for parents, children, and grandparents. Although divorce affects children of all ages, preschoolers are at greatest risk following divorce; boys seem to have a harder time than girls, and the fallout for children generally is worst during the first year of breakup. Cross-cultural studies reveal similar problems for children of divorced parents. Sources of support to help children cope with divorce include the extended family and friends, membership in a religious community, financial security, and intrafamily communication.

However, it is not so much the divorce itself as it is the manner in which parents conduct themselves and the poverty (especially for women) that cause the greatest stress on children of divorced parents. Existing laws do not address the crisis of divorce adequately, as attested by the incidence of child snatching by the parent denied custody. Another problem faced by many mothers is the awarding of custody to fathers on the basis of their greater financial security and access to legal services (which many women cannot afford), even when these fathers have not been the primary caretakers of the children. Although the increasing interest of fathers in parenting their children is to be applauded, to award them custody primarily on a class basis is a cruel punishment of mothers, who have assumed the major burden of child care throughout history, highlighting the need to address many women's economic inequality.[9]

Single Fathers

Fortunately, divorce courts increasingly confer joint custody of children, and more fathers willingly assume both the joys and responsibilities of child care. One result is the growing percentage of fathers (divorced, separated, never married, or widowed) who are raising three or more children under age 18. Among single fathers, most have a higher annual income compared with single mothers.

Fathers who do assume full-time parenting responsibility face stereotypes about that role, struggle with the same issues as single mothers, and may have fewer support groups. Most important for divorcing couples is to remember that they are divorcing each other, not their children. Fathers who parent successfully after divorce are able to distinguish being a father from being an intimate partner, elevate their love for their children over any anger at an ex-partner, prioritize children's needs over adult rights, and attend to the fatherhood role as well as financial responsibility. During custody conflicts, divorce counseling can help prevent such abuses as (1) awarding visitation rights to a father who abused his partner and children and (2) an angry mother charging a nonabusive father with child molestation as a means of denying him visitation or joint custody rights.

Teenage Parenthood

The problems and hazards of single parenthood are increased for a teenager with no job and an unfinished education. The infants of teen mothers are also at increased risk of death, battering, and other problems exacerbated by the poverty of most adolescent parents. Increasingly, teenage mothers do not automatically drop out of high school because of pregnancy, do not marry only because they are pregnant, and do not give up their babies. Hospitals and social service agencies are now establishing collaborative programs with high schools, which include an emphasis on health, sex education, parenthood, and career planning.

There is also growing recognition that the prevalence, problems, and financial hazards of teenage pregnancy will not subside until values and opportunities for women in society change. Consider this question about would-be teen mothers: If she is poor, lacks helpful family role models, feels unloved, sees little prospect of happiness through career or an education, receives cultural messages that her major role in life is motherhood, and is disadvantaged with limited access to contraception, *why wouldn't motherhood and the unconditional love of a child and firsthand experience of empowerment* in caring for a child seem like a reasonable choice?

Counselors and others working with young mothers repeatedly note that these girls see mothering as their only chance for fulfillment. Bolstered by outdated Freudian theory regarding gender roles, a young woman who has little chance of other contributions to society says in effect, "But I can produce a baby." In fact, some young women request pregnancy tests not because they fear they are pregnant but because they want assurance of their fertility. So even if a girl does not plan to conceive, once pregnant she finally finds meaning in her life; she now will be important and necessary—at least to a helpless infant. Current efforts to reform welfare will probably fail if they do not consider these issues and emphasize the joint responsibility of mothers and fathers for the children they produce. Kay S. Hymowitz[10] in her book, *Marriage and Caste in America*, writes that marriage may pose a larger social divide than race; in 2006, young two-parent families in the top quintile with postsecondary education had an average income of $88,000; while the average income of those in the bottom 20% (mostly single) was only $5,200!

Stepfamilies and Adoption

In addition to the high rate of divorce and teen pregnancy in North America, there is a high rate of remarriage and increasing presence of blended families. As with any major transition, families in these situations face many challenges and need support through crises in order to reap the potential riches of new family structures while avoiding the pitfalls, especially for children. There is now a growing body of literature on this topic, including the need for community-wide approaches to helping such families.

Adoption is another parenting issue ripe with opportunity and danger for the child, parents, and entire groups. For instance, a married woman who cannot bear a child and wants to adopt might sacrifice her marriage if her husband does not want children. A single person desiring parenthood usually faces many more challenges during the adoption approval process than a heterosexual couple with the same desire. Anyone, married or single, who attempts interracial adoption in the United States, including Native American tribal rights, must navigate not only the usual hurdles but also national debates on the topic. While acknowledging the importance of racial identity, emphasis should be on the common humanity and needs of all children for nurturance and love in a stable family, needs that are rarely met in institutional settings or with frequent shifts between foster families. Fortunately, more affluent people—whether infertile or not—are pursuing adoptions from among the world's children who need a loving home.

Lesbian and Gay Parenthood

The contemporary stresses of parenthood include those of gay, lesbian, bisexual, and transgendered parents. There is probably no group of parents more misunderstood than gay parents. The myth and fear is that they will bring up their children to be gay. Another myth is that gay men are much more likely than straight men to abuse children. As a result, lesbian and gay parents may lose custody of their children for no other reason than their sexual identity. Gay people of both sexes may be denied adoption if their sexual identity is known. For example, community protest in Massachusetts resulted in the removal of a foster child from the home of two gay foster parents, only to have the child abused 6 months later in a "normal" foster home. In case of a medical emergency in a nontraditional family unit without legal status, the nonbiological parent may be denied access to emergency or intensive care units if hospital rules state "family only." Crises around gay parenthood might decline with reflection on the following facts: The vast majority of parents are heterosexual, yet these straight parents have reared millions of gay people. Necessary role models of either sex and/or sexual identity are needed for all children in many social contexts besides the home. Also, the majority of child sexual abusers are heterosexual male relatives (see Chapter 6).

Surrogate Parenthood

Legal, ethical, and emotional controversy continues over this technological response to the desire of childless couples for children. Proponents cite the Bible to support their position, and opponents note that the last time human beings were bred for transfer of ownership was during slavery. These parenting and infertility debates will most likely continue. But we should note that infertility rates are highest among low-income racial minority groups, due in part to greater exposure to various hazards, whereas lower rates among affluent women are traced largely to later age at attempting pregnancy. Surrogate babies, therefore, are usually born to poor women and paid for by affluent white couples. In the United States, the price of a surrogate arrangement is usually many thousands of dollars, while women in poor countries are paid much less or nothing at all. And although procreation is a right, this right cannot be exercised at the expense of the primordial right of a woman to the child she has nurtured and birthed.

The *preventive* approach to infertility that has spawned surrogacy includes removal of environmental and workplace hazards affecting fertility and child care provisions that would allow career women to have children at earlier ages without compromising their jobs. The controversy in wealthy countries surrounding this issue has resulted in tighter licensing standards and the banning of surrogate motherhood and sex-selection techniques in Canada, while in the United States, there is a move toward such federal regulation of birth technology, especially for protecting the rights of children.

The complexity of this issue is compounded by a resurgence of 19th-century *natalism*, which emphasizes the biological reproduction role of women. Natalism's seductive power is dramatized in the stories of two Montreal couples who began in vitro technology; one couple followed through for years at enormous financial and personal cost, whereas the other dropped out in favor of adoption and a more global (versus individualistic) approach to their desire to care for children (see *The Technological Stork*, Canadian Film Board). But among those parents who in good faith choose adoption, after weathering the crisis of infertility, some are confronted with the loss of their adopted child to biological parents, whose rights are almost always favored by courts, sometimes apparently irrespective of the child's best interests. One couple who faced this crisis made meaning out of their loss by successfully advocating for a change in laws to more fairly protect the rights of all concerned in such cases.

Fatherhood in Transition

Our discussion of parenthood is incomplete without considering the changing notion of fatherhood, especially in regard to prevention of parent–child crises. The changing role of fathers is related to several factors: (1) the necessity for most mothers to work outside the home, (2) financial and other risks of single parenting to all concerned, (3) increasing realization of the benefits to children of being reared by two parents rather than one, and (4) growing awareness by fathers of what they miss emotionally through marginal involvement in parenting.

However, there are strains in this transitional process. Several factors work against contemporary fathers' assuming a more active role in child rearing: (1) continued sex-role socialization at home and in school, (2) continued gender-based inequality in the paid labor force, (3) the tenacious notion that it is more appropriate for a mother than a father to take time from a job on behalf of family needs, (4) lack of role models for male participation in child care, (5) gender-based stereotypes in such professions as nursing and child development, and (6) some women's continued ambivalence about men's active participation.

Because child care is the only arena in which women routinely have exercised control, it is unlikely that they will readily give it up so long as their limited access to other areas of power continues. Language is a barometer of our success here; for example, we still may hear that mothers "take care of their children," whereas fathers "babysit" or "watch" them. Fortunately, this stereotype is changing as stay-at-home fathers assume responsibility for full-time child care. In North America and worldwide, the poverty of children usually mirrors the poverty of their mothers. A 1993 United Nations Human Development Report[11] on 33 countries that keep gender-based statistics reveals that no country (including rich nations like Canada, Germany, Switzerland, and the United States) treats women as well as it treats men.

A social health index measuring, among other items, child poverty and teen suicide reveals that the United States lags behind Western European countries in policies and practices that address the needs of working parents. For example, Western European countries grant paid work leave for attending to family issues, whereas in the United States many cannot afford to take the unpaid family leave available—and this, only to workers in companies of 50 or more employees. Poverty and inadequate child care services are not just issues for welfare mothers; they adversely affect increasing numbers of intact families and struggling parents. Some corporations are also realizing greater business returns, more employee satisfaction, and reduced absenteeism as a result of providing child care benefits. As Sarah Ruddick[12] suggests, children, women, men, and the whole social order would benefit by balancing domestic and public work between women and men.

PHYSICALLY AND MENTALLY HANDICAPPED PERSONS

Becoming a parent can be the occasion of crisis, even if everything occurs as expected. The birth of a handicapped child, however, presents a serious threat to the parents' image of themselves as successful parents. Frequently, the parent asks, "What did I do wrong? What have I done to deserve this?" Parents conclude mistakenly that something they did or failed to do is responsible for their child's handicapped condition and for his or her future as an adult.

Because the parent–child bond is strong, a child's physical or mental handicap may be the parent's handicap as well. The intergenerational aspects of handicap suggest that crisis points and continued care of a handicapped person extend well beyond childhood. The degree of handicap and parental expectations of a normal child influence the likelihood of crisis for concerned parents. Handicaps vary greatly, from Down syndrome to hydrocephalus (characterized by an enlarged head containing excessive fluid), gross deformity or minor physical deformity, to developmental disabilities that surface later, such as a learning disability or hypothyroidism.

Initial Crisis Points for Parents

Whenever the child's handicap becomes known, a parent's usual response includes anger, disbelief, a sense of failure, numbness, fear for the child's welfare, guilt, and an acute sense of loss—of a normal child, and of a sense of success as parents. The parents' initial reactions of disbelief and denial may be compounded unnecessarily by medical personnel who withhold the truth from them. Seventy to eighty percent of developmentally disabled children also have physical disabilities, but parents should not be encouraged to believe that when these physical conditions are remedied, the mental condition will be cured as well.

PARENTING A HANDICAPPED CHILD

Edgar and Jean knew that their daughter Anna was different. But all children are different from one another in one way or another. They did not think much of Anna's particular differences, and they did not question her pediatrician. When Edgar and Jean took Anna, now age 6, for kindergarten evaluation, they were told bluntly that she required special education. The news came as a shock. No psychological or social services had been made available to these parents. Anna's physician had been noncommittal. Finally, the grandparents and a sister convinced them to seek help from a child guidance service.

A child's physical or mental handicap can be a source of crisis for a parent even before the child is born. When medical tests reveal a fetal handicap, parents face the decision of whether to abort the fetus. An infant born with devastating brain damage can now be kept alive through advanced medical technology. Like the spouse and children of an elderly parent who is dying, parents of a handicapped infant are caught in the middle of passionate public debates on life-and-death issues such as whether it is morally justifiable to sustain physical life by extraordinary means when brain death is certain. Parents of unborn children who are certain to die now face another moral dilemma—whether to carry the infant to term in order to donate healthy organs to other infants. Sensitive health care workers will make themselves available to parents who need to work through these dilemmas with compassionate guidance.

Successive Crisis Points for Parents of a Handicapped Child

Parents of children who are developmentally disabled or otherwise handicapped can experience crisis at many different times. The most common among these are when

- When the child is born
- When the child enters school and does not succeed in a normal classroom
- When the child develops behavior problems peculiar to the handicap
- When the child is ridiculed or sexually abused
- When the child reaches adulthood and requires the same care as a child
- When the child becomes an intolerable burden and parents lack resources for necessary care
- When the child needs institutional care but parents cannot go through with it out of misplaced guilt and a sense of total responsibility
- When the child is rejected by society, reminding parents again of their failure to perform as expected
- When parents decide on home-based care instead of the publicly funded institutional care that their child was entitled to, only to discover they are now ineligible for such funds as they plan for the continued care of their adult child after their own deaths

Signs of crisis are easily identified in most parents of handicapped children. These are:

1. *Feelings:* They may deny their feelings and displace their anger onto doctors, nurses, or each other. They feel helpless about what to do. Essentially, they feel they have lost a child as well as their role as successful parents.
2. *Thoughts:* Expectations for the child may be distorted. The parents' problem-solving ability is weakened; they lack a realistic perception of themselves as parents and sometimes expect the impossible. In short, they deny reality.
3. *Behavior.* Sometimes parental denial takes the form of refusing help. Sometimes help is not readily available, or parents are unable to seek out and use available help without active intervention from others.

EXAMPLE: MONA ANDERSON AND FAMILY—DOWN SYNDROME

Mona Anderson's experience illustrates these signs of crisis and the manner in which a maternal health nurse successfully intervened. Mona, age 31 and married for 10 years, wanted a child for several years before she finally became pregnant. Her baby girl was born with Down syndrome. When Mona was tactfully informed of this by the physician and nurse in the presence of her husband, she became hysterical. Initially, she refused to look at the baby. Whenever the nurse attempted to talk with her about the baby's condition, she denied that she could give birth to a "defective child." The nurse allowed her this period of denial but gradually and consistently informed her of the reality of her child's condition. During this time, Mona's husband was also very supportive. Neither he nor the nurse insisted that Mona see the baby before she was ready.

When Mona felt ready, the nurse brought the baby in, and Mona broke down, crying, "All I wanted was a normal baby. I didn't expect a genius." Mona continued to grieve over her loss of a normal child. Gradually, she was able to talk with the nurse about her hopes for her child, her sense of loss, and what she could and could not expect of her baby girl. Although the nurse could not answer all of Mona's or her husband's questions, she referred them to a children's institute for genetic counseling. They were also given the name and number of a self-help group of parents of children with Down syndrome.

The nurse was also helpful to other members of Mona's family who were drawn into the crisis. Mona's sister had had a baby 2 months previously. She concluded, wrongly, that she could not come to visit Mona with her normal baby because such a visit would only remind Mona again of her "abnormal" baby. The nurse counseled the family members against staying away, as it would only support Mona's denial of the reality of her child's condition.

The nurse, in the course of her usual work in a maternity ward, practiced successful crisis care by supporting Mona through her denial and mourning periods, offering factual information about the reality of Down syndrome, and actively linking Mona to her family and outside specialty resources for future help that go beyond the scope of this book. Such sources should also be easily available in pediatric clinics and waiting rooms. Because hospital stays after delivery are only a day or two, a visiting nurse plus respite care should be available in a situation like Mona's.

Crises of Handicapped People

Besides crises around parenting a handicapped child, any person, child or adult, with a handicap is more vulnerable than others to additional stressors, trauma, and potential crises. For example, physical limitations may prevent some handicapped people from protecting themselves in cases of domestic dispute, rape, or robbery. Lack of access to public transportation and buildings affects mobility for some. Others cannot take care of their own financial security and other requisites for a healthy self-image.

Another vulnerability of people with mental handicaps is that their grief following the loss of a loved one often goes unnoticed (see Chapter 3 for "Loss, Grief, and Bereavement"). The alienation and feelings of powerlessness associated with such vulnerability can also lead to unhealthy coping, such as excessive drinking.

ADOLESCENCE AND YOUNG ADULTHOOD: DANGER AND OPPORTUNITY

Opinion regarding the age span of adolescence varies in different cultures and according to different theorists. The Joint Commission on Mental Health of Children in the United States considered youth up to age 25 in the program it recommended for youth in the 1970s. The extent of adolescence is influenced by such factors as (1) length of time spent in school, (2) age at first marriage, (3) parenthood or the lack of it, (4) age at first self-supporting job, and (5) residence (with or apart from parents). In general, adolescence can be considered in two stages: early and late. Late adolescence overlaps with young adulthood, particularly for those who prolong vocational and educational preparation into their early and middle twenties.

Developmental Challenges and Stress

During early adolescence, psychologist Erik Erikson[13] cites achievement of "ego identity" as the major developmental task. Adolescents and young adults must give up the security of dependence on parents and accept new roles in society, including work responsibility and a capacity for intimacy. Adolescents typically struggle with issues of independence and freedom from family, for example, needing material and emotional support from family while perhaps resenting their continued dependence on parents. Interdependence—a balance between excessive dependence and independence—is a mark of growth during this stage.

Developmental tasks during late adolescence include finding and adjustment to independence and developing a capacity for intimacy in one's sex role, for example, finding and holding a satisfying job; succeeding in college, technical training, or graduate school; and adjusting to a lifestyle such as marriage or communal living.

Success with the developmental tasks of adolescence is influenced by what happened during infancy and childhood, including transitions such as toilet training, weaning, and starting school. An unhappy childhood is the usual precursor to unhappiness as an adolescent or young adult. Successful completion of the tasks of adolescence or young adulthood is accomplished only if parents know when to let go and do not prevent the young person from making decisions she or he can make independently. Among affluent families, the term "helicopter parent" describes parents who overschedule their child's day, hire tutors to assure admission to elite colleges, and hover over their children, which may stunt their opportunity to confront life's challenges toward eventual independence. Yet some young people may face new opportunities or terrifying threats with insufficient support. Successful transition to adulthood is rooted in the soil of opportunities to explore and the gift of healthy relationships.

US society has been described as youth oriented. This does not mean that Americans particularly value younger people; rather, it may signal a devaluation of older people. As youth violence and gang activity attest, services for both normal and troubled young people are grossly lacking in many communities. The youthful population in every community should have access to emergency hostels, where young people can go if abused by their parents or are seeking refuge from conflict. Housing for youthful offenders should be in special facilities with a strong community focus, not with hardened criminals. And all schools should provide suicide prevention programs. The lack of specialized services for disturbed children and adolescents needing psychiatric hospitalization has reached crisis proportions in many places, a problem exacerbated by the "second cousin" status of crisis and mental health services in the health care system, and the epidemic of misuse of psychotropic drugs for young children and college students (see Chapters 3 and 7).

In their search for identity and meaning, many young people turn to religion for a sense of belonging, with some caught up in age-old religion-inspired wars and ethnic hatred. As a young multicultural adult, Iboo Patel[14] wrote poignantly about the positive role of faith and his identity as a Muslim, an Indian, and an American. The Interfaith Youth Core he founded in Chicago is an inspiring account of how informed and idealistic young people can reduce religion-based hatred and reap the fruits of peaceful religious pluralism. His example could be replicated in families and among youth groups worldwide to help heal our divided world.

Sexual-Identity Crisis

While many adolescents are at increased risk of destructive behaviors toward self and others, gay, lesbian, bisexual, and transgendered youth are at even greater risk, especially of suicide. Though complex factors intersect during all adolescent crises, homophobia in mainstream North America is commonly assumed to underpin the crises and chronic problems faced by gay youth. Anthropologist W. L. Williams's[15] studies among Native people of North American, Pacific, and Southeast Asian cultures reveal how these people revere androgynous members of the community as "higher" because the spirit from which all life (human, animal, plant) emanates has blessed the person with *two* spirits; hence, the person is respected as a "double person," with particular roles and contributions to make in religion, the family, the workplace, and the community at large. Thus, "difference is transformed—from *deviant* to *exceptional*—becoming a basis for respect rather than stigma" (p. 267). From his fieldwork with the Lakota, for example, Williams notes that the *berdache* (androgynous men) are the first choice to become adoptive parents when there is a homeless child—a marked contrast to nearly universal policy in most North American jurisdictions, which forbids such adoption, allegedly to prevent sexual molestation.

Activists and others in the GLBT community know firsthand the enormous costs of homophobia to *all*—those who are stigmatized, victimized, and deprived of an opportunity to live peaceful and fruitful lives, as well as those who have accepted the notion that these "different" people are also evil. But the highest price is paid by adolescents during the vulnerable developmental stage of discovering their sexual

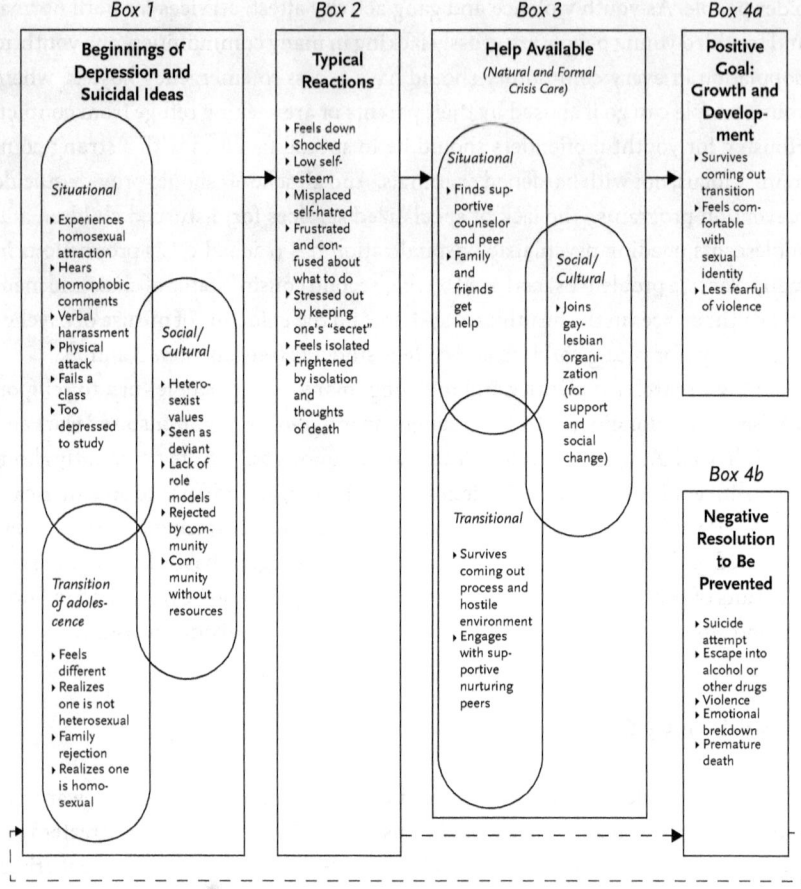

Figure 9.1 The Crisis Paradigm: Sexual Identity Crisis

identity in a homophobic mainstream society and coming to terms with who they are without engaging in self-destructive behaviors. Figure 9.1 illustrates the sexual-identity crisis that many lesbian, gay, bisexual, and transgendered youth experience. It depicts the Crisis Paradigm applied to this at-risk group of adolescents, highlighting both the danger and the opportunity to move beyond homophobia toward a more egalitarian value system, as espoused by many pre-Columbian Native communities. The good news is that attitudes and policies about sexual identity are changing worldwide in favor of equality and safety for all.

EXAMPLE: ROBERT—A GAY HAITIAN YOUTH

An immigrant in Boston describes an encounter with a fellow immigrant, Robert: "One day while I was riding the T (Boston subway) I was approached by a young man asking for money. Although his clothes were dirty and he looked as though he had not showered that day, something about him made me want to know his history. So I asked him, 'If you don't mind, could you tell me how you got in this situation.' He looked at me as though stunned that someone would want to hear *his* story. And so he smiled and explained with a heavy accent that he was originally from Haiti, which we all know is a country in turmoil. His parents wanted to send him to the United States to live with some relatives he had in Boston. Leaving his family and all that he knew behind, Robert left what he called home. He explained that he was still very young... around 13 or 14 and that people do this all the time. Fortunately for him, he finished high school and went to a community college in Boston. Life seemed to be going great. He met a guy friend with whom he explored his sexuality. His relatives did not accept this, due to the fact that homosexuality is considered a huge dishonor to one's family within the Haitian community. Slowly things got worse with his relatives. His uncle would beat him whenever he thought he was going out with his gay friends. Therefore, Robert moved in with his boyfriend. He explained that they never used protection and how they began to use drugs. He was not sure whether it was through sharing needles or the unprotected sex, but somehow he contracted the HIV virus. He gave me the most serious look as he told me that he could never return home and was simply waiting to die."

Let's consider the cross-cultural *commonalities* and *unique* features of Robert's crisis.

Commonalities

1. As with other immigrants, Robert suffers the loss of his native country and proximity to parents and homeland.
2. Robert struggles with education and jobs in an economy less than supportive and friendly to "outsiders."
3. As with most others in the gay community, Robert experienced a sexual identity crisis in discovering his homosexuality.
4. Like millions of others, Robert was in crisis on learning he is HIV positive and all that news of this serious illness entails.

Unique Features

1. The cultural value of the Haitian community regarding homosexual orientation, compared with growing acceptance of gay identity in the United States, Canada, and other countries.
2. Robert's sense of isolation in realizing that he could not return home to his family of origin, given their values about sexual identity, and feeling abandoned in a foreign culture as he faced the prospect of an untimely death from AIDS.

Helping Young People

As members of the human community, we all have a role in the care and protection of children—our future for good or ill. Parents, teachers, pastors, youth directors, guidance and residence counselors, primary care providers, and school nurses are in especially powerful positions to help or hinder young people in their quest for identity and a meaningful place in society. Help may mean simply being available and attentive when a young person is upset and wants to talk; offering information the person needs for making decisions about career, education, or marriage; guiding young people in the use of counseling and other resources when in crisis; and strongly advocating for youth suffering neglect, abuse, or other injustice.

The crisis care principle of doing things *with*, rather than *to* and *for*, troubled people is particularly important when helping the young (see Chapter 3, "Decision Counseling"). Because a major developmental task of adolescence is finding a unique place in society and achieving healthy interdependence, inattention to this principle can defeat the purpose of the helping relationship. Certainly, a young person in trouble needs a caring adult to help with certain decisions, for example, how to protect oneself if sexually active. As in work with troubled adults, a teenager in crisis should participate in any decision affecting him or her unless that is clearly impossible under certain circumstances. Some adults assume that young people are incapable of making decisions and accepting responsibility; or, in contrast, some adolescents may be forced into decisions and responsibilities they may not be ready for. Either extreme attitude causes trouble. Crises and ongoing problems such as drug abuse, delinquency, and violence can often be avoided when young people have the support they need for healthy development.

FAMILIES AND COMMUNITIES IN CRISIS

Although social relations are important during a crisis, often the members of a person's family and social network are themselves in crisis. Crisis researchers consider family troubles in terms of sources, effect on family functioning, and type of event the family faces if the source of trouble is within the family itself—usually more distressing than external sources such as a flood or racial prejudice. Often, an individual in crisis may precipitate a family crisis. For example, if family members make suicide attempts or abuse alcohol, the family usually lacks basic harmony and healthy functioning.

Family and crisis care pioneer R. Hill[16] notes that family troubles and distress can result from *dismemberment* (loss of family member), *accession* (an unexpected addition of a member), *demoralization* (loss of morale and family unity), or a combination of all three. These stressful events are often associated with crises. Death and hospitalization are examples of *dismemberment*. Unwanted pregnancy, a source of crisis for the girl or woman, is also an example of *accession* to the family and therefore a possible occasion of family crisis as well. A person in crisis because of trouble with the law for delinquency or drug addiction may trigger family *demoralization* and crisis. Divorce and the addition of children, stepparents, and stepfamilies also lead to dismemberment and accession. Together, these changes in family role and relationships may be experienced as loss and significant stress. Divorce, suicide, homicide, illegitimacy, imprisonment, and institutionalization for mental illness are examples of *demoralization* and *dismemberment* or *accession.*

The nuclear family (father, mother, and children) is the norm in most Western societies, whereas the extended family (including relatives) is the norm in most non-Western societies. Among immigrant Mexican women in the United States, for example, relatives of the family of origin are more important sources of emotional support than friends. It is now widely recognized and accepted that the traditional nuclear family form is being replaced by a variety of family forms. This includes an increasing role of grandparents or other relatives assisting with child rearing.

Communal or "New Age" families may provide more avenues of support for some people than do traditional nuclear families. A current variation on these themes is the cohousing approach, which is designed to address some of the family issues faced by all. Cohousing was initiated by a Danish divorced mother seeking greater support for rearing her children. Developed from the utopian ideal put forth by Thomas More (1516/1965) in the 16th century, the concept encompasses several features intended to

- Provide privacy through separate, self-contained units for individuals and families
- Relieve isolation and alienation and promote community by an arrangement of clustered homes, a shared common house, a shared garden, play and work space, community dinners, and perhaps a computer center
- Encourage diversity by welcoming a broad range of residents and lifestyles
- Promote a sense of ownership and empowerment by participatory planning and design from the start

Pioneered primarily in Denmark and adapted to US culture by Katherine McCamant and Charles Durett during the 1970s and 1980s, the Cohousing movement highlights the advantages of traditional village life in contemporary communities (see www.coho.org). Hundreds of Cohousing communities exist in Western Europe and North America or are in start-up stages. A similar "village" concept has been replicated across many US cities. It is modeled after Beacon Hill Village in Boston, where aging homeowners in five-level houses recognized their need for assistance but resisted moving to institutions for "assisted living." By organizing among themselves for transportation to medical appointments, grocery shopping, and other business they were able to stay in the homes they loved—at least temporarily—barring a major medical event. But at life's end, hospice care is now widely available in homes.

Increasingly, people call on friends and peers for essential material and social support that traditionally came from one's extended family. However, these new family forms can also be the source of unanticipated conflict when lines of authority are unclear, when opinions differ about privacy and intimacy, and when the group cannot reach consensus about how to get necessary domestic work done, or meet children's educational and medical needs, plus their socialization toward responsible adulthood. Whether or not stressful events lead to crisis depends on a family's resources for handling upsetting events and meeting the emotional needs of all family members.

With its unique position in society, the family is the most natural source of support and understanding for most people when in trouble. But for some, "family" is also the arena in which some persons endure the most acute distress or even abuse and violence. All families have problems, and all families have ways of dealing with them, with varying degrees of success in problem solving—often depending on available resources. Despite the burdens many face traceable to family stress, discord, or abuse, crisis workers can enhance individuals' prospects of moving beyond their family troubles. Adults in troubled crisis-prone families should take the lead in obtaining crisis prevention and counseling service, while also remaining watchful of being labeled as "dysfunctional" or beyond repair. Crisis prevention in families is often tied to public policies regarding health care, affordable housing, and gender equality in wages and child care.

A family's vulnerability to crisis is influenced by how it defines a traumatic event. For some families, a divorce or a pregnancy without marriage is considered nearly catastrophic; for others, these are simply new situations to cope with, often affected by religious and other values. Similarly, an upper-middle-class family experiencing financial loss typically has other reserves to draw on. In contrast, for a poor family, financial loss can be the "last straw." But we also need to look beyond the family for influences on family disharmony and crisis vulnerability. For example, welfare reform policies requiring mothers with inadequate job skills to work for poverty-level wages and unaffordable child care may result in children already at risk facing even greater odds in healthy development. Overall, these policy failures and the continuing pattern in numbers of children born to single mothers shine a light on this pattern: Falling birthrates over five generations correlate with the improvement in women's educational and economic status, regardless of race or ethnicity. It is easier, of course, to blame women for their dependency than to address the socioeconomic and cultural origins of welfare dependency.

Blaming families in crisis traced to deeply rooted social problems is more significant when considering that the United States is the only industrialized country without a national family policy regarding maternity and paternity leaves, child care, and flexible work schedules. In contrast, most Western European parents can take such leave *with* pay. Vulnerable and stable families themselves, with their concerned neighbors and friends, might turn the tide on this issue through systematic action aimed at crisis prevention in whole communities, such as organized gangs and danger to children.

EXAMPLE: THE PAGE FAMILY AND CRISIS COUNSELING

Donald Page, 44, and Ann Page, 39, had been married for 20 years and had four children: Alice, age 20; Michael, 18; Betsy, 14; and Gary, 9. Donald worked in a local automobile factory. After 2 years in military service, he returned home as a disabled veteran. Ann worked as a secretary prior to their marriage and returned to work when her husband joined the service. When Donald returned, the Pages moved to a small farm on the outskirts of a large city. They leased the farmland, and Donald stayed at home most of every day doing odd jobs around the farm. He did few routine household chores, even though Ann worked full-time outside the home. The Pages had a bleak social life, and in general their marriage and family life were strained.

The Page children felt isolated because it was difficult to see their friends except during school hours. Alice had a baby at age 17 and dropped out of her junior year in high school. She and her mother quarreled constantly over responsibility for the baby, who lived in the family home. After 2 years of this fighting, Alice's parents asked her to find a place of her own, which she did. Ann, meanwhile, threatened to report Alice to child protection authorities if she did not start assuming more responsibility for her child. Ann really wanted to keep Alice's baby herself, for she had wanted another child. Alice also talked about giving her baby away to her mother.

Betsy, meanwhile, was reported to be having problems in school, and teachers suspected her of taking drugs. Betsy had been belligerent at home, refusing to do chores and staying out late. Finally, Betsy ran away from home and was returned by police after 3 days. Donald and Ann were advised by police and school authorities to seek help for Betsy. They did not follow through and continued alone in their struggle to control her behavior. Michael tried to help both Betsy and his parents, but he felt pulled between the two parties. Gary was the "spoiled" child and occasionally asked why everyone was fighting all the time.

When Betsy's school problems heightened, she was threatened with expulsion and a week later ran away again. This time when police found her, she threatened suicide if she was taken home. Police therefore took her to a community mental health emergency service, where she saw a crisis counselor; she begged to be placed in a detention center rather than go back home. After several hours with Betsy, the counselor was able to persuade her that she could help her and her family make things more tolerable at home and that a detention center was no place for a girl her age, at least not until other alternatives had been tried.

Betsy's parents, meanwhile, were called and asked to come to the crisis clinic. Betsy felt hopeless about anything changing at home, although she expressed the wish that somehow things could get better. She particularly hated two situations: (1) her father and mother fighting about what she could and could not do and whom she could and could not see and (2) her mother's and Alice's constant fighting about Alice's baby. If these situations at home did not change, she said she just wanted to die.

The Pages agreed to a contract for eight crisis counseling sessions that were to involve the entire family, including Alice. One of the sessions was with the parents, Alice, and Betsy only. Another session was with the parents, Betsy, the school guidance counselor, principal, and homeroom teacher. The following goals were established for the counseling sessions:

1. Improve communication among all members of the family and cut out the contradictory messages Betsy was receiving
2. Help family members detect signs of distress among themselves and learn to listen and support one another when troubled
3. Work out a mutually agreeable program of social outlets for Betsy
4. Work out a plan to divide the chores in a reasonable and consistent way among all family members
5. Arrive at an agreeable system of discipline that includes rewards and punishments appropriate to various behaviors
6. Help Alice make satisfying decisions regarding herself and her baby
7. Develop a plan to work cooperatively with Betsy's teachers and the guidance counselor to resolve Betsy's problems in school

Family members agreed on various tasks to achieve these goals. For example, Donald and Ann would set aside some private time each day to discuss their problems and disagreements about discipline—out of the children's range of hearing. Betsy agreed to follow through on certain chores around the house. If she failed to do so, Ann agreed not to pick up after her and to discuss disciplinary measures with Donald. Alice would seek individual counseling to assist her in making a decision about herself and her child.

Two of the counseling sessions were held in the home, which the counselor observed was quite crowded. One result of this meeting was that the family found ways of ensuring individual privacy in spite of cramped quarters.

The threats of Betsy's suicide attempt and school expulsion were crisis points that moved Donald and Ann to work on underlying problems in their marriage. These problems made parenthood more difficult than it might otherwise have been. After eight crisis counseling sessions the Page family existence was less disturbed but by no means tranquil. However, Betsy was no longer in danger of being expelled from school, and she at least preferred her home to a detention house. Donald and Ann Page agreed to marriage counseling after termination of the crisis counseling contract in an effort to make their future years as parents less burdensome. The attention directed to dealing with marriage and family problems may decrease the chance that Betsy will follow in her sister's footsteps and become pregnant out of wedlock.

INTIMATE RELATIONSHIPS: BEGINNINGS AND ENDINGS

Basic human needs and the prevention of destructive outcomes of crises form an interdependent network of individuals, families, and communities in dynamic positive relationships. Human needs in regard to the self and the social network include privacy, intimacy, and community. Leading a reasonably happy life requires freedom from excessive strain, a balanced fulfillment of needs in all three areas.

Privacy, Intimacy, Community

A person can seldom have too much privacy if social needs are being met. The problem of too much privacy may negatively affect our need for intimacy and community. When social needs are seriously lacking, the result may be suicide by an isolated person who is lonely and feels rejected by others.

The excessively dependent and clinging person is too insecure to be alone in his or her private world. A person afraid of ever being alone most likely has been stunted in full psychosocial development, so that his or her capacity for privacy is unawakened. Typically, such a person does not recognize how unfulfilling an overly dependent relationship can be. For example, a man completely dependent on his spouse is a prime candidate for a suicide attempt when his wife threatens to divorce him; the wife is also deprived of essential privacy and feels exhausted by her partner's excessive dependency.

Intimacy as a basic human need implies a close bond between two people who trust each other for affection, reciprocity, and willingness to stand by when in distress without expectation of reward. The emphasis here is on psychological and social intimacy, although a sexual relationship may also exist. Whether married, single, or living with someone of the same or opposite sex, intimate relationships are essential to a happy, productive life. Sexual relationships alone do not necessarily imply intimacy.

The social and emotional bonds between people in a healthy intimate relationship are significant for the health of the entire community. Most common of these relationships are courtship, marriage, and deeply committed friendships outside marriage. Entering into such a relationship has important social and psychological ramifications. Common relationship endings with crisis potential include divorce or widowhood, but other less official disruptions of close bonds can be equally traumatic and crisis prone. The change in role and status from single to married, from spouse to divorcee, from associate to friend, or from friend to forgotten one, typically includes feelings of loss, mourning, insecurity, and vulnerability to crisis, particularly among adolescents.

Excessive Dependence on Intimate Attachments

Because intimacy with others is an integral part of our lives, deep emotion and importance are attached to intimate relationships. Some people have unrealistic expectations of those they love and may behave in unusual ways when the bond is threatened or broken. Others may have such deep fear of possible rejection that they repeatedly resist offers of friendship, love, and intimacy. Crisis can occur at the beginning of attachments or when the intimate relationship is disrupted, as in divorce, death of a spouse, or betrayal by a friend.

Relationship expert Howard Halpern[17] discusses "addictions" to people—a topic routinely noted in newspaper "advice" columns. It addresses the excessive need to be attached to someone special. For such "needy" persons, remembering Halpern's maxims and those described in other self-help books can help buffer the crisis potential when breaking out of addictive, co-dependent, or other destructive relationships; for example

1. You can live—and possibly live better—without the person to whom you are attached.
2. A mutual love relationship should help one feel better, not worse, about oneself.
3. Guilt is not reason enough to stay in a relationship.
4. Some people die of destructive relationships. Do you want to be one of them?
5. If someone says, "I'm not ready for a relationship," or "I'm not going to leave my spouse," or "I don't want to be tied down," believe it.
6. The pain of ending a relationship, like other crises, will not last forever. In fact, it will not last as long as the pain of sustaining it.
7. We are whole and valuable as individuals apart from particular relationships.
8. When we end a destructive relationship, we open our lives to new possibilities.

Impact of Individual and Family Crises on Whole Communities

In small communal or religious groups, the deprivation of individual needs or rebellion against group norms can mushroom into a crisis for the entire membership. Social and economic inequities among racial and ethnic groups or police brutality can trigger a large-scale community crisis. The risk of crisis for these groups is influenced by:

- Social and economic stability of individual family units within a neighborhood
- Level at which individual and family needs are met
- Adequacy of neighborhood resources for social, housing, economic, and recreational needs
- Personality characteristics and strengths of the group's members

In psychologist Abraham Maslow's[18] "hierarchy" of needs, beyond hunger, thirst, and protection from the elements, other needs emerge, such as social interaction and pleasant surroundings. When these basic needs are unmet, people are increasingly crisis prone. Worldwide, poverty is rampant, and people suffer from hunger, war, and other disasters. Slum landlords take advantage of people already disadvantaged; for example, threatening to cut off essential utilities for persons who cannot pay skyrocketing rates, leaving them vulnerable to death by exposure. Emergency medical and social services may be inadequate or inaccessible in complex bureaucratic systems.

Similar deprivations exist on North American Indian reservations, among migrant farm groups, and in sprawling cities with shantytowns (especially in the Southern Hemisphere), where millions of the world's poorest people eke out a way to survive. As a result of the personal, social, and economic deprivations in these communities, crime becomes widespread, adding another threat to basic survival. Another crisis-prone setting is the subculture of the average jail or prison. Physical survival is threatened by poor health service and danger of suicide. Prisoners fear rape and physical attack by fellow prisoners. Social needs of prisoners go unmet to the extent that the term *rehabilitation* does not apply to what happens in prisons. This situation, combined with community attitudes, unemployment, poverty, and underfunded mental health services, leaves ex-offenders highly crisis prone after release from prison (see Chapter 1, "Revolving Door" and Chapter 6).

Natural disasters such as floods, hurricanes, and severe snowstorms and real or threatened acts of terrorism are other sources of community crisis (see Chapter 8). In one small town, families and children were threatened and virtually immobilized by an 18-year-old youth suspected of being a child molester. Another small community feared for everyone's safety when three teenagers threatened to bomb the local schools and police station in response to their own crises: The teenagers had been expelled from school and were unemployed.

Communities in crisis have several characteristics in common with individuals in crisis. First, within the group, an atmosphere of tension and fear is widespread. Second, rumors run rampant during a community crisis. Individuals in large groups color and distort facts out of fear and lack of knowledge. Third, normal functioning is inhibited or at a standstill. Schools and businesses are often closed; health and emergency resources may be in short supply. However, as is the case with families, traumatic events such as war, school violence, and terrorist attacks can also mobilize and strengthen a group or nation (see Chapter 8).

Singles, Isolation, and Divorce

Considered within the privacy, intimacy, and community dynamic, excessive dependency on intimacy usually results in a neglect of basic needs for privacy and community. On the other hand, remaining attached to people who are not good for us is often linked to one's fear of social isolation.

Social opportunities, especially for the single person who has moved recently to a new community, are often lacking. In many communities, social events are organized around couple relationships. Consequently, a single person may find it extremely difficult or impossible to feel comfortable in a tightly knit society demanding that people participate as couples. Many communities now have singles organizations in which single people of any age can make friends and enjoy a wide range of social activities. Fortunately, the single state is now accepted by many as a fulfilling lifestyle, making it easier for the single person to establish social contacts in a new community.

A person not single by choice and unable to make friends easily is likely to be crisis prone. Psychotherapy may be indicated for a person who is chronically unhappy or depressed about being single; if living alone, that person is also at a greater risk for suicide. In general, the risks of isolation and crisis responses like suicide are greater when the person is single because of divorce, separation, or widowhood.

Divorce is particularly hazardous when the burden of care and support of young children falls entirely on one parent and when older people divorce and their value system has no place for divorce. The crisis potential of nonmutual divorce actions is high because of (1) lack of expectation; (2) contradiction of deeply held values; or (3) widespread absence of social support structures for these special groups. Consider the following example of what divorce can mean to an older person.

EXAMPLE: HELEN—DIVORCE

Helen, age 64, was not allowed to continue working in the same government agency as her husband, Tom, when they had married decades earlier. It was understood and accepted then that a husband should have the advantage of career development, and the wife should tend the home and children. Giving up her fledgling career as a civil servant was not a problem for Helen, as it was also understood and expected that marriage was for a lifetime and that her future economic support was secure. When Helen was 60, Tom, then age 64, left her for a woman 25 years his junior. Helen felt devastated and suicidal, saying over and over to her friends and two adult children that somehow it must have been her fault. She said repeatedly that Tom's death would have been preferable to a divorce.

Helen had a hard time acknowledging to anyone but her family and closest friends that she was divorced. She felt ashamed and frequently referred to herself as a widow. Helen could not understand how her daughter Caroline, also divorced, could be so apparently unruffled by the event. (Caroline had no children, worked as a writer, and preferred her single life.) Helen's only marketable job skill was babysitting. She was also a good gardener and cook but had no paid work experience in these fields. Besides being mateless at age 60, Helen barely escaped homelessness. By a stroke of luck, she obtained the marital home and was able to rent one room so she could pay taxes and utilities. There was no legal provision, however, for her to receive benefits from her husband's pension.

Despite these hardships, Helen scraped by and came out of her depression after 2 years. She now takes advantage of senior citizen travel packages such as Road Scholar and attends adult education classes. She is attractive, charming, and dearly loved by her friends and family, and she acknowledges at times that she may be better off without Tom in spite of occasional loneliness. Two years ago, Helen turned down the marriage proposal of a courtly but sickly older man. Although she was fond of this man, she resisted tying herself down to what she anticipated would eventually turn into a nursing role, especially after she had adjusted to her new freedom.

The harsh realities of some singles are contradicted by stereotypes of swinging singles with a carefree existence. The single state without children does provide greater freedom to pursue a career or engage in other activities, but the hazards of single parenthood speak for themselves. Every lifestyle has its advantages and trade-offs; for example, greater freedom and less responsibility may be balanced against greater insecurity in old age. Social research in the last century, beginning with Durkheim[19] a century ago, consistently reveals that marriage is in fact more advantageous and ego protective for men than it is for women. But women and men who have never married are better adjusted and are less at risk for suicide than those who have lost a spouse by any means. The hazards to individuals in these transition states might be modified by contemporary rites of passage, such as divorce ceremonies and acceptance into widows' clubs. Lacking such social supports can leave single people in a permanent liminal (transitional) state, as they are never quite reincorporated into the community in their new role.

From Privacy and Intimacy to Community

People who feel in charge of themselves and capable of living in their private world are at a great advantage as they reach out and establish intimate attachments. They may have a mature marital relationship or a small circle of intimate friends to rely on. This enables them to establish and enjoy additional relationships in the work world and larger community.

Such a healthy scenario can be halted in many situations: (1) if a person feels too insecure to establish intimate or communal attachments; (2) if a person is handicapped by mental illness, has been institutionalized for a long time, or has a history of rejection by family and others; (3) if a couple establishes an intimate attachment that is essentially closed and turned inward, thus limiting need fulfillment from the larger community; or (4) if a small communal group (for example, a religious cult) turns in on itself and fails to relate to the larger community. In all of these situations, healthy interaction is halted; an extreme example of this is the mass suicides of some cult groups.

Just as individuals in crisis are entwined with their families, so are families bound up with their community. An entire neighborhood may feel the impact of an individual in crisis. In one small community, a man shot himself in his front yard. The entire community was affected by this man's crisis—to say nothing of his wife and small children. Of course, the murder or abduction of a child invariably incites communitywide fear on behalf of other children. These situations call for a crisis response to the entire community, including special sessions for school children. Violence prevention targeted to schools, children, and teachers demands planning similar to disaster preparedness (see Chapter 8).

CHRONIC PROBLEMS AND CRISIS VULNERABILITY: BOUNDARIES AND DISTINCTIONS

Psychiatrist Norris Hansell[20] was an early proponent of social network strategies for people in distress. Social network approaches are ideal venues for persons with chronic emotional and social problems and address how these issues intersect with the repeated crisis situations faced by some individuals and families. As noted in Chapter 2, "chronic crisis" is essentially a contradiction.

Dr. Hansell expounds on this issue, especially in his description of the "Seven Essential Attachments" (pp. 31–49). The ideal of living comfortably with our family and community may seem unreachable for someone who seems to be in a perpetual rut with "one thing after another" popping up repeatedly with little noticeable progress. Every individual or family experiencing frequent crises related to chronic or deep-seated problems might benefit from a "network" approach to end what may seem like a "revolving door" or unending and hopeless situation. Family therapy is also indicated in these cases.

Social Network Influences on the Individual

A child born into a chaotic, socially unstable family may find it difficult to settle into a hostile world. Such a child is more crisis prone at developmental turning points, such as entering school or beginning puberty. The child's family, in turn, is affected by the surrounding community. Both the child and the family are influenced by economic and employment opportunities; racial, ethnic, or other types of prejudice; the quality of available schools; family and social services; and recreational opportunities for youth. When a sufficient number of individuals and families are adversely affected by these factors, the whole community is more prone to crisis.

Thus, the idea of individuals, families, and communities interacting underscores the importance of addressing human crises in a social framework. Psychiatrist Seymour Halleck[21] suggests that it may be unethical for a therapist to spend professional time focusing on a single individual in prison who has made a suicide attempt. A more responsible approach is using professional skills to *influence the prison system that contributes to suicidal crises*. As violence escalates and the subcultures of US prisons explode with overcrowding and more violence, the crises in these communities will only increase as long as the socioeconomic and cultural roots of aggression and violence are ignored (see Chapter 6).

Extending this argument to the home, emergency treatment of abused or troubled children without explicit attention to family factors is simply inexcusable given what is known about crisis care. The tragic death of 5-year-old Rebecca Riley in metropolitan Boston received national attention as malpractice; her parents were criminally charged in her death from adult-only drugs, while the attending psychiatrist apparently ignored the tumultuous parental problems in her family, including intimate partner abuse. Work with survivors of abuse and sexual assault supports similar conclusions: These individuals' crises originate from society's values about women, marriage, the family, and violence (see Crisis Paradigm, Chapter 1, Fig. 1.1). In this and similar complex social situations, everyone should expect a *social network approach* instead of overreliance on drugs, which are no substitute for resolving deep-seated family issues.

SOCIAL NETWORK AND GROUP APPROACHES TO CRISIS CARE

Among families in crisis and professional providers, why should they pay close attention to this topic? Clients and crisis counselors who have experienced the success and rewards of social network strategies with individuals and families have described it as a "miracle" compared with some other help-seeking efforts. Just sitting in the same room with key players in complex or repeat crisis episodes opens their eyes to things they never considered—nor was there time for it in a typical 15-minute individual appointment for yet another crisis.

Social approaches to crisis intervention never underestimate the interactional network between individuals, families, and other elements. Success in crisis care involves helping distressed persons to reconnect themselves in harmony with an intimate partner, family, and the larger community. In practice, this might mean, for example,

- Relieving the extreme isolation that led to a suicide attempt
- Developing a satisfying relationship to replace the loss of one's partner or a close friend

- Reestablishing ties in the work world and resolving job conflicts
- Returning to normal school tasks after expulsion for truancy, drug abuse, or violence
- Establishing stability and a means of family support after desertion by an alcoholic parent
- Allaying community anxiety concerning bomb threats or child safety
- Identifying why a client complains that "no one is helping me" when, in fact, five agencies (or more) are officially involved but not meaningfully connected to others in the network

People experiencing "repeat" crises or who may feel hopeless in a confusing mental health system should know that in each of these instances, an individual, psychotherapeutic approach is often used but *alone will seldom result in change if the social roots of the problems are not considered upfront*. And if a person is receiving care in several different agencies, a family member might ask the primary care provider a question like this: "My child is not getting any better... Why can't we all get together and see if we can get to the bottom of things?"

Anyone in a troubled family experiencing seemingly endless problems should know that a social strategy for this kind of situation is appropriate. And considering that the evidence supporting it is so extensive, one wonders why so many mental health practitioners rely primarily on individual approaches—including psychotropic drugs—to crisis resolution. The reasons are complex, of course, and related to issues such as the medicalization of life problems, political and economic factors influencing illness and its treatment, and the influence of the pharmaceutical industry in a culture featuring a "new pill" for problems that demand more for successful crisis resolution (see Chapters 1 and 3).

The lay public and families should note that increasing numbers of practitioners are choosing social strategies for helping distressed people. In an era before biological psychiatry (brain science) became dominant, the experience of social psychiatrists suggested that *social network techniques are among the most practical and effective available to crisis workers*. Psychiatrist and crisis pioneer Norris Hansell referred to network strategies as the *screening-linking-planning conference method*. This method was developed and used extensively in community mental health systems in Chicago and Buffalo on behalf of high-risk psychiatric patients and others. Social psychiatrist Paul Polak[22] called it *social systems intervention* in his community mental health work in Colorado.

The use of network strategies in resolving highly complex crisis situations is unparalleled in mental health practice. Their effectiveness is based on recognition and acceptance of the person's basic social nature. These network techniques should not be neglected in favor of excessive reliance on medications, a pattern traceable in part to cost containment measures and the dominance of biological psychiatry. As noted in Chapter 3, psychoactive drugs are often highly effective but rarely are sufficient without other forms of therapy.

Successful crisis care builds on faith in a person's social network and ways to mobilize these people on behalf of a distressed person. On the other hand, a crisis counselor's lack of conviction about social strategies translates into a negative self-fulfilling prophecy; that is, the response of a distressed person's social network members is highly dependent on what the client and counselor *expect* will happen. This means approaching the distressed individual, his or her family, and other involved providers with a positive attitude that conveys an expectation of a cooperative response and that each person in the network has something valuable or essential to offer the distressed individual.

Social Network Strategies and Referrals

Families and individuals dealing with chronic problems that intersect with repeat crisis episodes should know that successful social network intervention usually requires the skills of crisis or mental health specialists. For time and other reasons, this means that they must be *open to and accept referrals* by primary care providers who cannot apply this strategy in a 15- to 20-minute clinic appointment or busy emergency department (ED). *Refusal of such referrals can only prolong the cycle of repeated crisis episodes* rooted in chronic problems that demand more than ED visits for chronic problems, drives up health care costs, and contributes to a "revolving door" through EDs for lack of adequate mental health services. Its relevance supports the worldwide trend toward community-based primary care, as discussed in Chapter 1, even as a shortage of primary care providers looms.

Putting social network strategies into operation involves several steps, briefly listed here (see www.crisisprograms.org for further discussion and illustration of this important crisis care strategy):

1. *Clarify with the client and others the purpose of a network strategy and their active participation in it.* This is especially relevant for persons experiencing repeated crises and their relationship to chronic stress. Suggestions for a network conference can be introduced like this: "John, you've been coming here for some months now, each time with a new crisis around an old problem, it seems. We don't seem to be helping you with what you need. And you say other agencies aren't helping you either. I think we should all get together and try to figure out what's going wrong. Whatever it is we're doing now doesn't seem to be working." A positive presentation like this usually elicits a positive response.
2. *Identify all members of the social network.* This "laundry list" should include everyone involved with the person either before or because of the individual's crisis, for example, in networking with Alice (see next section).
3. *Identify the "symptom bearer" for a family or social network.*
4. *Establish contact with the resource people identified and explain to them the purpose of the conference.*

5. Convene the client and network members.
6. Conduct the network conference with the distressed person and with his or her social network.
7. Conclude the conference with an action plan for resolving the crisis or other problem.
8. Establish a follow-up plan
9. Record the results of the conference and distribute copies to all participants.

EXAMPLE: ALICE—EXCERPT FROM NETWORKING SESSION

MR. ROTHMAN (by telephone): Mrs. Barrett, this is Mr. Rothman at the crisis clinic. Your daughter Alice is here and refuses to go home. Alice and I would like to have you join us in a planning conference.
MRS. BARRETT: So that's where she is. I've done everything I know of to help that girl. There's nothing more I can do.
MR. ROTHMAN: I know you must feel very frustrated, Mrs. Barrett, but it's important that you join us even if it's agreed that Alice doesn't go back home.

After a few more minutes, Mrs. Barrett agrees to come to the clinic with her husband. (Alice is age 34, has been in and out of mental hospitals, and cannot hold a job. She and her mother had a verbal battle about household chores.)

Mrs. Barrett threatened to call the police when Alice started throwing things. Alice left and went to the crisis clinic. During the session at the clinic, the conference leader addresses questions to those attending and facilitates discussion:

TO ALICE: Alice, will you review for everyone here how you see your problem?
TO MR. HIGGINS, THE COUNSELOR FROM THE EMERGENCY HOSTEL: Will you explain your emergency housing service, eligibility requirements, and other arrangements to Alice and her parents?
TO ALICE: How does this housing arrangement sound to you, Alice?
TO ALICE'S PARENTS: What do you think about this proposal?

Crisis and mental health professionals as well as clients who agree to a networking conference are very confident in them because the strategy usually yields highly positive results. Its success can be traced to two key factors: (1) the power and effective implementation of *group process* techniques and (2) *active client involvement* in every step of the process. The client's empowerment and implied responsibility for self-care are powerful antidotes to hopelessness and a failure to follow through on recommended treatment. For example, a client can scarcely continue to protest that no one is helping when confronted with six to eight people whose explicit purpose is to brainstorm together about ways to stop the crisis cycle and help more effectively. Nor can agency representatives continue to "blame the victim" for repeated suicide attempts or lack of cooperation when confronted with evidence that part of the problem may be:

- Lack of interagency coordination
- Cracks and deficits in the system that leave the client's needs unmet
- Lack of financial resources to pay rent and utility bills
- Previous failure to confront the client (individuals and family) in a united, constructive manner

In the case of 5-year old Rebecca Riley (see next section), if a social network conference had been convened by a professional social worker or psychiatric nurse practitioner and attended by the prescribing psychiatrist, Rebecca's untimely death by overdose of psychotropic drugs meant only for adults might have been avoided. Instead, based on the biological psychiatry paradigm, the focus of treatment was the diagnosis of "bipolar illness" ascribed (unbelievably!) since age 2, with minimal attention addressed to serious family issues made public nationwide after the child's death. Psychiatrist Dr. Diller's statement of "moral culpability" fueled intraprofessional controversy regarding the responsibility of those providing the "science" (i.e., biological psychiatry) that allowed Rebecca to die. This case and its protracted legal facets drew national attention while attention to parental and professional responsibility continues.

As increasing numbers of discharged psychiatric patients call crisis hotlines for routine support, the social networking technique suggested here is *more relevant than ever*. Social network strategies are also effective in avoiding unnecessary hospitalization. Certainly, individual help and sometimes hospital treatment are indicated for a person in crisis. But once the person enters the subculture of a hospital or psychiatric unit, the functions of the natural family unit are often disrupted or minimized. In the busy, bureaucratic atmosphere of institutions, it is all too easy to forget the family and community from which the individual came, although some hospital staffs do excellent work with families. Even when social network members (natural and institutional) contribute to the problem rather than offer support, they should be included in crisis resolution to help the person in crisis clarify the positive and negative aspects of social life. Steps of the social network intervention process are illustrated in Figure 9.1 (www.crisisprograms.org).

Here is a final observation for readers who are new to this approach or feel intimidated by it. Social network principles—if not all the steps outlined here—can be applied in varying degrees. In noninstitutional crisis settings, for example, some of the steps may be unnecessary. The example of Ramona illustrates a very simple version of network intervention in a highly charged situation. Years of special training are not required for success in network techniques. Yet professionals and others trained in group process should be comfortable in applying this method even in complex situations.

EXAMPLE: RAMONA—NETWORKING IN A SHELTER FOR ABUSED WOMEN

Ramona was one of a group of eight abused women in a shelter with no overnight staffing. This shelter, like most, screens its residents for acute suicidal tendencies, addictions, and mental disturbance. Ramona became suicidal nevertheless, and one night she locked herself in the parlor to protect herself from acting on her suicidal tendencies with kitchen knives. When she slept, she did so on the office sofa so she would not have to be alone. Ramona had not told her fellow house members why she did these things, although the other women did know that she was suicidal. Tension among the residents grew because they did not understand Ramona's behavior. They were afraid that if they asked about it, she would become more suicidal (see Chapter 4 regarding this popular myth). One of the residents said she would leave the house if the staff did not get rid of Ramona.

Assessing the total situation, Diane, a volunteer staffer who was also a registered nurse trained in crisis intervention, called a meeting to discuss the problem. She explained to Ramona that other residents were worried about her and asked, "Are you willing to meet with them and explain what's happening with you?" Ramona replied, "Sure," and eagerly jumped off the sofa. The volunteer added that she had experience with suicidal people and was not afraid to discuss suicide. This brought a sigh of relief and a "Thank God!" from Ramona. (Ramona was on the waiting list for admission to a local hospital psychiatric unit for treatment of other problems.)

In the group meeting, Ramona explained her behavior as self-protection, not hostility, as her fellow residents had perceived, and shared with the group that she felt most protected and least suicidal when another resident had simply gone for a walk with her. Ramona also reassured everyone that in the event she hurt herself or died, it was her responsibility, not theirs. All residents expressed relief at having the problem openly discussed and agreed to keep open future communication with Ramona instead of trying to second-guess her.

Crisis Groups

The idea of helping people in groups developed during and after World War II. Because so many people needed help and resources were limited, it was impossible to serve everyone individually; group therapies were instituted. This experience, along with the success of the method, established the group mode of helping as often the method of choice rather than expediency. Whether or not workers use group modes in crisis intervention is influenced by their training and experience. Attitudes have been strongly influenced by psychiatric practice models that emphasize individual rather than social factors.

As is true of social network techniques, success in working with groups depends on the conviction by counselors and clients that the method is appropriate in the crisis intervention process. Group work is indicated in several instances:

1. *As a means of assessing a person's coping mechanisms.* Interaction in a group setting can reveal behaviors that may have contributed to the crisis situation.
2. *As a means of crisis resolution.* For the group members in crisis, the number of helpers is extended from one counselor to the whole group. The process of helping others resolve crises restores a person's confidence and can relieve a member's fear of going crazy or losing control.
3. *As a means of relieving the extreme isolation of some individuals in crisis.* For persons almost completely lacking in social resources or the ability to relate to others, the crisis group can be a first step in reestablishing a vital social network. The Madrigal[23] group work with traumatized combat veterans revealed bonding with other veterans—not "outsiders." This affirms the place of group support as one aspect of comprehensive crisis care.
4. *As a means of immediate screening and assessment.* This is especially useful in settings where large numbers of people come for help and the number of counselors is limited. This is the case in some metropolitan areas where the population is more crisis prone due to housing, financial conditions, employment, violence, and physical health problems.

As fruitful as crisis care in groups might be, and recognizing that for many it may not substitute for an individual counseling session, unfortunately, many professionals and clients in crisis seem reluctant to use it as a valuable approach to comprehensive crisis care.

MIDDLE-AGE TURNING POINTS: GROWTH, SADNESS, OR DECLINE?

The term *middlescence* has been applied to those past adolescence but not yet in senescence. J. S. Stevenson[24] identifies two stages in this period of adult life: *middlescence I*, the core of the middle years between 30 and 50, and *middlescence II*, the new middle years, extending from 50 to 70 or 75. This division contrasts with the US Census Bureau and popular opinion, which define middle age as the time between the ages of 45 and 64. Until recently, little attention has been paid to the middle years except in the negative sense of stereotypes about being "over the hill," sexually unattractive, unhappy, and depressed.

People in midlife are literally caught in the middle: They have major responsibilities for the young and the old. They are the primary figures in society's major institutions: family, business, education, health and social service, religion, and politics. Besides doing most of the regular work of society, they are also its major researchers, with the understandable result that they have focused their research primarily on groups other than themselves.

Because little attention has been given to the midlife period, it is not surprising that many popular notions about midlife are the result of myth and folklore. Considering also the influence of medicalization, this major life passage is often recast as a "disease" to be "treated." The reality is that most people in midlife:

- Are happier than they were when younger
- Lead highly productive and satisfying lives
- Have stable jobs and have met the major challenges of education and parenthood
- Are securely settled in a community in purchased rather than rented housing
- Enjoy a network of satisfying social relationships
- Have more disposable income and financial security than either the young or the old
- Enjoy good health and feel physically and mentally vigorous

In general, middle-agers today have more options than in earlier times because they are healthier. Census data reveal that North American and Western European women who are age 45 can expect to live 35 more years and men, 29 more years. Popular beliefs about middle age lag behind these statistical predictions.

Many, however, experience midlife as a threat. If a midlife person is married and has children, familiar parenting roles may no longer fill one's day; spousal roles may need redefining. If not single by choice, a middle-ager may see the chances for marriage as decreasing. Men may be threatened by a diminished sex drive and leveling off of career advancement opportunities. Women in careers face the same threat, while those without careers must meet the challenge of returning to school or resuming an interrupted career. The onset of menopause may threaten a woman's sense of feminine identity and attractiveness. Some men and women may perceive their lives at middle age as quickly slipping away before achieving what they want for themselves and others.

The success of men and women dealing with these midlife changes depends on:

- Psychological health and general outlook on life
- Lifelong preparation for this stage of human development
- Social support and economic security

Some people are trapped into the false security of living as though life were an unending fountain of youth. Such people may avoid healthy preparation for the developmental tasks of midlife. Or if they are socially isolated and lack the financial assets necessary to pursue education and leisure activities, midlife can increase their crisis proneness. Despite the advantages middle-aged people have, this developmental passage may be as hazardous as other transitions, though not as much as popular stereotypes would have us believe.

Among all the myths associated with middle age, none is more widespread than that of female menopause as a disease. Significant efforts to undo this stereotype include publications such as *Our Bodies, Ourselves* by the Boston Women's Health Book Collective,[25] which has been translated into many foreign languages. It is now widely accepted that menopause is a natural transition state, not a disease, despite bodily and mental changes such as hot flashes and a changing view of self after the child-bearing age. Not only does menopause not require medical intervention for distress in most instances but estrogen replacement therapy, so popular in the past, has drastically declined in use due to various complications found from long-term studies. Menopause support groups can sometimes take the place of estrogen replacement therapy during this important transition state. In such groups, women receive factual information and support in coping with the physical, social, and psychological changes accompanying menopause.

Men undergoing the climacteric could benefit from similar support groups. Coming to terms with middle age may influence some men who cope with changes in themselves by establishing liaisons with younger women.

GROWING OLDER: CHALLENGES, RISKS, AND JOY

It has been said that we are as old as we feel. Many issues regarding middle age apply to old age: psychological outlook, social support, and economic security influence the crisis proneness of older people. The retirement issues noted in Chapter 8 also apply to elderly people at special risk for crisis. For example, minority elders have lower incomes than white elders; three fourths of those below poverty level are female; older women earn much less than older men; low-income elders are more likely to have limiting chronic conditions than high-income elders. Among those wishing to remain in the workforce, some experience age discrimination. With the federal cutbacks in domestic programs since 1981, greater burdens of caring for increasing numbers of elders fall on women. Typically, those caring for impoverished and chronically ill women are underpaid, overworked, and overwhelmed.

The needs of elders are being addressed through the work of advocates such as senior legislators and the American Association of Retired Persons (AARP). A recent emphasis on gerontological research and graduate training programs in universities also contributes to the long-range welfare of seniors. Many of the myths about old age are an extension of those about middle age: Old age is a disease, and old people are uniformly needy, dependent, and asexual.

ATTITUDES TOWARD SENIORS

Despite increased political advocacy and advances in gerontological research, ageism and stereotypes about old people persist. Cultural values and the policies and practices flowing from them do not change rapidly. Old people are not as highly valued in mainstream North American society as they are, for example, in some Native communities and most non-Western societies. Recent social emphasis on the small nuclear family has virtually displaced the extended family arrangement in most Western societies. Grandparents, aunts, and uncles are rarely integrated into a family home.

Most children, therefore, routinely have only two adults (their parents) as role models and supporters. In cases of death, desertion, or divorce, children are even more deprived of adult models. Fortunately, this is changing with attempts to get children and old people together—for example, through nursing home visits by groups of children and other intergenerational volunteer programs in schools. Healthy attitudes toward aging are also helped by books that highlight the extraordinary rewards of growing old, especially by those with a keen sense of spirituality and life purpose, and who nurture personal relationships and accept the fact that some goals may remain unaccomplished due to physical or mental infirmity.

Older people experience even greater hardship than children do by their exclusion from the nuclear family. They feel—and often are—unwanted. They may be treated as guests (essentially invisible) with no significant role in their children's families. When older people, because of health or other problems, do live with their grown children, additional tensions arise. The older person may become impatient and irritable with the normal behavior of grandchildren. Space is sometimes insufficient to give everyone some privacy, or the old person may seem demanding and unreasonable. For these reasons, some older people prefer a "retirement community" to living with their adult children.

SERVICES FOR ELDERLY PEOPLE

Stress can be relieved and crisis situations prevented when special public health and social services are available to families caring for an older person. As a parallel to child care needs, many workers and advocacy groups for elders are demanding inclusion of elder care in benefit packages. Some programs combine child care and elder housing services under a single administrative umbrella, thus fostering important intergenerational contact. In many areas of North America, outreach workers from the public office for aging make regular contacts with older people in their homes. When housekeeping and other services are available, outreach programs serve a pivotal role toward success in the prized goal of "aging in place" and can help to prevent crises and avoid the institutionalization that many dread.

Where public and affordable private services are lacking, the lives of many older people can take on a truly desperate character. The situation is particularly acute for the older person living alone who (for physical or psychological reasons) is unable to get out. Senior citizen centers now exist in nearly every community.

We should make every effort to encourage older people to use these services. This may be the only real source for keeping active physically; for establishing and maintaining social contacts; and for preventing emotional, mental, and physical deterioration. Some people need help—money and transportation—to get to senior centers or counseling to convince them to use the services. Other services for seniors in many countries include volunteer programs; Life Line (24-hour security service that alerts police and fire services in emergency situations); Meals on Wheels, which makes and delivers hot meals to the incapacitated; and similar public and private organizations available to isolated and distressed elders.

Visiting nurses, a key resource for helping to keep frail elderly people in their homes, can detect stress or suicidal tendencies. Responding to the high percentages of older people compared with younger ones able to care for them, there are increasing "all-inclusive care" housing developments providing leveled services from independence to semi-independent, to assisted living, and nursing care—most including fitness centers and some with on-site comprehensive medical care.

All agencies for aging persons should maintain active contact with the local crisis center for consultation and direct assistance in acute crisis situations to prevent tragic deaths like that of Marjorie Jones and her developmentally disabled adult daughter, Rose. After the death of her elderly husband, Marjorie Jones was overwhelmed caring for Rose alone. She had resisted neighbors' offers of assistance. After a postal worker became concerned and alerted authorities, she and her daughter were found dead in their trash-filled home in a middle-class neighborhood. The neighbors anguished about what they might have done to avoid this tragedy. These deaths suggest the need for more proactive social services following loss, as well as for people caring for any disabled person. It also illustrates the need for community education about how to offer neighborly help or make early referrals without invading the privacy of people who may feel too proud to ask for or receive assistance.

EXAMPLE: ANTON CARLTON—HOME CARE

Anton Carlton, age 77, lived with his wife, Marion, in a rundown section of a city. He was nearly blind and had had both legs amputated, due to complications of diabetes, and with his wife Marion survived on a poverty-level income. Marion, age 68, was able to take care of Anton. Then she was hospitalized and died of complications following abdominal surgery. Anton was grief stricken. After Marion's death, a visiting nurse came regularly to give Anton his insulin injections and arrange for help with meals.

One day, Anton's house was broken into, and he was beaten and robbed of the few dollars he had. The nurse found him with minor physical injuries, but he was also depressed and suicidal. The local crisis center was called and an outreach visit made. The crisis outreach team assessed Anton as a very high risk for suicide. Anton, however, insisted on remaining in his own home. The services of a volunteer group for shut-ins were enlisted for him, especially to provide for an occasional visitor.

Homemaker services were also arranged. A week later, Anton was beaten and robbed again, but he still refused to move out of his home. The nurse inquired about a senior citizen housing project for Anton. They refused to accept anyone as handicapped as Anton, although he did consider leaving if he could move to such a place. After a third robbery and beating a few weeks later, Anton agreed to move to a nursing home.

Institutional Placement of Elders

In Anton's case, a nursing home placement was a means of resolving a crisis with housing, health care, and physical safety. However, admission to a nursing home is itself an occasion for crisis for nearly every resident. And while some people do well in a nursing home, for many, institutionalization marks the beginning of a rapid decline in physical and emotional health. A new nursing home resident will invariably mourn the loss of his or her own home or apartment and whatever privacy it afforded, no matter how difficult the prior circumstances were. New residents resent their dependence on others, regardless of how serious their physical condition may be. These problems are less acute for those whose health status does not require such complete dependence. A person placed in a nursing home by family members may feel unloved and abandoned. Some families do abandon an old parent, often not by choice but because they cannot handle their own guilt feelings about placing the parent in a nursing home, no matter how necessary that placement might be.

The most stressful time for a nursing home resident is the first few weeks after admission. The new resident's problems are similar to those of people admitted to other institutions: hospitals, detention facilities, or group homes for adolescents. Crisis intervention at this time will prevent many more serious problems later, such as depression, suicidal tendencies, withdrawal, refusal to participate in activities, and an increase in physical complaints. James Richman[26] and other researchers reveal that a significant number of older people simply give up after retirement or admission to a nursing home and die very soon thereafter. Hopelessness in these cases is the forerunner to death. Elderly people admitted to nursing homes should be routinely assessed for suicide risk. Besides having to deal with feelings of loss, resentment, and rejection, some people placed in nursing homes do not get a *clear, honest statement* from their family about the need for and nature of the placement. This contributes further to the person's denial of the need for nursing home care (see Chapter 7 for crises associated with Alzheimer's disease—for the one afflicted as well as family caretakers).

Retirement and the realization of old age are times of stress but need not lead to crisis. Societal attitudes toward old age are changing, so this stage of life is now anticipated by more and more people as another opportunity for human growth. In some societies, retired people are called on regularly to work several weeks a year when full-time workers go on vacation. There are many other opportunities in progressive societies for older people to remain active and involved. Many crises in the lives of elderly citizens can be avoided if they are accorded more honor and some postretirement responsibilities.

How we treat our elderly citizens can account for the marked difference in death rituals in traditional and modern urban societies: In modern societies, some people are dead *socially* (by forced retirement or familial rejection) long before physical death occurs. Society needs therefore only to dispose of the body; no rituals are needed to transfer social functions. This cross-cultural observation invites further consideration of the final passage we all face: death.

DEATH: THE FINAL PASSAGE

Dr. Elizabeth Kubler-Ross's[27] description of death as the final stage of growth brought this typically painful topic to broad public attention. As the marker of life's end, it is the most powerful reminder we have that we have only one life to live and that to waste it would be folly.

Death has been a favorite topic of philosophers, poets, psychologists, physicians, and anthropologists for centuries. Many books crossing all disciplines have been written about death. There is even a science of *thanatology* (study of death and dying). Yet death is still a taboo topic and many are very uncomfortable discussing it. This is unfortunate because it means the loss of death as a "friendly companion" to remind us that our lives are finite. Such denial is the root of the crisis situation that death becomes for many. Vast and important as the subject of death is, here the topic is limited to its crisis aspect for the general reader and for health care providers who regularly confront death and dying among patients and their families facing the reality of death.

Attitudes Toward Death

Death is not a crisis in itself but becomes one for the dying person and survivors because of the widespread denial of death as the final stage of growth. As Tolstoy wrote so eloquently in *The Death of Ivan Ilyich*, the real agony of death is the final realization that we have not really lived our life, the regret that we did not do what we wanted to do, that we did not realize in and for ourselves what we most dearly desired. This fact was borne out in research by psychologist Dr. Lisl Goodman,[28] who compared top performing artists' and scientists' attitudes toward death with a group who were not performing artists or scientists but similar in other respects. She found that the performing artists and scientists were less fearful and more accepting of death, and much less inclined to want to return to earth after their death if they had a chance. Having led full and satisfying lives, they were able to anticipate their deaths with peace and acceptance. They had "won the race with death."

Noted writer and humorist Art Buchwald[29] decided not to let death have the last word. He held court with friends and others and planned his funeral during his final months in hospice. There, in effect, death waited for him to invite his children and various well-known people like Carly Simon and Tom Brokaw to write eulogies that he included in his last book, *Too Soon to Say Goodbye*. He treats death with his famed sense of humor and offers the living inspiring ways to face life's final loss.

The denial of death, so common in US society, is a far greater enemy than death itself. It allows us to live our lives less fully than we might with an awareness and acceptance of death's inevitability. Through works of like those of Buchwald, physician Sherwin Nuland,[30] and many others, we have made progress in dealing with death openly. There are now groups and regular news sources dedicated to having that important "conversation" with loved ones *before* the final passage, rather than only during a person's last hours. Despite this progress, some health professionals and families still are reluctant to discuss the subject openly with a dying person.

This is changing through the promotion of living wills, advance directives regarding use of extraordinary treatment, and the public debate about physician-assisted suicide. For many, the assisted-suicide issue is primarily one of maintaining control over one's last days and not suffering unnecessary pain. More and more physicians and nurses are concerned about the influence of technology on care of the dying and the undertreatment of pain, and they avail themselves of courses on death and dying. Increased public awareness, a more realistic approach to death, and a loosening of denial's grip are now evident as people consider (especially through media attention) the prospect of dying in an institution attached to tubes and with no control over or conscious awareness of the process. Among families and the culture of medical institutions, there is growing change toward accommodating the notion of "negotiated" death. The Patient Self-Determination Act passed by Congress in 1990 facilitated such change by requiring health care institutions to inform patients of their rights to make advance medical directives. The Act encourages people to think about what treatment they wish if terminally ill, and it ensures honoring people's wishes for the kind of death they envision.

Many problems and crises associated with death, dying people, their families, and those who attend them in their last days might be avoided if death were faced more directly. Nurses, physicians, ministers, and families need to become open, communicative companions to those who are dying. Real-life stories in the magazine *Compassion and Choices* reveal the high emotional price dying patients pay when family and physicians avoid talking openly with them about their condition and end-of-life wishes. Yet such avoidance still occurs unless professionals have openly studied and discussed with families the needs of dying patients. Everyone concerned about this topic might benefit from physician Sherwin Nuland's books, *The Art of Aging* and *How We Die*. He has attempted to break through denial by his view on healthy aging and very blunt account of the physiological process of ending life.

Our inability or refusal to come to terms with death is a critical issue for all of us and for all crisis workers—not just on behalf of the dying. Why? Because death, as noted in earlier chapters, is a kind of prototype for *all* crisis experiences—that is, many crises arise directly from the death of a loved one, but all crises and life passages are like a "mini-death" in the *loss experience* common to them all. The successful resolution of crisis, then, is crucially connected to our coming to terms with *loss*. Helping others through their losses and finding new roles, new relationships, and emotional healing depends heavily on whether we are comfortable with the topic of death and our own mortality. A healthy attitude toward our own death is our most powerful asset in assisting the dying through this final life passage and comforting their survivors.

In a culture without strong ritual and social support around dying, the major burden of positively dealing with death falls on individuals. Sensitization to death and its denial in modern society and to ethical issues such as assisted dying is aided by reading literary and other works on the topic, for example, Goodman and Tolstoy, and by workshops focusing on denial of death through sensitizing exercises and group process. These carefully planned discussions can help us to treasure the preciousness of every moment. Coming to terms with our own death not only can change our life and eventual death but also lays the foundation for assisting others through death.

Helping a Dying Person

In US, Canadian, and other societies, instead of dying in institutions such as hospitals, more people are dying in their own homes or in hospice care. Ted Rosenthal,[31] a young poet dying of leukemia, struck out against the coldness and technology that awaited him along with death in a hospital. He tells his remarkable story of facing death and living fully until that time in *How Could I Not Be Among You?* On learning of his imminent death from leukemia, Rosenthal checked out of the hospital, moved to the country, and did the things he wanted to do before dying.

Dying people who are not able to die in similar self-chosen circumstances deserve to have the shock of their terminal illness tempered by those attending them. Crisis care for a person who has learned of a diagnosis of fatal illness begins with awareness of one's own feelings about death. Next in the helping process is understanding what the dying person is going through. Family members and everyone working with the dying will recognize the phases of dying described by Dr. Kübler-Ross from her interviews with over 200 dying patients.

Dr. Kübler-Ross identifies five stages of dying. Dying people do not necessarily experience all the stages she describes: denial, anger, bargaining, depression, and acceptance. Nor do these stages occur in a fixed, orderly sequence. Kübler-Ross's work is most useful for sensitizing health and hospice workers to some of the major issues and problems encountered by a dying person.

1. *Denial.* Typically, denial is expressed with, "No, not me," on becoming aware of a terminal illness. People deny even when they are told the facts explicitly. Denial is expressed by disbelief in X-ray or other reports, insistence on repeat examinations, or getting additional opinions from other doctors. Such denial serves to support the persistence of quack remedies. But denial may be necessary as a delaying mechanism, so the person can absorb the reality of having a terminal illness. Pressing someone to acknowledge and accept a bitter reality before he or she is psychologically ready may reinforce the need for defensive denial. Self-help groups are a contemporary substitute for traditional rites of passage through this important life passage.
2. *Anger.* When denial finally gives way, it is often replaced by anger: "Why me?" This is more difficult for hospital staff and family to deal with than denial, as the person often expresses the anger by accusations against the people who are trying to help. As possible targets of anger, it is important for all to understand that the anger is really at the person's unchosen fate, typically *not* at caretakers who must support the dying person and recognize that the anger will eventually pass.
3. *Bargaining.* Faced with evidence that the illness is still there in spite of angry protests, the person in effect says, "Maybe if I ask nicely, I'll be heard." This is the stage of bargaining, which goes on mostly with God, even among those who do not believe in God. Bargaining usually consists of private promises: "I'll live a good life," or "I'll donate my life and my money to a great cause." During this phase, it is important to listen and note any feelings of guilt the dying person may have or regrets that life was not lived as idealized.
4. *Depression.* During this stage of dying, people mourn their losses: of body image, income; people they loved; joy; or the role of wife, husband, lover, or parent. Finally, they begin the grief of separation from life itself. This is the time when another person's presence or touch of the hand means much more than words. Again, acceptance of one's own eventual death and the ability to be with a person in silence are the most helpful at this time.
5. *Acceptance.* This follows when anger and depression have been worked through. The dying person becomes weaker and may want to be left alone

more. It is the final acceptance of the end, awaited quietly with a certain expectation. Again, quiet presence and communication of caring by a touch or a look are now very important. The person needs assurance that he or she will not be alone when dying and that any wishes made, such as in advance directives, will be respected. Messages of caring will give such assurance.

Awareness and understanding of our own and of the dying person's feelings are the foundation of care during the crisis of terminal illness and death. Such understanding will be treasured by families of dying persons. Because dying alone is a dying person's greatest fear, communication with families is essential. During this final phase of life, families should not be excluded by machines and procedures that unnecessarily prolong physical life beyond conscious life. Family members who help by their presence will very likely become more accepting of their own future deaths. Denial of death and death in isolation do nothing to foster growth.

THE HOSPICE MOVEMENT

One of the most significant recent developments aiding the dying person is the hospice movement, founded by physician Cecily Saunders in London in 1967. Sylvia Lack, also a physician, extended the hospice concept to the United States. The hospice movement, now taking root worldwide, grew out of awareness of the needs of dying persons and the concern that these needs cannot be met adequately in hospitals engaged primarily with curing and acute-care procedures. A main focus of the hospice concept is the control of pain and the provision of surroundings that enhance the possibility of dying as naturally as possible. It consists of 10 components summarized by S. V. McCabe[32]:

1. Coordinated home care with inpatient beds under a central, autonomous hospice administration
2. Control of symptoms (physical, social, psychological, and spiritual)
3. Physician-directed services (due to the medical nature of symptoms)
4. Provision of care by an interdisciplinary team
5. Services available 24 hours a day, 7 days a week, with emphasis on availability of medical and nursing skills
6. Patient and family regarded as the unit of care
7. Provision for bereavement follow-up
8. Use of volunteers as an integral part of the interdisciplinary team
9. Structured personnel support and communication systems
10. Patients accepted into the program on the basis of health care needs rather than ability to pay

A growing emphasis on palliative-care research and service extends the hospice model, which is now widespread for persons facing death. The hospice movement is a promising example of a new awareness of death in modern society and the importance of supporting the rights of the dying. As more people select hospice care, however, the need for respite for families and more hospital-based hospices will also increase. Assistance for the dying person is supported by the "Dying Person's Bill of Rights," adopted by the General Assembly of the United Nations in 1975:

- I have the right to be treated as a living human being until I die.
- I have the right to maintain a sense of hopefulness however changing its focus may be.
- I have the right to be cared for by those who can maintain a sense of hopefulness, however changing this might be.
- I have the right to express my feelings and emotions about my approaching death in my own way.
- I have the right to participate in decisions concerning my care.
- I have the right to expect continuing medical and nursing attention, even though "cure" goals must be changed to "comfort" goals.
- I have the right not to die alone.
- I have the right to be free from pain.
- I have the right to have my questions answered honestly.
- I have the right not to be deceived.
- I have the right to have help from and for my family in accepting my death.
- I have the right to die in peace and dignity.
- I have the right to retain my individuality and not be judged for my decision, which may be contrary to beliefs of others.
- I have the right to discuss and enlarge my religious and/or spiritual experiences, whatever these may mean to others.
- I have the right to expect that the sanctity of the human body will be respected after death.
- I have the right to be cared for by caring, sensitive, knowledgeable people who will attempt to understand my needs and will be able to gain some satisfaction in helping me face my death.

On a hopeful note, listeners attuned to radio and other media are encouraged to have that "conversation" with their loved ones about their wishes when death calls. But despite the stories in *Compassion and Choices* and legislative measures in some countries, sadly, stories of dying with unwanted tubes and wires continue despite the decades-old UN document.

Throughout our lives, hazardous events and transitions can be occasions of crisis, growth, or deterioration. So in death, our last passage, we may experience either our most acute agony or the final stage of growth. Whether or not we "win the race with death" depends on

- How we have lived
- What we believe about life and death
- The support of those close to us during our final life crisis

REFERENCES, FURTHER READING, DISCUSSION GUIDE

REFERENCES
1. Blumenkrantz, D., & Goldstein, M. (in press). Seeing college as a rite of passage: What might be possible? In Hanson, C. (Ed.), *In search of self: Exploring undergraduate identity development*. San Francisco: Jossey-Bass.
2. Kimball, S. T. (1960). Introduction: *Rites of passage* (A. van Gennep, Trans.). Chicago: University of Chicago Press. (Original French edition published 1909)
3. LaFontaine, J. (1977). The power of rights. *Man, 12*, 421–437.
4. Spencer, P. (1973). *Nomads in alliance*. Oxford, UK: Oxford University Press.
5. Walker, A. (1992). *Possessing the secret of joy*. Orlando, FL: Harcourt Brace.
6. Straus, M. A., Gelles, R. J., & Steinmetz, S. K. (1980). *Behind closed doors: Violence in the American family*. New York: Anchor Books.
7. Golan, N. (1981). *Passing through transitions*. New York: Free Press.
8. Hogberg, U., & Bergstrom, E. (2000). Suffocated prone: The iatrogenic tragedy of SIDS. *American Journal of Public Health, 90*(4), 527–531.
9. Waring, M. (1990). *If women counted: A new feminist economics*. San Francisco: San Francisco Harper.
10. Hymowitz, K. S. (2006). *Marriage and caste in America*. Chicago: Ivan R. Dee.
11. United Nations human development report (1993). http://www.unitednationsdevelopmentreport.org. Retrieved January 22, 2014.
12. Ruddick, S. (1989). *Maternal thinking: Toward a politics of peace*. Boston: Beacon Press.
13. Erikson, E. (1963). *Childhood and society* (2nd ed.). New York: Norton.
14. Patel, E. (2007). *Acts of faith: The story of an American Muslim, the struggle for the soul of a generation*. Boston: Beacon Press.
15. Williams, W. L. (1986). *The spirit and the flesh: Sexual diversity in American Indian culture*. Boston: Beacon Press.
16. Hill, R. (1965). Generic features of families under stress. In H. J. Parad (Ed.), *Crisis intervention: Selected readings* (pp. 32–52). New York: Family Service Association of America.
17. Halpern, H. (1982). *How to break your addiction to a person*. New York: McGraw-Hill.
18. Maslow, A. (1970). *Motivation and personality* (2nd ed.). New York: HarperCollins.
19. Durkheim, E. (1915). *Elementary forms of the religious life*. London: Hollen St. Press.
20. Hansell, N. (1976). *The person in distress: On the biosocial dynamics of adaptation*. New York: Human Sciences Press.
21. Halleck, S. (1971). *The politics of therapy*. New York: Science House.
22. Polak, P. (1976). A model to replace psychiatric hospitalization. *Journal of Nervous and Mental Diseases, 162*, 13–22.
23. Madrigal, K. B. (2005). Treatment beliefs of combat trauma survivors with posttraumatic stress disorder. *Practicing Anthropology, 27*(3), 37–40.
24. Stevenson, J. S. (1977). *Issues and crises during middlescence*. Englewood Cliffs, NJ: Appleton-Century-Crofts.

25. Boston Women's Health Book Collective (2005). *Our bodies, ourselves: A new edition for a new era* (8th ed.). New York: Simon & Shuster.
26. Richman, J. (1993). *Preventing elderly suicide: Overcoming personal despair, professional indifference and social bias*. New York: Springer.
27. Kübler-Ross, E. (1975). *Death, the final stage of growth*. Englewood Cliffs, NJ: Prentice Hall.
28. Goodman, L. M. (1981). *Death and the creative life*. New York: Springer
29. Buchwald, A. (2006). *Too soon to say goodbye*. New York: Random House.
30. Nuland, S. B. (2007). *The art of aging*. New York: Random House.
31. Rosenthal, T. (1973). *How could I not be among you?* New York: Braziller.
32. McCabe, S. V. (1982). An overview of hospice care. *Cancer Nursing, 5*, 103–108.

FURTHER READING

Anderson, C. M., & Stewart, S. (1994). *Flying solo: Single women at midlife*. New York: Norton.

Arendell, T. (1995). *Fathers and divorce*. Thousand Oaks, CA: Sage.

Blumenfeld, W. J., & Raymond, D. (1993). *Looking at gay and lesbian life* (2nd ed.). Boston: Beacon Press.

Boston Women's Health Book Collective. (2005). *Our bodies, ourselves: A new edition for a new era* (8th ed.). New York: Simon & Shuster.

Brendtro, L. K., Brokenleg, M., & Van Bockern, S. (1990). *Reclaiming youth at risk: Our hope for the future*. Bloomington, IN: National Educational Service.

Chodorow, N. (1978). *The reproduction of mothering*. Berkeley: University of California Press.

Corea, G. (1985). *The mother machine*. New York: HarperCollins.

Doress, P. B., & Siegal, D. L. (1987). *Ourselves, growing older*. New York: Simon & Schuster.

General Assembly of the United Nations. (1975). Dying person's bill of rights. *American Journal of Nursing, 75*, 99.

Goodman, L. M. (1981). *Death and the creative life*. New York: Springer.

Hansell, N. (1976). *The-person-in-distress*. New York: Human Sciences Press.

Hill, R. (1965). Generic features of families under stress. In H. J. Parad (Ed.), *Crisis intervention: Selected readings* (pp. 32–52). New York: Family Service Association of America.

Lack, S., & Buckingham, R. W. (1978). *First American hospice*. New Haven, CT: Hospice.

Lopata, H. Z. (1995). *Current widowhood: Myths and realities*. Thousand Oaks, CA: Sage.

Luhrmann, T. M. (2000). *Of two minds: The growing disorder in American psychiatry*. New York: Knopf.

Mahoney, S. (May/June 2006). The secret lives of single women. *American Association of Retired Persons*, 50–74.

McCabe, S. V. (1982). An overview of hospice care. *Cancer Nursing, 5*, 103–108.

McCamant, K., & Durrett, C. (1988). *Cohousing: A contemporary approach to housing ourselves*. Berkeley, CA: Ten Speed Press.

McHugh, P. R. (2001). The DSM: Gaps & essences. *Psychiatric Research Report, 17*(2), 2-3, 14–25.

McKenry, P. C., & Price, S. J. (Eds.). (2000). *Families and change: Coping with stressful events and transitions* (2nd ed.). Thousand Oaks, CA: Sage.

Mitford, J. (1963). *The American way of death*. New York: Simon & Schuster.

Nuland, S. B. (1995) *How we die: Reflections on life's final chapter*. New York: Random House.

Parad, H. J., & Caplan, G. (1965). A framework for studying families in crisis. In H. J. Parad (Ed.), *Crisis intervention: Selected readings* (pp. 53–74). New York: Family Service Association of America.

Pillemer, K., Moen, P., Wethington, E., & Glasgow, N. (Eds.). (2000). *Social integration in the second half of life*. Baltimore: Johns Hopkins University Press.

Rathus, S. A. (2006). *Childhood voyages in development* (2nd ed.). Belmont, CA: Thompson Learning.

Sidel, R. (1996). *Women and children last: The plight of poor women in affluent America*. New York: Penguin Books.

Sommers, T., & Shields, L. (1987). *Women take care: The consequences of caregiving in today's society*. Gainesville, FL: Triad.

Spar, D. (2006). *The baby business: How money, science, and politics drive the commerce of conception*. Boston: Harvard Business School Press.

Tolstoy, L. (1960). *The death of Ivan Ilyich*. New York: New American Library. (Original work published 1886)

West, C., & Hewlett, S. A. (1999). *The war against parents*. Boston: Houghton Mifflin

Wolin, S. (1993). *The resilient self: How survivors of troubled families rise above adversity*. New York: Random House.

World Health Organization. (1994). *Maternal and child health and family planning: Traditional practices harmful to the health of women and children* (Resolution WHA 47). Geneva: World Health Assembly, 47th.

DISCUSSION GUIDE

1. After reading this chapter, reflect on your current phase in the life cycle and consider these points: What did you experience in earlier phases that was particularly helpful or harmful in your development? For example: Tender support? Or perhaps physical or sexual abuse?
2. How has this chapter helped you (and those close to you) prepare for and avoid possible hazards or crises during later life phases?
3. If you are middle aged or older and/or have a friend or relative in this life transition point, have you experienced any stressful interaction based on gender or other stereotypes about aging? If yes, how did you feel and respond to such an experience? For example, did you confront the offending individual, just "let it go" as "part of growing older," or confide in a trusted friend about any upsetting aftermath of such stereotyping? How comfortable would you feel discussing this with family or a friend?
4. Although the code of silence and denial about death is lifting, consider organizing a small group discussion in which people might benefit from sharing fears and/or end-of-life planning, with a goal of escaping some of the most painful facets of death and dying.
5. Since death is a fact of life, consider what can be learned from traditional societies and the role of rituals in one's final days.
6. What are the ethical issues to be considered in prolonging the life of a dying person with no hope of recovery by using advanced medical technology despite the expressed will of family members?

Conclusion

Vision for Global Action: Research, Education, and Practice

Learning from history, together we can make a difference across several fronts

CHAPTER OUTLINE

National Conference on Crisis and Violence Issues   299
Power of the "Critical Mass" for Effective Action   300
National/International Survey Data: Update via The Delphi Technique   302
Education and Practice Initiative—Launching Ideas   303
Maintaining Hope and Solidarity   305
References and Further Reading   306

Over the years of practice, research, and teaching on this book's topics, I have had the good fortune of observing idealistic interdisciplinary work on behalf of people in crisis, as presented here. Among dedicated and skilled mental health and social service workers, there is little new among these pages about ideal crisis care. But for them and new readers, I hope the book will affirm and support our best efforts together. Team support and self-care are keys to fruitful outcomes of the stressful but rewarding work with people in crisis—this, despite the threats and injuries sometimes suffered from disturbed clients or verbal/emotional abuse by one's own colleagues. My hope in this concluding chapter is to inspire leadership by professional and lay readers to act on their knowledge, power, and experience toward progress on this urgent topic.

Another observation has been the relative isolation of some providers who work long hours serving distressed persons with very challenging health and mental health issues. They experience firsthand the personal and social costs of underfunded (and therefore often understaffed) crisis and mental health services in the larger health arena—compared nationally, for example, with assumed billions routinely spent on war and national defense.

But it is not only the caretakers who endure the shortfall in funding and staffing; most important, these deficits affect outcomes for the everyday person in distress or crisis whose care may be seriously compromised when seeking help in the emergency department and primary care settings. This speaks to the core purpose of this book: to offer basic information for people in distress or danger, information that caretakers should provide across the life cycle in diverse situations. To prevent shortchanging people on these occasions, the book offers guidelines about *what to expect* from health and human service providers, and what we all can do to correct shortfalls and improve any substandard crisis care. The chapters' Discussion Guides may be especially helpful for this task.

NATIONAL CONFERENCE ON CRISIS AND VIOLENCE ISSUES

Since the 1985 workshop on violence convened by Surgeon General C. Everett Koop, those of us attending (only 150 from across the United States) were buoyed with enthusiasm and determination to apply outcomes of this workshop in our respective institutions and practice arenas. This included expectations of financial and other supports necessary for implementing the 1985 ideals across teaching, research, and practice domains in the health and social service arena as depicted in Chapter 1 and Figure 1.2 (the Continuum of Mental Health Services).

But despite the notable progress since then, including the goal of providing 24/7 crisis care in all communities, the centuries-old plague of violence continues with daily media inundations of murder, civil strife, and other dangers faced by individuals, families, and entire communities in serious distress and conflict worldwide. Readers will have noted my several references to historian Santayana and "learning from history." In that vein, my vision includes professionals and their clients revisiting the community mental health ideals of the 1960s and 1970s, plus a carefully planned and orchestrated follow-up of Dr. Koop's 1985 workshop, dubbed something like "The Surgeon General's Workshop on Crisis, Violence, and Public Health—30 Years Later."

In the larger health and medical arena it is useful to consider how determination, scientific knowledge, public health initiatives, consumer demand, and government support have nearly eliminated a crippling disease like polio worldwide. Today, it is worth noting that vaccination for preventable diseases is assumed as a necessary health measure and rarely questioned for its life-saving impact; it is supported financially and routinely applied to enhance protection of infants and others. On 24/7 crisis care with *prevention* as a key theme, it is a different story.

POWER OF THE "CRITICAL MASS" FOR EFFECTIVE ACTION

It is noteworthy, I think, that following the 2013 passing of Dr. Koop, several obituaries have cited his pioneering work on child health, HIV/AIDS prevention, and other health issues—all very important. But in obituaries of this pioneering physician, there was not a single reference to his major accomplishments on violence prevention as documented in the 1986 *Report* published by the US Public Health Service and US Department of Health and Human Services.[1]

To me, this signifies much lip service and publically stated regrets (but less consumer and provider action) about tragic deaths, often traceable to inadequate preventive mental health service, as in 24/7 crisis care and follow-up counseling. Unfortunately, client demand and public action may not follow verbal regrets to correct this notable lapse from historic ideals regarding crisis care and prevention of violence toward self and others in today's troubled world.

Reflecting on what we have been able to do since the recommendations from the 1985 Workshop, supported at the federal level, I am reminded of the biblical "critical mass"—that is, what is needed to move forward on the important issue of safety during individual crisis episodes or family and community disturbances, and preventing violence toward self and others under stress. Typically, collaborative efforts are necessary for making a difference on this issue—that is, providers and consumers in strong partnerships where lay and professional wisdom and contributions are valued.

Connecting the Dots

It is now well established that "upstream" sociocultural, religious, and civic organizations and political factors are typical underpinnings of the crises experienced by many individuals in distress or danger. "Connecting the dots," therefore, has been a major theme of this book. And so, practitioners in the crisis field—already knowledgeable about crisis care and danger potential—need assurance from their clients and colleagues that their daily challenges are on the "front burner" of national and international action on an issue affecting millions of victim-survivors and prospective perpetrators of violence in response to distress and crisis.

Pivotal to success in supporting this upstream vision is the power of professional, religious, and other powerful groups to "turn the tide" around the "opportunity and danger" of *individual* crisis situations to encompass *whole populations* of persons in crisis or distress—*a key tenet of public health*. I believe we need a contemporary "crusade" directed to powerful players who together might turn the tide on the continuing global crisis of violence and abuse. To that end, I propose a larger reach by each of us through professional, religious, civic, and governmental groups that can effectively address the topics this book. These include, for example, the following:

- American Association of Colleges of Nursing
- Canadian Nurses Association
- American Association of Suicidology
- American Psychiatric Association
- Sigma Theta Tau International (nursing)
- American Psychological Association
- American Association of Counseling Psychology
- Association of Primary Care Providers
- National Association of Social Workers
- American Association of Nurse Practitioners
- The heads of major religious groups; for example, Christian, Muslim, Jewish, and Hindu leaders
- The Departments of Health and Mental Health in state jurisdictions
- Heads or lay persons representing civic groups and consumers with a passion for engagement on crisis and violence issues affecting families and communities
- Philanthropic groups that might financially support this vision, for example, the Robert Wood Johnson Foundation and the Bill and Melinda Gates Foundation

The critical point here is to harness the power and prestige of these and other leaders, bolstered with lay input and scientific evidence to convince the United States and other countries to convene and financially support a conference akin to that led by Surgeon General C. Everett Koop decades ago—in essence, *a follow-up of that influential Workshop*. A first step in this endeavor would be appointment of a Steering or Development Committee—perhaps initiated by the president of one of these groups in concert with the current US Surgeon General elect, Dr. Vivek Hallegere Murthy, cofounder and president of Doctors for America. Significantly, Dr. Murthy is committed to integrating community-based prevention (assuming that this includes 24/7 crisis care) into the health care system. It is worth noting here that health care is one of the major domains of all societies, along with family, economic, education, sociocultural, political, and religion domains.

Despite progress, it sometimes appears that we are treading water instead of activating a vision for potential impact like that of the 1985 Workshop. For example, here is one group leader's presentation at the 1985 Workshop (paraphrased here): Mr. Surgeon General: Our group recommends as a policy issue that all health and social service professionals be taught and *examined* on violence issues as a *condition of licensure to practice*. Yet, as already cited, we are far from this ideal, when noting that as recently as 2012, a nurse participant in a federally funded research project said the only thing she remembered about violence issues from her nursing education was how to physically restrain a violent patient.[2]

In a related scenario regarding crisis care, a colleague who teaches an "elective" crisis course and therefore routinely searches for literature updates remarked that "there's nothing very new or different out there regarding the basics of crisis care." This point supports a key message of this book: the importance of learning from history and implementing ideal practice *guidelines published decades ago* (i.e., the AAS Organization Accreditation Standards Manual).[3] It also affirms the need for students embarking on careers in health and social services to be routinely taught the evidence-based "essentials" of crisis care. This includes the rich history of such care reaching back to centuries of community ritual practice and support across the life cycle. It encompasses fitting current crisis care standards (the "new clothes") of what elders over many centuries taught their young about responsibilities toward one another as they traverse the challenges of each phase of the life cycle from birth to death.

And so, let's consider, for example, the fact that among health and social service professional groups, nurses comprise the largest in sheer numbers in the United States and other countries. Nurses' commitment to the principles of holistic care and adherence to the ethic of the Hippocratic oath to "do no harm" leave me hopeful to imagine what progress on crisis and violence issues might ensue if these numbers were mobilized along lines of published ideals regarding education on crisis care.[4] To the extent that nurses move beyond their own historic struggles,[5] and the lessons of Paulo Freire[6] regarding oppressed group behavior, they could marshal their considerable power in knowledge and numbers to make a difference on the crisis and violence prevention issue.

I therefore cite Karen Daly, president of the American Nurses Association and survivor of HIV/AIDs from a needle stick injury on the job, and the American Nurses Association, and Paul Summergrad, President of the American Psychiatric Association, and colleagues they might enlist for prospective leadership to initiate and recommend a follow-up of Surgeon General Dr. Koop's 1985 Workshop on this current public health issue affecting many millions of individuals, families, and violence-plagued communities.

NATIONAL/INTERNATIONAL SURVEY DATA: UPDATE VIA THE DELPHI TECHNIQUE

Evidence for convening such a follow-up of the 1985 workshop might include an update of the national database obtained from the 150 participants Dr. Koop invited to the 1985 workshop, with these major goals: (1) Support the continued excellent crisis care delivered daily by already professionally committed providers against the odds of underfunding and so on, as already discussed. (2) Convene and implement outcomes of a national/international effort through an updated 30-year follow-up of the 1985 Surgeon General's Workshop.

For current evidence warranting such an update, a valuable first step might be data-gathering via the Delphi survey technique[7] employed for the 1985

Workshop in its pre-Workshop planning. A major goal of Delphi surveys is to ascertain the collective wisdom of a group with varying opinions of workshop participants on an issue of public concern—in this case, crisis and violence issues. After each of three iterations, invited participants representing professional and lay groups are asked to consider the opinions of others and reconsider their own positions until consensus emerges about how to address the issue. The US Public Health Service cited major values of this approach: (1) It reveals a shared sense of purpose among participants with no prior contact with one another. (2) It serves to clarify various positions in advance, so the Workshop's action phase can proceed as soon as it is convened. (3) It would help to keep invited participants interested over the year's planning phase. On a very hopeful note for today, Dr. Koop's Delphi survey resulted in an "unusually generous response" supporting my recommendation of its use 30 years later for another step forward on this topic[1] (p. 84). One example of influential follow-up of the 1985 Workshop and other initiatives is the ANA Position Paper regarding essential content in nursing education curricula.[8]

Prior to the 1985 Workshop, using the "Delphi survey" technique, participants were asked to answer questions over the course of three iterations with the aim of reaching consensus regarding opinions and ideas for action on three major questions regarding violence: (1) What is the role of education? (2) What should be done in research? (3) What should be done about the delivery of medical, health, and social services?[1] (pp. 84–91). One notable outcome example following the 1985 Workshop and related initiatives is American Association of Colleges of Nursing (AACN) Position Statement, *Violence as a Public Health Problem*.[8] Another is the *Ten Point Coalition*, a faith-based group of Christian clergy and lay leaders in Boston, with a particular focus on troubled and high-risk youth and alternatives to violent gang life.[9]

EDUCATION AND PRACTICE INITIATIVE—LAUNCHING IDEAS

Complementing the Delphi survey technique, and building on the notable initiatives by the AACN, the AAS, and Ten Point Coalition, my vision for current evidence-based teaching and practice ideas includes the following framework for a large-scale study using the quasi-experimental design.

Organize and engage an interdisciplinary research-planning committee to develop a proposal, obtain funding, and implement a crisis education project that would span at least 5 years with collaboration by committed experts in the crisis field and their respective institutions for stability and support, and working collaboratively with consumer groups for launch and implementation. A quasi-experimental project might look something like this with two groups of participants: (1) clients served in the emergency department; (2) emergency department nursing staff serving these clients:

- Identify at least two major medical/health care centers with state-of- the art emergency departments and linkages to comprehensive mental health services for follow-up referrals from crisis care in the emergency department.
- Obtain baseline data from the emergency department clients served, including type of crisis, life-threatening risk status, family and community supports, and other factors.
- Describe the type and extent of mental health services available at the engaged institutions to which emergency department clients are referred.
- Obtain an accurate and comprehensive medical and psychosocial record of prospective study participants' mental health status on admission, with invitation to participate in the long-range study.
- Explain to potential study participants what will be expected over the 5-year period, their free decision to join the research pool, and the potential benefits to themselves and the crisis care research and practice field.
- Obtain their "informed consent" to participate, as required of all US medical research institutions, and any stipend or other compensation for their time and participation in the study. This includes institution policies regarding "protection of human subjects" as federally required for this type of research.
- Describe what client and nursing staff participants will be asked to contribute over the 5-year period, that is, baseline and follow-up data; for example, for clients: an interview each year to track and compare current mental health status, their crisis experiences, and sociocultural and related factors with baseline information obtained at study outset; for nursing staff: educational preparation for the job, years of experience, their perceived competence in crisis care, and other factors.
- Keep a record of emergency department staff turnover and perceived reasons for stability or instability, incidence of workplace violence, continuing education opportunities, fluctuation, and other relevant data.
- Design and conduct a comprehensive crisis care education program for emergency department staff of the participating institutions; coordination and analysis with baseline data.
- Keep a record of emergency department staff concerns, stability, and related factors influencing emergency department crisis care and mental health follow-up of client participants in the study.
- Identify any intervening variables that might influence outcomes of education and crisis care.
- Compare baseline information and study outcomes from aforementioned data sources (clients and nursing staff) among the two participating institutions, for example, reducing the incidence of the "revolving door" phenomenon in emergency departments (see Chapter 1).
- At end of 5-year period, analyze data to ascertain comparative influences of formal crisis care education, experience, staff support, job satisfaction, staff turnover rates, and potential influences of education and training vis-à-vis

crisis care ideals on the mental health status of client participants and their satisfaction with care received.

MAINTAINING HOPE AND SOLIDARITY

Obviously, this is just a start-up idea for obtaining evidence-based data concerning the intersection between crisis care education and its potential influence on nursing and other service outcomes in emergency departments of major medical centers. The outcomes of a study like this would complement other research, for example, Susan Reverby's historical study of American nursing, *Ordered to Care*.[5] It also speaks to Paulo Freire's[6] work on oppressed group behavior and its relationship to gender in an occupation dominated by female workers. Finally, it supports my several references in this book to historian Santayana and the power and potential influence of learning from history.

We already know a lot about crisis and the needs of clients in crisis and the persons caring for them. And most nurses also know about violence and abuse within their own ranks—ranking just behind police and firefighters on rates of injury on the job, with nursing assistants bearing the brunt of that burden.[2]

The challenge is to apply more widely what we know and never forget that more positive outcomes of our own and others' crisis situations are more likely when we work collaboratively as members of a supportive team rather than going it alone. Readers are referred to *Crisis Education and Service Program Designs* for a fuller coverage of crisis education and training guidelines and examples.[4]

My vision of a "crusade" on this issue requires buy-in by the groups cited here and others in a strategic position to lead and make a difference—that is, professional, religious, governmental, and philanthropic leaders to recapture and build on the 1960s and 1970s ideals of 24/7 crisis care and comprehensive mental health services in every community. This may require community demand of tax and philanthropy sources for continued funding of the peace-promoting services. Such measures based on consumer expectations and demand might come within striking distance of taken-for-granted funding, for example, of the US Department of Defense.

Strong arguments can be made for "defense" of our family, friends, and neighbors and their caretakers aiming to prevent interpersonal violence and abuse at home, in schools, and work. Supporting such strategic action is the now well-established fact that crisis prevention and early intervention is less costly in human and financial terms (and life-saving vis-à-vis suicide and violence) than later treatment of mental health pathologies traceable to lack of crisis care early on.

But none of the envisioned programs discussed here and elsewhere will happen without collaborative strategic action by concerned stakeholders versed in principles and strategies of social change—keeping in mind the swathes of people struggling daily for the basics of food, clothing, and shelter. There are successful preventive models out there such as ROPE (Chapters 6 and 9), the Ten Point Coalition of religious leaders in metro Boston offering an alternative to violence-prone youth gangs out of their basic need of "belonging" through the turbulent phase of adolescence (see www.tenpointcoalition.org). Programs like these deserve widespread adoption and necessary financial support for replication across nations and cultures. They should become as commonly expected as vaccination in childhood—that is, an integral facet of successful child rearing and a peaceful nonviolent launch into responsible adulthood.

My hope for this book is that we continue to build together on what we already know, and thereby save both time and unnecessary suffering. Learning from history, successful current models and other sources are key in addressing crisis, distress, and danger among ourselves and others.

REFERENCES AND FURTHER READING

REFERENCES

1. Koop, C. E. (1986). *Surgeon General's work on violence and public health.* Washington, D.C.: Health Resources and Services Administration, US Public Health Service.
2. Hoff, L. A. (in process). *Violence against healthcare workers: A contextual analysis.*
3. AAS. (2011). *Organization accreditation standards manual* (10th ed.). Washington, D.C.: American Association of Suicidology.
4. Hoff, M., & Hoff, L. A. (2012). *Crisis education and training program designs: A guide for administrators, educators, and clinical trainers.* New York: Routledge.
5. Reverby, S. M. (1987). *Ordered to care: The dilemma of American nursing, 1850–1945.* Cambridge, MA: Cambridge University Press
6. Freire, P. (1989) *Pedagogy of the oppressed.* New York: Continuum
7. Hasson, F., Keeney, S., & McKenna, H. (2000). Research guidelines for the Delphi survey technique. *Journal of Advanced Nursing, 3,* 1008.
8. American Association of Colleges of Nursing—AACN. (2014). Retrieved at www.aacn.nche.edu/publications.
9. Ten Point Coalition (2014). Retrieved at http://btpc.org/about.php.

FURTHER READING

Lusane, C. (2011). *The Black history of the White House.* San Francisco: Open Media Series, City Lights Books.

INDEX

abortion, 253
abstractness, 235
abuse. *See also* violence
  childhood sexual, 92, 117
  coping with, 197
  crisis care and follow-up counseling for survivors of, 134–135
  "downward spiral" and, 127, 128f
  elder, 137
  inquiring about, 133
  not always entailing physical injury, 147
  often originating from bias, 116
  by one's colleagues, 159
  physical health and social consequences of, 221
  sexual, 129
  substance, 57, 197, 198–199
abused men, having more freedom to leave, 120
abused persons
  as brave survivors, 64
  potential for growth, development, and empowerment, 123
abusers
  holding accountable, 121
  violence prevention programs for, 145
abusive behavior, complexity of, 123–129
abusive husbands, trials of women who kill, 120
abusive men, facets of any program for, 163
acceptance
  by the dying person, 292–293
  replacing denial, 60
accession (an unexpected addition of a family member), 266–267
acquired immunodeficiency syndrome (AIDS)
  dementia complex, 192

easier for people to favor suicide, 194
people afflicted with, 191
perspective of people living with, 189
statements from people with, 188
women and children with, 195–196
action plan
  concluding a conference with, 280
  effective, 72
  as problem-oriented, 68
  talking it through to an, 66–67
active crisis, state of, 35, 37
active participation, by the person in crisis, 228, 280
acute anxiety, 45
acute crisis, 91
acute distress, signals of, 181–182
acute emotional upset, activating, 242
acute medical situation, including emotional crisis, 14
addictions
  crisis care of persons with, 197–200
  living with, 189–190
  to people, 272
  physical toll extracted by, 192
adolescence, developmental challenges of, 37, 262–265
adolescents
  harming themselves, 83, 84, 90
  pregnancy as an avenue of escape, 249
adoption, 256, 257
adult children of alcoholics, self-help groups, 200
advance directives, 290
advanced practice registered nurses (APRNs), 75
aging in place, prized goal of, 286
AIDS. *See* acquired immunodeficiency syndrome (AIDS)

AIDS Action Committee (AAC), 189
alarm reaction, 60
alcohol
   antidepressant drugs taken with, 105
   dependency on, 199, 214
   as an excuse for violent behavior, 161
   legalizing, 73
   suicide with, 89
ALS (Lou Gehrig's disease), John diagnosed with, 88
alternative lifestyles, 120, 121
Alzheimer's disease (AD), 201
ambiguity, arising from an acute crisis state, 91
ambivalence
   around a life or death decision, 129
   in high-risk behavior, 109–110
   in low-risk behavior, 106
   in a person's life-or-death decision making, 101
   strong in moderate risk behavior, 108
   weighing life and death, 94–95
American Association of Colleges of Nursing, 167
American Association of Retired Persons (AARP), 285
American Association of Suicidology, 83
American Foundation for Suicide Prevention (AFSP), 83, 96
American Indian reservations, poverty rampant, 212
anger
   at death, 292
   encouraging alternate expression of, 103
   following loss, 45, 60
   violent impulses and, 157
anthropological definitions of crisis, 243
antisocial behavior, primary prevention of, 165–167
anxiety, 38t, 41, 45, 75, 85, 104, 192
approaches, to crisis, 21–23
assailant, excusing, 127
assault and homicidal danger assessment tool, 158, 159t
assessment
   of dangerousness and violence potential, 156
   process, 46–48
   questions, 51t
   techniques, 38t
assisted-suicide issue, 290

attitudes
   changing, 34, 55, 56
   judgmental, 130
   toward death, 289–291
   toward seniors, 285–286
   toward work, 213
authoritarian approaches, using rigid, 180

Bangladesh, collapse of a clothing factory in, 228, 230
bargaining, with death, 292
battered woman, signals of distress, 137
battering, of women worldwide, 117
behavior. *See also* self-destructive behavior; violent behavior
   following through with a crisis resolution plan, 15
   of parents of handicapped children, 260
   signaling acute distress, 182
behavioral clues, of the suicide prone, 83
behavioral functions, controlling impulsivity, 15
behavior problems, of a child, 253
belief systems, influencing suicide, 87
benefit-cost ratios, inhuman language of, 238
berdache (androgynous men), 263
bereavement, reactions from, 60–61
Best Practices Registry, 96
bicultural groups, 148
binge drinking, on college campuses, 245, 247
biological psychiatry, 281
biomedical approaches, to social problems, 124
biophysical response, 181
bipolar illness, 105, 180–181, 281
bisexuality, strong association with suicide risk, 84
black men, violence and recurrent trauma among young, 153
blaming
   families in crisis, 268
   victims, 126–127, 128f
blended families, increasing presence of, 255
bond, establishing, 157
borderline personality disorder, 105, 150
Boston Medical Center, Violence Intervention Advocacy Program, 25
both-and approach, 163, 223

boundaries, in decision counseling, 62
boys, youth violence prevention and, 117, 152–155
bridge builder, role as, 7
bullying, continuing to create terror in schools, 152
burnout, preventing among crisis workers, 20

Cambodian genocide survivor, 220–221
caretakers
 morbidity and mortality rates, 202
 at risk, 196–197, 305
 women as, 209
Center for Advancement of Youth, Family, and Community Service, 155, 242
Center on Housing Rights and Evictions (COHRE), 224
chemical restraints, 4–5, 180
chemical tranquilization, 73, 76
child (children)
 with AIDS, 195–196
 damaging effects of alcoholism on, 199–200
 death of, 250–252
 dependent and needy, 249
 disturbed, 74
 having surgery, 187–188
 illness or behavior problems of, 253
 infected with the AIDS virus, 195
 interaction with older people, 286
 in international sex trade, 117
 loss by death, 49t
 miscarried or stillborn, 252–253
 mourning the death of, 251–252
 neglect of, 199, 211
 prioritizing needs over adult rights, 254
 witnessing violence, 117, 153
child care, 136, 210, 268
childhood, moving to adulthood, 212
childhood sexual abuse, 92, 117
child life workers, advice to parents, 188
child-resilience, protective influences on, 154
child snatching, 254
chronic crisis, no such thing as, 51–52
civil order, breakdown of, 117
client decision-making, facilitating, 71t
clients, potential danger from, 159
clues
 about intention, 85
 behavioral, verbal, and emotional, 83
 PCPs recognizing, 111
 to suicide and life-threatening crises, 5, 95–96
"Code of the Street," interrupting, 153
cognitive aspect, of crisis resolution, 15
Cohousing movement, 267
collaboration, restorative justice and, 164–165
commonalities, with others experiencing crisis, 221
communication
 central to health care providers threatened at work, 157
 critical to uncovering interpretations, 235
 as emotional crisis prevention, 236–238
 as a first step in helping, 57–59
 no substitute for simple, direct, 83
 pivotal to understanding inner pain and turmoil, 58–59
 as a suicide sign, 99
communication channels, keeping open, 157, 161
communication problems, of suicidal people, 82–83
communities
 assuming responsibility for children, 155
 in crisis, 266–271
 impact of individual and family crises on, 272–273
community-based services, as a failed policy, 24–25
Community Mental Health Acts of 1963 and 1965, 24
community planning, homelessness and, 221–224
Compassion and Choices magazine, 291
Compassionate Friends, 252
Comprehensive Mental Health Assessment (CMHA), 138
connections, sudden loss of, 32
constraints of managed care, 180
context
 for asking sensitive questions, 133
 cultural, 148
 of violence, 124, 125
continuum, of mental health services, 23f
continuum or path to suicide, interrupting, 92, 93

Index [309]

contracts. *See* no-suicide contracts; service contract
control, fear of losing, 20
controlling, authoritarian responses, by adults, 155
conversation, with loved ones before death, 290
coordinated care, versus the "revolving door," 24–26
coping
  ability, 39, 62
  effective and infective, 48, 49t
  mechanisms, 283
  strategies, 62–65
cosmetic surgery, as a booming business, 186
counseling, for suicidal persons, 106
counseling sessions, with a distressed family, 270
court-appointed guardian, anger at having, 201
crib death, 250–251
cries for help, 41
criminal justice system, denying a decent standard of treatment to criminals, 160
crisis
  as danger and opportunity, 15–16, 19–20, 174, 243
  defined, 1, 14, 242
  development of, 32–37, 44
  diverse approaches to, 21–23
  duration and outcomes of, 37–40
  emergency medical care and, 176–177
  feelings and other responses during, 45–46
  final decision about suicide during, 103
  during health status transition, 181–182
  interplay with stress and illness, 18
  keeping communication open, 236
  manifestations of, 44
  no such thing as chronic, 51–52
  as not inevitable, 35
  not occurring in isolation, 18
  origins, 44
  over SIDS, 251
  "plumage" and distress signals, 7
  preventing through education, 2
  prevention, 23, 247, 268
  recognizing an impending, 41–44
  resembling an earthquake, 17
  resolving constructively, 18
  response, 58, 276
  service plan, 27
  services, 23–24, 198
  on the threshold of, 31
  what it is not, 15
  why people go into, 32
  workers, 26, 268
crisis assessment levels, 44t
crisis care
  as a basic human right, 202
  basic steps in, 27–28
  continuum of mental health services, 24
  coordiinated care vs. "revolving door," 24–26
  of disaster survivors, 225–227
  in diverse health care settings, 28, 175–180
  in emergency setting, 70
  in hospitals and nursing homes, 178
  by non-specialists in, 3
  as opportunity, 198
  for people intentionally injuring themselves, 23
  of people with addictions and eating disorders, 197–200
  planning, 67–71, 106
  in primary health care settings, 177
  principles, 198, 266
  process, 176
  in psychiatric or residential settings, 178–180
  saving time and effort spent later, 65
  social network and group approaches to, 277–283
  for victim-survivors, 134–135
crisis counseling, 17, 102–104, 106
  example of, 269–271
  results of, 208
  sessions, 111
  short-term, 208
crisis counselors, 133, 183, 219
crisis experience, 40
crisis flags, ignoring taking a heavy toll, 73
crisis groups, 282–283
crisis hotline, 24-hour telephone service, 3
crisis intervention
  with assailants and those threatening violence, 161–163

being developed in many schools, 154
described, 17
early, 23, 24
economic implications of, 24
essential element of comprehensive
   health care, 177
focusing on timely problem solving, 20
life-saving actions for, 102–104
prescription drugs place in, 75–76
promoting growth and avoiding negative
   crisis outcomes, 22
in psychiatric and residential
   settings, 178–180
recognized as third of three
   revolutionary phases, 20
social approaches to, 277
tandem approach to, 125
with troubled youth, 154
crisis management, 14, 16
Crisis Paradigm, 22, 22f, 55, 264, 264f
"crisis plumage," 41, 235
crisis points, for parents of handicapped
   children, 259, 260
crisis resolution
defined, 14
essential elements of
   successful, 182–184
follow up after, 64–65
guidance aimed at health, 2
heart of successful, 18
positive, 55, 62, 64, 192–193
crisis theory, pioneers of, 3
critical incident stress debriefing
   (CISD), 227–228
Critical Incident Stress Management
   (CISM), 227–228
critical juncture, after multiple losses, 47
critical life events, 7, 51
critical life passages, 247
"critical mass," power of effective
   action, 300–302
cross-cultural perspective, of suicide, 87
cry for help, 94–95, 129
cult groups, mass suicides of some, 276
cultural norm, violence sometimes excused
   as, 146
cultural relativism, 121, 146, 148, 246
cultural sensitivity, by crisis workers, 19
cultural values, sensitivity to
   immigrant's, 221

culture and lifestyle, action plan consistent
   with a person's, 68
culture shock, 178, 180

Daly, Karen, 302
danger
assessing, 157
avoiding, 18, 19
of crisis, 1, 21, 22f
of a family breakdown, 16
identifying immediate and
   future, 131–134
risk of assault and, 157–158
Danger Assessment Tool, 159
danger signals, detecting early, 5
death
attitudes toward, 289–291
burial and other rituals, 248
of a child, 250–252
as the final passage, 289–293
debriefing, with colleagues, 227
decision counseling, 62–63
decision making, regarding a move, 218
decisions, making with the person in
   crisis, 67
de-escalation and/or restraint, applied, 25
dehumanization process, 156
deinstitutionalization, 24, 223
delayed grief reaction, 252
Delphi survey technique, 302–303
dementia, 192, 194, 201
demoralization, 266, 267
denial, 57, 232, 290, 292
dependence, on intimate attachments, 272
dependency conflict, 231
dependency needs, 68
dependent and clinging persons, 271
depression
among victims, 127
importance of treatment for, 96
indicating risk for suicide, 101
relationship to suicide, 95
while dying, 292
destructive forces, meeting challenges
   of, 234
destructive relationships, 153, 272
detention setting, physical and social
   constraints of, 162
developmental tasks, during late
   adolescence, 262

developmental transition, to middle age, 46
diagnosable mental illness, compared to a crisis state, 45
Diagnostic and Statistical Manual of Mental Disorders (DSM), 45, 127, 231
dialogue, providing opportunities for, 164
direct questioning, in the context of a trusting relationship, 137
disadvantaged groups, reducing crisis vulnerability of, 22
disasters
   cultural differences in response and recovery, 235
   of human origins, 117, 228–229, 233, 238
   job and home loss following, 224–227
   learning from, 233–236
   natural, 225t, 273
   natural compared to human origins, 229–230, 238
   planned, 230
discipline, 144, 150, 155
disclosure of facts, by medical personnel, 253
discrimination and repressive policies, 56
disequilibrium, after terrorism, 232
dismemberment (loss of family member), 266, 267
disordered homeless, case management and treatment of, 223
distress
   faces of, 31
   offering basic information for people in, 299
   origins of, 55
   recognizing different faces of, 30–52
   signals, 41
distressed persons, 8, 41, 174
distressful events, typical responses to, 55
distressful situation, 14
divorce, 253–254, 274
domestic violence, mandatory reporting of, 135
double person, 263
double standard, regarding male and female sexual expression, 149
Down syndrome, child with, 260–261
downward spiral
   from culture and rigidly defined social roles, 127, 128f
   to depression, 233
   interrupting, 21, 129
dropout rates, in US high schools, 211
drugs, complicating original symptoms, 75
drug treatment
   appropriate use during crisis, 75–76
   for depression, 105–106
drug use, added to the debilitating effects of AIDS, 195
dying person, 196, 291–293
"Dying Person's Bill of Rights," 294
dynamic plan, 69

ecological hazards, 152–153
education and practice initiative, 303–305
ego identity, achievement of, 262
elder abuse, 137
elderly homeless, 222
elderly people. *See also* older people
   moving to a group residential setting, 217
   services for, 286–289
emergency, defined, 15
emergency and acute-care settings, 176
emergency medical treatment, 102
emergency setting, example of crisis care in, 70t–71t
emotional attachments, establishing more stable, 63
emotional breakdown, 18
emotional coping, occurring through grief work, 227
emotional crisis, as normal, 7
emotional expression, fostering, 63
emotional needs, importance of, 176
emotional or mental illness, as not crisis, 15
emotional pain, symptoms signaling, 180–181
emotional recovery, from traumatic stress, 230
emotional scars, among disaster survivors, 226
emotional wounds, satisfactory healing of, 147
emotions, interfering in a person's cognitive functioning, 45
empathic engagement, with a distressed person, 63
empathy, 66, 71t
empowerment
   client's, 280

expressed by female emergency department patients, 135–136
of survivors, 128
of a victim-survivor, 134
enemies, as people like ourselves, 236
environmental racism, 228
ethical issues, suicide and the right to die, 87–89
ethnic cleansing and tribal wars, 228
ethnocentrism, 148, 236
events, putting in order, 42
evidence-based data, 305
excessive drinking, 57. *See also* binge drinking
ex-offenders, highly crisis prone after release from prison, 273
explicit statement, to others of intent to commit suicide, 99
extended family, norm in most non-Western societies, 267
external resources, 99

failure, possibility of, 31
families
　actions and motives of, 40
　affected by drug use, 27
　bound up with their community, 276
　in crisis, 266–271
　strain affecting the entire, 33
　troubles and distress, 266
　violence in and beyond, 122–123
family counseling program, 250
family life, maintaining a stable, 16
family members
　being honest with the resident of a nursing care facility, 202
　burdened with insurance and other obstacles, 26
　as first responders, 27
　greatest risk of attack from, 147
　tempting to avoid dealing with, 68
family violence, 122, 147–148
famines, in African countries, 228, 234
Farm Aid Rural Management, 215
fatherhood, in transition, 257–258
fathers, 39t, 254
fear, 20, 85, 162, 208
Federal Emergency Management Assistance (FEMA), 226
feelings
　about crisis, 15

experienced during a crisis, 45
including adequate time to express, 68
managing, 41
open expression of, 63
of parents of handicapped children, 260
refraining from expressing, 82–83
signalling acute distress, 181
female circumcision. *See* female genital mutilation (FGM)
female deviance, 56
female genital mutilation (FGM), 148, 244–245
female menopause, as a disease, 285
female violence, context of, 119
feminization of poverty, 210
"50-minute session," as ritual, 246
first responders, family members as, 27
flexibility, as key to averting a crisis, 34
flexible work schedules, family policy regarding, 268
focus, inability to, 47
follow-up, agreement for, 69
follow-up counseling, examples for planning, 106
follow-up plan, 69, 71t, 280
follow-up services, linkage to specialty, 134
forensic work, criticisms regarding prediction in, 155–156
formal crisis care, 26
friends, 40, 190
front lines, human service providers on, 46
functional level, action plan appropriate to, 68
futility, climates of, 153

gang members, employing, 212
gangs, initiation into, 247
gastrointestinal symptoms, from emotional upheaval, 47
gay, lesbian, bisexual, or transgendered (GLBT) relationships, 120
gay community, civil rights of, 191
gay Haitian youth, 264–265
gay men, more vulnerable to violence, 120
gay parents, 256
gender barriers, making communication difficult, 63
gender-based harassment, vulnerability to, 209
gender-based inequality, in the paid labor force, 258

gender-based stereotypes, in
     professions, 258
gender influences, on violent behavior, 144
gender roles, allocation of rigid, 152
general health care situations, 175
general health practitioners, hesitating to
     deal with emotional issues, 177
geriatric care manager, guidance from, 202
"get even" approaches, 164
girls, rates of violence increasing, 117, 144,
     151–152
globalization, 210
"going postal," 207
gold mine explosion, in Canada, 228
grief, 60, 61, 197, 261
grief counselor, 48
grief experts, 60
grief work, 61, 177
group counseling, for men who batter, 164
group mode, of helping, 282
group process techniques, 280
groups
     helping people in, 282
     power to "turn the tide," 300
group therapy, recommending, 109
group work, indicated in several
     instances, 283
growth, in the midst of pain, adversity, and
     turmoil, 20
guilt, 60, 61, 84, 85
guilt trips, avoiding, 112
gun lobby, 153

handicapped child, 258, 259–261
handicapped people, crises of, 261
handicaps
     intergenerational aspects of, 258–259
     living with or caring for a person with
          significant, 196–197
harms of wrongdoing, 164
hazardous events or situations, 38t, 48, 50,
     51, 247
hazing, 245
health, maintaining or regaining, 232
health and criminal justice agencies, 26
health and emergency providers, communal
     responsibility to prevent suicide, 89
health care, as a basic human right, 202
health care providers (HCPs), 86, 122,
     130, 134, 158. *See also* primary care
     provider (PCP)

relative isolation of some, 298
threatened at work, 157
what to clearly expect of, 8
health care settings, triage questions, 132
health care workers, detecting and
     preventing a full-blown crisis, 180
health insurance, 24, 33, 45, 74, 206
health professionals, 117, 122
health service protocols, 148
health status, 174, 180–182
health workers, assaulted as "part of the
     job," 161
heart attack, vulnerability to, 36
"helicopter parent," 262
help, 41, 72
helping
     communication as a first step, 57–59
     a dying person, 291–293
     young people, 266
heterosexual males, violence committed
     by, 116, 117
hidden messages, considering, 194
hierarchy of needs, 273
high-lethal methods, for suicide, 97
high-risk settings, working alone in, 162
high-risk suicidal behavior, 109–111
"highway" or continuum, suicidal behavior
     viewed as, 92
HIV/AIDS, diagnosis of, 191
HIV and AIDS, crisis and chronic
     illness, 188–196
holistic health care, 14
Holocaust, 48, 233, 234
home-based crisis care, 26–27
home care, example of, 287–288
homelessness, 221–224
homicide risk, 103, 155
homicides, 117, 162
homophobia, 263
honor killings, custom of, 149
hope, maintaining, 305
hopelessness, as forerunner to death, 288
hospice movement, 293–295
hospitalization
     avoiding unnecessary, 281
     enforcing a routine of dependency, 182
     like being stranded in a foreign country
          or culture shock, 178
     for suicidal person, 89, 93
hospitals, 3–4, 93–94, 176, 178
     psychiatric, 5, 27

hostility, expressing feelings of, 61
housing
   for abused women, 136
   "all-inclusive care," 287
   costs skyrocketing in cities, 223
   for youthful offenders, 263
"Housing First," 224
human beings, 57, 60
human connections, 57
human crises, addressing in a social framework, 277
human development, turning points in, 243
human needs, 32, 105, 271
human potential, for both good and evil, 228
human rights, basic, 6, 189
human rights perspective, framing violence in, 121
human rights violations, 118–119, 148
hyperactive child, caring for, 124–125

iatrogenic tragedy, 251
illness
   avoiding, 232
   of a child, 253
immediacy, of a person's stress, 48, 50
immediate danger, 101
immigrants, 137, 218, 219, 221
impact, recoil, and post-trauma phases, of disaster crisis care, 224
impact phase, of natural disaster, 225t
impulsive behavior, history of, 98
incest victim, 147
in-depth assessment, 134
individual, psychotherapeutic approach, 278
individual and public crises, in terms of human meaning, 235
individual and sociocultural factors, explaining violence, 124
industrialization, 243
inequalities
   between men and women, 151–152
   between rich and poor, 222
inpatient psychiatric care, 24
insanity, 147, 160
institutional barriers, to promotion and economic security, 210–211
institutionalization, marking beginning of a rapid decline, 288

institutionalized racism, 100, 234
institutional placement of elders, 299
institutional settings, goals in, 179
institution-based care, most costly, 23f
institutions, busy, bureaucratic atmosphere of, 281
insurance. *See* health insurance
integration, after terrorism, 232
intense feelings, associated with loss, 61
intensive care unit, environment of, 182
interaction factor, as crucial influencing violence, 156
interdependence, 66, 262
interdisciplinary framework, dynamic, 21–22
Interfaith Youth Core, 263
intergenerational welfare dependency, 210
International Decade for National Disaster Reduction, 226
international nuclear capacity, 234
international response, to disasters, 237
interpersonal violence, 119, 148
intervention, 4, 73, 186, 220
intimacy, 262, 271, 272
intimate relationships
   beginnings and endings, 247, 271–276
   essential to a happy, productive life, 271
   excessive dependency in any, 120
investigative procedures, 235
irresponsibility, learned, 153
isolation, 103, 265, 274, 283

jails and prisons, 25, 273, 277
job security, meaning security at home, 206
Joint Commission on Mental Health of Children in the United States, 262
joint counseling session, 183
Judeo-Christian tradition, suicide and, 87
judgment, withholding about behaviors, 19
judgmental attitude, 130

Kaposi's sarcoma, 194
Kitchen Table Alliance, 215
knowledge as prevention, framework of, 6

laboratory tests, of gastrointestinal symptoms, 76
Lakota Sioux, 150, 154
last straw, determining, 50

law(s)
  organization for a change in, 166–167
  trouble with, 41
leaders, harnessing the power and prestige of, 301
learned behavior, 117, 151
learned irresponsibility, 153
learning from history, 299
legislators, contacting, 166–167
lesbian, gay, bisexual, and transgendered persons, violence among, 119
lesbian and gay parenthood, 256
lesbian women, at risk for AIDS, 195
lethality assessment, 95
lethality of method, 97
lethal weapons, 98, 103
Level 1 assessment, 42, 44t
Level 2 assessment, 43–44, 44t
life
  final responsibility for, 89
  as meaningful and worthwhile, 194
life and death levels, of danger during crisis, 132
life crises, human development transition states as, 242
life cycle
  challenge and rewards through, 242–243
  navigating and growing through challenges across, 242–295
  phases of, 216
  transitions, 248
life events, critical through normal, 242
Life Line, 287
life-saving intervention strategies, 138
life's problems, interpreting in a medical framework, 127
life-threatening behavior, screening for, 43
life-threatening crises, 5, 7
life-threatening illness or addiction, events following diagnosis of, 191
life-threatening situations, approaching, 43
listening, 63, 226, 235, 236–238
lives, bringing stability and organization into, 57
living wills, 290
local support groups, providing housing and hospice care, 193
long range risk, 101
Los Angeles Suicide Prevention Center, 3
loss
  acute sense of, 259
  coming to terms with, 291
  as a common theme, 59–60
  making meaning out of, 232–233
  pain of, 221
  of purpose, 153
  sense of, 45, 217
Love Canal tragedy, story about, 233
low-lethal methods, for suicide, 97

male and female roles, stereotypical, 37
male dominance, 145, 149–150
male promiscuity, 149
males, socialized not to express feelings readily, 186
manageability, of survivors, 233
manipulators, 93
manufacturing jobs, widespread loss of, 212–213
marriage counseling, 270, 275
mastectomy, as a crisis point, 186
material-arrangement tasks, 248
maternal practice, 236
maternity and paternity leave, family policy regarding, 268
Meals on Wheels, 287
meaning
  of a physical act, 101
  of a problem, 62
  of self-destructive behavior, 90
  of self-injury, 102
  of suicidal behavior, 83
  of traumas in cross-cultural perspective, 233
meaningfulness of survivors, 233
meaningful work, success hinging on, 213
means, availability of for suicide, 98
mediation and nonviolent conflict resolution programs, 55
medical emergency, in a nontraditional family unit, 256
medical emergency treatment, 16
medical expenses, accumulating, 33
medical intervention, prolongation of life with sophisticated, 248
medicalization, 127, 231, 246
medically nonserious self-injury, as a life-and-death issue, 101
medically nonserious suicide attempt, HCP's response, 102
medical or health related crisis, 183

medical programs, refusing to follow life-sustaining, 92
medical-psychiatric-neurological evaluation, 183
medical tests, revealing a fetal handicap, 259
medication use, during crisis, 73–74
"Medicine Wheel," application of, 154
men, undergoing the climacteric, 285
menopause, as a natural transition state, 285
mental health and crisis care, "second cousin" status, 24
mental health commitment, example, 88–89
mental health crisis care framework, 42–44
mental health laws, 89, 99
mental health services, 6, 23f
mental illness, 6, 85
mentally ill persons, 158, 222
messages, of suicidal people, 82
middle age, 248, 283–285
military personnel, sexual assaults committed against, 117
miscarried or stillborn child, 252–253
mobbing, creating terror in schools, 152
moderate-risk suicidal behavior, 108–109
monetary compensation, 230
moranhood, 244
More, Thomas, 267
mothering, as only chance for fulfillment, 255
mother role, 47
moves
  anticipated, 216–217
  unanticipated, 217–218
multi-cultural societies, 148
multi-ethnicity, of North American, European, and other societies, 87
multi-faceted "wave," of the same underlying problem, 51
multiple losses example, 46
multiple sclerosis (MS), diagnosis of, 33
murder, not occurring in a cultural or social vacuum, 161
Murthy, Vivek Hallegere, 301

name, relinquishing, 245
natalism, resurgence of 19th-century, 257
national health program, lack of, 222
National Institute of Mental Health, ideal of 24-7 crisis services, 3

National Institute on Alcoholism and Alcohol Abuse, 199
National Strategy for Suicide Prevention, 96, 102
National Suicide Prevention Lifeline, 3
National White Ribbon Campaign, 127
Native American people, tradition on wife battering, 127
natural crisis intervention, 28
needy persons, 272
negative associations, with expressing feelings during childhood, 63
negative crisis outcomes
  avoiding, 55, 194
  example of, 35–37, 38–39
neglect
  prevention of and learning from, 230
  of victimization, 122
negotiated death, accommodating notion of, 290
network conference, conducting, 280
networking, in a shelter for abused women, 282
network strategies, 278, 279
"New Age" families, 267
Nigerian Nurses and Midwives Association, 245
no-fault divorce laws, increase of, 254
no-lose game, engaging in, 93
nonviolent approaches, to conflict resolution, 151
normal activities, resumption of, 61
normality, of physical symptoms, 76
normal response, after exposure to horrors of war, 231
no-suicide contracts, 103
notions, about people in crisis and how to help them, 18–20
nuclear arms, stockpiles of, 236
nursing care facilities, typical services, 202
nursing homes, 178, 288

obligations, achievable for offenders, 164
obsession, with work, 209
occupational security, challenges of, 211–212
occupation-based stress, 206
offenders, supporting, 164
older people. *See also* elderly people

crisis proneness of, 285
divorce of, 274
living alone, 286
"one more thing," 32, 36
one solution, to a problem, 100
one-stop health service centers, more needed, 144
one thing after another scenario, 50
opportunity
    Chinese character for crisis representing, 20
    of crisis, 1, 193
    failing to grasp, 21
    grasping, 18
    for growth and development through crisis 22f
    for learning new skills, 16
    for psychosocial growth, 75
    taking advantage of, 19
opportunity and danger, facing, 14
origin, of stress, 56
Overeaters Anonymous, 197
ownership, of women, 150

paid work, 209
pain, control of, 293
pain medication, providing adequate, 194
pain of loss, acceptance of, 61
palliative-care research, growing emphasis on, 294
panic reactions, avoiding the contagion of, 226
parental modeling, of nonviolent responses to stress, 154
parent-child relationship, nonreciprocal, 249
parenthood, common crisis points, 249–258
parents of handicapped children, signs of crisis, 260
past, influenced by, 153
pathogenesis, 232
pathologizing, everyday stressful life events, 231
Patient Self-Determination Act (1990), 290
patriarchal values, 145
Patriots Day bombing (2013), of the Boston Marathon, 232
patterns of behavior, lapsing into neurotic, psychotic, or destructive, 40
pauperization, of mothers raising children alone, 153

PCP. *See* primary care provider (PCP)
peace and acceptance, terminal patients arriving at, 190
pediatric PCPs, referrals to child psychiatric specialists, 136
people in crisis
    facts highlighting urgency of prevention and crisis care, 116–117
    forced out of home and country because of war or ethnic cleansing, 206
    generally capable of helping themselves, 19
    helping themselves, 67
    life-saving actions for, 102–104
    as normal from the standpoint of diagnosable illness, 19
    objectifying, 236
    outcomes possible, 39–40
    plan developed with, 67–68
    from sudden illness, 182–183
People in Crisis: Clinical and Diversity Perspectives, 2
people-to-people small-town approach, in Wyoming, 211
perceptions, signaling acute distress, 182
perpetrator
    accountable, 119, 146, 163
    described, 123
    excusing on grounds of psychopathology, 145
    in VRP triangle, 66
persecuting, the suicidal person, 87
persecutor role, switching to, 66
personal and social-psychological strategies, 166
personal coping ability, loss of 38t
personal crisis manifestations 51t, 191–192
personal freedom, less ritual implying more, 244
personality, 36, 100, 156
personal problems and public issues, 6–7
personal responses, questions assessing, 50, 51t
persons. *See* people in crisis
person's life, celebrating, 248
phases
    of crisis development, 32–33
    of dying, 292–293
physical battering 49t
physical illness, 100, 175

[318] *Index*

physically and mentally handicapped
    persons, 196–197, 258–259, 261
physical restraint, perceived as a form of
    punishment, 179
physical strength, differences between
    most men and women, 120
physical symptoms, 45, 47
physical toll, exacted by AIDS or
    addiction, 192
physical violence, accompanied by verbal
    abuse, 147
physician. *See also* primary care provider
    (PCP), arranging for home health
    services, 34
physician-assisted suicide, 88, 290
pioneers in crisis theory, 3
planning, 69, 98
point of no return, in response to
    unendurable psychological pain, 90
police patrol ride-along experience, 6
positive crisis resolution. *See* crisis
    resolution
post-suicide meeting, convening, 112
posttraumatic period, 32
post traumatic stress disorder
    (PTSD), 221, 230–231
poverty
    on American Indian reservations, 212
    causing stress, 254
    feminization of, 210
power and control, 122, 163, 164
power-coercive strategies, 56
precipitating factor, in crisis, 50
precrisis state, 19, 39–40
predicament, 15
prescription drugs
    abuse or misuse of, 4
    misuse and overdependence in
        dispute, 74
    place in crisis intervention, 75–76
    suicide deaths caused by, 102, 106
    used as restraint, 25
prevention, less costly than treatment, 177
preventive approach, to infertility, 257
preventive intervention, 184–186, 202,
    214
preventive public health measures, 229
primary care protocols, screening for
    abuse, 133
primary care provider (PCP). *See also*
    health care providers (HCPs)
    expectations for, 76
    mandatory reporting by, 135–139
    pediatric, 136
    recognizing significant clues after the
        fact, 111
primary prevention, 23, 224
priorities, setting, 67
prisons. *See* jails and prisons
privacy, intimacy, community, 130, 271
private work, women doing, 209
problems
    ability to solve effectively, 32
    helping in coping with, 64
    searching for boundaries of, 62
problem-solving approaches, creative, 36
problem-solving process, 28
problem-solving skills, 63
professional assessment, indicated for
    depression, 85
professional strategies, 167
professional success, achieving, 16
promotion
    institutional barriers to, 210
    leading to suicide, 207
protocol, when encountering a person in
    impending crisis, 41
providers. *See* health care providers (HCPs)
psychache, deemed to be unbearable, 90
psychiatric assessments, 28
psychiatric crisis specialists, 4
psychiatric diagnosis, 127
psychiatric disorders, distinguishing from
    crisis, 19
psychiatric facilities, searching patients on
    admission, 179–180
psychiatric hospitals. *See* hospitals
psychiatric patients, discharged, 25,
    281
psychiatric specialists, *DSM* used
    worldwide by, 45
psychiatric treatment, denial of, 28
psychiatrists, 75
psychic pain, victimized patients
    sharing, 166
psychological abuse, effects of, 147
psychological functioning, 15
psychological recovery, depicting
    survivors, 229
psychosocial or affective tasks, 248
psychotherapy, 17
    compared to crisis intervention, 20

psychotherapy (*cont.*)
  described, 106
  ongoing, 111
  rite of, 246
psychotic process, may or may not be present in suicide, 91
psychotropic drugs
  as chemical restraint, 25
  in combination with other treatments, 74
  danger of prescribing without a referral for counseling, 100
  discovery of, 20
  misuse for children, 277, 281
  overreliance on, 4
  for suicidal persons, 104–106
psychotropic medication, on an emergency basis, 104
psychotropic substance use, historical context and questions, 73–74
PTSD. *See* post traumatic stress disorder (PTSD)
public, educating, 166
public issues, debating and acting on, 235
public work, men doing, 209
punitive versus rehabilitative measures, counterproductivity of, 164
purity, cultural value of, 149
purpose, loss of, 153

quasi-experimental project, idea of, 303–305
questionable practices, regarding violence and abuse, 144
questions
  asking, 41–44, 63
  assessing type of plan and action timetable, 66–67
  considering key, regarding decisions, 62
  with implications for suicidal persons, 88
  in regard to suicidal behavior, 83
"quiet" crises, 208
Quincianara, in Spanish-speaking groups, 247

racial and economic justice, 167
racial minorities, comprising largest percentage of poor women and children, 210
racial minority groups, continuing struggle, 84
racism, 153

rape, fear of HIV infection following, 195–196
rape victims, majority know their attackers, 117
rapport, with the person in crisis, 57
rating scale, limitations of, 95
"rational suicide," 194
Reach for Recovery self-help group, 186
reality, accepting, 64
reason and research, action based on, 55
redundancy, 248
reeducation and attitude changes, 55, 56
referrals, 76, 279
refugees, 218, 219–220, 221
rehabilitation, not applying to prisons, 273
reintegration, encouraging, 164
reinvestment, in the new community, 218
relationships
  contributing to the patient's condition, 15
  between crisis and stress, 17
  ending, 271
  keeping open, with friends left behind, 217
religion, young people turning to, 263
renegotiable helping plan, 69
rescuer role, in VRP triangle, 66
residential change, 216–221
resilience, enhancing, 18
resolution of the immediate problem, 17
resource people, establishing contact with, 279
resources, 44, 56
respect, showing to all parties, 164
restorative justice, signposts of, 164–165
restraining orders, not preventing murders of women, 163
restraints, placing in, 179
retaliatory violence, escalating violence, 136
Retired Senior Citizen Volunteers, 219
retirement, 215, 216, 248
"revolving door," 4, 25, 158
rich and poor, gap widening globally, 213
rights
  determining one's own death, 88
  of suicidal people, 89
risk assessment, criteria and dynamics in, 156–157
Risk Assessment Tool: Suicide, 106, 107t
risk level, determining, 101

Rite of Passage Experience, 155, 242, 305
Rites of Passage (van Gennep), 244
rituals
   accompanying status changes, 242
   as aids to healthy development and happiness, 243–246
   comparing, 246–249
   death, 289
   making public what is private, 244
role expectations 39t, 100
role modeling, fostering emotional expression, 63
role models, for male participation in child care, 258
role transitions, crisis state occuring during, 31
roots
   of the problem, 163
   of violence, 124
   of youth violence, 152–154
rules of the game, changing, 34

safe water campaign, preventing epidemics among the Asian tsunami refugees, 229
salutogenesis, 232
Samburu of Kenya, 244
SAMHA (Substance Abuses and Mental Health Services Administration), 83
Sandy Hook Promise, 153
Santayana, George, 6, 299, 305
Saunders, Cecily, 293
savior tactics, 89
scale, attempts at precise measurement of little value, 100
scapegoat, tendency to, 112
school shooting tragedies, 154
Schweitzer, Albert, 237
scientific jargon, 235
screening assessment, 283
screening-linking-planning conference method, 278
seclusion, perceived as a form of punishment, 179
secondary prevention, 23–24
secondary trauma, 227
secularized society, ritual holding a paradoxical place in, 246
secure refugees, for victims terrorized or threatened with their life at home, 145
security, dramatic moves from, 206–207
self-actualized individuals, 20

self-blame, among victims, 127
self-blaming, curtailing, 64
self-care
   losing one's ability for, 201
   personal attention to, 128
self-defense, female violence primarily in, 119–120
self-destruction, material and physical circumstances making possible, 92
self-destructive behavior. *See also* violent behavior
   aspects of, 90–91
   chronic, 198–200
   communicating their distress, 99
   engaging in several kinds, 101
   overlapping features of, 90
   reinforcing, 102
self-destructive lifestyle, giving up, 199
self-destructive people
   essential services for, 102–104
   facts and feelings about, 83–84
   groups of, 91–92
   nearly everyone having contact with, 85
   recognizing typical behaviors of, 89–92
   requesting departure from the usual roles of patient and health service provider, 86
self-determination, people's basic need for, 20
self-evaluation tool, crisis care plan as, 67
self-help groups, 104, 186
self-injury, 86, 91
self-mutilating activity, engaging in, 92
self-sufficiency, actively fostering, 20
self-supportive, ability to be, 206
seniors, attitudes toward, 285–286
"sense of coherence" (SOC), 48
sensitization, to death, 291
serious illness
   caretakers of people with, 196–197
   example of, 174–175
service contract
   for a battering situation 139t
   egalitarian aspects of sabotaged, 65
   elements of, 72
   purpose of, 72–73
Service Contract framework, 138
services for suicide prevention, types of, 102
"Seven Essential Attachments," 276
severe emotional pain, 45

severe emotional trauma, 133
sex organs, men having surgery on, 186
sex partner, informing, 192
sex-role socialization, continued, 257
sex-role stereotyping, avoiding in child rearing, 145
sexual abuse, example of, 129
sexual behavior, irresponsible, 192
sexual decision making, as a complex process, 192
sexual expression, men's inability to control, 150
sexual identity, 31, 32
sexual-identity crisis, 85, 263–265
sexual identity minority groups, violence among, 119–122
sexually transmitted diseases (STDs), 175
shelter system, lives saved by, 165–166
sick role concept, 86
signals
　of distress, 43
　recognizing, 50
significant others
　inability to communicate stress to 38t
　inclusive of the person's, 68–69
　knowing what to expect from crisis care providers, 27
　resources and communication with, 99–101
　role of, 101
　trust and hopeful expectations of, 19
　as vital to the planning process, 68–69
signs
　of high risk, 110
　of suicide risk, 96, 97
singles, isolation, and divorce, 274–275
Sioux. *See* Lakota Sioux
situational factors, 156
sleep, inducing, 106
sleeping pills, 75, 89
sleeping position, for infants, 251
sleep loss, relieving, 104
social action
　as crisis prevention, 55
　violence as, 125, 146
social and cultural barriers, making intervention more difficult, 56
social and economic inequalities, 152, 208–209
social and emotional bonds, between people, 271

social and political actions, pivotal to a positive crisis outcome, 235
social and political struggles, negotiating, 57
social attachments, reinstating, 198
social beings, humans as, 14
social change, 55, 56
social class continuum, 124
social contacts, identifying new, 69
social/cultural milieu, determination of, 44
social health index, 258
social illnesses, not fitting the traditional sick role-helper model, 86
social isolation, 217, 219
social network
　inclusive of the person's, 68–69
　influences on the individual, 276–277
　linking the person to, 64
　members of, 14, 279
　sessions, 183–184
　strategies and referrals, 279–282
social network intervention, 198, 281
social network strategies, 276, 279–280, 281
social obligations, synchronizing with diabetes, 182
social opportunities, for the single person, 274
social or gender factors, internalizing, 57
social-psychological roots, of conflict, 86–87
social relationships, resumption of, 61
social services, proactive following a loss, 287
social skills, improving, 63
social sources of stress, resisting, 56
social supports, loss of external 38t
social systems intervention, 278
social ties, reestablishing, 104
societies, varying in beliefs and policies, 229
sociocultural context, 4, 55
sociocultural origins, of crisis, 22–23
sociopolitical strategies, 166–167
solidarity, maintaining, 305
solutions, 36, 62, 198
spillovers, of violence from home to workplace, 161
spirituality, as a coping tool, 233
spoils of war, 117, 151
staff burnout, 176

state-sponsored neglect and preventable harm, survivors of, 228–229
statistical indicators, viewing with caution, 156
statistically significant incidences, statements of, 235
stepfamilies, adoption and, 255–256
stereotypes. *See also* cultural relativism
  about couples in alternative lifestyles, 120–121
  gender-based in professions, 258
  male and female roles, 37
  of swinging singles, 275
stereotyping, 145, 148
stillborn child, 252–253
straight parents, reared millions of gay people, 256
"the straw that breaks the camel's back," 32
stress, 15, 17, 33, 206
stressful events, 45, 48, 50–51
subjectivity, of the crisis experience, 16
substance abuse, 57, 197, 198–199
Substance Abuse and Mental Health Services Administration (SAMHSA), 96
success neurosis, 208
sudden infant death syndrome (SIDS), 250–251
Sudden Infant Death Syndrome Foundation, 251
sudden loss, of a person or thing considered essential, 32
suffering, process of, 60
suicidal adolescent, example, 179
suicidal behavior, 90, 106–108
suicidal crises 38t, 103, 277
suicidal ideas, questions about, 97
suicidal or homicidal thoughts, 41
suicidal patient, emergency room interview, 58–59
suicidal people
  detecting and responding to despair of, 83
  engaging actively in the process, 98
  follow-up service for, 106
  messages of, 82
  psychotropic drug use for, 104–106
suicidal response, to multiple stressors, 187
suicidal women, 84
suicide
  assisting another in the act of, 88
  cutting across class, race, age, and sex differences, 85
  defined, 91
  detecting clues to, 95–96
  ethical issues and, 194
  gay, lesbian, bisexual, and transgendered youth at risk of, 263
  helping family and other survivors, 111–112
  highest rates in the US among older White males, 84
  immediate and long-range risk of, 93, 96–101
  immediate danger of committing, 110
  impossible to predict in any absolute sense, 96
  international range of, 84
  interrupting the path to, 82
  key facts about, 85
  life-threatening risk of, 133
  not an illness or an inherited disease, 91
  not inevitable, 92
  occuring most during periods of socioeconomic and family turmoil, 85
  path or "highway" to, 92–95
  as a process, 92
  rate for all ages and groups in the United States, 84
  reaction to, 81–82
  requesting assistance in committing, 194
  risk levels, crisis care, and follow-up counseling, 106–111
  social, psychological, and cultural context of, 84–87
  stigmatizing sort of death, 83
  threatening, 83, 91
suicide attempts
  high-lethal 38t
  history of, 98–99
  majority who succeed having a history of previous, 85
  stemming from feeling rejected, 200
  those who make, 91
suicide continuum or trip, interrupting, 92
suicide or violence toward others, no such thing as absolute prediction of, 8
suicide plan, 97–98
suicide prevention, understanding ambivalence basic to, 94
Suicide Prevention Resource Center (SPRC), 96
suicide rates, national, 84

suicide risk
    assessing, 93–94, 95, 96
    increasing fivefold with a gun in the home, 103
    Risk Assessment Tool: Suicide, 107
suicidology, 90, 96, 106
Summergrad, Paul, 302
supplies, needed to avoid crisis, 50
support, needed during crisis, 1
support group, joining, 76
supportive relationships, losing at work, 207
Surgeon General's report (1986), 167
"The Surgeon General's Workshop on Crisis, Violence, and Public Health--30 Years Later," 299
surgery
    children having, 187–188
    crises regarding, 186–187
surprise reactions, rooted in failure of triage questioning, 43
surrogate parenthood, 256–257
survival plan, for an abused woman, 136
surviving, struggle for purposes of, 57
survivors
    guilt as an emotional response, 191
    helping to accept the reality of what has happened, 226
    presenting to PCPs with physical ailments, 111
    referring to all those left behind, 111
    searching for meaning, 234
    separating panic-stricken from the rest after disaster, 226
    spending extraordinary energy trying to answer the question, Why? 112
    of suicide, feelings common among, 85
symbols, power for conveying values, 149
symptom bearer, identifying, 279

tahara (purity), 148
tandem approach, 23, 124
Tarasoff case, from the University of California, 162
teaching career, paralyzed by fear of responsibilities, 31
team, working collaboratively, 305
team approach, value of, 2
teamwork, in crisis care, 4
technology
    a double-edged sword, 238
    potential for both good and evil, 228

teenage children, risks in keeping on ADHD drugs, 74
teenage mothers, financial inequality, 246
teenage parenthood, 255
teen pregnancy, 210
temporary insanity pleas, 123
Ten Point Coalition of religious leaders in metro Boston, 306
tension, 34, 36
terrorism, 232, 273
themes, influencing interactions with people in crisis, 59
those in a position to help, goals of, 40
thoughts
    of parents of handicapped children, 260
    signaling acute distress, 182
threats
    of assault or homicide, 157
    to job, home, and financial security, 206–209
    of loss of a person or thing considered essential, 32
    of outing one's mate as a powerful tool of control, 120
threshold, of crisis, 31
time, keeping open, 157
time frame, for a good crisis care plan, 69
time limitation, to the crisis experience, 37
timetable, as part of any action plan, 67
torture, physical health and social consequences of, 221
traditional rites of passage, 247–249
tranquilizers, taken during crisis, 75
transitions, normal life-state, 32
transition states, hazards to individuals in, 275
trauma, 133–134
traumatic events
    assisting individuals through, 212
    causing an initial rise in level of anxiety, 33
    crisis not necessarily following, 17
    each person's unique perception of, 235
    emotional responses to, 191
    perception of, 64
    unanticipated, 242
traumatized people, linking to self-help and advocacy groups, 231
travelers, risks to, 218
Travelers Aid, 219
treating, for violent behavior, 144
triage questions, 42–43, 131–132

Triage tool, 131, 134
trusted confidant, discussing questions and fears with, 207
tunnel vision approach, to problem solving, 100
turmoil and pain, rebirth of peace following, 17
turning points, 198, 199, 242–243
24/7 crisis care and psychiatric treatment, patchy access to, 158
two-level assessment process, 42

unconscious, Freud's discovery of, 20
understanding of a crisis, helping a person gain, 64
unemployment, as occasion of emotional crisis, 213
unexpected events, vulnerability of persons facing, 7
unhappy childhood, precursor to unhappiness, 262
unintended consequences, giving attention to, 164
United Nations, 118, 294
United Nations Decade for Women conferences, 118, 210
universal human need, for self-mastery, 86
upset people, myths about, 18
"upstream" factors, underpinnings of crises, 300
urban neighborhood, death and life of, 212
urban stress syndrome, 153
usual self, changes in one's, 181

vaccination, for preventable diseases, 299
values, assumed in this book, 19–20
value systems, using to recover from traumatic violence, 233
verbal abuse, 120, 147
verbal responses, to assessment questions 51t
vicarious traumatization, 166
vicious cycle, becoming locked in, 36
victimization
  history as grounds for temporary insanity pleas, 123
  key facts and issues about, 116–118
  recognizing risk and future danger levels of, 129–130
  screening for, 43
  by violence, 116
Victimization Assessment Tool, 132, 132t, 134

victimization experience, realities and complexities of, 128
victimization status, identification of, 134
victimized workers, redressing the neglect of many, 161
victim-rescuer-persecutor (VRP) triangle, 65–66, 65f, 86–87
victims and offenders, equal concern and commitment to, 164
victim-survivors
  blaming, 121, 126–127, 128f
  including a variety of persons, 122–123
  legacy of disbelieving, 150
  majority knowing their abusers, 116
  making contact with relatives, friends, and other resources, 226
  people with AIDS and others facing a life-threatening illness, 193
  poignant testimonies and tragic lives of, 237
  reassurance of, 135
  reluctant to report abuse if the climate is unreceptive, 130
  resistance as an "ego" threat, 157
  some not acknowledging cause of their physical injuries, 136
  suppressing emotional pain of abuse and violence, 127
  violence and abuse from the perspective of, 116
  working toward the restoration of precrisis self, 164
violence. *See also* abuse
  as an abuse of power, 146
  accidental or intentional, 232–233
  approaches to understanding, 125–126
  begetting violence, 136, 155, 162
  being ready to talk directly and empathically about, 130
  in and beyond the family, 122–123
  centuries-old plague continuing, 299
  choices, action, and inaction regarding, 238
  chosen, 125
  complexity of, 123–129
  as a control strategy and a solution to conflict resolution, 121
  crisis care and follow-up counseling for survivors of, 134–135
  defined, 146–148
  defining as a moral act, 125

violence *(cont.)*
  double standard and gender relations, 149–150
  efforts to end the plague of, 144
  exerting physical force and power over another, 147
  explaining in person's level of understanding vs. psychiatric/medical language, 123
  fewer depictions of accountability, 146
  as a human rights violation, 118–119
  interpreted in psycho-sociocultural and feminist terms, 146
  key facts and issues about, 116–118
  layers of, 146
  learned and reinforced, 164
  as learned behavior, 151
  mandatory reporting issues, 135–137
  no such thing as absolute prediction of, 132
  not inevitable, 238
  as an occupational health hazard, 159
  originating from bias, 116
  originating in gender inequality, 152
  before or during pregnancy, 119
  primary prevention of, 165–167
  psychiatric disorder and, 160–161
  racially motivated, 234
  within relationships tending to escalate, 117
  as a response to stress, 125
  as a social act, 146, 147
  as a social phenomenon, 122
  victims needing public acknowledgement, 237
  youth violence, roots of, 152–154
Violence Intervention Advocacy Program, 25
violence-laced remarks, 5
violence prevention programs, for abusers, 145
Violence Recovery Program at the Fenway Community Health Center in Boston, 121
violent behavior. *See also* self-destructive behavior
  empirically impossible to predict, 156
  example of, 144
  intended to control another person, 125
  past, 158
  psychiatric and biomedical influences on, 124
  social and institutional factors influencing, 162
violent home, considered a form of child abuse, 117
violent men, programs for, 163–164
violent persons, 125, 162–163
visiting nurses, detecting stress or suicidal tendencies, 287
vital connectedness, helping victim-survivors with a view to, 135
volunteer programs, for seniors, 287
vulnerability, 18, 22f, 41
vulnerable state, 32, 38t

wage disparities, 210
war on drugs, 74
war refugees. *See* refugees
war trauma, responses to, 232
welfare recipients, lacking education and training to escape poverty, 210
welfare reform, 211, 268
WHO. *See* World Health Organization (WHO)
women
  abused, 48, 136, 137–138, 139t
  with AIDS, 195–196
  as caretakers, 209
  doing two thirds of the world's work, 210
  experiencing greater stress around appearance, 195
  having a fair trial on self-defense grounds, 120
  incidence of violence by increasing, 151–152
  left behind for younger women, 245
  marriage across cultures and, 245–246
  as a minority group, 152
  ownership of, 150
  postmenopausal, 248
  providing most care for acutely ill and dying, 196
  rates of violence by increasing, 117
  restraining orders not preventing murders of, 163
  retaining last names after marriage, 246
  suicidal, 84
  verbal abuse by, 120

violence against, 117, 118–119
  violence by, 119–122
  work and welfare reform, 211
work
  paid and unpaid, 209–211
  Western society's attitude toward, 213
workaholics, plunging into
    depression, 206
work disruption, from the local to global
    scene, 212–215
"work eventually," aim of, 211
workfare, 211
work hours, cutting down on, 36
working parents, policies and practices
    addressing needs of, 258
working people, needing hope, 207
workplace
  safety, 6
  violence and abuse in, 159–161
Workshop on Violence and Public Health
    in 1985, 122
World Conference on Injury Prevention
    and Safety Promotion, 118
World Health Organization (WHO), 83,
    84, 118, 149

young people
  helping, 266
  services for, 263
  transition to adulthood and economic
    self-sufficiency, 212
  violence and antisocial behavior
    among, 152–154, 157

www.ingramcontent.com/pod-product-compliance
Lightning Source LLC
LaVergne TN
LVHW022036260326
834688LV00060B/736